The United States–
Mexico Border

The
United States-
Mexico
Border

A POLITICO-ECONOMIC PROFILE

by
Raul A. Fernandez

UNIVERSITY OF NOTRE DAME PRESS
NOTRE DAME   LONDON

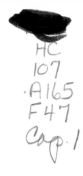

Copyright © 1977 by
University of Notre Dame Press
Notre Dame, Indiana 46556

Library of Congress Cataloging in Publication Data

Fernandez, Raul A   1945–
   The United States-Mexico border.

   1. Southwest, New—Economic conditions.   2. Texas—
Economic conditions.   3. Mexico—Economic conditions.
I. Title.
HC107.A165F47   330.9'764   76–22409
ISBN 0–268–01914–2

Manufactured in the United States of America

Contents

The United States—
Mexico Border

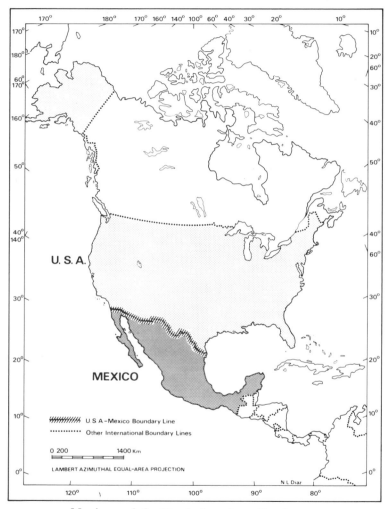

Mexico and the North American Continent

Introduction

This book is a study of the political economy of the United States-Mexico border region. Some specialists may not be impressed with my method of presentation and analysis. Historians may find themselves uninspired by the dearth of *new* historical data. With the exception of the last three chapters, much of the material utilized has appeared in print before. On the other hand, "traditional" economists may view my effort to expand the understanding of current economic developments on the Mexican border via a historical examination as fruitless. The task I have set is that of organizing and giving coherence, with the aid of theory, to a body of historical data already, for the most part, available.

My theoretical conviction is that a realistic quantitative and qualitative determination of economic systems aimed at specifying *conditions for change* cannot be arrived at by using the ahistorical tools and concepts of "neoclassical economic theory." Rather, any such attempt must incorporate institutional and historical elements. The extreme formalization of neoclassical models and their emphasis on characteristics which are common to all economic systems, rather than those which are peculiar to each, have obscured an understanding of the process of social change and development. More correctly, the shortcomings of economic "science" arise from the reduction of "sociology" to individuals; the reduction of "psychology" to rational calculation; the determination that society is a harmonious whole; and the equation of class differences with differences in innate individual talent.

The tight molds imposed by the implicit societal assumptions of neoclassical theory have become more and more of an obstacle in the minds of a generation of young economists who recognize that the "sociology" and "politics" of an adequate economic science must pass beyond "individual consumers" and "G" (government). The concept of the individual consumer is itself a historical product. So, an economic science that purports to be general in its scope cannot impose concepts based on the notion of "individuals" in societies where the concept is not present in concrete reality. Similarly, the narrowness of rational calculation—so central to the "psychology" of modern economic theory—has come under widespread attack. One of the graver consequences of this formal reductionism is the freedom of the "theorist" to collect data (numbers) based on the given taxonomy and to statiscize the result. A contemporary example of this practice is the recent flood of literature showing the superiority of white over nonwhite students on the basis of something that is measurable, i.e., intelligence. This crude empiricism—rampant in economics and in the "other" social sciences—is the result of an unfortunate confusion between what is factual and what is truthful.

Social forces more complex than the ones depicted in formal models have been at work in the process of emphasizing formalization, statistization, etc. During the last two decades, the social sciences have engaged in a race to be classified as "hard sciences." Part of this tendency has been motivated by the orientation of fund-granting agencies in the United States: the road to formalization and statistization has been cleared by the availability of funds for the support of this type of research. The consequence is that a pecking order has been established with the "harder"—or more formal—disciplines at the top and with everyone vying for first place. In this manner a form of curricular imperialism of the most pedantic kind has become fashionable, with economics as its standard bearer. Within each discipline the result has been a ridiculous and destructive separation of professionals into "hard heads" and "soft heads," with obvious connotations. This separation parallels the confusion between the ability to collect statistics and the production of meaningful results. The implied rationale is that capacity to quantify concepts and operations places the social sciences on a par with the physical sciences.

These pitfalls of the social sciences have rendered social science incapable of understanding the economic plight of racial minorities in the United States. Years of sociological, psychological, political, and geographical research into the conditions of Mexican Americans, for example, has not shed much light on the social origins and persistence of their plight, much less provided solutions to their problems.

II

I hope to demonstrate that the study of the process of economic change in and around the border area between Mexico and the United States is a topical as well as an authentic area of social scientific inquiry. In brief, an adequate study of the history of the border economic processes must shed some additional light on the determination of the economic systems of the two countries as well as the economic and political relations between them.

The boundary between the United States and Mexico is unique for a variety of reasons. The first important contemporary characteristic is the development of a string of population centers extending from the Gulf of Mexico to the Pacific Ocean usually named "border towns." This denomination is almost never applied to any of the population centers on the American-Canadian border; in fact, the American-Canadian border is, more often than not, referred to as the "boundary." The word "border," and especially the phrase "border town," has negative connotations which imply conditions of unsettlement and hostility. Additionally, the population concentration in the area is far from an ordinary situation: the area that is called northern Mexico has had the highest population growth rate of any region its size since the mid-fifties.

A second factor which makes the presence of these cities somewhat incongruous is their origin: the border towns appear to have no other economic-geographic raison d'être than the fact that they were set up as cross points on the border line. With few exceptions (El Paso–Juarez being perhaps the most important), the cities that are called border towns defy the canons of economic-geographic location theory and owe their existence quite literally to the existence of the border line.

The Mexican border is a unique contemporary example of the contrast between rich and poor nations or, as it has commonly been put, between "developed" and "underdeveloped" nations. Above and beyond the particularities of this situation, the adjacency of these two nations may serve to illustrate and perhaps to emphasize in a manner not obvious in other situations, the kinds of ties that have developed and are developing between advanced and backward nations. This example may also serve to illustrate forcefully such a relationship's projected path of development.

Thirdly, the study of this area cannot avoid two historically crucial developments: the expansion and conquest (1836–48) of a large area of Mexican territory by the United States; and a continuous saturation of the southwestern states by Mexican immigration, especially since the turn of the century. I will show that this latter development is clearly bound up with the adjacency of two vastly different socio-economic fabrics and, as such, it is unique although not without historical precedent. Although it is impossible to disregard direct and indirect references to the situation of the Chicano population of the Southwest, the methodology used does not allow an interpretation of Chicano history based on cultural difference or cultural oppression.

Meaningful research and analysis that guides subsequent political and social action must be grounded on the material forces and social relations of production which ultimately define the historical course of any group of people. To remain at a level of explanation which blames one racial or cultural group for having committed cultural genocide meets the requirements for moral indignation, but goes no further. Indeed, such methodology leads to the conclusion that the history of mankind is nothing but "an erratic series of cultural genocides."

To proceed with this kind of approach can lead into several blind alleys: one would be the assumption of complete cynicism at the "horrible pageant" of mankind and the taking of an ahistorical, "existential" posture with regard to the "evil nature of man"; another one would be the acquisition of a spiritual satisfaction based on the philosophical notion that "one's culture is as good as that of the white man's," regardless of the facts of oppression. A third road is traveled by a social strategy characterized by moralistic idealism where the slogan would be that all nations (which are viewed as equivalent to cultures) have equal rights to exist in a sovereign way, regardless of their concrete historical character; that is, regardless of the fact that "nations" are not eternal entities. A colony, or a nation, is a sensible concept when it is rooted in real material and historical circumstances, but not when it only serves a rhetorical purpose. Therefore, one must ask whether it makes sense to speak of a colony or a nation in relation to the Chicano people. Does it have a defined territory or an economy of its own? In what sense is it possible to speak of a nation during the present epoch, i.e., is a Chicano nation going to fulfill the historical role of nation-states in previous centuries?

III

The methodology that I utilize is that of historical materialism. The fundamental aspect of historical materialism is that the development of the history of mankind depends on the development of the contradictions between the forces of production and the social relations of production, on the material conditions of life (base or mode of production), and on its ideological conceptions (superstructure). Classical Marxism endeavored to determine the fundamental features of capitalism, and to demonstrate that it was a historical mode of production that arose in a determinate historical moment; that capitalism embodied inherent contradictions which would eventually destroy and transform it into a different mode of production; and that capitalism manifested specific traits which distinguish it from previous forms of social production. The backbone of Marxist social theory is that the critic can arrive by way of the theory of successive modes of production at a correct analysis of classes in a concrete situation.

This constitutes the theoretical framework, or the "paradigm," that is adopted here. The application of this general theoretical framework to the concrete case of the United States-Mexico border area should concern the delineation of modes of production coexisting side by side within a unified economic system. For this reason, I have placed a special emphasis on the analysis of feudal remnants in land tenure late in the nineteenth century in the otherwise capitalistic Southwest. Secondly, it is crucial to identify the specific manifestations of the development of monopoly capitalism in the border area, an aspect that is emphasized in the analysis of migration. Finally, I have attempted to show the importance of the relationships which arise from the uneven economic development of different social formations. Although I have not attempted to write a "history" of the border area, the chapters are written in an order which implies a certain chronology and periodization.

The First Stage

The first period extends from 1848 (or 1836 in the case of Texas) to approximately the turn of the century. This early stage is characterized by the head-on collision between two different socio-economic formations. The social economy that was predominant in the northwestern part of Mexico during the Spanish and Mexican periods can best be described as a variant of feudalism. This is true in terms of class relations (basically *patrones* and *peones*), in terms of the forms of

ground-rent, and in terms of the pattern of "economic behavior" of the landed aristocracy. Contact and conflict between
this social formation and the American (predominantly capitalist) system begins much before 1848, or even 1836. The
contact begins in three major ways. The development of commodity circulation within the United States economy and the
presence of the more backward Spanish borderlands brought
a variety of tradesmen into the Southwest, especially through
the Santa Fe Trail but also by sea along the California coast.
The increasing social division of labor within the former
American colonies brought fur trappers and other independent entrepreneurs down the rivers and mountains of the
area. And finally, the onset of major cyclical depressions in the
burgeoning northern capitalist centers sent successive waves of
colonists into the as yet non-American territories. By the time
of the conflict of 1848, the *economic* border—the front lines of
contact between the two predominant modes of production—had been lowered close to what the Treaty of
Guadalupe-Hidalgo would declare as the official international
boundary line.

After the War of 1848, the battle moved from the economic
sphere to the political and judicial levels. During the few ensuing decades, two important developments took place. First,
numerous Spanish and Mexican landowners lost their property in land in a variety of ways, but more often than not
through fraud, litigation cost, nonrecognition of Spanish land
titles, and a variety of legal technicalities. These were the
responsible agents for this political and economic reverse.
Secondly, the Hispanic (as well as Anglo) landowners who
survived this legal defeat succumbed to the onslaught of
competition in agriculture brought by the newly arrived Anglo
entrepreneurs, and to a number of other socio-economic
changes as well as some natural catastrophes.

The most significant element of this first stage is the victory
of one system of production and land tenure over a more
backward system. The proclamation of a legal border could
not prevent the continuing flux of new boundaries of economic contact and conflict. From the first moment of its exis-

tence, disturbances arose around the international border line. Some of these were generally economic in nature: for example, the problems arising from the establishment of a Free Zone around the border by the Mexican government. The significance of the Free Zone is enormous as it became the target of attack by American business and political leaders for many years. The smuggling that developed across the line in the 1860s, 70s, and 80s was blamed on the existence of this area, and was regarded as hostile behavior on the part of the Mexican government. Also, the existence of the Free Zone was tied in with the "cattle raids" and "Indian depredations" which plagued the border for several decades. The economic tensions led to military action and numerous incursions by American troops into Mexico during those years. It is not an exaggeration to state that the outbreak of another war between the two countries was a distinct possibility at several points. It is also fair to say that the subsequent easing of tensions in the area occurred in direct relation to the decision by the Mexican government under Díaz to facilitate American economic penetration both in the border area and in the Republic at large.

The Second Stage

If the first stage was characterized by the defeat of one economic system by another, and by the expansion of the economic battlefront, the second stage was molded by the full development of capitalist relations of production north of the border and by a process of American intervention in the area south of the border, a development which took place at varying speeds.

As opposed to a feudal system, capitalism is characterized by the existence of a labor force which is free to hire its labor services to an employer. Capitalism cannot survive if everybody is an employer: there have to be workers. It is precisely the manner in which the labor force was provided to satisfy the necessities of capitalist development in the Southwest which is crucial to an understanding of the border during this second period. The take-over of the Spanish land grants described previously had an important effect on subsequent economic development because, even though the transition represented a change in methods of production and reproduction (investment), the large landholdings which were typical of the Spanish and Mexican periods were largely left intact. Large monopolies in the land, decried at the time by Henry George, were part of the historical legacy of the Spanish colonization of the Southwest, and they became an important determinant in the development of agriculture and in the shape that the labor force was organized to meet the needs of this nascent agribusiness.

The particular process of capitalist development in the southwestern United States resulted in one of the most spectacular mass movements of people in the history of mankind: the mass northward migration of people from all corners of Mexico, and even Central and South America. This movement has taken a variety of forms: it has been regulated and unregulated, legal and illegal, seasonal and secular. It is fair to generalize that the adjacency of Mexico provided the opportunity to construct an economy that would easily be able to turn the supply of labor services on and off, at will. When the need for labor has been intense (in times of war, for example), the economy of the southwestern United States has readily relied upon cheap Mexican labor. On the other hand, every period of recession in the United States has been characterized by the intensification of Border Patrol activity and even by coercive repatriation.

Beginning in the 1880s, significant economic interest began to develop in the western half and south of the international boundary. American companies acquired huge acreages of irrigable land in the Mexicali district; cattle magnates and mining enterprises moved deeply into the states of Sonora and Sinaloa.

With the overthrow of Díaz and the years of the Mexican revolution, the political significance of American economic penetration in the border area was exemplified by a number of agrarian edicts designed to keep foreigners from owning land in the vicinity of the Mexican border and, later on, by the expropriation of American enterprises and the development of a nationalistic policy of industrial development for the entire country. One of the more specific policies designed to stem the tide of American economic expansion in the border area was the intense colonization efforts by the Mexican government in the territory of Baja California. Ironically, this colonization process was to become yet another factor (though a minor one) in the aforementioned northern migration.

The power of American business around the border did not exactly succumb to the pressures inflicted by the Mexican revolution between 1911 and 1920. Rather, it played a powerful if not decisive role in the eventual outcome of the revolution. Although the United States was officially neutral and enacted embargoes on horses, food, and supplies across the border, these measures were eased whenever the tide seemed to be turning toward interests which were considered favorable to American capital. The United States also served as a sanctuary for some revolutionary factions, while others were designated as "bandits" and "raiders."

During the second stage, the economy of the border area began to change at a rapid pace. The population increase and the particularly intense growth of urban centers brought about a disparity between the need for and the availability of the most basic social services. It also generated a tremendous unemployment problem since jobs could hardly be expected to keep up with the quadruplication of the population since 1940. Unemployment not only affected the urban centers, but the agricultural areas as well where, during the Second World War, American capital had invested heavily in the production of "winter vegetables."

The Third Stage

The first stage deals with the process that led to the legal establishment of a border that was already being established economically. The second stage is the epoch of coincidence of the legal with the actual economic border. The present stage is one where the legal border is, in *some* ways, a fiction, and has been left behind by the advance of the integration process. This rapid movement is part and parcel of a new dimension of the international business scene usually referred to as "the rise of the multinationals," "worldwide sourcing and dedomiciling," etc. This is an ongoing process, manifesting itself in a veritable mass exodus of labor-intensive industries from the developed countries into low-wage developing ones.

The multinational corporation, or "the highest stage of corporate development," came into the United States-Mexico border area in the form of the Border Industrial Program (BIP), which was instituted in 1965 and was in full operation in 1967. The primordial role that the BIP was supposed to assume was the alleviation of widespread unemployment prevalent along the 2,000 mile common border with the United States. The Border Industrial Program is, today, no longer limited to the border, and there are numerous plants in other states, such as Yucatán and Aguascalientes.

As the economic border progresses beyond the international line, the effects of this international line are still felt. Once again, a phenomenon of unique dimensions has appeared in this area of the world: the border town. It has already been pointed out that we hardly ever refer to cities on the international boundary with Canada or, for that matter, to cities on international borders in other parts of the world as border towns. The occurrence of a "border town" is brought about by a host of factors, the principal one being the contrasts which exist between the two countries facing each other across this line.

The present border area and the border towns included in it are continuing the trends of rapid growth, urban sprawl, high unemployment, and squalor experienced during the 1950s and 1960s. The economy of these towns is increasingly shaped by the presence of American industry, the transport of vegetables northward, the flow of tourists southward, the flow in both directions of contraband items (including weapons), the flourishing of prostitution, and the dynamics of illegal traffic in hard drugs. These items effect a deepening of the elements of social cleavage and the disruptions already present in this semimodern, semibackward atmosphere.

i: Material Basis of Culture in the Old Borderlands

What was the operative system of social economy in New Mexico and California during the Anglo conquest, and how had it evolved from Oñate's early *entrada* of the late 1500s? This chapter attempts to sketch the requirements of a minimal answer to that query and further seeks to specify the direction of internal change within this social fabric.

In analyzing patterns of social change and social structure in New Mexico, it is necessary to mention two stages of colonization, which can be separated by the Pueblo Revolt of the 1680s. During the first hundred years of colonization, the Spanish arrivals in New Mexico basically applied the same approach to the Pueblo Indians that had been implemented elsewhere in New Spain (Mexico). As such, the conquest of New Mexico forged the last link in a northward chain of conquest and colonization. The social relations of production which the Spanish colonists ideally desired to construct in the new territory were contained in the proposal advanced by one of the candidates considered by the Crown for the colonization project. Juan Bautista de Lomas y Colmenares, a rich miner from the Zacatecas region, asked for: the title of *adelantado* for his family in perpetuity as well as the appointment of governor-captaincy for six generations; the prerogative to bestow three *encomiendas* in perpetuity as well as any others for six generations; forty thousand vassals in perpetuity with attendant rights to the lands, water, and woods under their jurisdiction; a nobiliary title such as count or marquess; a ten-year monopoly on the raising of livestock in the region; and a few other items. This proposal was accepted in principle by the viceroy in Mexico. Even though he was empowered to authorize it, the viceroy, beset by inner doubt or scruple, forwarded the proposal to the king who refused to authorize it.[1] The fact that a request almost entailing the creation of a new sovereign principality could be seriously considered reflects two aspects of colonization in New Spain. As colonization progressed towards the northern frontier of New Spain, the royal authorities came to rely more and more heavily on colonists wealthy enough to effect the process. On the other side of the coin, this process allowed the more prosperous colonists an increasing power to acquire and develop enormous estates. These estates—or *latifundios*—became the norm of land tenure in northern New Spain during the sixteenth and seventeenth centuries.

When the conquest of New Mexico had been effected, *encomiendas* and *repartimientos* formed the basis of colonial production. As an institution, the encomienda dates back to the colonization of Castile during the retreat of the Moors.[2] Its appearance in New Mexico reflects the traditional assignments granted to a Spanish conqueror—in this case to some of Oñate's top soldiers—of supervision over land near an Indian community whose population was required to perform labor on these lands for the benefit of the encomendero.

Additionally, large landgrants were given to the more prominent Spaniards. Through the encomiendas, the Pueblo villages contributed an annual tribute in kind to the leading colonists, usually consisting of maize and cotton blankets. The repartimiento—or apportionment of labor required from the Indian population living near an encomienda—was utilized to the fullest extent by the settlers living on farms and ranches. Although a nominal sum of money was expected in exchange for Indian labor, there is enough evidence to suggest that the colonists did not comply with this requirement but, rather, simply appropriated the fruits of coerced, enforced labor. During the early years of the encomienda's development in

New Spain, the distribution of labor, and not necessarily the distribution of land, influenced the placement of encomiendas. Consequently, defined boundaries between encomiendas did not exist and, with the exhaustion of precious metals, some of the early encomiendas were transformed into large farm estates.

The encomiendas and repartimientos required the native inhabitants to till the soil, tend livestock, work in mines, and carry burdens in addition to the obligatory tribute. In New Mexico, there was little question of mining after initial explorations demonstrated the absence of gold or silver and, as a result, New Mexico was not characterized by the opulence and splendor that had typified earlier outposts such as Zacatecas. The general relative poverty of the New Mexico colony has led to questioning the view that here as well as elsewhere Spanish Mexicans lived comfortably off the coerced labor of their Indian serfs.[3] A number of problems are involved in this issue: first, though the tribute accruing from the encomienda did not amount to much, coerced repartimiento labor was clearly of greater economic importance to the Spanish-Mexican settlers. Here, as well as elsewhere in New Spain, the colonists lived off the labor of their Indian charges. Whether they lived *comfortably* or not is an outside conditioning factor which does not alter the pattern of subjection characteristic of the society.

The social relations of the early New Mexican province were feudal in character. Historically, feudal or tributary societies emerged at a time when the development of production and the degree of human knowledge and control of natural forces were at a fairly undeveloped level. Consequently, natural catastrophes affected every member of the society, regardless of class, rank, or status. Plagues and drought were the natural enemies of European feudal systems; the absence of rich minerals in New Mexico and its position as a weak frontier outpost surrounded by a hostile environment made this society poor as a whole, but did not eliminate class relations.

In feudal societies, the need to cooperate against the forces of nature, and the physical proximity due to geographical isolation (lack of development of means of transport) bred a definite form of paternalism where the lord truly cared for his vassals and serfs. This aspect of precapitalist society was, of course, reinforced by tenets of religious alienation which rationalized the modus vivendi. The nature of class relations in precapitalist societies can be favorably compared (from a romantic point of view) with the atomization and competitive mentality prevalent in a fully developed capitalist society. In this light, it is possible to refer to the "benevolence" of feudalism as specifically superior to that of capitalism.[4] Social *analysis*, however, should strive to look not only at the daily exposition of benevolence or lack thereof, but at the long-term path of a society's development, and at the material chances of escape from a position of coerced servitude. In feudal situations, then, benevolence may be viewed as an instrument of continued domination, and not as an idyllic virtue from older, better times.

In the case of New Mexico, the question becomes academic. Raids by nomadic tribes and disease decimated the Pueblos after 1665. With their numbers depleted, the labor requirements of the Spaniards became harder and harder to meet. Finally, the Pueblos rose in revolt in 1680, exterminated most of the colonists, and drove the survivors out of the upper Rio Grande Valley for the next twelve years.

The revolt of the Pueblos aborted a process of development in land tenure patterns that had spread over all of Mexico by the end of the seventeenth century. This process can be described as an official sanctioning—embodied in property rights—of the results of a trend toward indiscriminate use of land present from the beginning of the Conquest. In the sixteenth century, the process of land occupation in New Spain had been highly irregular. The only consistent characteristics of land occupation were the drive to acquire larger and larger portions of land; the appropriation and stewardship of communal Indian lands; and the stockmen's use of grazing lands, usually available to all inhabitants of a town. By the beginning of the seventeenth century, Mexico had experienced a de facto division into a conglomeration of extensive estates primarily devoted to cattle and sheep raising. Throughout the seventeenth century, this subdivision became legally sanctioned: the obligatory settlement of land titles became a new source of revenue for military expenditures in the eyes of the Spanish sovereign, and a tax was levied upon the newly required settlement of property. This measure was fought by most landholders since it directly affected their pockets, but in the long run, and despite erstwhile monetary impoverishment, the status and predominance of the large estate was secured. While in most of New Spain, landholders were obligated during the seventeenth century to define and legalize their property, the settlers in the northern provinces were specifically exempted because of frontier conditions.[5] This whole process came to a grinding halt in New Mexico. This is not the whole story on the formation of large estates in Mexico, but we will have occasion to return to this point later.

Twelve years after the Pueblo Revolt, the Spanish Mexicans returned to the upper Rio Grande Valley. At this time, Spanish landgrants became of prime importance in the history of the borderlands. However, the significance of the Spanish landgrant system has usually been approached a posteriori, i.e., via the violations of Spanish juridical systems that Anglo invaders effected. No adequate examination has been made either of the influence of the land tenure system on the internal dynamics of Hispanic society in the Southwest or of the internal variations that occurred from area to area. The fact that the society of the Southwest was conquered by an alien nation, and that the resulting cultural conflict became explicit in many ways (one of them being the struggle over land titles) has deterred attention to possibly conflicting elements in patterns of land tenure and other, concommitant economic peculiarities in the two opposing societies. Had Hispanic land titles been recognized and respected, would this land tenure system have survived the impact of the invader's institutions? The answer to this question entails an investigation of the property relations prevailing in New Mexico during the eighteenth century.

The Spanish crown (and later the Mexican government) allowed three types of landgrants in the northern provinces:

individual grants given to important people or sold to those with financial means, joint grants to groups of individuals, and community grants given to a group of settlers. Relatively few individual grants were issued during the Spanish period in New Mexico, and those usually went to prominent citizens. Joint grants were usually issued to a group of families who were generally accompanied by a larger group of families and individuals. In the main, the initial grantees allowed the accompanying people small residential lots and small portions of irrigable land to cultivate. These people usually provided the bulk of the labor force required by the initial grantees, who were usually engaged in livestock production. In town or community grants, land was allocated in three forms to each settler: residential lots, farming or irrigable lands, and common land, usually for grazing purposes. The particular topography of the terrain dictated the layout of most farmsteads in thin strips of land on both banks of the Rio Grande.[6] The incentive to stay close to one's farmland, and the absence of fertile soil and/or water away from the river generated a string of small strips farther and farther along the banks of the river. This situation eventually had a dispersal effect on the towns of early New Mexico, despite the constant threat of hostile Indians. It also yielded the phenomenon of squatting in the outlying areas.

From this very basic outline of land distribution in eighteenth-century New Mexico, what can we say about the social relations that emanated from it? Some speculation leans toward the view that the legal apparatus was a model of judicial wisdom since it granted some land proprietorship to the poor as well as to the rich.[7] Additionally, this view suggests that town and joint grants provided an important stimulus for communalism by making some of the building and defensive tasks obligatory for everyone. Empirically, of course, this kind of analysis is utopian and romantic in the extreme. During the eighteenth and nineteenth centuries, the colonized area of New Mexico became characterized by the presence of two basic classes—the patrones and the peones. The patrones were not only those holders of individual grants who chose to include servants in their holdings; it seems that in many villages, the *realengos* (common lands) designed for the pasturage of every neighbor came to be generally utilized by two or three large livestock owners in the village. The rest of the settlers became laborers in their de facto haciendas and, occasionally, kept some cattle themselves. The livestock owners became the patrones upon whom the majority of others were dependent for work.

To understand the transition from early settlements which appeared to have a more varied stratification to the simple pattern that resulted, one must look at two aspects of their social formation: first, the nature and tendencies of small, agricultural farmsteads within the larger social formation and, second, the history of the relationship between stock raising and agriculture in this mode of production.

From the beginning of the allocation of land, the small tiller was doomed to eke out little more than subsistence from his plot. The amount of land that he could cultivate was regulated by law, and the absence of primogeniture rights made the size of the plots decrease over generations. Given the availability of water and the degree of technical development, there was simply little possibility for the expansion of agricultural production toward larger areas away from the river. These factors were bound to prevent the expansion of agriculture, either in an extensive sense, or in the sense of gradual improvements in yield due to the application of more sophisticated scientific farming. The small proprietor could, at best, succeed in maintaining his rights of property; in the end, he generally became indebted and secured his livelihood by laboring on the large ranches. His formal independence and, in some cases, his property ownership, were hardly conducive to further economic growth.

The subjection of the small tiller by large ranchers occurs in New Mexico and, in this sense, there is considerable similarity to the process that established the large haciendas and the patron-peon relationship in northern Mexico. Earlier, we described the events leading to the de jure consolidation of the large estates (haciendas) in New Spain during the seventeenth century, but the de facto build-up of such large estates was only hinted at.

From the beginning of colonization in New Spain, colonial laws and regulations attempted to contain any desire for independent fiefdoms that might arise from the possession of large areas of land. Within a century of the Conquest, however, the economy of New Spain had become highly dependent on stock raising, and this dependence led to the formation of the large Mexican hacienda. A number of reasons have been advanced for the growth of cattle raising in Mexico. One initial—and purely functional factor—was the service that cattle haciendas provided for the mining centers in terms of the basic supplies of meat, animals, and hides. A second factor was, certainly, the tremendous demographic toll Mexico took in the sixteenth century, which severely restricted the availability of manual labor. Stock raising was favorably viewed because of its low labor requirements.[8]

Despite regulations that appeared to restrict the development of large estates, Mexico suffered the same fate in this regard as Spain. The stock raisers' growing power allowed them to make a sham of existing regulations by conniving with municipal authorities—other cattle raisers—to secure their private use of common pasture lands. Even though the viceroy tried, at first, to interfere, the process was too massive to be contained. For a time, the stock raisers maintained an appearance of respect for the integrity of the law while, through their association, the *Mesta,* they worked out the details of their private use of common lands.[9] Coupled with this was the tremendous numerical growth of cattle and sheep in the entire region during the first hundred years of conquest, a biological wonder due to the untouched pastures of Mexico. The growth of cattle caused the destruction of Indian farmlands, and in turn caused an abandonment of villages and whole valleys by the dispossessed local population during the sixteenth century. This phenomenon can easily be compared with a foreign invasion or a natural disaster. Numerous abuses also arose from the old Spanish practice of allowing cattle to graze on crop fields after the harvest was completed.

By the time a pasture-cattle equilibrium had been reached, the haciendas held an entrenched position; mining dropped back in the ranks of economic activities, and former miners turned into wealthy stockmen. This pattern also emerged in northern Mexico where it was reinforced by the tendency of the central Spanish government to rely on rich men to carry out the initial colonization project. Extensive areas of northern Mexico were populated by large flocks in the seventeenth century. The process which elevated stock raisers into a position of undisputed dominance in New Mexico was roughly similar to the process that had occurred earlier farther to the south.

Certainly, different areas of New Mexico were characterized by different degrees of patron and livestock raiser predominance.[10] Even in the case of New Spain, it is not true to claim that the hacienda penetrated every aspect of the social system, since whole areas—such as the valley of Oaxaca—were different in structure. Still, hacienda formation was the dominant and decisive one. Thus, in New Mexico the patron-peon relationship was, empirically and tendentially, also the dominant pattern of social relations, although it was obviously not the only one.

Doubts on this score have been cast by reports indicating that people of all classes enjoyed a substantial diet of animal meat. To confuse the ability of a social formation to feed or not feed all its members at a certain point in time says little about the social relations and the direction of change. It is well known, for instance, that some groups of African hunters and gatherers consume considerably more meat on a daily basis than the average European or American—in fact, the designation the "original affluent society" has been coined for this situation.[11] In the fourteenth century, the citizens of Frankfurt enjoyed a diet of meat and poultry that has been unequaled since.[12] What can we infer about social relations from these material facts other than that they are contingent factors?

A specific instance of the development of patron-peon relationships in New Mexico is the *partido* system. This system began in the late eighteenth century and remained in effect until the beginning of the twentieth century. Its life course seems to have been closely tied to the life cycle of the area's sheep industry. Basically, the livestock proprietor would turn over a breeding herd to a tenant. The renter was bound to return twenty lambs for every hundred ewes in the original group at the end of a year. The lessee also rented rams, sold the lambs and wool through the owner, and was responsible for any losses and the usual costs of operation. He was also obliged to return, upon demand, a breeding herd of the same size and age as the one he had originally obtained. The tenant received the proceeds of the sale of wool, the excess lambs, and grazing rights on the owner's lands for all sheep under his supervision (at a specified rate, of course). As such, the partido system held little hope for small independent livestock operators. Based upon the existing control of grazing resources, its stipulations were intended to maintain the separation between large and small owners.[13]

A good deal of sociability developed, in New Mexico during the colonial period, especially among the rich. The large, extended families saw a good deal of each other and interclass relations were personal in nature. What local changes were brought about by Mexico's independence from Spain? In the very basic sense of social production that we have spoken about—the foundation of social relations on the ownership of productive resources—the sheep industry's tendency towards predominance intensified and began to expand its area of operation. During the Mexican era, the migration pattern followed the movement of large flocks of sheep. Much more evidence is available on the development of patron and partido systems during this time. The Mexican government advanced the process of settlement, and a sizable number of large individual grants were issued during this period. Mexican independence, then, provided additional stimulus to the area's land-based dominant class and an expansion of its domain.

California was another major area of Hispanic conquest and colonization in the Southwest. In California, as in New Mexico and parts of Texas and Arizona which were occupied at this time, stock raising became a principal item of material production.[14]

Within this common denominator of economic production, some differences of timing in development of similar social relations of production emerged, especially between California and New Mexico. California history shows a different chronology from that of New Mexico.[15] When the colonization of California began in earnest, the New Mexico settlement could claim a history of two hundred years. The reasons for this late colonization were very specific, and were apparently concerned with the fears of the Spanish crown regarding the possible intrusion of Russians and even Englishmen in the territory.[16] At any rate, the colonization of California began in the last third of the eighteenth century.

Although the legal history of property relations in the California settlement is very similar in form to that of its older cousin to the east, its content varies considerably. To begin with, the Spanish government granted very few landgrants of any size to individual settlers. So conservative was the Spanish government, that between the year 1782 and the end of the Spanish period, only twenty individual landgrants had been issued. The other side of this situation was the tremendous role, and land control exercised by the "mission system" in California during these years and well into the Mexican period. This system, as it developed in California was never known in New Mexico. From the founding of the first New Mexican mission—the mission of Friar Ruiz in Puaray in 1581—through the subsequent founding of numerous others, their role in New Mexico was almost imperceptible.

In carrying out its assignments to introduce New World Indians to Christianity as well as European culture, the Roman Catholic Church depended upon the effectiveness of its missionaries who belonged to various religious orders. They were as aggressive in their spiritual conquest as the soldiers had been in their physical conquest. Almost from the beginning, the Church accompanied the invading forces in the Southwest; each expedition numbered priests among its members. As soon as a territory was settled, Jesuits (and later Franciscans) took up residence and began their work among the colonists and Indians. None of the clerics seems to have questioned the legitimacy of Spanish rule in the Southwest, although early in the Conquest the Christian voice was the only one raised against the cruelty of the encomienda and repartimiento.[17]

The Jesuit order was responsible for the first missions in the Southwest. The Jesuits were characterized as being well-organized and militant, with an efficiency that yielded economic power. Their success aroused the jealousy of other orders as well as the suspicion of the Crown. The king of Spain, protective of his power, had the Jesuits expelled from the New World colony in 1760, and replaced them with the Franciscans, an order somewhat more harmonious with the Spanish absolutism of the eighteenth century.[18]

In general, the relations between Church and state in the New World were sufficiently harmonious to allow the Church to become quite wealthy. Having seemingly converted numerous Indians in the sixteenth century, the Church became involved in other matters, notably, the acquisition of property and wealth. Tithes and parochial fees provided a small share of the Church's income: the principal source of wealth was furnished by legacy. The wealthy were expected to leave part of their wealth to the Church when they died. Not leaving a legacy for the convents constituted an immoral, irreligious act, and this sin of omission placed the soul's final salvation in jeopardy. Over the decades, the Church accumulated vast estates. Banks were extremely rare and the ruling groups had little liquid capital, but loans could be obtained from the monasteries.[19]

Nowhere was the influence of the mission felt as in California, where, in 1822, the Church held the largest portion of desirable land and, consequently, almost all the livestock. What kind of social organization was adopted by the Franciscan missionaries to administer this wealth? What historical role did this power and social organization play in the long run? The missionaries of California confronted a different situation than those in New Mexico. In New Mexico, as in large parts of

Mexico and South America, the Indian population was concentrated in native towns and villages and the missionaries were able to take the faith to them. In contrast, the California Indians were dispersed, and the missionaries were compelled to bring them to the faith under the cover of the mission and its adjoining lands. This measure permitted the maximum use of a few clergymen in the administration and supervision of the Indians. The center of each mission was a church or chapel, built by the doubtful converts. Surrounding the church were the living quarters, schools, warehouses, and prison facilities for unruly Indians. Mass was a daily procedural requirement, after which the Indians went to work in the fields from sunrise to sunset.[20] Once the Indian had been brought into the mission on whatever pretext and once he evidenced the vaguest tendency toward conversion, he became a virtual slave whose contact with his pagan relatives was to be prevented at all costs.[21]

Under the mission system, the California Indians were clearly subjected to coerced, compulsory labor which bore a striking resemblance to slavery. The neophytes performed physical labor in handicraft production, agriculture, and construction. While mission work was not exorbitantly strenuous, this qualitative aspect of labor must be viewed in terms of the missionaries' primary objective to keep Indian recruits continuously occupied. The Indians were not spared brutality and arduous work, however, because in addition to the tasks performed on mission lands, neophytes were "loaned" out to work in the presidios and for individual Spanish soldiers. While the Indians were supposed to receive some remuneration for this work, in fact they received no payment for their labor. In this capacity, the Indians performed a number of tasks, ranging from errand boy and cowboy to ditch-digger, i.e., they did all the work the soldiers were supposed to do.[22]

The mission system was basically a series of concentration camps where Indians were relocated for the purpose of providing labor services and for the destruction of their native religious beliefs. While some Indians acquired certain skills, the mission system failed to prepare the vast majority for an existence beyond the scope of their native culture. This occurred not necessarily because of the evil intentions of Franciscan monks, but because the mission—as a conductor of a mode of material production which developed in Spain and later in Mexico—was not adequately equipped to do otherwise.

Economic life within the mission compound revolved around the somewhat mutually exclusive constraints of discipline and productivity. While the padres were concerned about introducing domestic animals and cultivatable products to make the missions self-sufficient, this was a short-term goal tempered, in the long run, by the need to maintain a strict level of discipline and spiritual advancement. To develop individual skills to a maximum degree and to attempt the achievement of a high volume of production would have run counter to the mission's idea of spiritual advancement.[23]

In California, the missionaries never held titles to the land they acquired, nor did they apparently envision its appropriation by the order. However, since specific social and physical conditions motivated considerable expansion of the de facto use of the best lands, little else was left for lay individuals. To illustrate this phenomenon, it is sufficient to mention two instances of territorial expansion. The grazing lands of San Gabriel Mission, although not contiguous, extended from the pueblo of Los Angeles to the mouth of the San Gabriel and Santa Ana rivers, and eastward through La Puente, Santa Ana del Chino, Jurupa, San Bernardino, and San Gorgonio—a total distance close to seventy miles. In the north, the grazing lands of Mission San Carlos extended from Carmel Valley and its surrounding hills and mountains—as well as from the mouth of the Salinas River—up to Chualar.

The expanse of mission livestock range and wealth made it difficult to attract new settlers to the area. As a result, the mission system came under incessant scrutiny during the Mexican period. It appears that the padres were a fairly insignificant political obstacle. Thus, the mission system came to an end in 1833 with the secularization and distribution of its land and livestock holdings to private landgrant holders. The secularization of mission lands marked the second major period (pre-1848) in the history of land tenure practices and social relations in California—the era of the *ranchos*.²⁴

Few colonists had settled in California before 1822, and only thirteen new grants were made by the Mexican government between 1822 and 1833. After the secularization of mission lands, a massive process of carving up the area began. Between 1833 and 1846, approximately eight hundred new grants involving upwards of 8 million acres of the best land were distributed at a feverish pace. Property in land and its accompanying livestock became so highly concentrated that, by 1848, it is estimated that forty individuals held virtually absolute control over the economic and political affairs of California.

In California, the predominant economic unit was transferred overnight from the Franciscan mission to the rancho. The size and number of these ranchos and the social relations they engendered became important for several decades. The institution of the rancho has been traditionally compared with that of the medieval English manor. Each rancho was, to a large extent, self-sufficient. Even though a great deal of production related to livestock was utilized for export purposes, these exports satisfied the luxury needs of the ranchos and did not play a significant role in the daily reproduction of life.²⁵

If the institution of the rancho has been compared with the English feudal manor, the generalized social relations that accompanied it have been likened to the slave South. During the mission system, the predominant forms of labor were religious forced-labor and peonage in the presidios. As the ranchos became organized, a situation closely resembling that of New Mexico developed with a small, solid, landed aristocracy at the top and a mass of former mission Indians at the bottom. Paraphrasing a ranchero, the Indian tilled the soil, pastured cattle, sheared sheep, cut timber, built houses, paddled boats, made bricks and tiles, ground grain, slaughtered cattle, and dressed their hides for market, while Indian women worked as servants, brought up the children, and cooked every meal. Was this not slavery?

In California, a form of debt-peonage also became operative

during this period. Before an Indian could move from place to place, he was required to prove that he had been legally discharged by and was not in debt to his employer. This practice persists and indeed typifies the relationship of many contemporary South American rural landowners to their servants of the land. In addition to this veiled, coercive apparatus designed to secure a stable labor force, outright seizure and physical coercion were not unknown, and there was also some traffic in Indians. In conclusion, then, the methods used to coerce labor to produce and maintain the ranchos way of life was more extreme than European feudal relations. Class relations in California, as in New Mexico, were not limited to two classes—patrones and peones. Although in New Mexico, a middle strata of petty agriculturalists clung precariously to life, in California, the rancheros (*gente de razón*) were the patrones; the Indians hovered between peonage and slavery; and the Mexicans (and other mixed groups) occupied the middle strata. In effect, this meant that the Indian's unpaid labor served as the real basis of the economy; the Mexicans were the artisans, vaqueros, and foremen of the ranchos, as well as petty craftsmen in the scanty villages; whereas the *gente de razón* owned the means of production and occupied all the political and military positions. This situation, popularly depicted as idyllic, was far from utopia except for a few privileged families. The same social structure, at least in Southern California, continued for a few decades after the Treaty of Guadalupe-Hidalgo until it met its demise.

Before proceeding to an empirical and theoretical summary of the material basis of production and traditions in this area, brief mention must be made of Spanish colonization in present-day Arizona and Texas.

Arizona was settled as early as 1696, when Father Kino founded a number of missions including San Xavier del Bac, near present-day Tucson. By the end of his work, around 1712, twenty-five years of quiet was shattered by the discovery of silver in Arizona. After this brief silver boom, Arizona's economy came to be dominated by livestock production, insofar as the state was populated by the missions and some haciendas. However, from the middle of the eighteenth century onward, the area was the target of constant campaigns by warring Indians that made the maintenance of this frontier next to impossible. With the coming of Mexican independence and the disappearance of the defensive presidios, the area was abandoned and, from 1822 to 1862, suffered neglect and obscurity.[26] In the case of Texas, even though more definitive developments took place than in Arizona, its future course makes it more appropriate to be examined in a different essay.

The mode of production that developed and prevailed in most of Europe during the Middle Ages (feudalism) produced many of the forms that, with differences in location and time, the Spanish attempted to transplant in the New World. In many cases they succeeded. In a feudal mode of production the basic form of obtaining an economic surplus occurs through the appropriation of unpaid labor performed by serfs on the land. Whereas capitalism historically develops in and is based upon urban centers, feudal societies of production are based on the countryside. Since capital is mobile and ubiquitous, profit rates in different areas of production tend to become equalized; in contrast, land is immobile and fixed, and rents deriving from it tend to differ depending on fertility and other natural conditions. The study of the forms that ground rent took in Spain and Western Europe are important for an understanding of the developments that took place in northern New Spain.

Rent—in the form of labor services—was one of the oldest and most commonly practiced ways of securing agricultural surplus. It is probably correct to suggest that there is a chronology from labor rent, passing through rent-in-kind, to money rent. As far back as the fourth century B.C., the Chinese had learned to identify these three kinds of agricultural surplus. Whether labor rent is a more or less exploitable method than another form is also problematic. The Chinese philosopher Mencius considered labor services to be superior to others in that they provided the peasants subject to this service with the largest degree of stability, whereas the other two lent themselves more to the landowners' injudicious exactions, because the time required to work for the master was traditionally fixed and bore no relation to physical phenomena.[27] It provided the peasant ability to regulate the intensity of labor as the expectations of his master also varied. When labor services as agricultural rent emerged, the appearance of surplus paid in kind occurred, usually in the form of agricultural products, or in some cases, handicraft production.[28] It is not uncommon to find coexisting forms of labor rent and rent-in-kind, however. Money rent is characterized by the direct producer turning over part of a market product's price to the landowner. A surplus of products in their natural state ceased to be the norm, and the money-form took its place. Historically, the transition to money rent signified a step away from the earliest forms of feudalism toward the direction of a full-fledged monetary-market economy, though the latter is not necessarily a predominantly capitalist social formation.[29]

This is so because the feudal or capitalist character of a mode of production is determined by society's class relations or relations of production and not by the widespread existence of trade or money. If the existence of trade or money is considered the differentiating specification for capitalist development, the economic interpretation of history falls by the board, since we must assert that capitalism has always existed.

Also, within predominantly feudal European social formations, specific forms of land tenure concommitant with the direct exaction of ground rent by the upper class were common: typical examples are the proprietorship of small parcels; different forms of tenant-holding and sharecropping; and, in rare cases, independent owner-cultivators of medium-sized lots. Historically, these forms tended to disappear as feudalism gave way to capitalism. In the case of the proprietorship of small land-parcels, this was so because rural domestic crafts—a normal income supplement—were eventually destroyed by the development of large-scale industry, because methods of cultivation depleted the soil; because of the usurpation of common grazing lands; and because of competition—either from larger plantations or large-scale capitalist enterprises.[30]

The self-propelled estate where a peasant cultivator engaged in independent production was also bound to disappear: eventually he tended to become a small capitalist farmer exploiting the labor of others, or he lost his means of production and became a wage-laborer. Finally, with regard to the different forms of sharecropping, the crucial question is whether the relationship was, formally, a modern "business enterprise," or whether the substantive situation was otherwise, and the tenant holding arrangement merely a covert subterfuge for a more explicit form of rent-extraction.

Tenant-holding forms should *not* be confused with the case of independent capitalist cultivators who rent out the land and whose success is insured by social circumstance. Again, this is not to say that, on occasion, successful capitalist development cannot arise from the former. Whether any of these methods of sharecropping can lead to successful capitalist production is a rather determinable matter—statistically and historically.[31]

Of course, this kind of arrangement is suggestive of the possibility of breakdown of existing relations of production. This may be so because, although the tenant farmer may lack enough capital for self-sufficient management, the expropriation by the landlord goes beyond the old forms of rent, and interest on capital can appear. In other words, the direct producer or tenant, whether he simply utilizes his own labor or the labor of others, can now claim his income in his capacity as a capitalist rather than as a simple laborer. Conversely, the landlord can claim his share as a lender of capital as well as a landowner. Further, there was no dearth of this kind of economic arrangement in agricultural societies in their tributary state. A case in point is Spain where only slightly dissimilar forms appeared through the period of the *Reconquista.*

Spain was, of course, the source of the social institutions that were literally to find fertile ground in the soil of the New World. By the time of the Catholic kings, Spain had instituted the dramatically uneven distribution of income and wealth that was to develop so rapidly in New Spain. Despite the onset of commercial navigation, ownership of land and rents constituted the backbone of the Spanish economy. Spain, in its own particular way, was a society where commerce and capital were secondary to land ownership as the source of income and wealth.[32]

The basic feudal elements of medieval Europe and Spain were reproduced in New Spain. There is little to indicate that the developments that took place in the northern provinces were different from those that took place in the central valleys of Mexico. The hacienda system, with its patron-peon relationships developed later in New Mexico and California, but followed the same course as in Mexico and Spain. Purported differences between the California rancho and the New Mexico hacienda occur more in the way of nomenclature than in any significant matter. Of minor importance are, first, the rapidity with which the ranchos developed in California. But once it is explained that the groundwork had been laid by the more important role played by the missionaries in California, the speed of the transformation ceases to be a matter of concern. Second, the more intense racial overtones in California are due to empirically different circumstances. It is interesting to note that the colonization of Spain after the Reconquista shows a reverse trend. The first two centuries of colonization were characterized by a harsher relationship (outright expulsion and/or slaughter) toward the conquered Moors than those employed during the last few centuries of the colonization process. Otherwise, the basic mode of rent extraction was patently the same in California, New Mexico, Mexico, and Spain.

There are strong similarities—especially between California and New Mexico and the northern sector of Mexico—regarding the manner of colonization: expressly through subcontracting labor to political or military leaders of the Conquest, as well as through the rapid institution of large latifundias as the representative unit of social economy in the area. Again, there was nothing procedurally original in this process: rapid colonization by a few military leaders more or less anxious to settle the land among themselves typified the colonization of Andalusia in southern Spain during the thirteenth and fourteenth centuries.[33]

Perhaps one of the most popular misconceptions about New Mexico is the notion of presumed communalism. This misconception arises from the legal separation which existed between the land assigned to and independently cultivated by the individual peasant and the assurance of common water and grazing resources. In combination with the historical necessity to repel attacks from neighboring nomads, these factors presumably fulfilled the prerequisites of communal living. Communal organization for the purpose of defense cannot, in the long run, be viewed as substantial proof of a communal mode of production, anymore than footraces among communal people can be construed as evidence of competitive capitalism. These arguments are purely formal and do not advance any serious understanding of social change. Further, in the specific case of New Mexico, any communal preoccupation with defense was clearly secondary to the necessities of subsistence survival. This is clearly evident in the dispersal of colonial settlements and the dissolution of the towns—usually because the townspeople were more worried about being closer to their individual plots of land than to each other.[34]

Secondly, the existence of common lands disappeared in New Mexico, as it had earlier in Mexico, Spain, Poland, and Rumania, by a process of unswerving similarity. Private individuals (livestock owners in the cases of Spain, Mexico, and New Mexico) usurped the use of common lands until, eventually, free peasant proprietors were subjected to various forms of rent-exaction, while those who usurped the lands came to eventually control or acquire not only the communal lands but the lands of the peasants themselves. This was precisely the practice employed by the hacendados and rancheros. Of course, in some cases the legal protection extended to pueblos and settlements had positive results: in Spain, many towns were able to establish a measure of peasant independence during the Reconquista period; in Mexico, there were cases where the efforts of the townspeople in defending the integrity of the *ejidos* (communal lands) against the onslaught of the large landholders were successful. These efforts did not come to fruition in the northernmost settlements.

In my estimation, most of the confusion regarding this aspect of the history of the Southwest can be traced to its historians' concentration on three interrelated modes of interpretation: formal-cultural, legal, and institutional.

Formal-cultural interpretations generally focus on superficial or, in the final analysis, insufficient data to justify their claims. A common example of this approach is the description of inferior mental attitudes held by individual members of Spanish society. The "correct attitude"—as held by the historian—should embrace a certain willingness towards risk and uncertainty, since these facets are essential to the development of a business mentality. The opposite tendency—embodied in the notion of communalism—utilizes the same basis for argument: in both cases an explanatory structure is based on mental attitudes. Whether a business mentality or a communal disposition is preferred depends on the choice, or prejudice, of the individual historian. The failure to include the basis of *choice* between various subjective conceptions of what idyllic society is and was opens up a Pandora's box of relative choice. We enter a realm where the notion of historical progress is eliminated and one conception of the idea is as worthwhile as any other.

Other writers have been concerned with specifying the precise legal jurisdiction regulating the process of settlement in the area under study. Their activity cannot be condemned; on the contrary, it is a highly valuable task insofar as its practicioner does not fall into the error of regarding the letter of the law as the deciding factor of actual social relations during this period. Legal canons surrounding the issue of property in the land are important, not because they indicate that under the Spanish and Mexican governments every peasant was an independent cultivator, but because the study of subsequent developments reveals the manner in which laws were observed, i.e., where traditional practices supported by economic power prevailed over written legislation.

Of the three modes discussed, institutional history has perhaps been the most successful method used in identifying important structures in the history of the Southwest. This approach has specified the mission, the pueblo, and the presidio as the crucial institutions in the colonization of the Southwest. It is perfectly proper to speak of these institutions as the dominant instruments of conquest and initial settlement, but their discussion provides little understanding of the evolution of classes, the possibilities for and forms of economic surplus that originated in these societies and, finally, the directions for change which stem from this kind of social economy.[35]

The combination of cultural, institutional, and legal emphasis has implicitly produced a view of the Southwest as a peculiarly unique example of Spanish colonial society, sometimes referred to as the "Spanish borderlands."[36] My own interpretation is that nothing could be further from the truth. The basic socio-economic life of the northern provinces closely resembles the rest of Mexico and Latin America, and the same holds true—with slight variations—at the institutional level. There is no reason to believe that the land system of California and New Mexico would have had a future different from the process of latifundia and peasant exploitation that has characterized history south of the Bravo since 1848.

From this combination of historical and economic analysis, what are the main conclusions that can be drawn about the material substratum of life in New Mexico and California?

The strongest conclusion is the identification in both instances of a society which, in its process of development, resulted in a feudal form of social economy, characterized by a fairly rigid class structure and based upon possession and legal ownership of the land and by a separation in the distribution of this land. The coexistence of latifundias and minifundias and the predominance of the hacienda made this social economy indistinguishable from the rest of the Mexican social structure. By their nature, these aspects of the mode of production prevented the development of socially productive labor forces and the concentration of capital (though not of wealth) as well as the progressive application of technology in the agricultural sector.[37]

ii: Development of Commodity Circulation in the Southwest

Despite centuries of physical isolation, the old Southwest maintained an interesting array of trade ties with surrounding economies. Although the existence of trade has been popularly interpreted as a characteristic of "modern" societies, this is hardly the case, and such conceptions generally occur from viewing contemporary trade forms as the transactional norm. Trade between groups, clans, or societies has existed from the earliest times. It usually makes its first appearance as occasional exchange, and is linked to the extremes of scarcity or abundance in a primitive economy. Slightly more stable forms occur when surplus production becomes more or less consistent; silent barter, ceremonial gifts, etc., are stepping stones to and the initial manifestations of historical—rather than incidental—exchange.

The stage of "trade" proper, as it is commonly referred to, arises when the societies engaging in exchange are no longer self-sufficient; when trade is not reduced to a surplus which can be disposed of after the groups' needs have been fulfilled; when the surplus is no longer limited to a few specialized items since different societies have become specialized in production; when regional specialization forces the interdependence of adjacent groups; and when each group can no longer satisfy all of its own needs. In other words, trade in this form coincides with the appearance of markets and craft production.

In this form, trade necessitates the tradesman or merchant.

This individual makes his living by buying certain commodities at a price which is hopefully below their true value and selling them at a price which is hopefully above their true value. Consequently, trade develops and merchants thrive in conducting transactions between people living at different stages of productive development. People who enjoy the same level of economic development are less prone to enter into such unfavorable deals. As a general rule, trade is the result of uneven economic development and differences in productive ability.[1]

Before the Spanish *entrada* into New Mexico during the 1600s, trade had already taken place between earlier groups of regional settlers. In his first expedition, Coronado observed the existence of commerce between the Plains Indians and the Pueblos. The Plains Indians, skillful tanners of buffalo and deer hides, exchanged these goods on a regular basis for Pueblo corn, cloth, and pottery. Long-distance trade, so typical of the Old World at the time of the 1492 discovery, also existed in the New World during this period, primarily between the two major civilizations of the continent—the Aztecs of Mexico and the Incas of Peru. From Peru, a northward flow of metal and alloys—bronze, compounds of silver and gold, copper, gold, etc.—were exchanged for Aztec goods: precious stones such as amethysts, emeralds, and obsidians, weapons, dyes, embroidered clothing, and jewelry. In itself, trade was obviously not the product of Spanish influence on her new colonies.

However, Spain did impose trade regulations which became increasingly significant over time. In the case of Southwest settlement, as well as the rest of Spanish America, revolutions of independence marked a turning point in the development of commodity circulation or trade.[2] To understand this transition, we will explore the pattern of trade relations before 1821 in the specific case of the Southwest.

Beginning with New Mexico, it is possible to see at least three major aspects of trade affecting this frontier society. The first was the commerce that developed with surrounding groups of nomadic Indians. From the Comanches, Kiowas, and other groups, the New Mexicans obtained beef meat, tallow, and buffalo and deer hides, usually in exchange for knives, axes, muskets, liquor, and vegetables, especially corn. This trade relationship became quite organized, and traders from various New Mexican settlements congregated annually at the Taos fair where exchange took place. Additionally, numerous merchants from New Mexico ventured into Indian territory to engage in trade with the Kiowa and Comanche. Kiowa trade was conducted by a group called the *ciboleros*, or buffalo hunters (since these traders were also engaged in buffalo hunts as a part-time occupation). A more active intercourse developed with the Comanche, giving rise to the term Comanchero trade. This exchange involved, as it developed, a considerable amount of horse and cattle rustling at the Comanche end of the trade route in Texas. Trade with Indian nations became a vehicle for French-Spanish trade. French goods made their appearance in New Mexico in the mid-1700s. These commodities originated with the French in Louisiana, passed through the hands of the Pawnee Indians, and were then traded to the Comanche, who finally brought them to the Taos fair.[3]

The trade between New Mexican merchants was strictly regulated by Spanish authorities, who entertained their private policies of gift exchange and other forms designed to maintain good relations and peace on the frontier. A significant number of traders had no permission to engage in commerce, and the Spanish authorities did not encourage this trade.

The second aspect of trade in the Southwest settlement involved a commercial relationship with the rest of Mexico. The towns of New Mexico such as Santa Fe, were at the northern end of New Spain's network of communications: the Camino Real, or King's Highway. The Camino Real allowed the residents of New Mexico to maintain contact and receive subsistence supplies from the closest settlement on the road —Chihuahua, two hundred and fifty miles to the south.[4]

During the early period of settlement, Chihuahua became the center (and the Camino Real the avenue) of supply for the missionaries and other inhabitants of the northern provinces. A caravan service—similar to the long-distance caravans of antiquity—developed, at first, on an irregular basis from Mexico City to New Mexico. The trip occurred every three years and generally took six months in one-way transit. From Mexico City northward, the caravan carried mission supplies, missionaries, new settlers, baggage mail, and what was at first illegal private merchandise for exchange. During this early period, two forms of profit-making developed: one was based on the exchange of merchandise between different points on the route; the second was based on profiteering by caravan contractors involved in mission supply service. From New Mexico, a southward flow of local products initially included coarse dress fabrics, drapes, blankets, hides, and candles. As further trade developed, the northward supply of merchandise included boots, shoes, chocolate, sugar, liquors, paper, and ink. New Mexico was becoming a transactional center for the exchange of Indian and Spanish goods. By the mid-eighteenth century, an independent trade had developed between the merchants of Chihuahua and the New Mexicans, and an annual caravan moved between these two points. The times of arrival and departure from Santa Fe were arranged so that New Mexican merchants could visit the annual fair in Taos where trade with adjacent settlements took place. In terms of trade, the economy of New Mexico came to be monopolized by, and indebted to, the few Chihuahua merchants who had achieved a commercial monopoly through their receipt of royal licenses. The only other beneficiaries in New Mexico were large livestock owners who sometimes drove their own flocks of sheep to sale in the Chihuahua market under military protection.[5]

In addition, an active trade in slaves existed in New Mexico during most of the colonial period. Some traders engaged in this activity because it was far more profitable than trade in skins. It is also possible that some marginal settlers risked the dangers of reprisal to supplement their meager existence by hunting Indian men and women and exchanging them for various products. These slaves were usually traded to enemy Indian tribes or to wealthy Spaniards in the south who utilized them as servants and peons.

The case of California was somewhat different from New Mexico. The latter depended on the Indians for beef, tallow, and hides. On the other hand, California was self-sufficient in these items and used its surplus for export purposes.[6] Although California was settled by the Spanish toward the end of their domination of Spanish America (that is, during the most liberal period in trade regulations), a number of circumstances prevented the development of trade and outside communications. The overland south-north routes into California were desert routes, which effectively prevented the development of a well-trained path from mainland Mexico to California. California commerce during the colonial period can be reduced to a few items: hides and tallow exported to Mexico through the port of San Blas, and the provisioning of wine, flour, and grain to the occasional ships from other nations which put ashore in California. The latter were usually American ships engaged in the exchange of sea otter skins with a commercial house on the Chinese mainland. The California missions became far more prosperous than their New Mexican antecedents and did not have to depend on supply services as did the latter.[7]

In terms of colonial settlement, Texas had a more irregular history than either New Mexico or California. Texas was finally occupied during the 1720s, after a century of tentative colonization and retreat. Though sparsely populated throughout the colonial period, the impact of commerce and trade on the Texas settlement was perhaps more profound than in the previous cases. This was due, in part, to the size of the population involved and, more significantly, to the proximity of French settlements in Louisiana. Indeed, the geographical proximity of the French colony caused an active commercial exchange between the inhabitants of both areas. Although commercial intercourse was regulated by law, most trade was clandestine in character; smuggling enjoyed a high popularity during this period. The situation became accentuated after the Louisiana Purchase. As was the case in New Mexico, the supply services were managed by private merchants and government officials, usually for their personal gain. This official corruption generated a great deal of friction between state and Church authorities throughout the eighteenth century.[8] Although cattle multiplied with incredible speed on the Texas plains, livestock production did not become as integral a part of the social economy as had been the case in New Mexico and Spain. Smuggling, Indian slave trade, prostitution, and other such activities typical of border communities left an early imprint on Texas society. Despite its small population, the high degree of interaction with outside economies brought about the formation of an apparently complex society marked by a variety of "service" occupations (traders, interpreters, prostitutes, etc.).[9] Here, as in the nineteenth century, the history of Texas reads like a tabloid of adventure and exploit.

As a whole, the history of commodity circulation in the Southwest reflects Spain's colonial policy. Of course, all colonial powers sought to effectively control their trade with the colonies, but the degree to which Spain sought to regulate and appropriate the benefits of colonial possession was greater. Spain's colonial policy reflected the relative degree of backwardness into which she had fallen shortly after the discovery of America. Whereas in England and Holland commercial capitalists came to have an increasing influence in state trade policies, this was not the case in Spain. From the seventeenth century onward, England and Holland began to pursue a policy of "free trade" designated to benefit the domestic economic interests in ascendancy. The defeat of these interests in Spain during the sixteenth century left an absolute monarchy based primarily on landed interests who were occupied in colonial and world trade only insofar as their domestic position remained unthreatened. A typical policy of the Spanish crown was the institution in Sevilla of the Casa de Contratación (or House of Trade) in 1501. The Casa de Contratación had complete authority over commercial affairs with the colonies, and came to dominate commercial activities completely, since all colonial trade had to pass through the city of Sevilla. For many years, a ship could unload its cargo only at this port and a loading ship going to the colonies was required to pick up the goods at Sevilla. Although a change in ports from Sevilla to

Cádiz was effected later, all commerce still had to be transported by Spanish ships, and all colonial trade had to pass
through a single town in Spain. Instead of placing trade in the
hands of monopolies, the Spanish government attempted to
effect a monopoly over trade.[10]

Trade regulations were as forbidding in the colonies themselves; neither foreigners nor their vessels could enter colonial
ports, under penalty of death and loss of property. This trade
regulation was added to manufacturing regulations which
prohibited the production and cultivation of products that
might endanger already existing production in the mother
country.[11]

As we have noticed in the Southwest, these policies resulted
in smuggling, a flourishing contraband trade, and the slow,
grinding process of colonial development. Toward the end of
Spanish rule, the Crown attempted to ease trade regulations.
Certain cargo to the mother country could be carried to British
vessels, and some trade was allowed among the colonies. These
measures were prompted by the pressure of British interests
and, in addition, by the imperative of colonial revitalization.
Unfortunately, these measures were accompanied by a number of taxes and tariffs: Spain's renewed attempt to exact a
maximum colonial profit. The remedy was too small and came
too late. Napoleon's invasion of Spain coincided with the increasing discontent of a Creole class who wanted its share of
the profits following other wars of independence in Spanish
America. In Mexico, the alignment of the classes that ended
Spanish domination was not as strongly dominated by commercial interests as it was in the rest of the colonies. This was
partially because of the fear that a movement toward independence would become a social revolution from the bottom up (as
Hidalgo and Morelos had hoped). Consequently, landed
interests played a more important role in Mexico's independence. However, *the necessity to eliminate commercial restrictions
became an objective element in the final dissolution of political ties with
the Spanish empire.*[12]

The independence of the Latin American republics was
immediately followed by the *elimination of trade restrictions, the*

rapid intensification of commerce, and the accessibility of Latin American nations to foreign commercial and industrial interests. The pattern of economic and commercial development in the Southwest after 1821 reflected these trends which had occurred in the rest of Mexico and South America. The story has been told, not by the historians of South American trade, but in the diaries, legends, and even the folktales of the American West. One instance of this popular history is the entrance of the fur trappers into Mexican territory after 1821.

As early as the sixteenth century, Spanish explorers recognized the abundance and utility of furs in the area known as the Southwest. But since these explorers were mainly interested in the wealth to be obtained from gold and silver mining, large-scale ventures in fur trapping and trading really began with the American frontiersmen.

After the Louisiana Purchase of 1803, Spain began to use the fur trade as a diplomatic tool. By loosening the restrictions on trade in the area northwest of New Mexico, Spain was able to maintain Indian dependence through the exchange of pelts and other articles. In this manner, the Indians served as a buffer between the Spanish and American settlers, since the Spanish realized that the Indians had more to offer the Americans than they themselves did.

Southwest trade in the early 1800s generally consisted of coarse furs (buffalo and deer hides) and, for a number of reasons, did not develop further until the 1820s. High freight costs made the exportation of furs unprofitable; and, additionally, the warm climates of Spain and Mexico hardly accentuated their market value. Further, most Spanish colonists were too busy trying to subsist agriculturally to have much time for trapping. Of course, the main reason was that until 1821, Mexico was still owned by Spain. Before Mexican independence, a number of trading expeditions left the Missouri settlements for Santa Fe, but most were seized and imprisoned by the Spanish authorities. By enforcing severe penalties for trapping and the mere possession of furs, Spain hoped to promote and protect her own trade between central Mexico and the northern province.

During the first years of Mexican independence, Mexican officials were largely preoccupied with sustaining their power and developing their country. Consequently, no effort was made to enforce the old Spanish restrictions concerning fur trapping. Trade to the Santa Fe region developed rapidly, with Taos and Santa Fe as the centers for trapping and Indian trading operations. Merchants would bring goods to Santa Fe, and then return to Missouri with furs. In this way, the Santa Fe trade and the fur trade developed symbiotically.[13]

In 1824, the extensive trapping out of Taos and Santa Fe came to the attention of Mexican officials. Soon after, Americans were prohibited from trapping out of Mexican streams. Because of this prohibition, trappers began smuggling furs. Taos became a strategic location for traders: the streams of the Southwest were not easily navigable, thus overland transportation had to be relied upon. Because of Taos's remote location, furs could be taken out or supplies smuggled in without attracting the attention of Mexican authorities. Its proximity to the Santa Fe Trail was another asset. These qualities made Taos a perfect supply base for the overland route.

Since "foreigners" were prohibited from trapping beaver in Mexican territory, some men found it easier to become Mexican citizens than to risk smuggling penalties. Most of these men applied for a trapping license within one year of citizenship. They were also the men who gradually acquired vast amounts of land and contributed to the "bloodless conquest" of New Mexico by the United States.

The years between 1825 and 1833 are known as the Golden Era of Beaver Trapping. During this time, swarms of trappers operated out of Taos and Santa Fe, and the competition for beaver streams increased. There was a rapid expansion of trade between Missouri, Santa Fe, and Chihuahua, in addition to extensive traffic between New Mexico and California. "Trailblazing" to California, accredited to such famous "mountain men" as Jedediah Smith and Kit Carson, brought trappers into more promising beaver grounds and uncovered a convenient route to Pacific ports where furs could be marketed.[14]

Most of the beaver fur in North America was used in making men's hats. In the early 1830s, when silk began to be imported from China and, subsequently, more fashionable than fur, the price of beaver dropped. Although the decline in the price of beaver did not result in the decline of the fur trade, it did change the nature of the trade throughout the far West. After 1832, with the increased popularity of buffalo robes, the buffalo became the most sought-after animal. Unlike beaver pelts (which few Indians trapped), buffalo hides could be traded with the Indians. This meant that the fur trade could be carried out at trading posts and, in the mid-1830s, the stationary trading post became a dominant feature of the fur trade.

The impact of fashion, in concert with other factors such as the replacement of beaver with seal or rabbit fur, and the most obvious reason of all—the depletion of beaver streams cause by heavy unrestricted trapping—relegated the 1840s fur trade to the unimportant role it had played during the Spanish period. Once again, coarse furs dominated the trade and trapping became obsolete.[15]

Individual or small groups of trappers dominated the Southwest trade. In California, however, mountain men often held this occupation. Trapping in California was carried on by Hudson Bay Company, a large British firm which ran trapping expeditions throughout North America as well as Hawaii.

The early period of British fur trapping was characterized by poor relations between the Mexican government and the Company. No inquiries into Mexican land rights were made and the California government was so weak that Company officials held it in high contempt. No governmental protection was necessary since the wilderness in which the Company worked was far from any settlement, and the small number of beaver made trapping them impractical for the individual trapper. The Company attempted to extract the fur quickly in case there was an unreasonable border settlement. After 1838, the Company made an attempt to establish better relations with Alvarado's government. The Company was beginning to branch out into various agricultural areas, including cattle raising. Naturally, such an endeavor would be totally impossible under a hostile government.

By 1840, friendly relations had been established, but the agricultural plans never materialized, and California, which did not have a large beaver population to begin with, had lost almost all of its beavers.[16]

The colorful stories of mountain men roaming the West in search of fur occupy a significant role in American folklore. Often, however, these stories are not historically accurate. The available literature about the fur trade is rather poor. Writers seem overly concerned with legends rather than with the economic foundations of southwestern commerce. Research is inadequate in terms of the role of the fur merchant, the price of fur, the cost of other commodities, and the role of the American Indians.

In conclusion, the men who did the trapping should be mentioned. Although these mountain men have become historical heroes, responsible for opening an unsettled region to commodity circulation, in reality, they did not contribute to any significant change in the region's economy. They did explore, and caused the attendant destruction of resources, contributing to the alienation of the Indians. The trappers often remained in the area after 1840. Many became Mexican citizens, while others served as guides for the American government and for individuals going west. Their knowledge of the area's geography and the Indian tribes made them a valuable source of information to people who came later. However, the trappers were, first and foremost, men in search of a profit. While colorful, the lore which has grown up around them should take a backseat to economic considerations in social science research.

Equally important in the development of Southwest commodity circulation was the formation of the trade route known as the Santa Fe Trail. In 1821, William Becknell, traditionally known as the "Father of the Santa Fe Trail," took a trading expedition from Franklin, Missouri—a new river town—to Santa Fe. The route he followed was one of two commonly used routes, both of which crossed the plains to the

Big Bend of the Arkansas. From there, Becknell followed a tortuous mountain route over Raton Pass and across into New Mexico. Wagons could not, however, follow this route, and on his return trip Becknell bypassed the Raton Mountains and discovered a short cut across the Cimarron Desert, a flat, suitable area. On his trip, Becknell had carried his trade goods on pack animals and had reached Santa Fe by mid-December. Successful in selling out at a profit, he promptly returned home in January with news of the changed attitude of the authorities in New Mexico.

Encouraged by Becknell's reports, several expeditions left Missouri for Santa Fe in the spring of 1822. Becknell himself went along, taking three wagons—the first caravan ever hauled to Santa Fe and back—and established the Santa Fe Trail as a road. Although the caravan nearly proved disastrous (wagons had to go sixty miles without water), this cut-off proved more practical than the old one and other freighters soon began assembling in Franklin. Within a few years after Becknell's 1822 journey, annual caravans were traveling the nine hundred mile route from Independence, Missouri—the newly favored starting place—through dangerous Indian Territory to Santa Fe. Later, Council Grove—a city one thousand miles further west—became the starting point. The freight was transported in huge Conestoga-type vehicles, pulled by three or more yokes of oxen or teams of mules, and carried more than five thousand pounds of merchandise. These vehicles of early freighting trade came to be known as "Santa Fe trains." From the New Mexican bases of Santa Fe, Taos, and Albuquerque, beaver hunters could now exploit the area of the Southern Rockies. Thus, the widespread commerce of the prairies began. One of the most famous accounts of this commerce is the journal of a Santa Fe trader, Josiah Gregg. During eight expeditions across the Great Western Prairies, he recorded events and compiled them with his personal interpretations in a book. The first draft of *Commerce of the Prairies* was completed in 1843 and provides an eye-witness narrative history of Santa Fe during the 1830s.[17]

Traders had to contend with the burdens of travel, wagon

tools, official graft, and the attacks of Southwest Indian tribes. When Indian raids threatened the Trail, teamsters would travel closely together driving several wagons abreast. The caravans varied in size from year to year, but usually consisted of fifty wagons or less. At night, they would corral—or circle—and guards would be stationed. The rate of travel over the Santa Fe Trail averaged about fifteen miles a day and round trip passage usually took two to three months. Once in Santa Fe, the cargoes of textiles, lead, hardware, cutlery, glassware, and similar goods were traded for Mexican silver, mules, pelts and hides, blankets, and other items in demand on the East Coast.

When New Mexico became an American territory in 1848, traffic and trade over the Santa Fe Trail underwent many changes. For example, during the Mexican regime, the caravans made only one round trip each spring and summer; but with United States soldiers, civil servants, and settlers demanding goods, teaming operations to Santa Fe were modified to allow regular year-round schedules.

One of the largest wagon-freighting firms to cover the Great Plains was headed by three veterans of the Santa Fe Trail trade. Russell, Majors, and Waddell, a firm that grew wealthy from war rumors, became responsible for the movement of freight from Missouri to Salt Lake City, where a political rebellion threatened to occur in 1859. In transporting supplies for the troops ordered by President Buchanan, the firm established what became a standardized plan for the movement of men, animals, and vehicles. Although the firm eventually ended in financial ruin, it established a pattern for the march of wagon freight across the plains. In fact, the increase in freighting volume continued until completion of the various transcontinental railroads.[18]

The Santa Fe Trail, the lifeline of New Mexico, also served a military function after Cheyenne, Comanche, and Kiowa raids occurred in Colorado, New Mexico, and Texas. The Trail provided a route for military supplies to California and New Mexico volunteers with additional subsistence goods for the rest of the population. Many of these "Indian depredations" occurred along the New Mexico stretch of the Trail, where General James Carleton appointed an expedition under the command of Kit Carson to stop the Indian uprisings. This military endeavor—known as the Battle of Adobe Walls—led to a reduction of Indian raids on the wagon trains using the Trail and resulted in an 1864 treaty signed by the three tribes and the United States government: the Indians agreed not to engage in any further warfare either against settlements or against the traders of the Santa Fe Trail and to remain otherwise nonbelligerent. Although the Army continued to escort wagons on the Santa Fe Trail until the end of the war, there was little or no conflict with the various Indian nations along the route.[19]

The Santa Fe Trail was not an exclusive relationship between the frontier towns of Missouri and those of New Mexico. In fact, Santa Fe did not become the southern terminal of the Trail but simply a watering hole in the southern flow of merchandise. The old trail to Chihuahua now became the vehicle of continuation for American trade bound for all destinations south of New Mexico. From Santa Fe, American merchandise reached Chihuahua and Durango; trade links were even established with Sonora to the west. As such, these "local" transactions became part of the developing trade and influence of the United States with all of Mexico. However, the relative importance of this aspect of trade within the totality of Mexico's foreign commerce has not yet been determined. As American merchants moved farther into Mexico, they encountered constraints of commercial control and, consequently, a considerable amount of friction and contraband trade developed between Anglo tradesmen and Mexican officials in the northern sector.

In California, wealth took the form of live beef cattle and, as the period of independence from Spain commenced, this wealth entered into a lucrative trade arrangement with foreign vessels. Cattle were slaughtered for a small amount of dried beef for local consumption, and hides, tallow, and horn for commercial purposes. Money was scarce in California at this time, and almost all transactions were conducted by barter.

The value of hides fluctuated between one and three dollars, and the hides themselves were referred to as "California banknotes."

In exchange for hides and other animal products, the *Californios* obtained a heterogeneous assortment of goods including liquor, cigars, sugar, spices, gunpowder, and furniture. Throughout the Mexican period, the hide and tallow trade provided the California rancheros with goods from the outside world and helped make California familiar in the East.[20]

Throughout the Southwest, all commercial activity had two major consequences. The first involved the utilization of a new trail between California and New Mexico that came to be called the Old Spanish Trail (although it had never been used by the Spaniards). These two provinces had never been in contact during the Spanish period and had remained in complete isolation from one another. The connecting path between these two settlements was originally established as a result of the fur expeditions from Santa Fe, when many trappers who came to California for pelts via rivers and streams found it easier to procure fresh mules and horses for the return trip.[21]

This mode of travel eventually developed into a lucrative two-way trade during the 1830s and 40s and brought blankets and other items to California in exchange for mules that would eventually find their way back to Missouri and beyond. Some of the same New Mexican traders who had previously engaged in slave and other trade with the Utah Indians became active on the Old Spanish Trail. Understandably, they were not welcomed by the placid landowners of Southern California, who treated them as they would any "foreigner." Trade on the Old Spanish Trail grew between 1830 and 1848, and disappeared rapidly thereafter.

The second major consequence of Southwest trading activity involved the development of communication routes reaching waves of colonists in the southwestern states. The importance of these colonists will be the subject of closer analysis in a later chapter, but one aspect of their migration is germane here. Just as the emergence of Santa Fe trade can be explained as a result of the pursuit of wider markets by American enterprises as well as in terms of Mexican independence, the appearance of colonists in the Southwest corresponds to the vagaries of American economic development.

By the time of Mexican independence, a large sector of United States economy could be identified as an internationally important center of industrial capitalism. Consequently, the United States began to suffer from those periodic crises which are the hallmark of a capitalist mode of production. What are now controlled recessions were previously known as depressions or, by yet another name, panics. Throughout most of the nineteenth century, two panics exerted considerable influence on the subsequent history of the Southwest. The economic collapse of 1819 gave tremendous impetus to the colonization schemes for Austin in Texas, and served to reinforce the flow of colonists migrating to Texas. Similarly, the crisis of 1837 was an important reason for the first flow of overland colonists to California.

In summary, what impact did independence from Spain and Mexico have on the economy of the Southwest in terms of trade development? As in any situation, the increase in commodity circulation carried an attendant disintegration of the simplicity of life that had existed before this time. But, as in every case, the appearance of commerce in a natural or subsistence economy had a disintegrating effect, limited by the nature of the producing community itself. In other words, whatever development or disintegration took place did so on the basis of the existing mode of production. This was certainly the case in New Mexico and California where the old class relations (which I have described in an earlier chapter) remained basically untouched. The traders, whatever their nationality, were regarded as foreign intruders within the traditional social fabric of these societies.

Secondly, as in the case of some localities in classical antiquity and in medieval Western Europe, the development of commerce in the Southwest was not conducive to the development of local industry and manufacturing, or to the growth of towns and handicraft industries. Commercial development only achieves these results under certain circumstances. The failure to do so is attributable to the fact that gains in long distance trade are often made not by simply exporting domestic products, but by promoting exchange between two or several backward, though unevenly developed, areas. In any given area, when less developed productive forces engage in commerce, there is a tendency toward monetary concentration in the hands of the merchants.

The development of commercial capital has been falsely associated with unremitting progress and the growth of urban centers. But these are empirical contingencies. Trade and commercial capital can also make their appearance among economically undeveloped, nomadic peoples—as evidenced by the Southwest before the Spanish invasion. In the case of the Southwest, manufacturing or industrial development did not occur as a direct result of increased commercial activity.

Neither commerce nor commercial capital should be confused with capitalism as a mode of production, since both commerce and commercial capital are much older than capitalism. The presence and development of commerce is an insufficient explanation of the transition from one mode of production to another. In fact, wherever merchant capital predominated in the history of capitalism in Western Europe, backward conditions and a stronger similarity to things past survived. It is fair to say that the development of merchant wealth has generally stood in inverse proportion to the general economic development of society. The history of Latin America is one large textbook example of this seeming paradox. Here, in twenty republics, a century and a half have passed during which the greatest accumulation of commercial wealth has been accompanied by the strengthening and persistence of social relations characteristic of the region before independence. The Latin American nations are all characterized as trading nations, as well as backward, semicolonial, and semifeudal nations. The monopolies that develop from the trade of backward societies have, at the basis of their existence, that very backwardness.[22] Insofar as this backwardness can be eliminated, the basis for trade exploitation will disappear and so will the monopolies arising therefrom.[23]

Wherever commercial capital has held sway, it has stood for all sorts of "illegal" enterprises, including robbery and piracy. In the case of the Southwest, the local expression of this aspect of commercial wealth was the excessive smuggling that developed, especially in Texas and New Mexico, after Mexican independence. Smuggling and contraband characterize the United States-Mexico border relations to this day.

In conclusion, the two most important and direct effects of the development of Southwest commodity circulation were, first, the unification of the area as one region and one market, especially as effected through trade on the Old Spanish Trail. Never before, despite legend and wishful thinking, had the areas of California and New Mexico constituted a materially unified area. This was done after independence in 1821, and was promoted by the spread of commerce in the western United States. Unification became an important precondition to the establishment of capitalism at a later date. Secondly, the trails opened by commodity circulation provided an avenue of escape for the newly dispossessed, those who sought relief from the crises of capitalist abundance. These colonists became the pivotal agents who would economically survive the political defeats of 1830 and 1848, and who would assist in the decisive implantation of a new mode of production in this old region.

iii: *The Victory of Capitalism*

How was the final defeat of feudalism in the Southwest achieved? What was the social significance of the Mexican-American War? The answers to these questions are both simple and complex: simple in that within a few years, a palpably different mode of the social organization of production predominated the economy of the Southwest; complex, in that with regional and chronological differences, a variety of social mechanisms and individual agents simultaneously influenced this change. In some areas, it is clear that economic forces—or differences in the methods governing the economic organization of production—were perhaps the most important determinants of social change; while in other areas (or at other times) purely economic factors are obscured, and legal (and/or extraeconomic forms of coercion) are clearly visible. As a whole, this situation is not surprising, if the process is one of social revolution: it is certainly more difficult to identify and to ascertain the impact of social forces in an epoch of upheaval and rapid flux than in an era of stability. This chapter will isolate the most significant elements effecting the transition from feudalism to capitalism in the Southwest. In doing so, a distinction will be made between economic and noneconomic processes and, at the same time, the economic aspect of basically noneconomic processes will be explored.

In reviewing the agents and agencies of historical change in the Southwest between 1821 and 1880, it is possible to identify four major contributors: the development of commodity circulation; the infiltration of independent colonists; the litigation over land titles; and the effects of usury capital. Since the development of commodity circulation has already been discussed, we will concentrate on the action of usury capital as the process that most clearly delineates the conflict between the two modes of production, recognizing that the importance of the remaining factors should not be dismissed.

Historically, the infiltration of colonists predates litigation over land titles and the development of usury capital by more than two decades, concurrent with the influx of traders after 1821.

In Texas, the era of American colonization began during the period 1819–21, when Moses Austin succeeded in obtaining (first from the Spanish crown and later from the Mexican government) the authorization to carry out a colonization project. The Panic of 1819 brought increased immigration to Austin's colony, and nursed a developing interest in other colonization projects.[1]

Between 1821 and 1836, the relationship between the American colonists in Texas and the authorities in Mexico City can best be recorded as a litany of vicissitudes. During this period, Mexico underwent what historians have referred to as the conflict between "federalists" and "centralists." In general, Mexican centralists encouraged the maintenance of colonial society; consequently, they derived their power from the landed aristocracy, the wealthy mine-owners, and the Church. They advocated a strong, centralized government under military rule, and tight control over local industry and commerce. The federalists formed the opposition and drew their members from the bourgeois classes. They represented independent commercial interests, incipient industrial enterprises, and advocated the elimination of Church privileges and the development of local autonomy in government.[2]

The Texas colonists were soon caught in the struggle between these two political forces. Many colonists entered Texas under the Colonization Act of 1824, enacted during one of the few periods when the federalists held governmental power. In addition, other colonists entered the territory under liberal contracts with the state authorities in Coahuila (the Mexican state that Texas was a territory of until 1836). After the federalists were defeated, the situation of various Mexican states deteriorated in terms of self-rule, and the future of those territories that hoped to become states became cloudy. By the early thirties, Mexico's colonial policy included firm military rule, the suspension of any promise of statehood, heavy duties on commerce, and restriction on further American migration into Texas.

Of course, most of what is now Texas had never been under effective Spanish control and other areas were, on the average, thinly populated. In Texas, American immigration had swollen the foreign population to more than fifteen thousand residents, and Americans vastly outnumbered the Mexican population. When the hostilities which eventually led to the independence of Texas began, the American residents had developed into a large settlement of self-employed colonists engaged in agriculture and commerce. Despite the presence of some slaveholders, the settlement was characterized by the absence of traditional bonds typical of Mexican society, and represented the transition to—if not the embryonic form of —an economy organized under capitalist modes of production. The settlement was certainly no longer characterized by feudalistic forms of land rent and peonage. But neither was it capitalistic, since the Americans were, with some exceptions, independent cultivators who did not employ wage labor in the manner of classical capitalist enterprise systems. Most importantly, the Texas settlement did not arise from the old society, but had grown side by side with it and independent of it. Consequently, its political independence from Mexico in 1836 was not incongruous with its history of independent self-development.

The War of Texas Independence did not set the territorial boundary with Mexico at the Rio Grande, but simply extended it to the Nueces River. Below the Nueces, the traditional way of life in the old Southwest, as explored in earlier chapters, remained uninterrupted until the war between Mexico and the

United States. In contrast, American settlers had clearly developed a different social economy. In summary, then, American colonists in Texas had not deposed the feudal system of the Southwest but, instead, acted as the harbingers of a new system which they implanted where the Spanish had not imposed theirs: the Texas settlement provides a case of erosion from without, not from within.[3]

Between 1836 and 1848, the section between the Rio Grande and the Nueces continued to be populated by Mexican immigrants. During this period, and for decades after the War of 1848, the lower Rio Grande Valley evidenced a system similar to the early California Settlement, with differences between various counties. After 1836, the role of the colonists diminished and other legal economic agents completed the economic transition.

In New Mexico, traders and colonists were virtually inseparable before 1848. A number of traders and fur trappers had acquired Mexican citizenship after 1821 in order to operate their businesses without the added restriction on foreign enterprise. In the later 1830s and 40s, some of these individuals were able to acquire landgrants from the Mexican government. However, these settlers cannot be categorized with the Texas colonists, since they identified themselves with the trend of large land acquisition occurring in New Mexico and California during this period. Former fur trappers and traders became land speculators and, as such, immediately affected the economic system of New Mexico. After facilitating the conquest of New Mexico by the United States, however, they continued their speculative ventures at the expense of Mexican property.[4]

California had a similar history in some respects. By the eve of the American occupation of California, Mexican and American residents had already acquired grants of the best land in the area. American landowners did not represent an immediate threat to the prevalent economic system then dominant in California, though some of them reinforced the rigid class structure of the state through marriage into important Mexican families and the further acquisition of landed wealth.

In general, a distinction should be made between American "farmers"—or those colonists who settled in Texas and became immediately antagonistic to the prevailing social economy —and American "landowners"—or those settlers who benefited from the existent order and did not welcome the erosion of land tenure systems.

With the exception of Texas, the Mexican Southwest underwent a unique pattern of historical development. The revolutionary power of a bourgeois state usually develops when the economic infrastructure has extensively modulated into a predominantly capitalist mode of production. In the Southwest, the converse occurred: an American victory in the Mexican-American War ensured a succession of political and legal forms alien to the native economy of the Southwest. An important consequence of this development was the legal battle over land ownership following annexation. The origin of this conflict began during 1820–48 and revolved around the manner of land distribution.

In California, some eight hundred grants of land were made to private individuals during this period. These grants collectively included over 8 million acres and were individually restricted to eleven square leagues. The availability of such large grants was facilitated by the secularization of mission lands and the last-minute rush for land titles before annexation.

The formal procedure for obtaining a landgrant began when the applicant filed a petition with the governor which included specific information on the individual and the land in question. The government then investigated the claim to ensure the Mexican citizenship of the applicant or the availability of the land. If the findings of the investigation were positive, the governor would issue a personally signed document to the applicant as title to the land being granted. The grant was then surveyed and its boundaries marked. A record was kept in the governor's office of all petitions, grants, and maps of land granted. In many cases, however, the failure to comply faithfully with the established procedure resulted in vague or overlapping boundaries.

To obtain a landgrant from the Mexican government, the

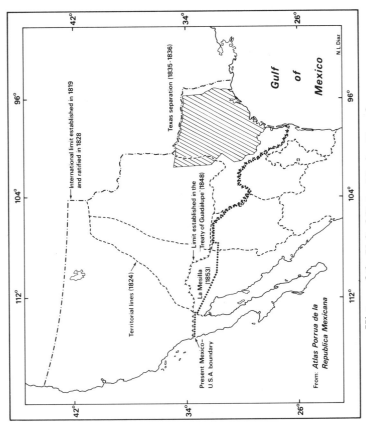

Territorial lines (1824)

International limit established in 1819 and ratified in 1828

Texas separation (1835-1836)

Limit established in the Treaty of Guadalupe (1848)

La Mesilla (1853)

Present Mexico-U.S.A. boundary

Gulf

of

Mexico

N.L.Diaz

From: *Atlas Porrua de la Republica Mexicana*

History of the United States–Mexico Boundary

applicant had to prove Mexican citizenship, although foreigners could receive grants if they were naturalized first. A map of the ranchos in existence at the time of the American conquest of California in 1846 indicates that one-eighth of the ranchos were located in the Sacramento and Upper San Joaquin River valleys and the majority were held by Anglos who had immigrated to California during the 1840s and become naturalized in order to qualify for ownership. Elsewhere, the rancheros were predominantly Spanish Californian. Several ranchos were held by christianized Indians who, under Mexican law, were considered citizens entitled to landowning privileges.[5]

Most of the land comprising the ranchos (that is, Mexican grants) lay in the southern part of California. In 1846, most of the northern territory was unoccupied and unclaimed by white individuals, as was most of the desert and mountain land throughout the state. Since ranchos rarely extended into the mountain regions, scarcely any of the area which irresistibly drew gold-seekers in 1848 was encompassed in rancho land.

Landgrant ownership was transferred in many ways and, certainly, on many occasions. Prior to the conquest of California by the United States, a grantee might lose his land if he failed to comply with the various terms on which he received it, such as the failure to occupy or cultivate the land. If an individual noticed this laxity and reported it to the Mexican authorities (at the same time making his own petition), and if governmental investigation upheld the secondary claim, then grant ownership was transferred to the second claimant.

The Treaty of Guadalupe-Hidalgo ceded California to the United States. Under the terms of this treaty, the United States pledged to respect all Mexican landgrants in California as the property of whoever owned them at that time. However, thousands of American settlers who came to California during the Gold Rush saw the best land tied up in ranchos; millions of acres of rancho land sat useless, land owned, but neither occupied nor cultivated. In their eyes, the rancheros were land monopolists and had no need of their vast holdings. Settlers like themselves, they reasoned, should be allowed to put some of this vacant land to better use. The Land Law of 1851 attempted to reach some resolution to the developing conflict between landowners and settlers. Under this law, a Land Commission was instituted to judge the validity of every claim to a landgrant brought before it. Any grants not brought before the Commission were automatically judged invalid and the area involved became public land open to American settlers.[6]

The Land Commission took several years to decide the validity or invalidity of landgrants. In the interim, a violent battle ensued between squatters and landholders in northern California. In most cases, the Land Commission's final decision favored the original claimant or grantee. By this time, however, the decision was essentially useless: if the original grantee had not lost his land to squatters, he had almost certainly lost it to the lawyers whose services he had engaged over several years while his case was pending, or else to moneylenders who had financed his litigation.[7]

Southern California remained basically unaffected by the change in government and land regulations. The influx of settlers during the Gold Rush was concentrated in the northern part of the state. There were two reasons for this development: southern California lacked the mineral wealth to attract miners; and southern California lacked good agricultural land to attract farmers, especially given the dearth of available water. As a result, land in southern California was generally devoted to cattle grazing.

In California, litigation over landgrants resulted in the ruin of many Mexican landowners, the spoliation of small Anglo-American settlers, the enrichment of some Mexican landowners, at the expense of others, but, most importantly, in the maintenance of large landholdings as the basic unit of California agriculture.

In concentrating on the failure of American law to recognize the property titles of its newly acquired citizens, some important details have been neglected. One point involves the nature of California's landholding class whose main interest and activity was the leisurely abuse of the Indian population. To defend the rights of California's landed aristocracy is as progressive as defending its direct descendant—the contemporary Latin American latifundio. The notorious racism of the vast majority of Anglo-American newcomers does not provide sufficient justification for the continued existence of an oppressive class as backward as the California rancheros. The tendency to do so constitutes a particularly one-sided example of nationalism.

Secondly, focusing on the losses incurred by landgrant litigation distracts attention from the original mode of acquisition where, under Mexican law, fraudulent, deceitful grants were chosen as the most effective assurance of aggrandizement in the transition from Mexican to American rule. The abuses suffered by new settlers under the Mexican landgrant system have also been ignored: many settlers were evicted—often through forged notices—from land which they had improved by its legal owner, who waited to claim it until it was improved. Thus, concentration on the vagaries of the litigation process has deterred attention from the final result of that process: *the maintenance of large landed property as a dominant element in California's economic landscape.*[8]

New Mexico provides a somewhat different case. In New Mexico, other methods besides litigation were employed to obtain ownership of the land. The imposition of American law made it difficult for some Mexicans to keep their land: the indigenous population, unfamiliar with the new landgrant statutes, could not easily defend themselves. The new land included a steep land tax which, because of the lack of a money economy, the Mexicans could not pay. The change to a currency-based system of trade extended an advantage to those who had a supply of capital—that is, to Americans with financial backing. Reclamation projects carried out by large companies also aided the transition by altering the ecology of the area: lowering the water level partially resulted in the demise of the small farmer. Finally, large tracts of land declared public were committed to the railroad companies or reserved as national forests. Consequently, the fight over land in New Mexico was not always peaceful; several conflagrations occurred, among them the Lincoln County War and the Colfax County War.[9]

The New Mexico experience both resembles and differs from California in this respect. Some large Mexican land-holders survived the early period of land title validation and, for a few years, became quite wealthy and powerful, especially through sheep-raising. Their eventual demise occurred through the onslaught of different forces. However, New Mexico's small agriculturalists suffered immediate harm under the impact of validation regulations and other measures mentioned above.

The Texas-Mexican experience with landgrant problems provides another variation: in some areas—such as Nueces County—large tracts which had been held by Mexican land-owners passed almost completely into American ownership by the time of the Civil War. Mexican landowners transferred their property under duress; many sold their land at a low price for fear it would eventually be confiscated. In Texas, more than anywhere else, the hostility between Anglo Americans and Mexicans had been long and heated; fraud, chicanery, and outright theft played a more significant role in the early transfer of land ownership from Mexican to American hands.[10]

Stressing the extraeconomic struggle over landed property in the Southwest deploys attention from a purely economic sphere, where the meeting of two systems of social production would eventually result in the victory of a capitalist mode. Even where Mexican landowners were immediately able to secure their holdings, they were eventually defeated. Validation and legal pressures were the products of an assault from without; the internal erosion proceeded at a slower, but firmer pace. If commercial capital had begun a process of disintegration, usury capital would deal the death blow to the old social formation of the Southwest. California and New Mexico both exemplify this process.

Prior to 1849, slaughtering cattle for their hides and skins sustained the economy of southern California. These were traded to Boston merchant vessels for manufactured goods produced on the East Coast. However, the population boom generated by the Gold Rush created a large market for beef in the northern counties. In 1849, California's Anglo population was only fifteen thousand; by 1852, it had soared past the quarter-million mark.

The ranchos quickly recognized this market for beef. In a letter to Abel Stearns, dated in the spring of 1849, Hugo Reid wrote from Monterey describing how the two could make a profit of twenty thousand dollars by shipping one thousand head of cattle from Los Angeles to the northern counties. Instead of transporting cattle by ship as Reid suggested, the ranchos drove them overland, up the coast, or through the San Joaquin Valley. The average herd numbered seven hundred to one thousand head, although herds of two thousand were not uncommon. Meat dealers' agents from San Francisco or Sacramento often traveled south to purchase cattle in Los Angeles, thereby releasing the ranchos from the somewhat risky business of driving the cattle north. Cattle sold for about seventy-five dollars a head in San Francisco, and thirty to forty dollars a head in Los Angeles. This was a considerable increase over the four dollars a head price in effect prior to 1849. The southern California "cow counties" were, in order of importance, Los Angeles, Santa Barbara, Monterey, San Bernardino, and San Luis Obispo counties. The most important of these counties, Los Angeles, was dubbed "Queen of the Counties" by the more prosperous northern cities. It was estimated that nearly thirty thousand head of cattle were annually sold out of Los Angeles during the seven year cattle boom.[11]

The cattle boom allowed the rancheros and their families to enjoy an opulent existence for a few years but, by the late 1850s and early 1860s, they were caught in a credit squeeze. During the bonanza years, many rancheros became indebted at high interest rates, expecting the boom to last indefinitely. Credit suddenly dried up, however, and the boom ended.

The lack of ready capital is a particularly interesting phenomenon. It would seem that the state should have been flowing with gold; but, in fact, most of the gold was shipped to the East to pay for goods purchased on credit in the interior. Most of the gold in circulation (ten and twenty dollar gold pieces) was coined privately along with the thirty dollar "slugs" issued by the assay office in San Francisco. Some examples of interest rates included:

1851   Juan Bandini borrowed $1000 at 4% per month.
1854   José Yorba mortgaged 17,000 acres of the Rancho Las Bolsas along with a vineyard for $5500 at 5% per month.
1854   Joaquín Ruiz borrowed $400 from Able Stearns for mortgage at 5% per month payable in one year.
1861   Julio Verdugo mortgaged his share of the Rancho San Rafael for $3445. In eight years the original debt had increased to $58,950, and he found himself a landless man.[12]

The demand for southern range stock began to fall as early as 1855 because of the influx of cattle from the Mississippi and Missouri valleys, and the importing of sheep from New Mexico. It is estimated that in the spring and summer of 1852, over ninety thousand head of cattle and twenty-five thousand sheep passed Fort Kearny en route to California. The following year, over sixty thousand head entered the state through major routes alone. During the late 1850s, the Midwest cattle drives greatly decreased, but this was offset by the influx of sheep from New Mexico, estimated to number one hundred thousand head during 1858 and 1859. The above factors caused a drop in the price of beef at the close of 1855. A bad drought in 1856 led many ranchos to sell their cattle at the lowest prices since the cattle boom began in 1849. By 1857, the cattle market in Los Angeles was completely glutted. According to a special federal census report in 1860, the more than 3 million cattle in the state were far beyond the "wants of consumption."

By 1860 all the ranchos were in serious financial difficulty because of delinquent property taxes, high interest rates, and the rancheros' financial ineptitude. Those rancheros who remained after a bad drought in 1860 and the flood which followed in the winter of 1861 were completely ruined by the infamous Great Drought of 1864. In 1860, grazing land in the area was assessed at twenty-five cents per acre; during and immediately after the Great Drought this assessment fell to ten cents per acre. The taxes of five-sixths of the property in Los Angeles County became delinquent in 1864. The great ranchos were sold to help pay off their owners' debts, mortgages, and delinquent taxes. Land syndicates usually purchased these large land holdings and subdivided them. The settlers who bought this subdivided land paid anywhere from $1.50 to $10 per acre.[13]

Was the demise of the California rancheros the result of a combination of purely fortuitous circumstances? In spite of any peculiarities exclusive to the region, what happened to southern California's rancho economy is not ·without precedent. When the development of exchange and monetary circulation has reached a certain level and a vast amount of social wealth is held in nonliquid amounts, usury and usury capital reaches its maximum development.

Historically, usury and commercial capital have appeared simultaneously with similar and slightly dissimilar effects. In different times and places, the development of trade and commercial capital has liberated the direct producer or the small agriculturalist from control by his lord or master as the development of exchange took place in a peasant economy. The reverse was also true: the development of exchange in the lord's economy intensified exactions from the peasants.[14]

In a similar fashion, the appearance of usury capital—where money is lent to the lord or landed aristocrat—can result in the impoverishment of the laborer or immediate agricultural producer. Usury has the added capacity to indiscriminately cause the impoverishment and destruction of rich landowners as well as the ruination of small peasant producers. In other words, "the usury which sucks dry the small producer goes hand in hand with the usury which sucks dry the rich owner of a large estate."[15] The pivotal power of the usurer in partially monetized economies rests in his ability to provide the means to pay taxes and other forms of monetary disbursement required of property owners.

Despite the popular conception of interest-bearing capital as the ultimate appearance of "capitalistic" social relations, it should be noted that money capital may or may not have a revolutionary effect on the old mode of production. It can and does disintegrate previous forms of production, although these paralyzed or crippled forms may survive for long periods of time. Only when other conditions are historically present can usury capital deal the final blow by ruining the landed aristocrat and transforming a small-scale producer into a wage laborer.

Returning to the California experience, it is evident that the demise of the rancheros at the hands of moneylenders is not an unprecedented, inexplicable phenomenon, but rather a well-precedented, theoretically comprehensible process. The complete and final defeat of the old mode of life was not, of course, accomplished by the influence of money capital. It was the sum total of a series of simultaneous developments—the struggle over land titles, high interest rates, competition with other producers, and natural catastrophes—which effected the transition.

Spanish and Mexican landowners were not the only victims of usurious interest rates; Yankee landholders who were old residents of southern California also had to sell their property in order to pay their debts. The influence of usury capital had an indiscriminate effect during this period. As economic theory would indicate, the wealth amassed by moneylenders was not qualitatively sufficient to effect a change in the mode of production. In fact, California lingered in a state of "under-development" for thirty years. Usury capital is not bent upon killing the goose that bears the golden eggs; it does, however, succeed in debilitating it.[16]

Some of the large landholders managed to alleviate their situation by leasing portions of land to gringo farmers willing to engage in capitalist agriculture. This method did not provide an effective remedy for the landowner's situation since general loan rates affected everyone equally forestalling capital intensive methods, immigration and, in the last analysis, capitalist farming. So, while usury capital did not ruin an existing class of small farmers, it restricted its ability to prosper.

In southern California, the late 1850s to the early 1880s were characterized by retarded economic growth.[17] As late as 1880, part of the original ranchos had survived taxes, mortgages, floods, and droughts only to disappear completely during the decade as a result of competition with other producers and the pressures of debts and mortgages. From the outset of the cattle boom, the ranchero cow counties had met competition from other producing areas able to undersell the southern Californians. These competitors included a number of Spanish and Anglo sheep raisers from New Mexico who drove their flocks through to the California markets. By the 1880s, California's traditional mode of life and production had been obliterated.

In New Mexico, the action of money capital is equally important, although the tempo and the focus of disintegration differs from California. As had been the case in California, the early period under Anglo-American occupation was favorable to the existing mode of economic organization. For almost thirty years after the conquest, Hispanic sheep owners were able to expand their territory into eastern Arizona, southern Colorado, and southwestern Texas. This movement was stopped by the economic competition and extraeconomic coercion of Anglo-American cattlemen converging on New Mexico.

Throughout this period and into the first year of the twentieth century, New Mexico's moneylenders applied a contained but firm pressure on Spanish landowners and American settlers alike. The demand for ready cash to meet a variety of obligations made many of the owners dependent upon the usurer's services. The ruinous effect of usury capital on landed wealth in New Mexico was not as visible as in California; in New Mexico, early recourse to litigation and fraud and, finally the war waged by Anglo-American cattlemen were empirically more decisive. However, the effect of usury capital on the poor can be clearly viewed in New Mexico as opposed to its relatively indistinct effect on California's dispossessed. The underclass of Old New Mexico—village dwellers and small peasants as well as the *partidarios*—continued to graze sheep on their small plots. As late as 1880, many partidarios survived in bondage to merchants and moneylenders instead of to their former patrones. With the advent of mechanized agriculture and the appearance of large-scale, commercially oriented sheep raising enterprises, those landholders who tenuously depended on moneylenders to stave off bankruptcy began to become wage laborers.[18]

Between 1880 and 1900, the area that had been annexed by the United States in 1848 had become predominantly capitalist. Whatever labor was utilized throughout the region was now wage labor, and accumulated wealth was acquired and utilized by capitalist investors in agriculture as well as in industry. This process was sealed by the development of rapid communication throughout the area advanced by railroad construction.

Although slavery was not an issue in the Southwest (1850 Compromise specifically avoided any reference to the issue), American settlers were very concerned with the Southwest's role in the Civil War. New Mexico remained loyal to the Union while Arizona joined the Confederacy. Significantly, the Mexican and Indian populations—those with no stake in the conflict—remained almost completely apolitical. After the Civil War, everything changed, when large investors became interested in the territories.

The corporations, as well as the individual Anglo settlers, considered Anglo-American ownership of the land an absolute necessity. In Arizona, this was accomplished through the Indian Wars. Unlike the New Mexico tribes, the Arizona Indians had been quite powerful, making it almost impossible for Mexicans or Anglo Americans to settle the territory. The Treaty of Guadalupe-Hidalgo did nothing to change this condition. By 1880, however, the reservation system was well underway, ensuring Anglo ownership of the land. After the confiscation of Indian lands in Arizona, large companies became the favored trustees. These companies made large-scale attempts at irrigation, and their success resulted in larger profits, particularly after the railroads opened up eastern markets. Until 1896 when the government also began irrigation projects, only

large companies could farm profitably. The growth of agribusiness had begun.

In New Mexico, the coming of the railroads also encouraged
the growing of crops for eastern markets. This farming did not
match Arizona's scale, however, as irrigation was limited.
Furthermore, cattle ranchers exerted greater control over the
land and opposed the spread of large-scale farming.

The cattle industry had been based on the "open range"
concept—that is, ranching on public land. Huge profits were
made in this industry, particularly during the Gold Rush,
when beef was in heavy demand. In the 1880s, a combination
of factors caused the end of the open range cattle industry in
New Mexico and Arizona. The 1886 blizzards killed large
numbers of cattle, and the invention of barbed wire allowed
owners to pen their cattle, thus making it more profitable to
own land than to keep it in the public domain.

The cattle industry did not constitute the first ranching
enterprise in New Mexico. Until the end of the Civil War,
sheep farming was an extremely profitable venture for some
members of the Mexican population. Between 1852 and
1858—the years of the Gold Rush—over five hundred thousand sheep were driven to California. After the Civil War,
however, California developed a surplus which drastically cut
profits. Wool remained an important source of income until
the 1890s, when the onslaught of drought, the removal of
tariff protection and the Panic of 1893 destroyed the industry.

The growth of the cattle industry had some significant results. It caused a great deal of animosity between Mexican and
Anglo communities as sheep herders and cattle ranchers
fought for control of the land. Besides this negative effect,
however, the industry positively benefitted both territories. It
was in part responsible for the great population growth of the
1870s and 1880s because as the cattle industry produced
astronomical profits in Texas, real estate companies began to
"sell" people on New Mexico. Coupled with the coming of the
railroad, the population rose by twenty-five thousand in New
Mexico during this period (an increase of 20-25 percent).
Cattle and sheep industries also generated a large flow of

capital into the area, accelerated by the railroad's guarantee of easy access to eastern markets. The growth of these industries was significant to territorial development during this era.[19]

The mining industry also played a role in the development of the Southwest. In New Mexico, this industry was not as important as in Arizona. After the Civil War, gold was discovered and produced much wealth in 1867 and 1868. In the ensuing years, however, silver played a much more important role, but in 1893 the silver market crashed and destroyed the industry. Copper mining, which was to play a significant role in the history of the state, did not get started until the twentieth century.

Arizona had a much large number of mines, particularly those owned by concentrated economic interests. The demand for labor caused a population boom in the mining towns, particularly after the advent of the railroad. Gold and silver were the major metals mined until the Panic of 1893. As in New Mexico, copper mining did not commence until the twentieth century. Significantly, large corporations played a more important role in the development of mining in Arizona because they had a larger influence than the small-scale operations of New Mexico.[20]

As discussed earlier, the Southwest's rapid growth was, to a great extent, caused by the railroads. Throughout the area, there was a pressing need for cheap freight transportation and, by the end of the 1870s, railroads were established. (Earlier attempts had been destroyed by the Panic of 1873.) Since handsome profits could be made constructing railroads, the rush to build them resulted in a surplus distinctive to many of the smaller railroad companies, adding to the growth of centralized capitalistic enterprises.

The railroads assumed monumental importance in ending the age-old isolation of the West. They opened up eastern markets to southwestern products and facilitated the import of heavy machinery used in mining. Other equally important capitalist developments took place in California and Texas during these years, but they properly belong in a separate chapter.

The geographic border of 1848 disappeared during the Mexican-American War and a new border was delineated. In economic and social terms, the border still existed north of the new juridical line, and this period witnessed the elimination of former economic and social distinctions prevalent in the area. Meanwhile, beginning in 1848, the area immediately adjacent to the border line became the center of economic conflict with the Mexican Republic, but this too is a subject for a later chapter.

iv: Establishment of a New Border

With the signing of the Treaty of Guadalupe-Hidalgo, a new border existed between the United States and Mexico. It took a few years to complete the work of surveying the boundary and, consequently, except for that portion traced by the course of the Rio Grande, the separating line was not defined for some time. A few years after 1848, the border lying between the Rio Grande and Colorado River was redefined. The Gadsden Treaty—as the purchase of this additional territory was called—was negotiated to obtain a convenient railroad route to the Pacific Coast as well as to obtain mineral rights to the area.[1]

For a number of years, the border line consisted of two major sections which met on the Rio Grande above El Paso: the line drawn from the Pacific Ocean to the Rio Grande, and the course of the river itself. Of the two, the former could not be geographically identified as an international boundary. The only settlements in existence at the time, and for a few years later, were on the Rio Grande. In 1853, only the States of Tamaulipas and Chihuahua had towns on the border with the United States. The population of these settlements was thin and almost nonexistent along the rest of the border. Many Indian groups displaced by the United States Army roamed over this unsettled area.[2]

Because of the lack of basic research on the border area during the second half of the nineteenth century, it is somewhat difficult to identify more than a few basic structures and events which played an important role in the socio-economic transformation of the region. To introduce the student of socio-economic transformations to three major focuses, it is necessary to isolate those themes which concurrently emerge from 1830 to 1910 in this northern area of Mexico. The first theme concerns the isolation in which the northern area of Mexico continued to survive thirty years after the Treaty of Guadalupe-Hidalgo. Based on the lack of efficient transportation, and affected by such momentous events as the French occupation of Mexico, the isolation of the northern area prevented any effective connection with the national economy as well as inhibited the task of frontier defense. At the same time, the economic control of production by large latifundista cattle raisers remained unchecked.[3]

Secondly, whatever the objective needs of the economic system and/or the subjective whims of its officials, the United States continued to entertain the idea of further occupation of Mexican territory.

Thirdly, though the period from 1848 to 1914 is known as one of world peace, it is precisely during this period that the newly formed border between the United States and Mexico became a bloody arena of cultural, racial, economic, political, and military conflict. For the borderlands, these years were characterized by chaos and turbulence.

Evidently, these three themes are separable only heuristically, and the same is true for the division of conflict into political, economic, and social spheres. The border area appeared as a result of the clash between two economic systems—a clash which eventually ended in military confrontation, expropriation, and social chaos. It would be the height of naiveté to believe that peace and calm could have ensued in the wake of such historical developments. The struggle that characterized the area can only be isolated for the purposes of clarification, understanding, and explanation.

The creation and development of the so-called Zona Libre provides a specific instance of the themes sketched above. For almost fifty years, beginning shortly after the Mexican-American War, a strip of territory along the northern part of Mexico known as the Zona Libre played an important role in the economic and political relations between the two countries. At the height of this development, the Free Zone extended for 1,833 miles from the Gulf of Mexico to the Pacific Coast and was 12.5 miles in width. The importance of the zone was based on tariff differentials which could be enjoyed within the zone. Although the zone was never completely free of tariffs, the differentials were large enough to provoke a great deal of national and international anguish and conflict.[4]

Shortly after the signing of the Treaty of Guadalupe-Hidalgo, a peculiar situation developed among the towns situated on both banks of the Rio Grande in that radically different prices prevailed on the two sides of the river. The usual explanation given for this development is that in the United States no taxes or restrictions of any kind were levied against internal trade, and there were minimal taxes on foreign goods. In contrast, on the opposite bank, the "old system" prevailed—setting heavy taxes on foreign goods while a variety of levies against internal trade led to a restricted domestic commerce. There were also heavy protectionist restrictions in Mexico on the number of commodities which could enter the country. As a result of this situation, different prices existed on each side of the border. On the Mexican side, higher prices were charged for goods of domestic production and consumption, and an even higher price was laid on foreign goods than on the American side. As a consequence of this disparity, people were either leaving Mexican towns and settling on the American side of the river or were actively engaged in smuggling goods across the border into Mexico. At the outset, two sets of commodities were involved in the controversy. One set involved locally (Mexican) produced provisions essential to the population, whose apparent dearness forced migration to the left side of the river; the second set consisted of foreign goods. The controversy surrounding the latter has never been made entirely clear. Arguments over the causes and consequences of the Free Zone are so tangled with political interest that it is imperative to begin any discussion by making careful distinctions between these different aspects of the problem.[5]

The situation of forced migration across the river to the United States developed quite early, and it became grave enough to force the central government of Mexico to authorize the importation of provisions through the border customhouses of Tamaulipas at reduced rates. This permit severely limited the flow of other goods—namely, those produced far away from the border, either on American's eastern seaboard or in foreign countries. The next crucial step was taken by the United States. In 1852, the United States passed an act by which foreign goods imported into the United States could be sent in bond to Mexico over certain specified routes. These goods could be held indefinitely in warehouses on the border and, if sent to Mexico, were exempt from export duties.

This move made the situation on the Mexican side of the river far more precarious. In relative terms, it also indicated that commercial houses on both sides of the border placed a greater importance on the prices of foreign goods than on locally manufactured provisions. Evidently businessmen involved in European imports and located on the left bank could exercise commercial predominance under the new act; they could smuggle European commodities into Mexico at a very low price, thereby ruining Mexican merchants as well as influencing English and other European sales in the area.

Out of this situation the Free Zone emerged. It was not only a response to the actions of the United States and to the prevalent practice of smuggling, but issued from the desire to strengthen the border settlement. To some extent, the Free Zone also served as a battleground for American and British commercial interests. At the state level, the forerunner of the Mexican Free Zone was established by the governor of Tamaulipas in 1858. For all intents and purposes, he established by decree what came to be known as the Free Zone. All foreign goods used in the frontier towns were exempted from federal though not from state and local taxes. The decree also allowed "in bond" warehouses in border towns. The struggle was obviously one between dealers in foreign goods on both sides of the river: British goods imported through ports at the mouth of the Rio Grande could sell more cheaply than the same goods that, having arrived at U.S. eastern seaports, had to be transported halfway across the United States. More importantly, European goods in the Mexican towns provided a spirited competition to many American manufacturers.

The institution of the Free Zone in Tamaulipas was intended to reverse the flow of smuggling towards the United States. Additionally, since tariff duties were not lifted outside the Republic, the Free Zone provoked a considerable amount of smuggling back into Mexico. The Tamaulipas legislation was confirmed and enacted into federal law in 1861. From then on, in the eyes of American officials, the existence of the Free Zone was intimately connected with smuggling, banditry, border violence, and hostility on the part of Mexico. Within Mexico, there was some opposition to the establishment of the zone, stemming mainly from interstate rivalries. It was the feeling of at least some important cabinet officers that the establishment of the Free Zone amounted to playing provincial favorites and caused undue damage to commercial interests in other states. These views never held much sway in Mexico, especially since many nationalistic officials viewed their coincidence with American interests as ample justification for dismissal.

A few years later, the Free Zone was extended to include the additional states of Coahuila, Chihuahua, and Sonora as well as the territory of Lower California. By the 1890s, the economic impact of tariff liberality in this area caused a decreased tariff differential. Secondly, new regulations such as the 1891 statute regulating import duties on commodities manufactured in the zone and coming into the rest of Mexico—whether of domestic or foreign raw materials—provided an impediment to the development of manufacturing interests inside the Free Zone.

The direct effects of the Free Zone were also influenced by changes in the relative productive power of the United States and other industrial countries, as well as by such historical events as the American Civil War. The impact of the latter was later confused with events caused directly by the existence of the Free Zone itself. Briefly, the outbreak of war in the United

States made the existence of free and neutral ports of paramount importance. The cotton trade, contraband war materials, and supplies of various kinds began to flow through Matamoros. Within three years, Matamoros had become one of the busiest *international* trading centers, with up to eighty ships anchored in its harbor at any given time. Between 1861 and 1865, the population of Matamoros grew from less than five thousand to almost forty thousand residents. Once the war was over, the trade in weapons and cotton declined rapidly, as did the wealth and business of the town. Within a decade, it barely counted five thousand residents.

The Free Zone was established with the purpose of alleviating the flight of Mexican citizens across the border. Some of its side effects were disastrous. The considerable smuggling into Mexico caused the consequent loss of treasury revenues and provoked some smuggling into the United States and the attendant protest of the American government. The existence of the Free Zone was one of the many factors causing serious friction between the United States and Mexico during this period. The controversy involved American nonrecognition of the Díaz government for almost two years and, in the 1870s, it became the central issue in all relations between the United States and Mexico. The United States viewed the existence of this Free Zone as an unfriendly act and, for some years, applied diplomatic pressure to have it removed. Beginning in 1870, the president's annual State of the Union address mentioned the evil nature of the zone as a base for smuggling across the boundary into American territory. The American press and governmental officials also connected the existence of the zone with the violence and depredations of Indians and cattle rustlers.[6]

A Mexican Border Commission instituted to investigate the situation in 1873 indicated that Americans, in making complaints of Mexican raids and the Free Zone, were seeking a pretext for annexation of Mexican frontier territory. This was not, by any means, an intemperate accusation. In the specific case of the Free Zone, its original purpose became reversed over time. By the mid-1870s, the decline in the price of American manufactured goods, coupled with the development of the railroads, had enabled American merchants on the Texas side of the river to successfully compete with Mexican merchants who dealt in European products. From being a barrier to the predominance of American imports, the Free Zone became a haven for those American manufacturers who were the sole beneficiaries of the liberal tariffs on foreign goods. Not only did American commercial capitalism dominate the area, but restrictions on manufacturing prevented the independent development of the area. Despite this reverse in the function of the Free Zone—which in fact had become detrimental to the best interests of Mexico—the government of the United States continued to use the Free Zone as an excuse for continuous harassment, threats of invasion, and military incursions into Mexico.

Before the Free Zone was established, the border area had been tormented by violence. The area between the Nueces River and Rio Bravo may be characterized as a no-man's land ravaged by guerrilla warfare and battles between Texas and Mexican regulars during 1835–48. The immediate causes of violence are interwoven in a variety of ways; in this area, racial tensions, the "lawlessness of the frontier," international questions, and the "economic battle" simultaneously occurred. For example, warring factions involved Texans against Mexicans, Texans against Texans, and Mexicans against Mexicans. One net result of this violence involved the partial rout of Spanish landowners seeking refuge in the towns.

Before the American Civil War, a number of major outbreaks had occurred and a continuous state of violence prevailed along the Rio Grande. Historians have referred to the first major outbreak as the Merchants' War.[7] The direct cause of this incident was closely related to the tariff issue. Before the Treaty of Guadalupe-Hidalgo became effective, American merchants had managed to introduce large quantities of their commodities into Mexico. Under the conditions of the treaty, no tariffs were to be levied against any of this merchandise. Mexican officials proceeded to levy some duties upon certain goods transferred from American warehouses at the signing of the treaty, and whenever payment was refused, they confiscated the merchandise. Quite a few incidents of this nature took place, naturally infuriating many American merchants who saw British interests behind the tariff situation. Their collective response was to organize the first "filibustering" band, led by a Mexican adventurer under the guise of creating an independent nation—certainly one without tariffs on American goods—out of the northern Mexican states. Prompted to launch the adventure, not only because of restrictive tariffs, but also because their first response—smuggling—had been stopped with unusual vigor by Mexican authorities, their several expeditionary excursions into Mexican border towns met with unremitting failure. More than anything else, the Merchants' War is important because it took place at a time when other "adventurers" were launching filibustering expeditions against Central America, Cuba, and other sections of Mexico. Secondly, from this date forward, the increase of expansionist filibustering in the area reached such proportions as to merit Rippy's characterization of the period up to 1878 as the "Golden Age of Filibustering."

A second source of friction concerned the activities of Indian "depredators." In reality, this classification is a misnomer: many raiding parties were composed of Mexicans, Negroes, and whites as well as Indians. The reason for "Indian" violence was, once again, connected with the fact that Indian groups were being as economically and culturally dislodged as the Spaniards and Mexicans. The Indians in these marauding groups were usually members of wandering "nations" seeking refuge in Mexico after they had been forced from the hunting grounds and fertile soil of lower Texas to the barren plains of Chihuahua and Sonora. It is hardly surprising that they were driven to violence and depredations. Under the excuse of punishing the raiders, however, parties of Texans repeatedly invaded Mexican territories, meeting reciprocal action by Mexican army chiefs. Another incident of violent attacks by army troops and armed civilians on both sides of the border occurred over the flight of slaves into Mexico (and probably the flight of peons into the United States). The pursuit of these fugitives led to numerous American raids into Mexico.

With the onset of the American Civil War, the attention of the United States ceased to focus directly on the border, and Mexican towns were able to prosper, partly because of the war and partly because of the Free Zone. After the war, however, American attention became refocused on the border.

As I have already mentioned, the American government viewed the Free Zone as a source of smuggling into the United States, and interpreted its establishment as an act of hostility by the Mexican Republic. In the 1860s and 1870s, when border raids and frontier agitation had become more frequent, the Free Zone became a center of controversy. Public denunciation and the "desire to pacify the frontier" were offered as the basis for America's nonrecognition of the Díaz government for almost two years.[8]

The Mexican response to these accusations was cool and perceptive. The 1873 Mexican Commission report indicated that claims of American losses were exaggerated and raids by Texas bandits were as much to blame as raids by Mexican bands. The issue exploded with the development of the "hot pursuit" strategy favored by generals as ample justification for the complete eradication of bandits and marauders from the border zone. In his memoirs, the ambassador to Mexico at that time (Foster) indicated that the practice might be explained as a plan to use pressure upon the Mexican government in order to present the alternatives of hostility or sale of the northern states of Mexico. Whatever its ultimate purpose, the appearance and development of banditry plagued the border area through at least fifty years of violence.

For a variety of reasons, between 1850 and 1900, the border area was a fertile ground for the development of banditry. Social scientists who have delved into the myths and legends surrounding this phenomenon have unearthed a number of factors and circumstances usually contingent upon the appearance of this social practice. The first prerequisite for banditry is proximity to a major geographical or political border, preferably the latter. The ideal situation for a *bandolero* is one where he can operate in a particular location and use another for refuge from legal extradition. There is also a close correlation between the appearance of banditry and the onset of a period marked by pauperization and economic crisis. Since the practice in question occurs, in our discussion, in rural, peasant areas, the expropriation of peasant lands provides ready evidence of pauperization. In this respect, a period of economic crises can result as a consequence of "surplus" rural population, due either to the expropriation of property or massive migration. As opposed to overpopulation, the concept refers to the existence of landless groups of individuals.[9]

During several decades of the nineteenth century, all of these factors were present along the United States-Mexico border. The border's proximity and the rough terrain surrounding it provided bandits on both sides of the border refuge and easy escape routes. Pauperization characterized several cultural groups inhabiting the area in the immediate vicinity of the Rio Grande and was especially true of many Indian groups in the area. In concert with the Indians and other dispossessed peoples (runaway black slaves, marginal white colonists), Mexican settlers who had either lost their land or been forced to abandon it created the "surplus" rural population which spawned the bandolero. This development occurred in California as well as in Texas, although, given the distance of California banditry to the California border, it is less important to our analysis.

The growth of banditry in the area was also caused by the coincidence of several forms of economic and social oppression. In Mexico, since most of the land was owned by large haciendas, the absence of settlement incentives inadvertently supported the border's "surplus" population and did nothing to mitigate the presence of bandits, cattle thieves, and other criminals. In the border area itself, American citizens fought with Mexican citizens; Indians fought against both; the rich were set against the poor; and governments on both sides of the border had to deal with their respective and collective tradition of criminality. With the advance of the railroads and the further penetration and establishment of industry below the border, the intensity of violence subsided.

During the construction of its transportation empires in the Southwest, the Pacific Railroad projects—the Kansas Pacific, the Atchison, Topeka, and Santa Fe, the Southern Pacific, and the Texas Pacific—received huge grants of public lands. Between 1850 and 1871, more than 150 million acres of public land were given to western railroads. In granting these large sections of land to the railroad corporations, the federal government took land from the public domain; former settlers suffered great losses of land in New Mexico and Arizona; and the incursion of people and commerce brought clashes of violence and destroyed the old ways.

During the 1870s, the United States began importing Chinese workers and exploiting their labor in railroad construction. Many thought that the Chinese could become a major labor force, but anti-Asian bigotry caused Americans to begin excluding them.[10] Although railroad companies like the Southern Pacific were more concerned with the financial advantage of Chinese laborers, immigration legislation totally excluded the Chinese after 1884. Railroad managers then turned to Mexicans as the next cheapest source of labor for railroad crews. When the demand for Mexican labor could no longer be supplied by Sonora alone, the United States recruited further into Mexico. The increased area covered by Mexican railroads made the importation of Mexican workers easier.

Mexico itself began railroad construction very slowly. During the Juárez administration (1867–72), the British were authorized to build a railroad between Veracruz and the capital. The program failed, however, because the rails laid with foreign money and skills were built to support foreign capitalists rather than to enhance national economic development. The rail lines grew in patchwork formation and were never designed as strategic national transportation networks.

When Juárez died in 1872, Sebastián Lerdo succeeded him to the presidency. Lerdo continued the policies of his predecessor, but refused to allow railroads to be built toward the north or to connect with North American tracks beyond the border, since connecting the two lines could give the Americans a military advantage. In America, powerful railroad interests were angered and Lerdo had to fight for reelection, which he won but did not maintain. Porfirio Díaz took advantage of the politically unstable situation in Mexico and was finally declared president. The base of Díaz's economic program was railroad construction; economically, railroad building and industrialization were the two most important innovative processes generating social change in Mexico during the Porfiriato.

Prior to Díaz's seizure of power, only four hundred miles of track had been laid. During his administration, the federal government began selling huge tracts of Mexican soil to foreign companies and native hacendados. In the northern states, railroad concessions were sold to the United States. Within three years after the Díaz recognition, concessions to America provided for the construction of five railroads in Mexico aggregating over twenty-five hundred miles and carrying subsidies of over $32 million. These lines went from north to south and provided a route to the interior of Mexico from which ore was transported to the United States. The Southern Pacific had been extended eastward as far as Yuma, Arizona, in 1877 and in 1881 was extended to Deming, New Mexico, and El Paso, Texas, connecting at Deming with the Atchison, Topeka, and Santa Fe. Other major railroads linked routes through the southwest region and, at the same time, work progressed rapidly south of the border. The Mexican Congress granted concessions with the stipulation that the roadbed would revert to Mexico at the end of ninety-nine years. Díaz kept his promises, believing at this time that North America would otherwise forcibly seize the railroad concessions.

Between 1880 and 1910, American and other foreign capital had financed the building of fifteen thousand miles of track. As communication and transport improved, the degree of lawlessness and banditry began to subside, although it did not altogether disappear. One of the more curious episodes in the long campaign of pressure and threats, which typified the conduct of the United States towards Mexico before Díaz, involved the roles played in the negotiation of railroad contracts by one Mariano Vallejo—a California farmer—and General Frisbie—Vallejo's son-in-law. The two acted as semi-official agents of the United States to the Mexican government; their plan was to force Mexico to sell some of its northern territories under threat of armed attack by the United States.[11]

In summary, the violence of this period was promoted by and affected both sides of the border. The United States utilized the issues of violence, cattle rustling, "Indian" raids, and the Free Zone, regardless of their inaccuracy, to successfully apply enormous pressure on the Mexican Republic in order to facilitate the growth of American investment enterprises in Mexico. In some cases, border "violence" can be recorded as ruthless economic competition. Much of the "cattle rustling" that occurred in the area usually referred to the practices of large Texas cattle owners who would launch "expeditions" against similar Mexican entrepreneurs south of the border. The amount of cattle rustling quickly diminished as the grazing property of northern Mexico passed into American ownership.

The railroads developed concurrently with the tremendous infusion of American capital into Mexico; this wave of investments was especially pronounced in some of the northern Mexican states immediately below the border, as indicated by the following tables.

Thus, the official border that separated the United States from Mexico was, to some extent, a fictional device. As in the case of the effective penetration of the old borderlands, the expansion of capitalism proceeded below the border set by the Treaty of Guadalupe-Hidalgo.

Of course, there were a few differences in the new process. First, the process of capitalist expansion below the border was erratic rather than continuous. The Civil War in the United States and the open resistance of Mexican authorities forced a slower pace. As the same time, expansionism had to consider the uprooted peoples who disrupted the frontier for many years. These early years of development in the border area took place under constant threat of forceful conquest by the United States. In the end, American business monopolies accomplished this goal without open resort to armed strength.

As the century came to a close, little economic development had taken place along the border in spite of United States' capitalist penetration. The railroads had only recently interrupted the isolation characteristic of the area, and the basic system of land tenure remained unaffected. During this period, the northern states of Mexico began to suffer from the alliance of two different economic systems: American capitalism, rapidly advancing into its monopoly phase, and the backward latifundismo which had become even more entrenched under the leadership of Porfirio Díaz. In this setting, the growth and development of the border towns and the border area began.

TABLE 1

Basic Calendar of American Economic Penetration
into Areas Adjacent to the Border

Early 1880s	William Cornell Green purchases the Cananea Mines and organizes the Green Consolidated Copper Company.
April, 1887–Sept., 1888	2,077 new mining claims and 33 stamp mills appear over all of Mexico.
1888	$30,000,000 is invested in mining. Solomon R. Guggenheim purchases several silver mines.
1890	Solomon and William Guggenheim build the first complete silver-lead smelting works in Monterrey, Mexico.

TABLE 2

Total U.S. Investments in Mexico by State in 1902

D.F.	$320,852,000 ($281,000,000 in railroads)
(border) Coahuila	48,000,000
(border) Sonora	37,500,000
(border) Chihuahua	32,000,000
Oaxaca	14,000,000
(border) Nuevo León	11,000,000
Sinalva	7,000,000
Durango	7,000,000
Veracruz	4,455,000
Guanajuato	3,000,000
(border) Baja Calif.	2,374,000

TABLE 3

U.S. Investments by Branch in 1902

Railways	70%
Mining	$95,000,000
Agriculture	28,000,000
Manufacturing	10,000,000
Banks	7,000,000
Smelting Refineries	7,000,000
Utilities	6,000,000
Total (1,177 companies, firms and individuals)	$500,000,000

TABLE 4

Mining Investments by State in 1902

Sonora	$27,829,000
Chihuahua	21,277,000
D.F.	8,430,000
Durango	6,520,000
Coahuila	6,000,000
Aguascalientes	3,682,000
Sinaloa	3,183,000

TABLE 5

Agricultural Interests by State in 1902

Oaxaca	$10,700,000
Sonora	3,733,000
Veracruz	3,513,000
Chihuahua	1,822,000
Tabasco	1,506,000
Chiapas	1,188,000

TABLE 6

Representative Firms in the Border Area

Mining

W.A. Clark Menator from Montana	Copper Mines	$ 220,000
	Sonora	222,000
		442,000
Creston-Colorado Gold Mining Company	Sonora	2,222,000
Greene Consolidated Copper Company	Sonora	7,500,000
Moctzume & Phelps Dodge	Sonora	2,000,000
Las Cruces of New York & Sonora Mining Co.	Sonora	444,000
Sinaloa and Sonora Mining & Smelting	Sonora	600,000

Smelting

American Smelting & Refining Company (Guggenheim)	Monterrey Nuevo León	6,000,000
″ ″	Coahuila	750,000
″ ″	Chihuahua	600,000

Haciendas, ranchos, and farms

Mrs. Phoebe A. Hearst	Chihuahua	1,333,000
Nelson Welle Company	Coahuila	436,000
Greene Cattle Company	Sonora	—
A.M. Sherman	—	500,000 acres

Source: Tables 1 through 6 were culled from James M. Callahan, *American Foreign Policy in Mexican Relations* (New York: Cooper Square, 1968).

v: Border Economy 1: The Framework of Migration

The purpose of the chapter is not to study Mexican migration in particular, or specific aspects of Mexican migration in detail but rather to place Mexican migration across the border in perspective in a threefold sense. First of all, by showing the intimate connection that existed and still exists between the pattern of agricultural landholding in California (the material dealt with in the first chapter) and the development of Mexican migration. Secondly, by showing how this landholding pattern and the need for cheap labor affect the whole of the phenomenon of migration to California much before the onset of massive Mexican migration. And thirdly, by showing how the occurrence of massive migrations was not unique to the border between the United States and Mexico, but became part and parcel of the web of relationships between rich and poor countries during and after the development of large capitalist monopolies in land and agriculture. There is already a vast and growing body of literature on such important specific topics as the Bracero Program, commuters, etc. In general, this literature deals primarily with Mexican migration and usually a very specific aspect of Mexican migration. By contrast, the intention of this chapter is to provide neither a summary of this literature nor a research contribution to it; it is rather an effort to set down a number of elements that must be included as constituent parts of a theoretical explanation of Mexican migration to the United States and to show the manner in which, historically, migration is organically connected with the earlier economic development in the former Mexican and Spanish northwest. Thus, the cursory treatment given to specific aspects of Mexican migration per se is not an indication of lack of regard for the importance of these topics, but a consequence of the conscious decision to examine *general* and not *particular* aspects as the title indicates.

To accomplish these goals, it is necessary to clarify the social property relations that characterize an advanced capitalist economy. The notion of private property is usually regarded as the sine qua non of capitalism. However, the much too general sense attached to the popular notion of private property disguises a deeper reality that characterizes any predominantly capitalist society. Property in the *means of production*, e.g., land, equipment, tools, etc., is the privilege of one group or class in the society. The other class is dispossessed and owns no property in this particular sense. Thus the only effective ownership that a person of the latter class can exercise is ownership over his/her own ability to labor, i.e., labor power.

Whenever and wherever this class separation does not exist, capitalism cannot develop. This is the reason why an economic "theorist" of the nineteenth century, Edward Gibbon Wakefield, was very critical of the early development of the United States. In his view, the ability of the potential wage-worker, who arrived as a migrant on the East Coast, to migrate into the interior of the United States and become a self-employed farmer was the gravest obstacle in the development of capitalism:

> Where land is very cheap and all men are free, where everyone who so pleases can easily obtain a piece of land for himself, not only is labour very dear . . . but the difficulty *is* to obtain labour at any price.[1]

One way to remedy this situation was to prevent all men from being free, as happened in the slave South. As the nineteenth century wore on, however, the waves of migrants arriving upon the eastern seashore vastly outnumbered the ability of migrants to settle in the interior. Therefore, the lack of a pool of "free labor" ceased to be a deterrent to the advance of capitalism, while in the South slavery was abolished.[2]

What were the parameters of a) ownership in land and b) availability of labor in the Southwest after the Anglo-American conquest and the establishment of the new border? As we have established in previous chapters the characteristic landed monopolies that prevailed in the Southwest during the Spanish and Mexican periods changed hands but remained largely intact in the transition from Mexico to the United States. From a feudal monopoly in the land the economy of the southwestern states was swiftly transformed into one characterized by capitalist monopoly of the land. To the heritage of the Spanish and Mexican period we must add a development in the American economy which was to reinforce the absence of the small farmstead in the far Southwest: the development of imperialist monopoly capitalism.

This development can be described in its general and particular manifestations. In its general aspects it consisted of the loss of importance, at the national level, of the small competitive firm, its replacement by the large industrial monopolies, the growing importance of financial institutions, the fusion of financial and industrial concerns and the growth of capital exports. In its particular aspect in the Southwest it meant the concentration of land ownership and the intervention of bank capital in the promotion and direction of agricultural production.

The concentration that already existed in the Spanish land-grants was augmented through a series of economic policies and events such as the railroad grants and land speculation which transformed the Southwest, especially California, into an empire of large farms. Thus, from the outset, whoever was not the owner of a portion of this empire was a landless peasant and potential wage-worker. In part, it was this pattern of land distribution coupled with a very low population density that made California and the Southwest, after aridity had been conquered by irrigation, dependent upon foreign migrant labor.

Carey McWilliams, writing in the late 1930s, could look back to the history of California agriculture and describe it as the history of Asian-American migration. Today Mexican migration seems to have always been the rule, but the fact that less than forty years ago a social critic could look back eighty years and refer not to Mexican but to Asian labor as the prototype suggests that there was nothing special about Mexican labor per se and that the fundamental needs for large masses of cheap labor were inherent in the growing agribusiness empire.[3] Asian labor was utilized in California agriculture after some of the crops that were earlier cultivated such as coffee, tobacco, and silk, were abandoned. Other early crops were not terribly dependent on large pools of labor. While some labor scarcity was already apparent in the 1850s, it was therefore, not yet critical. With the growing of specialized fruit crops in the 1860s and 1870s, immigrant Chinese workers became indispensable in California agriculture. But a combination of organized labor and small farming interests, appealing to racism, succeeded in driving the Chinese from the California fields. The large California growers, in search of a new source of labor, promptly found one in the Japanese, who became a prime labor pool from the last few years of the nineteenth century to the beginning of World War I. But the Japanese were to meet the same opposition as the Chinese and eventually shared the same fate. In desperation, California agribusiness began to import East Indian and Filipino workers. Asian labor continued to provide the bulk of the labor needs of California agriculture until "the discovery of the Mexican" in the mid-1920s.

As well as the social property relations that prevailed in the Southwest, importance should be accorded to the scientific and technical discoveries that made the production of certain crops economically possible. Among these were the development of refrigerator cars that permitted the transportation of fresh produce to distant markets and the development of large-scale irrigation. The change from wheat production to specialized deciduous fruits and truck gardening in California was dependent on these developments. But nothing equals in impact the influence that the growth of large-scale irrigation had on the Southwest as a whole. Large-scale irrigation signified in itself a tremendous development of the productive forces. In 1902, the Southwest, an area larger in size than the original American thirteen colonies, was little more than an unpopulated desert. In 1902, the Reclamation Act, which made possible the use of federal funds for the construction of large irrigation projects, was passed, marking the beginning of the modern economic development of the Southwest. Irrigation allowed the reclamation of millions of previously arid and unproductive acres and helped turn large portions of desert brush country into fertile orchards.

Such an expansion of acreage and the ability to grow cotton and truck produce in previously uncultivated areas in itself necessitated increased labor supplies. Large-scale irrigation meant, additionally, a new and increased over-capitalization of the land. Heavy capital investment, in addition to creating "agribusiness" by bringing banking capital into the agricultural enterprise, meant an increased demand for ever larger pools of cheap labor.

If these were the parameters in terms of productive forces and productive relations north of the border, what were the conditions south of the border at the time of the onset of large Mexican migration? A number of circumstances coincided in the Mexican economy around the turn of the century to condition the northward migration. One was the process of depeasanting agrarian Mexico that became especially rigorous during the Díaz regime. Throughout the second half of the nineteenth century Mexico suffered the pangs of its peculiar form of primitive capitalist accumulation.[4] The expropriation of the property of the Church and Indian communities are phenomena which must be understood as part of this process. The disentailment law, which presumed to create small agricultural holdings, in fact brought about the further concentration of land and the opening of a market in land transaction. The activities of the famous "compañías deslindadoras" also formed part of the process of primitive accumulation. The

Yaqui wars which deprived those Indians of their fertile lands in the Yaqui valley gave a "colonial" character to this process by producing the landless peasant.[5]

The railroads were the second element in the genesis of Mexican migration: they enabled the landless peasant to find a wage-earning job. They were instrumental in bringing the peasants to labor markets, such as the American operated mines of northern Mexico and eventually to the larger labor markets of the United States. If the process of depeasanting gave them their "freedom" to move and the railroads provided the means of transportation, the Mexican Revolution of 1911 sent them in droves across the border.

From the above description of the conditions at the onset of Mexican migration to the United States one might draw the conclusion that this movement of people was and is a unique phenomenon of modern economic history. Nothing could be further from the truth. One of the marks of the development of monopoly capitalism in the United States and Europe was the development of migration from backward to advanced capitalist countries as well as the appearance of a new wave of "white settler" colonialism. Germany at the turn of the century is an example of the generality of this phenomenon. This has been pointed out by Handman:

> Germany . . . presents an analogy with the agricultural labor situation of the Mexican in America. . . . Germany, particularly in the East, had large landed estates which needed additional seasonal labor in order to produce for a growing market. In proportion, however, as the cities and industrial life made calls on the working forces of the country, the large landowners and producers began to call in seasonal labor from (other) regions. . . . the result was that Germany before the War imported annually more than four hundred thousand agricultural laborers to harvest her crops.[6]

For American agribusiness north of the border the Mexican migrant was better than any previous migrant. The ideal immigrant was one who showed up for harvest work and who "disappeared" in the off-season. This ideal immigrant would not cost society the expense of bringing him up and would not become a public "nuisance." The early Asian migrants met the ideal requirements for only a brief period of time. Given the physical distance to their homelands it was natural that they should settle permanently in the United States. Worse yet, they promptly began to leave the workfields to settle either on small farms purchased with savings, or in cities where they became self-employed businessmen.

Given the formidable need for cheap labor that was felt during the early part of the century, the Mexican migrants appeared to hold superior qualities: availability in larger numbers and disappearance in the off-season made possible through easy return to Mexico. Although it turned out that some Mexican migrants, like their Asian predecessors, chose on occasion to settle in the United States, from the point of view of agribusiness Mexican migration was "better" than its predecessors. Also, important differentiations should be made within Mexican migration. The most important separation is between legal and illegal migrants. It is the latter type that most perfectly fits the "job description" of the agricultural (or industrial) hand. The illegal entrant is available in large numbers whenever and wherever he is needed and is completely at the mercy of immigration authorities when he is not wanted. The illegal migrant does not require education, training, or sustenance (except for the portion of the year during which he works), the costs of his rearing are borne by his home country; and because of his legal status—the fact that he can be deported at a moment's notice—he is likely to be a "loyal," if not an especially hard-working, laborer.

Not all the migration from Mexico has been illegal, however. The most famous example of legal migration is the bracero program, whereby the needs of agriculture in the Southwest were met through a legalized system of contract labor. Looking back at the history of sixty-plus years of Mexican migration, it appears that migration was very intense between 1910–30; it declined relatively between 1930–50, only to rise again in the last twenty years. It is during this last period that illegal migration became a factor of paramount importance in the economics and politics of the area. Strictly speaking the "illegal" phase in Mexican migration started during and after the Second World War.

Throughout these sixty years all the socio-economic conditions that were present at the outset have been of continuing influence. With the exception of an actual revolutionary war in Mexico, all the other factors remain in force in modified form: the capitalization of southwestern agriculture continues unabated: means of transportation to and from Mexico have improved considerably and, despite legal changes in land tenure in Mexico, the poverty of the small peasant still acts as a factor in his migration. One major new element has appeared in the whole framework: the development of urbanization along the United States-Mexico border.

This process of urbanization matches the urbanization of those Mexican migrants who have settled in the United States. From the perspective of the development of large towns in the Mexican border area two particular forms of migratory movements are of interest. One is the case of illegal migrants whose movement is facilitated enormously by the existence of large urban centers, which serve as bases of operations. The second type is the so-called commuter: a person who lives in Mexico but who crosses the border every day to work in the United States. Both of these types of migrants have contributed to the settlement of northern Mexico; and, conversely, they have made their appearance in the United States in large numbers *on the basis of* such a process of urbanization. As such, the "illegals" and the "commuters" are both *cause and consequence* of the rise of the border towns. It is in this sense that the urbanization of northern Mexico and the migration northward are inseparable. Whereas migration of all types provided for much of the urban settlement of the border area, now the border area in turn has become the source of a new and important form of migration.

vi: *Border Economy 2: Urbanization and Border Towns*

The urbanization brought about by the migratory process we have described was not peculiar to the northern border area of Mexico. Rather it was a particular manifestation of the general development of migration and urbanization in Mexico since the 1920s, and especially since World War II. Despite all of its important singular characteristics, the border economy of northern Mexico shares some fundamental aspects of the Mexican economy as a whole. An analysis of the problems confronting Mexico's north must therefore be preceded by a presentation of the outstanding socio-economic features of contemporary Mexico.

The Mexican Economy at the Crossroads

At present the Mexican economy is affected by some important "developmental" traits. Chief among these are: the monopolistic structure of the economy; the presence of perhaps the strongest "state-capitalist sector" in all of Latin America; an agrarian structure which preserves wide disparities of income and wealth among the rural population; cities filled with vast masses of the unemployed and underemployed; and last, but not least, a strong economic relationship with the United States, in which the latter country exercises dominance. These traits characterized Mexico ten years ago and, despite a decade of rapid growth, the evils connected with these structural elements have not been alleviated. In fact, conditions have worsened.

Monopoly—concentration in industrial production, agriculture and finance—constitutes the primary characteristic of Mexico's semicapitalist economy.[1] Of 135,000 industrial enterprises examined by the VIII Censo Industrial of 1965 a minute 0.82 percent accounted for 64.3 of the total production and 66.3 percent of the total capital investment for that year. The same monopolistic structure is present in the agricultural sector of the Mexican economy: in 1960, 3 percent of the farms (or 79,000 out of a total of 2.5 million) produced 55 percent of all agricultural produce and accounted for 80 percent of the increase in value of production since the 1950s (Table 7). Equally concentrated is the financial sector of the economy where six large commercial banks control 83.4 percent of all deposits. Hand-in-hand with monopoly, the state (the "public sector") has come to play an important role in all sectors of the Mexican economy. As of November 1973 there were over four hundred fifty state enterprises operating in Mexico some of which were the largest in the economy. Early in the 1960s the role played by the Mexican state was already impressive: at that time the state owned all of the nation's ten largest enterprises, 88.5 percent of the twenty largest and 82.5 percent of the thirty largest (Table 8).

The agrarian structure set up by the Mexican agrarian reform law allowed a surreptitious concentration of land which has permitted a relatively small number of landowners and farmers to benefit from credit facilities, price support programs, etc., while the vasy majority of the beneficiaries received a subfamily plot. But the predominantly monopolistic structure of the economy has not facilitated the absorption of an increasing surplus working force, and thus unemployment and income disparities have continued to afflict Mexico. In Mexico today the average income of the richest 5 percent of families is thirty-six times as great as that of the poorest 10 percent of families, whereas it was thirty times as great twenty years ago. The wealthiest tenth of the population receives over

TABLE 7

Proportional Distribution of Production and Resources, 1960

Type of Holding	Number of Plots	Value of Production	Value of Plots[a]	Culti-vatable Area	Value of Machinery	Irri-gated Area	% of Farmers Receiving Credits[b]	Contribution to Increased Production between 1950–1960
Total	100.0	100.0	100.0	100.0	100.0	100.0	51.5	100.0
Infra-subsistence	50.3	4.2	6.7	13.6	1.3	—	20.5	−1
Subfamily	33.8	17.1	13.8	24.5	6.5	3.9	28.2	10
Family	12.6	24.4	22.6	19.2	17.0	27.0	58.1	11
Multifamily Medium	2.8	22.0	19.3	14.4	31.5	31.5	62.6	35
Multifamily Large	0.5	32.3	37.6	28.3	43.7	37.6	75.0	45

[a]The value of the plot is composed of the value of the land, or fixed and semifixed capital, and of livestock. By plot is meant the ejidal plots (not the whole ejido) and the nonejidal plots.

[b]Based on a regional sample survey and judged not to be representative of the nation as a whole.

Source: Centro de Investigaciones Agrarias, *Estructura agraria y desarrollo agrícola en México*, vol. 1, p. 296, vol. 3, pp. 14–20.

TABLE 8

(A)

Mexico's Largest Industrial Firms, 1965
(measured by total production)

Firms	Control of Total Production (%)	
	(of the 938)	*(of the country)*
Top 10	17.7	11.0
Top 100	49.4	30.6
Top 300	72.2	44.7
All	100.0	62.0

(B)

Distribution of 938 Largest Industrial Firms
by Composition of Capital, 1965

Firms	Degree of Control of Total Production (%)			
	Foreign	*State*	*Private National*	*Total*
Top 10	50.0	20.0	30.0	100.0
Top 20	55.0	15.0	30.0	100.0
Top 50	48.0	22.0	30.0	100.0
Top 100	47.0	13.0	40.0	100.0
Top 500	31.0	7.4	61.6	100.0
All	26.7	5.1	68.0	100.0

Source: Taken from David Barkin, "Mexico's Albatross: the U.S. Economy," in *Latin American Perspectives* 2, no. 2, p. 67.

one-half of the income while the poorest one-half of the population enjoys 15 percent of Mexico's total personal income (Table 9). Thus the urban areas of Mexico—the "underdeveloped cities"—are the concentrated focuses of all the evils usually associated with "backwardness" or "underde-

TABLE 9

Distribution of Family Incomes in Mexico, 1950, 1958, 1963, 1969
(in percentages)

Deciles* (10% of Families)	1950 By Decile	1950 Cumulative	1958 By Decile	1958 Cumulative	1963 By Decile	1963 Cumulative	1969 By Decile	1969 Cumulative	Average Monthly Income (1969 price) 1950	1958	1963
I	2.7	2.2	2.2	2.0	2.0	2.0	2.0	374	437	457	518
II	2.4	6.1	2.8	5.0	2.2	4.2	2.0	4.0	472	545	745
III	3.8	9.9	3.3	8.3	3.2	7.4	3.0	7.0	527	638	865
IV	4.4	14.3	3.9	12.2	3.7	11.1	3.5	10.5	610	745	1,069
V	4.8	19.1	4.5	16.7	4.6	15.7	4.5	15.0	665	880	1,208
VI	5.5	24.6	5.5	22.2	5.2	20.9	5.0	20.0	760	1,140	1,528
VII	7.0	31.6	6.3	28.5	6.6	27.5	7.0	27.0	968	1,220	2,308
VIII	8.6	40.2	8.6	37.1	9.9	37.4	9.0	36.0	1,190	1,660	2,960
IX	10.8	51.0	13.6	50.7	12.7	50.1	13.0	49.0	1,498	2,632	11,615
X**	49.0	100.0	49.3	100.0	49.9	100.0	51.0	100.0	6,790	9,560	5,395
90–95%	8.8		10.7		11.6		15.0		2,450	4,124	17,850
95–100%	40.2		38.6		38.3		36.0		11,110	14,975	2,328
Total	100.0		100.0		100.0		100.0		1,385	1,935	
Gini Coefficient	0.50		0.53		0.55		0.58				

*Each decile represents 510,500 families for 1950; 640,510 for 1958; 732,960 for 1963; and 889,114 for 1969.

**The last decile at the top of the scale of income has been divided into two parts of 5% each.

Sources: Ifigenia M. de Navarrete, "La distribucion del ingreso en Mexico," in *El Perfile de Mexico en 1980–I* (Mexico, Siglo XXI editores, 1970). 1969–1970 family income survey with adjustments.

velopment": unemployment, underemployment, rapid urban growth, deterioration of social services, etc.

The degree of United States business influence on the workings of the economy can be gleaned from two separate but combined aspects of foreign investment in Mexico: foreign industrial capital and foreign loan capital. As a first approximation, Table 10 gives an indication of the importance of *direct* foreign capital among the largest Mexican enterprises. The abundance of large foreign enterprises is due to the rapid inroads made by the transnational corporations in Mexico in the last fifteen years. According to a Harvard University survey of the U.S. multinational corporations that account for the bulk of U.S. foreign direct investment in manufacturing, 162 of these companies were installed in Mexico in 1967 with 4.2

TABLE 10

Fifty Largest Companies in Mexico
(based on capitalization)
1970

Company	Principal Shareholder	Capital (million pesos)
1. Teléfonos de Mexico	Government	3,070
2. Banco Nac. Agropecuario	Government	1,500
3. Cía. Mex. de Luz y Fuerza	Government	1,361
4. Nacional Financiera	Government	1,300
5. CONASUPO	Government	1,000
6. Guanos y Fertilizantes	Government	1,000
7. Banco Nal. de Crédito Agr.	Government	850
8. Altos Hornos de Mex.	Government	800
9. Imp. de Papaloapán	Government	750
10. Cía Fundidora de Mty	Banco Nacional de Mexico (BNM)	675
11. Celanese Mexicana	BNM-Celanese	642
12. Financiera Banamex	BNM	640
13. Hojalata y Lamina	Garza Sada	580
14. ANDSA	Government	500
15. Banco de México	Government	500

Table 10 Continued:

16. Banco Nal. de Obras y Serv. Pub.	Government	500
17. Cervecería Modelo	BNM (P. Diez)	500
18. Soc. Mex. Cre. Industrial	Government	500
19. Banco Nacional de México	BNM	475
20. Cervecería Cuauhtemoc	Garza-Laguera	440
21. Fertilizantes Fosfatados	BNM-Government-Panamerican Sulphur	440
22. Tubos de Acero de México	Government	406
23. Asarco Mexicana	American Smelting	400
24. Banco de Comercio	Banco de Comercio	400
25. Celulosa de Chihuahua	Banco Comercial Mexicano	400
26. Cementos Tolteca	British Cement Mfgrs.	400
27. HYLSA de Mexico		385
28. Sears Roebuck	Sears	375
29. Financiera Bancomer	Banco de Comercio	360
30. Banco Nal. de Cre. Ejidal	Government	350
31. Cía Cigarrera la Moderna	Brown & Williamson	350
32. Cervecería Moctezuma	Banco Commercial Mexicano	330
33. Cía Industrial de Atenquique	Government	300
34. Cía Mexicana del Cobre	Government	300
35. Puerto de Liverpool		300
36. Fábricas Automex	Chrysler	300
37. Ford Motor Company	Ford	300
38. Kodak Industrial	Kodak	300
39. Volkswagen de Mexico	Volkswagen	300
40. Anderson Clayton	Anderson Clayton	290
41. Fierro Esponja	Hojalata y Lamina-Garza Sada	290
42. Unives	—	254
43. Cementes Anahuac	BNM—J Serrano	250
44. Diesel Nacional	Government	250
45. Lever de Mexico	Unilever (UK)	250
46. Cía Nestlé	Nestle	240
47. Cía Minera de Cananea	—	240
48. Valores Industriales		240
49. Industrias Unidas	Ing. Alejo Poralta	235
50. Cigarros El Aguila	British-American Tobacco	230

Source: Barkin, "Mexico's Albatross."

subsidiaries. Of the total number of subsidiaries, 225 were in the manufacturing sector; 143 were completely new firms while 221 were either acquisitions or branches of other previously established business.[2] The influx of multinational corporations brought about an accelerated pace of foreign investment and, during the 1960s the book value of private foreign investment increased from $1,080 million to $2,300 million in 1968—an increase of over 100 percent in the space of ten years. The trend of the investment pattern during these years was away from traditional sectors such as public services and mining and toward trade, tourism, and manufacturing. The quick pace of foreign penetration, especially as U.S. corporations made their way through direct purchase into the most dynamic sectors of local industry, was another characteristic of the 1960s. This trend occurred most notably in consumer durables, chemicals, electronics, department stores, hotels and restaurants, and the food industry, in which United Fruit, Heinz, and General Foods became very visible.

The process of denationalization and control can best be illustrated by the role of Anderson Clayton in the Mexican economy. Anderson Clayton's role in the Mexican agriculture places it among the top twenty corporations (government companies not included) when measured by reported capital. This company controls, through credit and marketing channels, the production of cotton, which is Mexico's leading export product. Anderson Clayton provides more credit for cotton production than the National Edijal bank gives to all of Mexico ejidatarios. The control over the production of cotton is made effective because the Mexican producers do not sell their cotton production in the international markets but do it mostly through Anderson Clayton (also through Hohenberg International, MacFadden, and other U.S. based enterprises) which monopolize the harvest and provide credit, seed, and fertilizers to the producers. The company also controls cotton production in the countries with which Mexico must compete: Brazil and the U.S. Anderson Clayton thus has engaged in cotton "dumping" to remind Mexico who is in control.[3] In recent years Anderson Clayton has branched out into Mexican production of cattle feed, chocolates, planting seeds, edible oils, and insecticides. Other U.S. corporations have joined Anderson Clayton in effectively taking over Mexico's agribusiness, from production and sale of machinery and fertilizers to the processing and merchandising of agricultural goods. Among the better known are John Deere, International Harvester, Celanese, Monsanto, Dupont, American Cyanamid, Corn Products, United Fruit, and Ralston Purina.[4]

A less visible form of foreign control is effected through foreign loan capital. The total foreign debt of Mexico has expanded considerably in recent years, reaching the figure of $11 billion in late 1972; $5 billion of this amount were credits by U.S. private banks; $1.47 billion came from the Export-Import Bank, the World Bank, and the Inter-American development bank; and $1.5 billion from European, Canadian, and Japanese banks. More than half (55 percent) of the foreign debt was absorbed by private American commercial banks. Between 1950 and 1972 the foreign debt grew at an average rate of 23 percent.[5]

There are several reasons for the large size and rate of growth of the foreign debt of Mexico. First of all, the application to Mexico, and to the rest of Latin America, of the economic policies propounded around 1950 by the Economic Commission for Latin America must be taken into consideration. The essence of the ECLA analysis is well-known. Mexico, Latin America, in general, and other primary-commodity producers had ceased to benefit from free trade and the international division of labor. This was due to factors such as "income inelasticities" for primary goods which, coupled with the effects of union demands in the industrialized countries, resulted in both a deterioration of the terms of trade and chronic balance-of-payments difficulties for most Latin American nations. The policy recommendation for the resolution of this thorny problem became known as "import-substitution industrialization" (ISI).[6] A policy to favor import substitution through protective tariffs on industrial imports was taken to be the direct route to industrialization. After flourishing from the late 1940s to the early 1960s, the policies of ISI were pronounced dead. ISI failed in its goals, and economic conditions had become, if anything, worse than before. Unemployment continued unabated; ISI industries had not penetrated the export markets; and the dependence upon the export of primary products became intensified, for now the import mix showed a higher degree of semifinished materials, spare parts, and machinery necessary for the maintenance of ISI industries.

The policies of ECLA during this period resulted in a true substitution of imports, although not in the sense ostensibly defended by ECLA theorists. The whole ISI period provided a resolution for a problem of markets confronting the predominantly monopolistic economics of the U.S. and other advanced countries. The chronic balance of payments difficulties of Latin American nations made their purchase of finished consumer goods in the United States a precarious and unpredictable activity. ISI provided market stability by bringing foreign capital (usually with foreign machinery and raw materials) into production in Latin America, where products that had been imported for half of a century were now produced and sold. In the meantime, new credits were issued for the importation of machinery and raw materials (this was the actual import substitution!) based upon the high expectations for growth in the ISI industries. It was not long before the new industries had passed their high growth-rate and new bottlenecks to development appeared in the form of "limited internal markets," which prevented the further growth of domestic industry.[7]

But in the end the policy of ISI did not improve balance-of-payment difficulties of Mexico. In place of consumer goods purchased directly from foreign producers, raw materials, intermediate goods, and capital equipment imports skyrocketed to provision the numerous factories catering to the sumptuary demands of the oligarchy and the affluent middle classes, comprising as much as 30 percent of the entire population. The chronic balance-of-payment problem became aggravated, moreover, by mounting repatriation of profits and other income by foreign investors, by the increase in the ratio

TABLE 11

Rates of Profit and Profit Repatriation in Manufacturing

| | % Profit | | % Profit Repatriation | |
	1969	1970	1969	1970
Latin America	12.0%	11.0%	6.0%	6.1%
Mexico	10.3	9.6	5.4	6.7
Argentina	12.4	7.8	9.0	7.6
Brazil	12.3	14.0	5.2	5.7
Chile	Loss	1.5	—	—
Colombia	10.8	8.6	4.6	5.9
Peru	7.2	8.3	4.2	4.1
Venezuela	16.2	14.2	6.0	8.4

Source: *Hanson's Latin American Letter*, Washington, no. 1392, Nov. 20, 1971.

and total volume of reinvestment of earnings rather than new foreign investment by foreign firms and, finally, by the practice of "over-pricing" and "over-invoicing" of transnational corporations. A brief digression on the last item is necessary to illustrate the power of the multinational corporations.

The obvious discrepancy between the official low rates of profit (see Table 11) made public for foreign companies and the eagerness with which foreign capital has gone into certain sectors caused the government of Colombia to commission an investigation of the subject. In the Colombian study it was discovered, for example, that a given amount of chemical product that sold for $100 in the world market, was "sold" by the parent member of a multinational complex to its Colombian subsidiary at an average of $255. The ability to perform this kind of operation is one of the great advantages that imperialism has obtained through the medium of the so-called multinationals. A growing portion of world trade is carried on presently by the branches of the multinational corporations; and the prices utilized in such transactions are bogus, serving the ultimate purpose of covering up and shifting profits from country to country.[8] The order of magnitude of the differential in profit rates accounted for by intracorporate transfer pricing is shown in Table 12. It should be noted that the multinational corporation is very *flexible* in its transfer pricing policies. In the case of sales of oil from subsidiaries to the parent company, the transfer of profits via overpricing usually favors the less developed country—a reverse practice which allows the parent companies to solicit larger benefits from the United States Internal Revenue Service.

In an effort to remedy balance-of-payment problems it is natural that governments in the capitalist world should welcome off-setting foreign investments. But the "nationalistic" policies of the PRI in Mexico, geared to presenting an image of an independent national capitalist class, have made the state the principal shareholder in a variety of institutions, and this situation has forced the state to utilize foreign debt as one of the means of its "Mexicanization" policy.

Mexico as a whole is thus characterized by a monopolistic structure that is both rural and urban; by the predominance of a state capitalist sector which appears to be in the clutches of the American commercial banks on which it must rely as sources of funding; and by an industrial-urban structure that is unable to raise (a) the level of employment or (b) the amount

TABLE 12

Profit Rates of Foreign Companies in Colombia, 1968

Type of Industry	Average Rate of Overpricing	Official Profit Rate	Effective Profit Rate
Pharmaceutical	155%	6.7	79.1
Rubber	40	16.0	43.0
Chemical	25.5	n.d.	n.d.
Electronic	16-66	n.d.	n.d.

Source: C.V. Vaitsos, "Transfer of Resources and Preservation of Monopoly Rents," Center for International Affairs, Harvard University, *Economic Development Report 168*, 1970.

of manufactured exports that well deserves the title of the "ciudad subdesarrollada."

The Mexican economy is thoroughly influenced industrially and financially by American-based multinational corporations and American banks. In its efforts to appear to free itself from the penetration of direct U.S. and foreign capital, Mexico had to give in to the control of international bank capital. To free itself of the balance-of-payments problem and the burden of the foreign debt, the Mexican government must strive to increase both its agricultural and manufactured exports. It must also try to increase revenue from foreign tourists, and strive to reduce the consumption of foreign goods by its citizens, while maintaining the pattern of consumption, production, and distribution of social wealth which predominates at present. The problems and contradictions of the economy as a whole find direct expression in the northern border area, and, as we shall see, the proposed remedies for the national ills are "at work" in this area.

The Basic Economic Life of the "Border Town" and Its Environs

The Mexican border states and the border zone itself have experienced a tremendous growth in population and urbanization over the last fifty years. This growth has affected the make-up of some very old towns such as Nuevo Laredo, and it has been the major force in the development of wholly new urban centers such as Tijuana. The eight major municipalities of the Mexican border are from west to east, Tijuana, Mexicali, Nogales, Ciudad Juárez, Piedras Negras, Nuevo Laredo, Reynosa, and Matamoros. Between 1950 and 1960 the total population of these eight centers increased by 83 percent, from less than nine hundred thousand to 1.5 million (data includes Ensenada). By 1970 the population had reached a total of 2.3 million persons or about 5 percent of the total population of Mexico. Between 1960 and 1969 the population rise in the northern border states (Baja California, Sonora Chihuahua, Coahuila, Nuevo León, and Tamaulipas) grew by

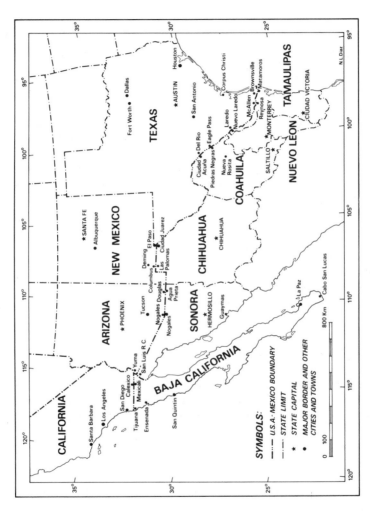

The United States–Mexico Border (1977)

45 percent in contrast with a figure of 31 percent for the nation as a whole. During the 1950s the rates of growth of the largest cities on the border surpassed that of the Federal District, and the growth continues unabated today. As shown in the previous chapter, this increase in population and rate of population growth has been due fundamentally to migration. In 1970, fully 29 percent of the border population came from other parts of the country, and foreigners accounted for another 2 percent.

The population of the northern states is concentrated predominantly in the cities listed above and several other urban centers. In this regard the northern states are more highly urbanized than Mexico as a whole. The outstanding example is the state of Baja California where 85 percent of the state's population is urban, living in localities of twenty-five hundred or more inhabitants.

The physical conditions of the area are such that the population is largely concentrated in four cities (Tijuana, Mexicali, Ensenada, Tecate) in the northern part of the state, the rest of the area being practically uninhabited. Only half a century ago the entire area of Baja California was practically uninhabited, but a number of historical events coincided to set off the growth that we still witness today. First of all, the continued fear of American attempts to annex Baja California caused the Mexican government to initiate various programs to encourage the settlement and colonization of the area during the 1910s and 1920s. As we have indicated, the penetration of the northern area of Mexico had proceeded apace during the regime of Porfirio Díaz and by 1885 "little that was Mexican remained" in Baja California.[9] As a reaction to the power of U.S. private interests in the area and various U.S. colonization projects, the government of Mexico realized that the only way to maintain sovereignty over the region was through a concerted colonization effort. Additionally, the licensing of gambling, the commercialization of vice, and opium refining became authorized activities that brought a large influx of population and gave to Tijuana the exotic character it still possesses.

As indicated in the previous chapter the origin of the growth has been such that these urban centers have never had the productive capacity needed to support such a large population. *The large concentrations of people in these towns perform the function of a large reserve of labor at the disposal of U.S. industry and agriculture.* The flow of labor services from Mexico into the United States has taken a variety of forms, but the specific flow from the border towns throughout the past decade and at the present time has been in the form of illegal migration and "commuters."

Illegal migration from Mexico is without a doubt the "best of all possible migrations." In the history of agribusiness in the Southwest the first preferred migrant agricultural workers were the Chinese and, later, the Japanese. Both groups seemed to make themselves scarce once the work duties ceased during the off-season. But this phenomenon turned out to be only an appearance, for the Chinese and the Japanese established themselves eventually as agriculturists and could not be depended upon to serve as a massive, highly mobile reserve of human labor. Their place was soon taken up by the Mexican migration. Since the motherland was much closer for Mexican migrant workers, it was anticipated that the Mexican migrant would be more apt to return to his homeland and not tend to settle in the United States. However, contrary to expectations, Mexicans not only settled in large numbers and became American citizens, but they also became highly urbanized. At this point, the *illegal* Mexican workers, apt to work in industry or in agriculture, raised at the expense of the Mexican economy, and easily deportable, came into the picture. Their presence has been felt especially since the end of World War II. At the present time the Immigration and Naturalization Service estimates that approximately 3 million illegal workers from Mexico come to work in the United States every year. These illegal workers have no recourse to the courts if they are exploited by employers and are willing to work for far lower wages than United States citizens can live on. Not all of these illegal workers make their permanent residence in the border towns, although the towns are used as a stopping point and base of operation.*

A source of labor more directly tied into the life of the border cities consists of the so-called green-card commuters. These are people who live in the border towns and who cross the border every day to work in the United States. The number of commuters varies a great deal from town to town. At the present time a conservative estimate places the number of green-card commuters at fifty thousand.[10] How important commuters' wages are as a source of labor revenue for workers residing in border towns is indicated in Table 13. In actuality, not only green-card commuters but many "illegal" workers cross the border every day to work in the United States, consequently accurate estimates of the total number of green-card holders plus illegals are unavailable at present.

TABLE 13

Mexican Border City Wages Earned in the United States

Mexican Border City	*Percent of Total 1960 Wages Earned in U.S.*
Matamoros	30
Reynosa	22
Nuevo Laredo	31
Piedras Negras	23
Ciudad Juárez	36
Nogales	19
Mexicali	21
Tijuana	33

Source: Secretaría de Comercio, *Programa Nacional Fronterizo,* Mexico, 1965.

*The reader is referred to the theoretical presentation of this material in the previous chapter.

The net result of the laboring activity of the large mass of workers concentrated south of the border is a depressing effect upon the wage rates and the maintenance of a higher-than-average level of unemployment in the areas of the United States bordering Mexico. Thus the fundamental aspect of the social economy of the border towns is the incorporation of a large pool of Mexican workers into the orbit of the American monopoly-capitalistic economy and the formation of a large reserve of competitive, unskilled and unorganized workers immediately south of the border. The most glaring economic appearance—a service oriented economy designed to satisfy the foreign visitor—is fully deceiving. The souvenir shops, peddlers, restaurants, night clubs, car watchers, barber and beauty shops, gasoline stations, store clerks, etc., are the visible facade that the border towns offer to the investigator. Beneath this facade one can discover something more elemental about the organization of material production in the United States.

The economic conditions that prevail in the *American* border area are a reflection of the fundamental aspect of the role of the laboring population in the economy. An indication of these conditions was the attention paid to border counties at the height of the War on Poverty in the late 1960s. The southern American border zone is characterized by the pressure of low-paid, foreign workers, small towns that depend on unsteady retail (and some wholesale) trade with Mexico, military establishments, agriculture based on irrigation, and higher than average unemployment rates. The basic categories of employment (military, agriculture, retail trade) are those where the organization of workers has traditionally been weakest. As opposed to the United States northern border with Canada—where industry, employment, union organization, and general economic conditions look like a cross-sectional reflection of the overall U.S. economy—the southern border appears to be a collection of aspects from the seamy side of the U.S. economy. This situation cannot be separated from the existence of Mexican underdevelopment.

Other Economic Activity across the Border Line

While the flow of labor resources northward is the principal element of the border equation, other elements are also important. Among these are the flow of Mexican workers' wages into retail establishments on the U.S. side of the border, the further dependence of this retail trade on purchases from a wider Mexican region, the flow of agricultural production from Mexican border states into the United States, the contribution of tourist dollars to the trade economy of Mexican border towns, the direct technological dependence of Mexican industry upon United States industry, and a host of illegal activities and enterprises.

A good portion of the income earned by residents of border towns is not spent in Mexico but in the United States. This is so regardless of the origin of the revenue. Thus the border towns provide not only a source of labor. The remuneration for this labor, and more, reverts back to American business, contributing to the uneven development of the area. A hypothetical Mexican family's binational shopping list is presented below (Table 14). The list indicates the relationship that exists between shopping patterns and differential availability of goods in retail stores on both sides of the border. The percentage of income that is spent on the U.S. side by Mexican nationals varies considerably. In one illustrative case it was estimated that the workers of American operated plants in Agua Prieta (Sonora) spent fully 52 percent of their gross income from wages in Douglas (Arizona) and other American towns.[11]

Expenditures by Mexican nationals in U.S.-side twin cities are not limited to local shoppers. The wholesale and retail establishments in these American border towns cater to a market that extends deep into Mexico. The town of Laredo on the Rio Grande, and also on a major highway that connects to the interior of Mexico, is one example of this far-reaching trade. It is said that wealthy Mexicans from Monterrey and beyond come to Laredo to make special purchases, mostly in the

TABLE 14

A Binational Shopping List

Buy in Mexico	Buy in U.S.
Services, including	Manufactured goods
Entertainment	Clothes
Physician's services	Cars
(particularly for	Car parts
Mexican-Americans)	Appliances
Dental Work	Canned goods
Some auto repairs	
Haircuts	
Staples	Poultry
Sugar	Eggs
Rice	
Most vegetables	American liquor
Tropical fruit	
Beef	American cigarettes
Baked goods	
Bottled beverages	
Liquor	
Beer	
Soft drinks	
Furniture	
Prescription drugs	

Source: David S. North, *The Border Crossers* (Washington, D.C.: Transcentury Corporation, 1970), p. 39.

clothing stores of this city. As a consequence, Laredo has the distinction of being the one U.S. city where apparel sales volume exceeds that of auto sales.[12] Nogales (Arizona), located on the Mexican West Coast Highway, attracts shoppers from several hundred miles south to its retail and wholesale outlets. Interviews conducted among businessmen in this city brought out the importance of purchases by Mexican nationals from as far away as Ciudad Obregón, Mazatlán, and Guadalajara. This pattern of trade obtains with variation in all border towns throughout the entire length of the border.

The border towns constitute the focal point of exchanges of agricultural goods flowing back and forth across the border. Recently, agricultural trade between the United States and Mexico has been on the increase. The Economic Research Service of the United States Department of Agriculture indicates that during 1973 agricultural trade between the United States and Mexico accelerated rapidly. U.S. agricultural exports to Mexico amounted to $254 million, 94 percent above 1972, and U.S. agricultural imports from Mexico totaled $706 million, up 32 percent. The U.S. is Mexico's principal supplier of farm imports. Mexico imports corn, grain, soybeans, fruits, vegetables, seeds, dairy products, poultry meats, and dairy cattle. At the same time, Mexico is the principal supplier of the U.S. domestic market for agricultural imports. The U.S. imports from Mexico cattle, beef, sugar, molasses, onions, tomatoes, melons, strawberries, fruits, and vegetables.

The obvious overlap between exports and imports is due in large part to the shipping of identical products back and forth across the border. Although this back-and-forth movement of commodities across the border reflects to some extent climactic conditions, e.g., the production of "winter vegetables" in Mexico, it is a relatively new phenomenon. As recently as the early 1940s the largest agricultural imports from Mexico by value were items not produced in the United States, such as bananas, coffee, chile, and henequen. The production of fresh vegetables for the U.S. market at this time was not as important as it is today. For instance, only a third of all the tomatoes produced were exported, although it should be pointed out that, even at

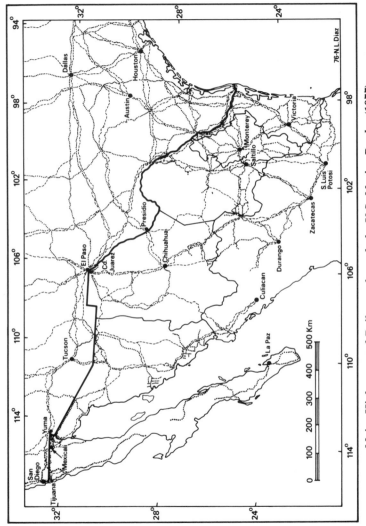

Major Highways and Railways through the U.S.–Mexico Border (1977)

this time, fully two-thirds of the production of two northern states (Sonora and Sinaloa) reached the American consumer. An important element in the appearance of the "winter vegetables"—and the two-way traffic of commodities through border towns—was the rapid development of "commercial agriculture" in the northern states of Mexico beginning in the early 1940s. With the building of the Pan-American Highway in Mexico the exports of tomatoes from the Mexican northeastern states increased from less than a million pounds in 1942 to 4 million pounds in 1943 and 14 million in 1944. Some of this early growth in production for export was based on the surplus production of small ejido parcels. By the late 1950s, however, full-fledged capitalist production of a variety of agricultural goods had developed—especially in Sonora, Sinaloa, and Tamaulipas. Thus a few small areas of northern Mexico have become pockets of California-like "agribusiness." Some of the crops that are produced in Mexico for export into the United States by Mexican workers, with the help of advanced agricultural methods and machinery are, during a different season of the year, produced in the United States for export to Mexico, sometimes by the same Mexican workers using similar mechanical equipment. The nature of this flow is such that the direct contribution to the economy of the border towns is negligible, except in the specific case of towns on the path of railroads or highways such as Laredo, Nogales, etc. In such towns a few jobs are generated for office workers, warehousemen, packers, and service fields related to trucking, primarily on the U.S. side of the border.[13]

Tourism is the main "industry" of the Mexican border zone. It is one of the most important "industries" of Mexico as well. Tourist dollars are the main source, directly or indirectly, of the personal income of most residents of the border towns. It is tourism that gives to the gaudy commercial enterprise the glaring predominance over other aspects of economic life and is, therefore, the most immediately perceivable element of economic life in the border towns of Mexico. Tourism, despite its arguable merits as an "industry" in a developing country, has been intensely promoted by the Mexican government in the border area, and this policy cannot be separated from the external financial situation of the country as a whole.

The border zone received 58 million visitors in 1970, who spent an average of fifteen dollars per person. Global border tourist spending in that year, amounting to $880 million, was the second most important item in the current account income of Mexico's balance of payments. The most important trading centers are *Tijuana, Mexicali, Ciudad Juárez, and Nuevo Laredo, which jointly accounted for 80 percent for all border income in 1970.* Although Tijuana is the most commercially active city, it is also the one with the highest level of outgoings, mainly as a result of the illegal import of goods and services by locally based companies, contraband, and the repatriation of profits and dividends by U.S. companies operating in the city. The phenomenon has become increasingly marked; income from 1965 to 1970 increased at an annual 18 percent and the outflow by 20 percent. The balance of border transactions in Ciudad Juárez from 1965 to 1970 moved down at a mean annual 4.4 percent, due to the slow rate of income expansion rate of expenditures (17.5 percent yearly). Mexicali is the second most important city in volume of income and outflow, and third as regards the balance. Income in Mexicali has grown steadily, with constant fluctuations in the outflow. Nuevo Laredo in 1970 accounted for 5 percent of total border transaction income and 5.5 percent of all outflow, contributing 4 percent to the national trade balance.

One last form of economic domination manifested in the border area is the phenomenon of technological dependence. To illustrate the situation I shall use the case of Monterrey, a major Mexican city which is not *on* the border, but whose proximity to the border makes it part and parcel of the whole "border syndrome." Monterrey has been primarily an industrial city, characterized by large scale industry since the 1890s. The natives of Monterrey have been favorably compared (apparently because of their "entrepreneurial spirit") with the Antioqueños of Colombia. The continuing growth of this city has come to depend, more and more, not on the talent and capacity for "self-sacrifice" of the local bourgeois class but on their utilizing, and becoming dominated by, the technology and facilities of U.S. corporations.

Technological dependence manifests itself in at least three fundamental ways. The first is the utilization by U.S.-located firms of some of the technically-skilled manpower which abounds in Monterrey (such as engineers, draftsmen, etc.) to work in the research and development of plants, machinery, blueprints, etc. Final sale of the product is in the United States, and the purchasing parties are charged as if all labor services had been performed at U.S. wages. The other side of the coin is the use by Mexican firms of technical advice and direction from special U.S. consultants to produce cheaper—and technically inferior—plants for production processes in Mexico. Secondly, industrial production in Monterrey has become increasingly dependent on the importation of entire used automated plants. This phenomenon, which is not exclusive to Monterrey or Mexico by any means, can be easily characterized as the "institutionalization of uneven technological development" between the United States and Mexico. Lastly, the two problems described above make it easier for other economic activities dependent upon the United States, such as wholesale distribution of imported machinery, to settle in Monterrey, rather than in other areas. The reason is that Monterrey's wholesale importers have more direct access to manufacturers' representatives than wholesale importers do in other areas. Thus domination breeds further domination.

Illegal Economic Activity

The economic complement of the above technical and economic flows, which give life to the border towns on both sides of the line, is the presence of a variety of illegal (or semilegal) activities. One has been historically inseparable from the border region: smuggling. As in times past, smuggling of goods to either side of the border is commonplace. The better known smuggled items are a variety of narcotic drugs that are transported from Mexico to the U.S.

Prior to World War II, the illicit market in the United States was the recipient of heroin and other opium derivatives[14] from various areas of the world. The Balkans, Turkey, and Persia accounted for considerable quantities. In the Far East, China and India were the principal suppliers. Opium grown in Mexico was less important. The laboratories which transform the opium into heroin were also geographically scattered. World War II brought about important changes in the patterns of trade with the United States. Shipping routes were affected by the war at sea and access to processing laboratories was denied by the war in Europe and the Far East. These war-caused restrictions did not, of course, apply to Mexico. An extensive common border and a heavy flow of automotive traffic between the U.S. and Mexico provided ready access to a limited crude opium supply being produced in the states of Sinaloa, Chihuahua, Durango, and Jalisco. The war-time demands for Mexican opium provided an incentive for increased production by Mexican growers. Today, consequently, it is estimated that Mexican opium is the major source of opiates currently being consumed in the United States' southwest.[15]

Heroin from France currently provides 80 percent of the United States heroin supply. French heroin production relies wholly on opium diverted from government-controlled crops in Turkey—which represents the major source of opium produced for the legitimate pharmaceutical industry in Europe and North America. Some noncontrolled fields are also producing for the illegal market. The illicit Turkish opium moves through several complicated routes which include Syria, Lebanon, and Corsica to France, where it is processed into heroin and shipped to the underworld in the United States through a web of channels and connections.[16]

The traffic in Mexican heroin, in contrast to the French operation, is not organized to any great degree. Usually it is carried on by numerous small operators located on or near the United States border, who cater to individual distributors in Texas, New Mexico, Arizona, and California. Aside from heroin, other drugs have flowed and continue to flow northward from Mexico: marijuana, cocaine, "dangerous drugs," etc. While the U.S. drug market may in itself be an interesting subject of study, its over-all economic impact on border residents and wage-workers is far less important than publicity —such as that obtained through Gordon Liddy's* Operation Intercept in 1970—would lead one to believe.

Less publicized, but probably more important from an economic standpoint, is the contraband into Mexico. According to popular sources, the amount of smuggling is substantial. Many commodities brought into the border area under a variety of arrangements become contraband to be taken into the interior of Mexico. To the extent that smuggling exists, it defeats the protectionist policies of the Mexican government designed to promote "national" industry. Unfortunately, there is no data on which to base a reasonable judgment of the effects of smuggling on the border towns or on Mexico as a whole.[17]

Far more important in the economic fabric of the border towns is the prostitution "industry." The commercial, *nonindustrial* character of most Mexican border towns makes them unable to provide employment for the masses of people that overflow into them. Such conditions drive the men into a variety of menial "service" occupations (shoeshine boys, etc.) and it forces women into prostitution. That this "business' is far from being fortuitous and disorganized is revealed by an estimate that places the total of *municipal revenues* for Ciudad Juárez derived from official prostitution at one million dollars per year, or half the total city revenues.[18] The economic domination of the United States economy over the Mexican economy is given an air of pestilence by the relation that exists between a thriving prostitution industry and the presence of tens of thousands of U.S. servicemen in bases along the border. The problem that arises from the quartering of soldiers and the need to provide for relief to their sexual needs is solved by "shifting" it over to the "lower forms of life" of Mexico. Again,

---

*Of Watergate fame. An account of Gordon Liddy's leading role in Operation Intercept, see "Gordon Liddy: He Bungled into the White House," *Rolling Stone*, July 19, 1973, San Francisco.

there is hardly anything new about this: the Brownsville incident over fifty years ago offered proof of the convenient "outlet" provided by Mexican women for the physiological needs of U.S. soldiers.*

Mexican Remedies

Under the combined stress of demographic explosion and economic deterioration, the Mexican government attempted in 1961 to institute a special effort to integrate its border region with the rest of the nation. The Programa Nacional Fronterizo (PRONAF) was begun in 1961. It provided some infrastructure in the way of buildings, paved roads, industrial parks with electricity and water, etc. This infrastructure was supposed to facilitate and promote the appearance of "import substitution" and the increase of the "tourist industry." Although PRONAF met with initial success it soon became apparent that it would not suffice to meet the unemployment situation in the area, so in 1965 the Mexican government established the Border Industrial Program (BIP) which came into full operation in 1967.

The BIP has received glorious publicity by both Mexican and American official sources.† And the Mexican government has reacted to what has been the clearest result of the BIP: the intensification of the economic dependence of the border towns upon the American economy. It has done so by means of a whole new program which purports to reintegrate the border economy into the national economy of Mexico. Since this new program (The Inter-Ministerial Commission for the Economic Development of the Northern Border Zone and Free Zones) is of recent vintage, not much in the way of data is

*The soldiers in that particular incident were black American soldiers. Would it be a surprise to find that at that time and for many years most U.S. Army Negro units were stationed near the Mexican border?

†See the chapter on the BIP in this book.

available. Thus the best that can be said is that perhaps it is too early to tell. However, a cursory examination of the various dispositions regulating this new program show that its two fundamental policies are: a) a program of duty-free imports of "enticement articles" presumably unavailable to Mexican residents on the Mexican side of the towns and b) the same aid extended for the import of machinery, materials, and equipment needed for the construction, operation, expansion, and maintenance of trade centers. The success of the first aspect of the program means that Mexican wage earners will no longer have to cross the border line to make special purchases since now the Mexican retailer himself can do it duty-free. The second aspect of the program is a rehash of the ISI policies discussed earlier. I fail to see how the program can have any direct effect upon either the massive unemployment and underemployment problem of the border or upon the domination of the economy of this area by the United States economy. Quite the contrary, in the light of the whole of the previous analysis, it would seem that this program, alone or pursued in conjunction with the BIP, will make matters *worse* in the long run.

The Border Syndrome

The border towns have become famous among people throughout Mexico for having the highest wage scales in the entire Republic. As a result, an increasing number of peasants in the interior are making the decision to sell their homes, their cattle, and whatever other belongings they may have, in order to migrate to the border area. They go there expecting to find a wonderful job awaiting them. But a very large percentage are disappointed to discover upon arrival the true state of affairs in border towns. The female is fortunate who finds a job in a factory; rarely does a male find one. Great numbers of unemployed peasants are thus stranded in the border towns. Some return to the interior. Most do not. They have nothing to return to—all of their possessions have been sold.

In the border towns, however, there is no "servant problem" or lack of cheap sex. Border towns are characterized by prostitutes, pimps, and demonstrations of every type of sexual perversion imaginable. The material conditions of subjugation to United States' economic interests are reflected in a degenerate atmosphere where people that are already the victims of poverty and oppression are forced by circumstances to become morally and physically degraded. This state of affairs goes on amidst a climate of callousness which does not allow even the traditional, if hypocritical, notions of immorality and shame associated with prostitution to surface. The same insensitivity is manifested in the majority of studies that deal with the border area and border towns: the fact that countless people are reduced to social behavior hardly distinguishable from that of animals appears to be accepted as something inevitable—an attitude quite in keeping with the tendency of modern social science to regard all that is *real* as *necessary*. I have called these historical and contemporary phenomena the border syndrome.

These aspects of the border economy are by no means unique to the border towns. The availability of cheap domestic servants of Mexican nationality—who may live in the border towns—is one of the "attractions" of western living in southern California; prostitution is not solely a border phenomenon but is also the lot of many Mexican women in the United States. The border syndrome therefore is something which does not arise from the nature of an imaginary line or the "character" of a city. It is instead a syndrome whose roots extend deep into the basis of economic exploitation and oppression and is but a reflection—perhaps the most palpably horrendous—of the division of the world between rich and poor nations today.

vii: Border Economy 3: The Border Industrial Program

The one process in the history of the border area which can be most closely identified with the existence of the border line is the development of the area's Border Industrial Program. Interestingly enough, it is through this program that the border area ultimately ceases to be a particular—if not an isolated—instance of economic development, and instead becomes a locus for the manifestation of structures and processes which are at play in the larger world. This is so because the Border Industrial Program is directly related to the appearance of multinational corporations, and to the ebb and flow of Latin America's post-war economic policies.

A multinational corporation "is multinational in the sense that it operates in a number of nations with the purpose of maximizing the profits not of the individual units on a nation-by-nation basis but of the group as a whole."[1] Its appearance and development must, of course, be understood in a context in which the export of capital was already a predominant aspect of international economic relations.

The development of the multinationals provides positive and negative results. Positively, it brings the results of technological advance to backward areas where it helps disintegrate the old organization of the economy. Negatively, it provides neither independence nor equality for the "underdeveloped" world. The international corporation is not very interested in building up the educational and technical skills levels of the nationals of a country falling in the "periphery." An increase in skills and educational levels has long been acknowledged as an important element in the process of economic development, and as such it has been the subject of considerable investment on the part of national governments in the 1950s and 1960s. Given the structure of the multinational corporation, investment in the educational infrastructure may easily result in a "brain-drain" toward the center countries. At its worst, this type of technically skilled migration may meet at the center with unexpected barriers: discriminatory practices based upon ethnic or cultural factors.

The appearance of the multinational corporation is a sign of the passage to collective capitalism and state capitalism. While doing so, it also affects the design for development of a country by its effect on tax capacity. In order to facilitate economic growth, governments must be able to invest in a variety of "infrastructure" investments which range from the educational programs mentioned above, to road paving, electrification, etc. A most important consideration in gauging the ability of a government to support these services is its ability to generate revenues through taxation. And this ability, in turn, will be affected by the multinational corporation's ability to play off particular levels of infrastructural development with given levels of taxation and to move facilities from one country to another. Whereas the national home base of the corporation is able to obtain some corporate revenue through taxation, this possibility is not so certain for poor countries, especially on a long-term basis. Finally, the multinational corporation represents a strong setback to the long-fought economic gains of the labor movement in advanced countries.[2]

The Border Industrial Program represents the entry of the multinational corporation into the economic development of the border area. It also can be viewed as a manifestation of a broad change in the economic policies of Latin American nations, which, not surprisingly, happen to coincide with the "best interests" of the corporation.

Postwar economic thought regarding Latin America by the ideologues of national capitalist development represented a reversal of the policies that had characterized conventional wisdom before World War II. Before 1945, the growth of most Latin American nations was seen as being dependent, according to a harmonious international division of labor, upon the production of primary commodities for more advanced manufacturing countries. The reversal in thought blamed this world-wide division of labor for the slow development of Latin America: "crecimiento hacia afeura" was to be substituted for "crecimiento hacia adentro."

In many politico-economic tracts, the losses in trade suffered by the export-oriented Latin American nations were amply described, and the emerging conclusions—the basis for postwar orthodoxy—were formed. Latin America, if it wished to develop and prosper, must develop its own industries and must become self-reliant. This was to be done by a variety of measures, but the one name that stuck to the policies followed during this period (roughly from 1950–70) was that of "import substitution industrialization," or ISI.

Current economic thinking about the economic lessons of the postwar period for Latin America (and for the rest of the backward nations) is taking the direction of a *new orthodoxy*. The lessons of the postwar period—up to and including the late 1960s—are seen as follows: a) import-substitution policies have outlived their usefulness; b) the unemployment problem of countries in Latin America has remained unabated because of the labor-saving characteristics of both foreign investment and local "import-substitution industries"; and c) planning and control oriented toward national self-development have become obsolete.

The new orthodoxy which is slowly emerging presents the following prescriptions to remedy Latin America's ills: a) import substitution is to be abandoned in favor of policies that promote the export of manufactured goods; b) planning and restrictions are to be deemphasized in favor of a freer utilization of the "market mechanisms" for national development; and c) foreign capital is welcome, but it will be subject to restrictions designed to "guide" its route so that its introduction will benefit the host nation. Mexico is one of the prime countries where these new prescriptions have been adopted. No longer is Mexico oriented to a development pattern tied to concepts of import substitution. President Echeverría indicated in late 1970 that import substitution was not an answer to Mexico's development, and that, additionally, Mexico needed a significantly increased export sector. The notion of "market" in this context implies two different but related ideas: the first is that profit forces should be allowed to operate which might bring foreign companies and investment into Latin America to engage in operations, thereby making international boundaries less of a barrier for "free enterprise." The second idea is that the "effective market" can be improved and its size increased through the medium of economic integration agreements.

In 1965, the Mexican government established the Border Industrial Program (BIP), which came into full operation in 1967. The primary goal of the BIP was "the alleviation of widespread unemployment prevalent along the 2,000 mile common border with the United States." The advantages of the program for Mexico were officially seen as: a) the appearance of new jobs, and larger incomes; b) the introduction of modern methods of manufacturing; and c) the increase in consumption of Mexican raw materials. The idea of establishing the BIP came from the Mexican Secretaryship of Treasury and Public Credit whose first officer, Octavio Campos Salas, had observed American plants assemblying goods for U.S. markets in the Far East.[3]

In his 1965 report to the nation, President Gustavo Díaz Ordaz announced the institution of the program as an answer to the prevalent unemployment on the northern border. This commitment was reaffirmed by Díaz Ordaz in his 1966 Report to the Nation. After setting up operational procedures for the processing of applications of interested companies, the BIP started in 1967 with seventy-two authorized American-owned plants. This number grew to 147 in 1969, and to 330 in 1972. It is estimated that border plants turned out more than $50 million worth of products in 1971, which represented an increase of more than 200 percent over 1969.[4] The BIP ceased to be a "border" program in 1971 when the Mexican government extended it to a twenty-kilometer-wide coastal strip and to the whole country in November 1972 (the so-called "in-bond" industries). In 1973, exports were estimated at approximately $400 million. The vast majority of the plants are located on the area bordering the United States. Major American corporations actively participating in the BIP include Magnavox, Litton Industries, Kimberly-Clark, General Instrument, Memorex, Samsonite, Republican Corporation, Sears & Roebuck, Motorola, and Hughes Aircraft.

The legal structure of the program is as follows. The Mexican government waived its duties and regulations on the importation of raw materials and capital equipment, as well as its restrictions on foreign capital, for foreign-owned plants located anywhere within a 12.5 mile deep strip of land along the U.S.-Mexico border as long as 100 percent of the finished products were exported out of Mexico. Industries which competed with Mexican exports are generally prohibited from participating. According to Mexican labor law, at least 90 percent of the employees must be Mexican citizens, although executives and technical personnel not available in Mexico can be excluded from the calculation of this percentage. If the company operating in Mexico under the BIP imports 100 percent of raw materials and components and exports 100 percent of product, then there are no sales in Mexico and, consequently, there is no corporate income tax, or any other tax associated with profits, sales, or dividends. It is also possible to escape municipal and state taxes, but this is usually negotiated at the local or state level. Foreign national and Mexican corporations with foreign stockholders are not allowed to own land within 100 kilometers of the border. This regulation has not been waived for the BIP and the interested companies are also required to pay the minimum wage for workers. The minimum wage varies along the border to reflect local conditions and is revised upward every two years by the Mexican government.[5]

The chief United States regulation relevant to the program is Section 807 of the Tariff Schedule of the United States:

Articles assembled abroad in whole or in part fabricated components, the products of the United States which a) were exported in condition ready for assembly without further fabrication . . . c) have not been advanced in value or improved in condition abroad except by operations incidental to the assembly process such as cleaning, lubricating, and painting. . . . A duty upon the full value of the imported article less the cost or value of such products of the United States.[6]

In other words, duties are to be paid only on the value added abroad. In the case of the Mexican assembly operations, the value added is essentially the wages paid to Mexican workers.

The initial purpose of this legislation was to maintain U.S. production by encouraging the use of U.S. components in foreign-made products. The actual result has been to encourage U.S. corporations to utilize low-wage unskilled labor in "underdeveloped" countries in the assembly of products for the U.S. market. This system exists not only in Mexico, but also in Hong Kong, Taiwan, Korea, and Haiti.

Economic Background and Scope of the BIP

On a more analytical level, the policy decisions establishing and promoting the BIP and its extensions have rested on an analysis of the growth process of the Mexican economy. This analysis showed the Mexican economy to be achieving high raw rates of growth while failing to solve a high unemployment problem as well as a pattern of extreme unevenness in the distribution of income and wealth. While the economy as a whole grew at an average rate of 7 percent a year during the 1960s, underemployment (based on earnings) was estimated to be higher than 50 percent of the labor force in 1970. Another estimate places open unemployment at 2.2 million man-years.[7]

During the 1960s, manufactured goods began to acquire a more important position in Mexico's imports. As has been the case in general with Mexican industrialization, this change was heavily directed toward capital intensive industries. Consequently, the net employment effect of the increase in manufactured exports was fairly insignificant, in part due to the relatively low ratio of employment to output. The promotion of "plantas maquiladoras"—as assembly plants are referred to—was supposed to bring about a structural change in this ratio because of relatively higher labor-intensity. Secondly, the development of assembly plants in specified peripheral areas was seen as part of the national effort to stimulate regional industrialization and to effect a decentralization of production facilities away from major industrial centers, particularly in and around Mexico City.[8]

Since its inception, the BIP has moved with vertiginous speed, but roughly one hundred firms began operating after the Tariff Commission's report became known. Of 147 plants authorized in mid-1969, 103 were in actual operation. The heaviest concentration was in Baja, California, where over seventy plants were assembling U.S.-made components. Of these sixty-eight in Tijuana and Mexicali. The remainder were mainly in Ciudad Juárez, Nuevo Laredo, and Matamoros.[9] Presently, the emphasis is on electronic products and textiles with fully 80 percent of the workers in electronic and textile plants. But many other lines are represented, including dismantling of scrap railroad cars, food processing and packaging, assembly of medical instruments, boats, and caskets.

The usual procedure is to set up two plants: one on each side of the border. Under this "twin-plant" arrangement, the products are initially processed in the U.S. plant, sent to the Mexican counterpart for assembly, and then returned to the American side for "finishing and shipping." The U.S.-side twin is by far the smaller of the plants. It employs very few workers and is designed mainly to fulfill the stipulations of the Tariff Schedule, which presumably requires that the goods be "finished" in the U.S.

> An example of the concept are the "twins of Transitron" an electronic component manufacturer, employing about 75 in Laredo and 1,500 in Nuevo Laredo, Mexico. "Finishing" could mean little

more than pasting on a label. Many plants on the U.S. side hire Mexican residents anyway. Attempts to organize are met by threats to move the rest of the operation to Mexico.[10]

The important centers of the BIP are located, not surprisingly, in "twin-city" locations along the border: San Diego-Tijuana, Calexico-Mexicali, Nogales-Nogales, Douglas-Agua Prieta, El Paso-Ciudad Juárez, Laredo-Nuevo Laredo, etc. Since 1967, the proportion of Section 807 imports coming from Mexico make it the largest foreign assembler of U.S. components for re-export to the U.S. Although wages in Mexico are not as low as in the Far East, the border zone operations have clear advantages over the Far East. The most important are lower transportation costs which can offset the difference in direct wage costs and the facility to supply the foreign plant with machinery and materials other than components.

The expansion of the zones of operation of the assembly plants program was encouraged from the beginning by the American business community in Mexico as evidenced by the following citation:

> Another idea that is rapidly making headway . . . is that of extending the Border Industrialization Program (meaning . . . plants which must export 100 percent of their production) to other areas of the country particularly those which have high job demand and little industry. Already ranked high as possibilities for such a program are the states of Yucatan and Aguascalientes.[11]

Success or Failure?

The performance of the BIP is best examined by analyzing the evidence against the proposed goals ("benefits for Mexico") in the areas of employment, income, technical training, and dollar inflow.

Employment. According to data prepared by the Mexican government, by January 1970 the BIP had created a total of seventeen thousand jobs. At the beginning of 1972, the number was closer to thirty thousand jobs. Although this may seem impressive in absolute figures, it is hardly a solution to the unemployment problem. To adequately evaluate the effect of the BIP on employment, it is necessary to digress for a moment to consider the causes of unemployment in the border area.

The region usually referred to as Northern Mexico is made up of six states: Baja California, Sonora, Chihuahua, Coahuila, Nuevo León, and Tamaulipas. Characteristics of these northern states that became pronounced in the early 1960s were: a) the growth of trade, tourism, and some manufacturing had produced such a large concentration of people in urban centers that the area had become the *most urban* of Mexico; and b) the area had a higher population growth than any region of comparable size had had in Mexico since 1940 (see Tables 15 and 16).

Three important demographic changes converged to bring

TABLE 15

Population Increases and Urban Proportions of Mexico
and the Northern Border States, 1949–1970
(Thousands)

| | Northern Border States | | Nation | |
	Totals	% Urban	Totals	% Urban
1940 Population	2,618		19,654	35%
1950 Population	3,763		25,791	43%
1940–50 % Increase	44%		31%	
1960 Population	5,541	64%	34,923	51%
1950–60 % Increase	47%		35%	
1970 Population	8,671		49,561	58%
1960–70 % Increase	57%		42%	

Source: Nathan L. Whellen, "Population Growth in Mexico," *Report of the U.S. Select Commission on Western Hemisphere Migration* (Washington, 1968), pp. 173–184.

TABLE 16

Population Increases in Northern Mexico, 1940–1970

	1940–50 % Increase	1950–60 % Increase	1960–70 % Increase	Projected 1970 Population (Thousands)
Baja California	187	129	112	1,105
Sonora	40	53	61	1,258
Chihuahua	36	44	54	1,892
Coahuila	31	26	33	1,209
Nuevo León	36	46	58	1,704
Tamaulipas	56	43	47	1,504
Regional Totals	44	47	57	8,672
National Totals	31	35	42	49,561

Source: See Table 15.

about these circumstances: the increase of births over deaths, the rural-to-urban shift, and the migration northward. Obviously there are important rural-to-urban as well as south-to-north "pull" factors which cannot be separated from the proximity and economic influence of the United States. Perhaps the most important economic factor is the higher wage rate obtainable in the border states. But it is also important to remember that Latin America has the highest rate of population growth of any of the major underdeveloped regions and that Mexico has the highest rate of population growth in Latin America.

The population increase of the border area has brought with it an unemployment problem. Since 1940, the population of the border states has quadrupled, but jobs have not kept up with the inflow of workers. The closing of the bracero program in 1965 exacerbated the unemployment situation because many braceros who could no longer work in the U.S. chose to remain in northern Mexico instead of returning to their points of origin elsewhere in Mexico. In 1966, unemployment statistics estimates "ran as high as 40-50 percent in several border cities." The incidence of underemployment in the agricultural sector was considered substantial, although reliable figures were not available. At this time, estimates showed three-fourths of the labor force engaged in agricultural pursuits. *The fact that the BIP has further stimulated this migration has already been noted. The employment situation may very well worsen as a result of further migration.* [12]

It is also important to specify the structural differences between unemployment in northern Mexico and the jobs provided by the BIP. Mexican government reports indicate that the sectors of the working force that are hardest hit by unemployment are young men and male heads of households. By contrast, women workers constitute the bulk of the labor employed by the BIP. Roughly, between 65 and 90 percent of the jobs are available for women. In one location (Agua Prieta), *more* than 90 percent of the employed workers are women. The kind of tasks in which women are engaged can be gleaned from the following citation about Rey-Mex Bra, a brassiere-making plant in Reynosa (McAllen), Texas:

> The production supervisor is in charge of hiring women and all are given a dexterity test which judges agility of fingers as well as mental reaction concerning sewing. Testing is based upon elapsed time and varies from operation to operation in the bra-making procedure which involves 22 separate steps on a sewing machine. Quality rather than quantity is being stressed at the plant as trainees are individually trained in one of the 22 steps. Following training, each employee will be expected to turn out three dozen bras per day for production of approximately 6,000 bras daily from the Reynosa plant when full employment is reached. [13]

A third crucial qualification that must be made to the "employment benefits" of the BIP is what traditional economists refer to as "seasonal employment"; i.e., there is no way of telling for how long an authorized plant will remain in actual operation. An indication of the "rate of attrition" in the BIP is given by the comment below:

> It was difficult to get an up-to-date list from any sources because of the constant movement of the companies. The lists provided by the

government offices were used as a starting point for visits, but it was found that many of the plants listed had already closed down and others, not included, had opened up. The greatest attrition was in the Tijuana area. Since Norris & Elliot made their last survey in November 1967, almost 50 percent of the companies then covered had closed their doors.[14]

Thus, in the first two years of the program, the rate of attrition was 50 percent. And predictions about the long-range employment effects of the BIP are vitiated by the typical "slash-and-burn" procedure of capitalist enterprise in backward countries. One hypothetical explanation for this attrition is that U.S. firms may undertake operations south of the border in order to postpone the necessity to scrap existing production methods in favor of more efficient techniques. Utilizing the lower wage costs of Mexican labor allows U.S. firms to ease the costs of switching to more capital intensive operations. Once the new equipment is installed, the need for low-wage labor power goes down, and the firms retreat back over the border leaving even greater numbers of Mexican workers unemployed and requiring more welfare assistance on the part of the Mexican government. Another hypothetical explanation would relate fluctuations in BIP to the relative economic stability of the "mother firm" in the U.S. Unfortunately, the data to test these hypotheses is unavailable at this time.

Income. The above characteristics of the employment produced by BIP are reflected in the income accruing to workers: *an intermittent source of low income accruing to female members of households.* Why a *low* income? It is well-known that since the Mexican revolution, the Mexican government has made a public commitment to maintaining a measure of social welfare as a mode of ensuring political stability. Several "analysts" have pointed to these social measures (especially minimum wage legislation) as one of the constraints upon, if not the main explanation for, the persistence of unemployment in backward areas.[15] In the Mexican BIP, high minimum wages have been unimportant because even though companies are required to pay wages 50 percent above the prevailing minimum wage rates to full-time workers, they are permitted to pay only *half the legal minimum* to on-the-job trainees. According to a Chamber of Commerce paper aimed at U.S. businessmen, one of the "bright spots" of the Mexican labor market is that "the definition of the training period tends to be liberal." How liberal is indicated by an interview with a Mexican girl who has been working for more than seven months for a firm in Nuevo Laredo and is still receiving half wages!

In the northern cities of Mexico, the daily wage is about equal to the American hourly rate, not allowing for on-the-job training liberality (see Table 17). It has been suggested that this

TABLE 17

Comparative Minimum General Salaries on
Assembly Plant Areas of Mexico

	1972-1973 *Dollars per Day*
BAJA CALIFORNIA	
Ensenada	4.308
Mexicali	4.308
Tecate	4.308
Tijuana	4.308
CHIHUAHUA	
Juárez	3.384
SONORA	
Nogales	3.160
TAMAULIPAS	
Nuevo Laredo	3.188
Reynosa	3.188
Matamoros	3.188
YUCATAN	
Merida	2.384

Source: *The Assembly Plants Program in Merida, Yucatan, Mexico* (Merida, 1973).

difference may be partially offset by a productivity difference, but this is not borne out by the evidence. The report of the American Chamber of Commerce quoted above indicates almost universal satisfaction with the performance of Mexican workers. Sixty-one of the sixty-three companies interviewed expressed satisfaction with the performance of Mexican workers and some pointed out that such matters as absenteeism and tardiness—of recent importance in the U.S—were not present in the border zones.

Technical Training. Another area of proposed benefit to Mexico is the training of Mexican workers, but there is little evidence to substantiate the claim that American industries will train Mexicans to replace U.S. managers and technicians. It is certain, at any rate, that *U.S. companies moving to Mexico may import virtually as many skilled workers as wanted.* Also, the utility of the technical training that comes out of BIP is dubious, for if older equipment can remain at least temporarily competitive when used by cheap Mexican labor, a number of firms locating in Mexico may find it advantageous to put new equipment into their U.S. operations and to use the old equipment in the Mexican operations. What this means is that even if Americans train a significant number of Mexicans, and even if Mexican industry comes to be in a position to capitalize on a source of semiskilled workers, many Mexican workers will be trained to work only in obsolete production methods.

Dollar Inflow. To the extent that American firms are paying Mexican workers, the result is a net dollar inflow into Mexico. However, it appears that "U.S. businessmen along the border like the program because over half of Mexican factory workers' wages . . . are spent on this side of the river."[16] Some estimates place the percentage of income spent by Mexicans on the U.S. side of the border at 40 percent. This represents, of course, the percentage of all income spent by all Mexicans in the U.S. zone. One specific study estimates that 39 percent of the BIP's workers' salaries are spent in the U.S.[17]

In summary, little can be said about the net effect on the

balance of payments of both countries. The total earnings of the plants are not known, nor are the total spent in the U.S., or the extent of U.S. sales to equip and supply plants in Mexico. Furthermore, we do not know the extent to which Americans substituted products of Mexican plants for goods previously bought in other countries or, conversely, the extent to which Mexican-American imports increased as a result of the improved competitive position of American products. There are a great many things unknown about the BIP. In the words of David T. Lopez:

> Exactly which manufacturers are being lured to Mexico is virtually impossible to determine before the fact, and the established plants are as easy to inspect as the Chinese Communist atomic plants. Photographers hired in Laredo, El Paso, and San Diego were all unable to come up with pictures inside existing plants. They said they were denied permission to enter the plants and shooed away by the guards.[18]

More recently, an official of the U.S. Custom Service has made public that many of the U.S. companies involved in the BIP have been fined for fake duty declarations at the U.S. border. The Service indicated that the alleged violations range from double invoicing and keeping two sets of books to concealing the true value and extent of their operations, to placing too low a value on goods declared for duty at the border. Customs officials felt that fraudulent duty declarations have become so prevalent at U.S. ports of entry that the agency plans to check the books of the 250 plus firms headquartered in the U.S. with border plants in Mexico.

Evaluation. The performance of the BIP, in terms of its proposed official goals, leaves much to be desired. It has had a composite unsubstantial employment record, and it may have, in the long run, reinforced the elements causing unemployment. It has produced an undistinguished record of personal income promotion, and has not been directed to the relief of the specific structural characteristics of the unemployed population of the area. Its contribution to the development of

Mexican "human capital" can best be described as nil, and the total dollar inflow emanating from the program is not clearly ascertainable. Finally, various sets of provisions protect BIP from almost any kind of taxation by the host country.

On a different level, BIP was supposed to alter existing output employment ratios in Mexican export manufacturing industries by introducing more labor-intensive technology, since this would contribute to the national effort of industrial decentralization. In terms of the first goal, "all results are not in." The one study that I am aware of concluded that the border industries are only slightly more labor-intensive than the average Mexican manufacturing export industry (127 workers per million dollars as opposed to 117 workers).[19] Beyond this, there is a reason to suspect the quality of official information on the actual production of border industries. Secondly, it would be misguided to view the development of the border industries as a farsighted effort to remedy the problem of urban congestion and industrial concentration around the Federal District. Between 1950 and 1960, the rates of growth of the three largest border cities—Mexicali (126 percent), Ciudad Juárez (111 percent), and Tijuana (153 percent)—far surpassed that of Mexico City (60 percent). Urban growth on the border constituted a "problem" before the BIP was instituted; the latter is therefore to be viewed partly as a short-run, stop-gap measure designed to alleviate rising unemployment.

In terms of the political and economic relationships of northern Mexico to the rest of the country, the BIP has signified an abandonment of the traditional Mexican policy of strengthening the local border economy against American business encroachment, and establishing ties of dependence between the northern area and the rest of Mexico. From the establishment of the Zona Libre in the nineteenth century, to the development of colonization projects for Baja California in the 1920s, and the institution of a border policy of the National Border Program (PRONAF) in the early 1960s, the governmental policy of the Mexican state was consistent in its application of a border policy of *containment* regarding the northern colossus (U.S.) and the *integration* of the Mexican border into the national economy. The existence of the Border Industrial Program constitutes an abandonment of this hope for Mexican national economic integration.

In the context of the change of policies by Latin American countries, what is the meaning of the border industries? The BIP is obviously a paradigm of a new panacea. It represents: a) the abandonment of import substitution in industrialization, b) changing emphasis favoring the workings of "the market," c) the "skillful manipulation" of foreign capital, and d) the development of economic integration across national boundaries. If the BIP is representative of the general results of the new panacea, the prospects for Latin America, as well as for the border area, are bleak. Finally, organized labor in the United States has been opposed to the existence of the Border Industrial Program since its inception, and this opposition has come through official publications and official declarations of the leadership of the AFL-CIO. It is the correct view of the AFL-CIO that the BIP is another instance of "runaway plants" being established where labor is not organized and paying wages abysmally low by U.S. standards at the cost of increased unemployment in the U.S. In this view, the BIP constituted the most dangerous "loophole" to minimum wage legislation in the United States.

Notwithstanding the above, the extent to which organized labor in the United States can exert enough pressure to limit and control the expansion of the BIP is limited by the role which organized U.S. labor has played as a partner in international adventures with the U.S. government. The leadership of organized labor has supported the foreign policy of the State Department since Gompers. And the relationship between the foreign policy of the State Department and the interests of the American corporation has been close. Thus organized labor is left in the paradoxical situation of standing up for imperialism and its necessary foreign policy. This explains the lack of enthusiasm with which organized labor has thus far protested against the BIP.

The analysis presented in this chapter utilized the relatively abundant amount of data on the BIP that was available in its early years. In recent years data has been rather scanty perhaps because the program has not had the often prognosticated results and because the 1974–75 economic recession has effectively eliminated some of the market for the products of the "maquiladoras." Also, it appears that the "unspoiled workforce" which lured companies to the border ten years ago has undergone some changes; thus North American companies in Mexico feel that "Mexican labor today—as did U.S. labor a few years ago—is killing the goose."[20] In fact, many feel that the goose is already dead and that it is only a matter of time before the border cities become ghost towns. Thus, between October 1974 and April 1975, thirty-nine U.S.-owned assembly plants closed down operations along the Mexican border, while many others cut their work force by as much as 50 percent. More than twenty-three thousand workers were laid off in less than ten months with employment down by 30 percent in Tijuana and Mexicali.[21]

Conclusion

How does the study of the history of the border help in understanding the present conditions of this area and what light does it shed upon its future? In my mind the study of the past is necessary to understand the present and to be able to change the future. The conception of the "border region" as a separate entity, i.e., a unique region that extends to the north and south of the international boundary line, has become a current notion for discussion and investigation. I intend to show the extent to which the previous analysis sheds light upon the validity of that conception. At the same time, I will try to clarify the basis upon which such a conception becomes appropriate to understand the future, i.e., the forces at work at the present time which tend to accelerate or retard the development of the border area as a separate, sui generis region. In doing so I will refer to such conceptions as "borderlands," "Southwest," "border region," "Aztlán," "Chicano colony" and "Chicano nation."

It is clear, from a variety of vantage points, that the border area stands up as unique not because of a developing pattern of homogeneity but, quite the contrary, because of the heterogeneity and diversity of the area. This is so whether we view the border area from economic, linguistic, or broadly defined cultural angles. In terms of the presence of different modes of social economy, one finds in the Sonoran Desert, for instance, the coexistence at the present time of hunters and gatherers, peasant agriculturists, and capitalist industrial urban centers. Diversity is also dominant in terms of the multiplicity of languages spoken by the various ethnic groups that inhabit the area. Thus, in a formal sense heterogeneity and diversity are fundamental to any basis of unity one finds in the border area.

The relative obscurity and paucity of data is a major obstacle to understanding the border area. This is true whether the information sought is historical, economic, or geographical. Whatever period or angle of approach is used, the attempt to provide an analysis and interpretation of the region has of necessity to be based on relatively scanty direct information. There are two distinct aspects to the problem. While much untapped data is known to exist in libraries and repositories throughout Mexico and the United States, scholars have only recently begun the sifting and weighing of this material. Secondly, few works have been devoted *directly* to the border region as such. This is evident in that there is only one bibliographical work devoted to sources for study of the border region.[1]

The definition of "border region" implied in this chapter is not exactly the same as the idea of the "Spanish borderlands" used earlier. "Border region" implies a larger territory than that comprised by the "Spanish borderlands." The concept of the "Spanish borderlands" has most commonly been utilized to describe that territory which is now part of the United States which was at a former time occupied and under the control of either the Spanish crown or the Republic of Mexico. However, this is not always the manner in which the notion of "Spanish borderland" is used; sometimes it is meant, in a very inclusive manner, to encompass all those territories north of the Mexican plateau that were known as the Provincias Internas. In that case it is possible to detect a close resemblance, territorially speaking, between the notions of "Spanish borderlands" and "border region." The latter must also be distinguished from the notion of the "Southwest" which has as many territorial definitions as there are writers on the subject, the geographic range covered in the literature being so narrow as to include only New Mexico and as broad as to include not only New Mexico, Arizona, California, and Texas, but Oklahoma as well. Equally distinct from the "border region" is the conception of "Aztlán" which enjoys much current popularity.

Common to both "borderlands" and "Southwest" history is emphasis upon the study of Spanish language, architecture, clothing, food, religion, etc. Some of the leading exponents of these fields of history have been also concerned with the study of the social institutions that were peculiar to the Spanish and Mexican civilizations that once occupied the area. Because of this concentration of "borderlands" and "Southwest" history, much of the available literature has been tinged, with notable exceptions, by at best a good deal of ethnocentrism and at worst a very backward form of racism. It is also unfortunate that some of the recent literature that has sought to set the historical record straight on the heritage of the Spanish-speaking people has fallen into the same trap of "culturism." The understanding of the historical development of this region should be something more subtle and complex than a polemic about which of the "cultures" represented in the area is superior.

The concept of culture central to the notions of "borderlands," "Southwest," and "Aztlán" is of little use in defining the basis for unity of the border region. Because this concept is widely used in so much of the literature, it is necessary to point out its shortcomings.

The utilization of a general notion such as "culture" by itself is not helpful for the purpose of defining a region. First of all, it usually refers to culture only in a formal sense, without paying proper attention to the social content of a particular culture. Culture is thus sometimes equated with literature and art, sometimes with the sum of the "values" and "status symbols" of a community of people and sometimes with other aspects of everyday life such as colloquial speech, mannerism, clothing, foods, and the like.

The most important aspect of any "culture" should be, however, the manner in which a society organizes the productive labor of its members. These production relations become crucial in determining many other aspects of the culture including values, literature, art, etc. Equally important for the study of a region is some knowledge of the material level of development of the same, i.e., the kinds of artifacts, material goods, and especially instruments of production that are available to the inhabitants of the region. The material level of development and the relations of production that are most characteristic of a region constitute the basic and most important elements of the social content of any culture and must serve as the foundations for the study of any given social-geographic region.

A definition of culture that is concerned with emphasizing the social content can thus be considered as having two mutually dependent aspects: formal and material. The formal aspects of culture would include such things as ideas (art and science), values, rules of personal behavior, social institutions, and, fundamentally, a given set of social relations in the process of production. The material aspect of culture, on the other hand, would be composed of all artifacts and material goods resulting from human activity in a given society. These two aspects are not separate but interdependent. This is so because what is produced in any given society is not merely a reflection of the physical needs of its members but is also an outgrowth of the values and interests of the group or groups that control the production process.

When seen in this light, it becomes clear that a historical account of "Chicano culture," must include the relations of exploitation that were characteristic of the Mission system in early California, for the failure to do so can result in the formulation of statements that are susceptible to reactionary and backward-looking interpretations. The social content of a culture is the basis upon which it can be said that the "Chicano culture" of today is still characterized by negative aspects. The abstract defense of an imaginary, entirely "good" culture, is nothing but the resurrection of the myth of the noble savage in a different disguise, and it serves to push into the background real differences and to obviate the concern for economic and political equality.

The "border region" should also be distinguished from the

question of whether or not a Chicano "nation" or "colony" exists as a nation within the United States. The question of Chicano nationality itself has on occasion been presented in recent literature in a confused, intertwined manner with the narrow cultural definitions discussed above. The elements that make up a nation are not those that enter into the definition of culture and are not necessarily those that add up to the determination of an economic region.

The concept of nationhood arose during the breakdown of feudal barriers in Western Europe and elsewhere with the development of commodity circulation and home markets and also with the acquisition and recognition of a common language and territory, all of which gave rise to the idea of a national character. Nations so defined may have acquired independence or they may still suffer from oppression from which they want to obtain independence by means of a national movement. Typical cases are the appearance of a variety of nations in Europe several centuries ago, the appearance of the Latin American nations, including Mexico, and the rise of national liberation movements and newly independent nations in the world today.

It is historically documentable that the kinds of economic and territorial unity implied by the concept of nationhood became present in the Spanish southwest only after the appearance of the Old Spanish Trail. This was the first time that there were any trade bonds between the otherwise isolated Spanish settlements of New Mexico and California. Any discussion of the possible existence of a nation in the Southwest, either in the nineteenth century or at the present time, must take as its point of departure the concrete development of commodity circulation in the 1820s. Aside from that, it should be indisputable that questions such as nationality cannot be settled on the basis of abstract norms but must be tied to economics, politics, history, and territoriality. Lastly, the examination of this question must take into account that in the present epoch the boundaries between nations seem subject to erosion. If in its beginnings capitalism provided the impulse for the breakdown of feudal barriers and thus helped form nations, at the present time its continuing development tends to destroy the independent character of nations.

Is it possible to refer to the border region as a nation or colony? In my estimation the answer clearly must be negative for a variety of reasons. In the first place, the border region includes large portions of both urban and rural areas of northern Mexico, in which several million people of Mexican nationality live at the present time. It is easy to make the argument that a large number of these people suffer under a variety of forms of oppression, but it is not possible to claim that their oppression, poverty, etc., has the character of national oppression. Secondly, it is difficult to conceive in what sense the region north and south of the border became an economic unity on the basis of a common economic life. The development of economic relations in this area coincides not with the development of commodity circulation in a "home market" corresponding to its territory but rather with the development of *foreign* economic relations between the United States and Mexico. Thirdly, the territorial region which is implied by the notion of border area is subject to as many geographical interpretations as the notion of the "Southwest." It is clearly not a well-defined territory in the economic and social sense that a nation must be.

Finally, and perhaps, the most important consideration of all, is the historical absence of a political movement of a national character, i.e., towards the formation of an independent national state in this area. A study of the struggles of the nineteenth century reveals that they constituted either struggles led by feudal reactionary elements against the intrusion of capitalism in the Southwest or struggles over the maintenance of communal rights of use and ownership. Even the latter represent struggles for precapitalist forms of organization, which occur precisely because of the savage manner in which the separation of the peasants from communally owned means of production was carried out by the bourgeoisie, but in no way do they represent the struggles of a developing national Chicano bourgeoisie.

The border region is to be defined neither as a culturally

homogeneous area nor as a nation. The bases upon which it is permissible to speak of the area as possessing a degree of cohesiveness are twofold—geographic and economic. In a geographic sense, north and south and across the whole length of the border, a certain homogeneity exists which is bound to influence the character of whatever human developments flourish. These basic geographic features are well known.

The western part of the border from about the thirty-eighth to the twenty-third parallel is essentially a geographic unit. *Climactically*, it is very dry, producing a reliance on massive irrigation for agriculture to prosper. In terms of *geological resources* the border area from the Pacific shores to a line running north to south from the Colorado Rockies to Zacatecas in Mexico has been for centuries (and is today) a rich mining area for copper, silver, gold, lead, tungsten, and several other minerals. *Agriculturally*, the aridity and similar climate of the area resulted in the cultivation of similar crops both north and south of the border. The boundary line runs approximately through the middle of this climactic, geologic, and agricultural area.

Geographic unity is enhanced rather than diminished by such other geographical features as the Sonoran Desert and the Rio Grande (Brave del Norte). In the case of the Sonoran Desert, a vast expanse of arid land which used to effectively divide the western border region has turned, with the development of technology and modern means of communication, into a unifying factor. In a sense it is the ability to deal with the problems peculiar to a desert which provides for such unity rather than further separation. In the eastern part of the border zone, the Rio Grande has also provided for a long time a feature of unification in an otherwise parched area. This is so simply because the Rio Grande is not the kind of torrential river which could ever become a serious obstacle. On the contrary, the history of the area shows that its inhabitants for years had closer contacts with each other that they had with the people of other regions of either the United States or Mexico.

A substantial foundation of economic forces and relations lies on this natural geographical base. These economic connections have already been described in some detail and will not be repeated here. It is necessary to present more explicitly, however, the raison d'être for the peculiar economic dependence between the United States and Mexico as revealed on the border zone.

Economically, the unity that is characteristic of the border region is based upon the uneven development of the areas north and south of the border and as such is ultimately a reflection of the uneven development of the United States and Mexico. The problem of uneven development, or, more correctly, the problem of imperialism, is specific to the twentieth century. Before the onset of the twentieth century, there were nations and territories that had not been brought into the world market. But these were not yet "rich nations" and "poor nations." This distinction appears in the twentieth century with the development of monopoly capitalism, i.e., with imperialism.

The separation of the world into poor nations and rich nations is not a natural sort of phenomenon. The explanation for it lies in the development and growth of monopolistic forms of capitalism in the more economically advanced nations, the ability of these monopoly enterprises to affect the economic life of the less advanced nations and, consequently, the persistence of poverty and backwardness and at best the appearance of warped development possibilities in the poor areas of the world.[2]

The relations of economic domination and dependence which exist between the United States and Mexico are but one concrete example of the general principle about the relationship of domination and dependence which exist between advanced countries and poor countries. As such, the basis of the economic unity of the border is founded on inequality, uneven development, and domination.

Can unbalanced, irrational growth provide the basis for the future integration of an area into some sort of formal economic region? The answer must once again be negative. The apparent economic unity of the border area cannot be seen in

separation from the inability of the Mexican economy to provide adequate employment for millions of people who must
therefore seek jobs in the United States as illegal workers.
Rational economic development for Mexico must entail the
ability to utilize these millions of human beings in productive
occupations in their homeland. But this possibility is unrealiz-
able for Mexico short of drastic economic planning and a
restructuring of the economic fabric of its society. Even if it
were possible to achieve such a change in Mexico, the absence
from the United States's Southwest of several million workers
could not be achieved short of important changes in the economic structure of the United States.

Even in the highly monopolized and state-directed economy
of the United States, profit considerations will always pose
some limits to the development of a truly integrated plan for
the Southwest—a plan that can allow for a genuine economic
development of Mexico and that can make the Southwest
economy independent of such a large pool of cheap labor.
Thus, to speak of a border economic regional unit *as we know it
today* can only imply the continuation of the status quo in both
the United States and Mexico. A better, more rational economic development future for this geographic area must signify the disappearance of the present economic elements of
unity, i.e., the disappearance of imperialism and uneven development.

Notes

I: MATERIAL BASIS OF CULTURE IN THE OLD BORDERLANDS

1. François Chevalier, *Land and Society in Colonial Mexico* (Berkeley and Los Angeles: University of California Press, 1963), p. 157.
2. Robert S. Chamberlain, *Castilian Background of the Repartimiento-Encomienda* (Washington, D.C.: Carnegie Institution, 1939).
3. George I. Sanchez, *Forgotten People: A Study of New Mexicans* (Albuquerque: University of New Mexico Press, 1949), chap. 1.
4. This is a dangerous road: from this ahistorical vantage point, slavery was also benevolent, more so than capitalism.
5. Chevalier, *Land and Society*, chap. 5.
6. O. E. Leonard, *The Role of the Land Grant in the Social Organization and Social Processes of a Spanish-American Village in New Mexico* (Albuquerque: Calvin Horn, 1970), chap. 5.
7. Rodolfo Acuña, *Occupied America* (San Francisco: Canfield Press, 1972), chap. 1.
8. Chevalier, *Land and Society*, chap. 3.
9. William Dusenberry, *The Mexican Mesta* (Urbana: University of Illinois Press, 1963). These generalizations regarding the northern territories do not rule out exceptions.
10. In this context, generalization is geared toward the identification of widespread and predominant patterns, especially those which held on balance the direction of social change.
11. Marshall Sahlins, *Stone Age Economics* (Chicago: Aldine Press, 1972), chap. 1.
12. Karl Kautsky, *La Cuestión Agraria* (Paris: Ruedo Ibérico, 1970), chap. 1.
13. United States Department of Agriculture, Soil Conservation Service, *A Report on the Cuba Valley,* Reg. Bull. No. 36, Cons. Economic

Series No. 9; see also *Tenant Herding in the Cuba Valley,* Reg. Bull. No. 37, Cons. Economic Series No. 10.

14. Livestock raising (whether in the form of sheep or beef cattle) was the most important material element of production during the Spanish and Mexican periods of the Southwest. In New Mexico, grazing sheep gained increasing economic importance from the mid-eighteenth century onward. In other areas, such as California and parts of Texas and Arizona, raising beef cattle became the primary economic activity. The development of livestock in this area formed the basis for the northward expansion of the colonial effort. The spread of Spanish influence, especially its religious impact, has usually been attributed to the presence of large, exploitable resources of precious metals and the resulting development of mining. Popular legend attributes the saying "donde no hay plata, no entra la religión" or "no silver mining, no religious conversion" to a Franciscan. While it is true that during the early stages of conquest, the haciendas and their resources were secondary to mining in economic importance, as northward expansion passed Zacatecas, mining became negligible and cattle raising haciendas became the key to economic sustenance.

15. Exploration of the California coast occurred as early as the sixteenth century, for a variety of reasons ranging from the search for a northward passage to the need for a port of call that would serve as a refuge for Spanish ships against pirates. These early Spanish ships were the famed Manila galleons, returning to Mexico via the California coast loaded with silk, spices, and other products from the Far East. Although Monterey Bay was discovered at this time, it would be over two hundred years before as notable a geographic feature as San Francisco Bay would be discovered.

16. Cecil Alan Hutchinson, *Frontier Settlement in Mexican California: The Híjar-Padrés Colony and Its Origins, 1769–1835* (New Haven: Yale University Press, 1969).

17. Under the domination of the priests, the Indians contributed to the imperial economy of Spain, worshiped as Roman Catholics, and dressed like Europeans. The mission system was utilized to minimize the threat of Indian revolt and to help hold distant frontiers against foreign claims and intrusions. As such, it became an important scheme for defensive colonization.

18. Herbert E. Bolton, "The Mission as a Frontier Institution in the Spanish-American Colonies,"*American Historical Review* 23 (1917/18).

19. Michael P. Costeloe, *Church Wealth in Mexico* (London: Cambridge University Press, 1967).

20. Carey McWilliams, *Southern California Country* (New York: Duell, Sloan & Pearce, 1946), chap. 1.

21. During the early years of missionary activity, Indians were

attracted to the missions by various means of enticement. As the years passed, however, the mission system began to take a large toll of Indian lives. From 1769 to 1833, 29,100 Indian births and 62,000 deaths were recorded by the California missions. As this trend developed, the missionaries—aided by colonial soldiers—conducted a more forceful recruitment by means of raids into "wild" Indian territory.

22. Varden Fuller, "The Supply of Agricultural Labor as a Factor in the Evolution of Farm Organization in California," in Hearings before a Subcommittee of the Committee on Education and Labor, United States Senate, Seventy-Six Congress; Part 54, *Agricultural Labor in California* (Washington, D.C.: Government Printing Office, 1940).

23. Ibid., p. 19787.

24. Lynn Perrigo, *Our Spanish Southwest* (Dallas: New Mexico Highlands University, 1960).

25. Robert Glass Cleland, *The Cattle on a Thousand Hills* (San Marino: The Huntington Library, 1951), chap. 2.

26. Odie B. Faulk, "The Presidio: Fortress or Farce?" *Journal of the West* 3, no. 1 (January 1969).

27. Ernest Mandel, *Marxist Economic Theory* (New York: Monthly Review Press, 1962), vol. 1, chap. 9.

28. Rent-in-kind signifies that the labor of the direct producer for himself and his labor for the landlord are no longer separate.

29. Karl Marx, *Capital*, 3 vols. (New York: International Publishers, 1967), 3:797.

30. Ibid., p. 807.

31. Ibid., p. 798.

32. The argument to the effect that there was feudalism in Europe but *not* in Spain is not an argument at all. This is the case because the very elements that give content to this mode of production—the absence of rapid communication, geographical isolation, and the basic immobility of the source of rent—can only entail differences in the ways in which the mode of production will manifest itself. (In different times and places, the juridical, ideological, and cultural expression of a fundamentally similar mode of economic production can take different forms.) Once this is positively clarified, the argument becomes one over equivocal presentations of the question. The same economic basis can show—because of numerous empirical circumstances, natural environments, racial relations, etc.—infinite varieties and gradations.

33. Jaime Vicens Vives, *Historia de España y América* (Madrid: Grijalbo, 1960), vol. 2, "Feudalism."

34. Marc Simmons, "Settlement Patterns and Village Plans in Colo-

nial New Mexico," *Journal of the West* 8, no. 1 (January 1969).

35. The presidio was a military post designed for provincial defense against foreign invasion, and for the preservation of internal order. The presidio received sufficient land to supply its garrison with food and furnish pastures for the king's cattle, horses, and other livestock. A line of presidios eventually spanned the entire North American continent from Florida to California. Some eventually became towns, as in the case of San Francisco. The presidios were essentially forts; from an institutional point of view, they were predated by a variety of fortifications that spearheaded the advance and protected the retreat of the Spanish in their struggle with the Moors on the Iberian Peninsula. From a wider perspective, they played a negligible part in the economic life of the colonies and dovetailed into the pattern of exploitation of borrowing mission Indians as domestic and field servants.

36. Burl Noggle, "Anglo Observers of the Southwest Borderlands, 1825–1890: The Rise of a Concept," *Arizona and the West* 1 (1959).

37. The development and application of science and technology to agriculture historically occurred with the expansion of capitalism (in the sense of capitalist class relations) to rural areas. This expansion occurred sporadically in most Western nations and usually lagged behind developments in urban, commercial, and industrial capitalism.

In the classical development of the capitalist mode of production, the application of machinery to agriculture has had to overcome more technical obstacles than in urban industry. In urban industry, the working place—the factory—is artificially and conveniently molded to the physical requirements of its machinery; in agriculture, the physical setting is usually the given, and the machinery has to be adapted, which is not always an easy or possible task. In urban industry, machinery represents a larger savings in the use of labor power since machines can be utilized on a 24-hour 365-day schedule; in agriculture, their utilization occurs on a seasonal basis. In terms of human requirements, typical urban industry under capitalism does not demand abilities greater than those possessed by a craftsman. With agricultural machinery, the problem is more complex, since considerable training is often necessary for its correct operation and maintenance. Despite these and other difficulties, the extreme social barrier to capitalist forms of agriculture in Europe, the United States, and South America has been the presence of large landholding monopolies. In this sense, landed property can act as a powerful deterrent to the development of productive forces, because the monopoly exercised over land allows its owners to exact a tribute in the form of rent for making land accessible for modern production.

II: DEVELOPMENT OF COMMODITY CIRCULATION IN THE SOUTHWEST

1. Karl Marx, *Capital,* 3 vols. (New York: International Publishers, 1967), 1: 325–337.

2. Tulio Halperín-Donghi, *The Aftermath of Revolution in Latin America* (New York: Harper & Row, 1973).

3. Max L. Moorhead, *New Mexico's Royal Road, Trade and Travel on the Chihuahua Trail* (Norman: University of Oklahoma Press, 1958), chap. 2.

4. Ibid.

5. Ibid.

6. Richard Henry Dana, *Two Years Before the Mast* (Los Angeles: The Ward Ritchie Press, 1964).

7. Cf. Helen Bank, *California Mission Days* (New York: Doubleday, 1951); also Edwin Corle, *The Royal Highway* (Indianapolis: Bobbs-Merrill, 1949).

8. Vito Alesio Robles, *Coahuila y Texas en la Epoca Colonial* (Mexico: Editorial Cultura, 1938), chap. 41.

9. On this point see, Alicia V. Tjarks, "Comparative Demographic Analysis of Texas, 1777–1793," *Southwestern Historical Quarterly* 5, no. 2, pp. 291–398.

10. For a variety of views on Spanish-South American relations, cf. R. A. Humphreys and John Lynch, eds., *The Origins of the Latin American Revolutions, 1808–1926* (New York: Alfred A. Knopf, 1965).

11. Ibid.

12. John Lynch, *The Spanish-American Revolutions 1808–1826* (New York: Norton, 1973), chap. 9.

13. David J. Weber, *The Taos Trappers: The Fur Trade in the Far Southwest, 1540–1846* (Norman: University of Oklahoma Press, 1968).

14. Robert G. Cleland, *This Reckless Breed of Men* (New York: Alfred A. Knopf, 1963).

15. LeRoy R. Hafen, *The Mountain Men and Fur Trade of the Far West* (Glendale: The Arthur H. Clark Company, 1965).

16. Cf. John Galbraith, "A Note on the British Fur Trade in California," *Pacific Historical Review* 24, no. 3 (August 1955), pp. 253–260; also Dale Morgan, "The Fur Trade and Its Historians," in *The American West* 3, no. 2 (Spring 1966), pp. 28–35, 92–93.

17. Josiah Gregg, *Commerce of the Prairies,* 2 vols. (New York: J. B. Lippincott, 1844).

18. Lynn I. Perrigo, *Our Spanish Southwest* (Dallas: New Mexico Highlands University, 1960), chap. 6.

19. Moorhead, *New Mexico's Royal Road,* chap. 4.

20. Leonard Pitt, *The Decline of the Californios* (Berkeley: University of California Press, 1971), chap. 1.

21. Cf. on this Eleanor Lawrence, "Mexican Trade Between Santa Fe and Los Angeles, 1830–1848," *California Historical Society Quarterly* 10 (March 1931), pp. 27–29.

22. The term "backward" does lead sometimes to regrettable misinterpretations. It is a grave mistake to view the relative low degree of productivity, technology, organization of labor, labor skills, etc. i.e., societal characteristics, as the result of the actions of individuals who are somehow inferior. Nothing is, in fact, further from the truth. For instance, in backward *societies* the low degree of division of labor signifies the ability of each individual member to perform dexterously a large variety of tasks; the opposite is true in advanced societies; so that backward or "simpler" societies are usually composed of individuals who are in a sense more "complex" than modern man because they are so much less interdependent.

23. Raul A. Fernandez and José F. Ocampo, "The Latin American Revolution: A Theory of Imperialism, Not Dependence," in *Latin American Perspectives* 1, no. 1 (1974), pp. 30–61.

III: THE VICTORY OF CAPITALISM

1. Lynn I. Perrigo, *Our Spanish Southwest* (Dallas; New Mexico Highlands University, 1960), chaps. 6–7.

2. Hubert Herring, *A History of Latin America* (New York: Alfred A. Knopf, 1965), chap. 19.

3. Perrigo, *Our Spanish Southwest*, chap. 7.

4. Warren Beck, *New Mexico* (Norman: University of Oklahoma Press, 1962).

5. William Robinson, *Land in California* (Berkeley: University of California Press, 1948).

6. On the question of litigation over Spanish landgrants see Leonard Pitt, *The Decline of the Californios* (Berkeley: University of California Press, 1966); Carey McWilliams, *Factories in the Fields* (San Francisco: Anchor Books, 1969).

7. Paul W. Gates, "Adjudication of Spanish-Mexican Land Claims in California," *The Huntington Library Quarterly*, no. 3 (May 1958); cf. also Paul W. Gates, "California's Embattled Settlers," *California Historical Society Quarterly* 41 (1962).

8. McWilliams, *Factories in the Fields*, chaps. 1–2.

9. Maurice G. Fulton, *History of the Lincoln County War* (Tucson: University of Arizona Press, 1968).

10. Curiously, the converse also applied: in some counties bordering on Mexico, the intense level of conflict served as a protective measure. As late as 1930, supposedly more than 50 percent of the

WREN THE INCOMPARABLE

SIR CHR: WREN.
Late Surveyor General of
the Royal Buildings.
He died the 22 of Feb 1723, aged 91.

I   PORTRAIT OF WREN BY SIR GODFREY KNELLER
IN THE NATIONAL PORTRAIT GALLERY

WREN

THE INCOMPARABLE

MARTIN S. BRIGGS

That incomparable genius my worthy friend Dr Christopher Wren
JOHN EVELYN 1664
A wonderful genius had this incomparable person
JOHN EVELYN 1681
That incomparable architect, Sir Christopher Wren
N. HAWKSMOOR 1728

LONDON
GEORGE ALLEN & UNWIN LTD
RUSKIN HOUSE · MUSEUM STREET

PRINTED IN GREAT BRITAIN
in 12 pt Fournier type by
SIMSON SHAND LTD
London and Hertford

CONTENTS

ILLUSTRATIONS

FIGURES

All the above illustrations are drawn by the Author

PLATES

9

ACKNOWLEDGMENTS

The Author's thanks are due to the photographers and others whose names appear in the list above, particularly to The Controller of H.M. Stationery Office for Plate XXIX, to the Royal Commission on Historical Monuments for the Crown Copyright of photographs marked *, to the National Buildings Record for those marked †, to the Director of the National Portrait Gallery for the Frontispiece, to Mr Quentin Lloyd for Plates LV and LIX, and to the Virginia State Chamber, U.S.A., for Plate LXIII.

I

EARLY YEARS

1632 — 1662

THE name of Wren is more widely known than that of any other English architect, indeed it may fairly be regarded as 'a household word'. Vanbrugh was a more picturesque figure, Inigo Jones is considered by some competent critics as a greater designer, Sir Gilbert Scott had an almost equally sensational and spectacular career. Yet Wren's fame is justified, and has been recognized in the tribute of many biographies, far more, in fact, than have ever been written about any other architect. The long series begins with the volume entitled *Parentalia* which, as its Latin name suggests, includes the lives of other members of the great architect's family—his distinguished uncle Matthew (1585-1667), who became Bishop of Ely, and his own father, another Christopher Wren (1591-1658), the Dean of Windsor. It was compiled by Sir Christopher's son, yet a third Christopher (1675-1747), and published in 1750 by Sir Christopher's grandson Stephen Wren. Although this work of filial piety is inaccurate in several respects, and lacks much personal information— such as the dates and even the fact of Wren's two marriages—it has served as the basis of all subsequent biographical studies. It was followed, after a long interval, by James Elmes' *Memoirs*, in 1823; then by lives written by Lucy Phillimore (1881), W. J. Loftie (1893), Arthur Stratton (1897) and Lena Milman (1908). The long interval between 1823 and 1881 is explained by the unpopularity of Renaissance architecture during the mid-Victorian period, when interest was focused upon the Gothic Revival and when Ruskin was the arbiter of English taste. In 1923 the bicentenary of Wren's death was celebrated by the publication of a splendid volume containing tributes from a number of distinguished writers, and produced, appropriately, by the Royal Institute of British Architects. In the same year appeared a lively critical biography by Sir Lawrence Weaver, in 1932 another by C. Whitaker-Wilson, and in 1937 a brief but masterly study by Geoffrey Webb. During 1951 were published John Lindsey's *Wren*, Ralph Dutton's *The Age of Wren*, and my own brief study for young people,

Christopher Wren. To these may be added several pamphlets, and more than one book describing the repairs to St Paul's Cathedral which were actually in progress during the Bicentenary celebrations, as well as monographs on many of Wren's chief buildings and on the rebuilding of London after the Great Fire of 1666. This imposing list of books affords in itself a proof of the high regard in which Wren's talent has been held, but far more significant is the fact that in 1923 the 'Wren Society' was founded to perpetuate his memory. No other architect has had the honour of a society being founded to celebrate his work; and the Newcomen Society, established in 1920 to study the history of engineering and technology, is hardly a parallel. The Wren Society undertook the ambitious task of locating, editing and publishing all important designs, engravings, documents, letters, building accounts, etc., illustrating Wren's architectural work. The fruits of their devoted labours, largely due to the two editors concerned, were duly published in twenty handsome annual volumes, the first appearing in 1924, the last in 1943, for even the Second World War failed to interrupt their orderly sequence; and with the twentieth volume the editors were justifiably able to regard their work as complete. As a result, far more is known of Wren's abilities and methods of procedure. Some buildings attributed loosely to him hitherto are now regarded as his no longer, whereas others may be added to his long list; but not very much has been added to our knowledge of his personality, his domestic affairs, or his career, apart from his professional work as an architect. Yet, in spite of these omissions, an enormous number of new facts relating to his architectural work have been revealed, and a consequent need has arisen to revise certain judgments and statements made by earlier writers who were denied the fruits of the Society's research.

Any biography of Wren must be primarily concerned with his buildings; but he was so phenomenally versatile, and he turned to architecture so comparatively late in life, that his earlier career as a scientist must receive due attention in these pages as in any previous book written about him. Yet, when all is said and done, he goes down to history as a great architect, even if he was a man who would have achieved fame in any walk of life, and it is as a great architect that he will be treated here. His output was prodigious, but that fact need not prevent a critical study of his designs without any cheap attempt to minimize his assured reputation.

He was born on October 20, 1632, in the old rectory of East Knoyle in Wiltshire, a pleasant village in gently rolling country, on the road running south from Warminster to Shaftesbury. His father, the Rev Christopher Wren, and his uncle, the Rev Matthew Wren, were the sons of

Francis Wren, a London citizen and merchant. Both boys attended Merchant Taylors' School. Here they attracted the notice of Lancelot Andrewes, then Master of Pembroke College, Cambridge, who subsequently became Dean of Westminster and then Bishop of Chichester (1605), Ely (1609) and Winchester (1619). Matthew entered Pembroke College in 1601, and Christopher (senior) was admitted to St John's College, Oxford, in 1608. The two brothers then rose rapidly in their clerical careers as a result of support from Andrewes, Matthew—the elder—being first up the ladder, and, after a sequence of rapid promotions, becoming Dean of Windsor in 1628. Christopher became Bishop Andrewes' chaplain, and then received successively the livings of Fonthill and East Knoyle, two villages less than three miles apart. It was while at Fonthill that he met Mary Cox, daughter and heiress of the local squire, and he married her in 1623. Nothing has been recorded about her except that she was the mother of the famous architect; but the careers of her husband and her brother-in-law Matthew Wren had so important an influence on his future that these family details loom larger than usual in a biography. Of the eleven children born to the rector and his young wife between 1624 and 1643, nine were girls, and among them only one (Susan, b. 1627) played any part in Christopher's life. Both the sons were named Christopher after their father, the first dying within an hour of his birth in 1631, and the second— the architect—being born in 1632. The fact that both boys bore the same name has led to some confusion among historians, but the date, and even the hour, of the second Christopher's birth appear to be quite definitely established, and are recorded, with other domestic events, in a copy of Helweg's *Theatrum Historicum* (1618), now in the National Library of Wales.

The rector of East Knoyle was a man of parts, widely read in the humanities, an accomplished orator, a competent musician and mathematician. Evidently he also possessed some knowledge of drawing and architecture, for in 1634 he was commissioned to design a building—to cost over £13,000 and therefore obviously of some size—for Charles I's queen. A detailed estimate for this, dated May 15, 1635, was reproduced by Elmes from the Clarendon Papers. The rector is also said to have designed a new roof for his church at East Knoyle. He was an affectionate father, but above all things he was a devoted loyalist, a Tory of Tories, and a staunch supporter of the Church of England by law established. His brother Matthew was equally conservative and loyalist in his sympathies. Both brothers profited at first by this devotion to Crown and Church, but both paid for it in the stern struggle of the Civil War and the

Protectorate that followed. Only Matthew lived to see the Restoration.

The younger Christopher thus appeared upon the scene in 1632 as the son of well-born, well-educated and comparatively prosperous parents. There was no 'chill penury' in the village rectory where he first saw the light, and he started with the initial advantage of being a parson's son, generally agreed to be the most favourable and stimulating circumstance for the production of talent. Of his childhood hardly anything is known until he went to Westminster School in 1641 or 1642. When he was three years of age, his father succeeded to the Deanery of Windsor just vacated by his elder brother Matthew, together with the office of Registrar of the Order of the Garter; and at the same time was presented by the King with the living of Great Haseley in Oxfordshire, some eight miles east of Oxford near the main road to London via High Wycombe. For most of his early years, therefore, the young Christopher divided his time between Windsor Castle and Great Haseley. According to *Parentalia*, 'his first Education in Classick Learning was (by reason of a tender Health) committed to the Care of a Domestick Tutor, the Rev. William Shepheard, M.A.'

In January 1641, when he was only nine years old and before he had entered Westminster School, he wrote a remarkable letter in Latin to his father which was eventually reproduced in *Parentalia*. Whether as an example of Latin composition or of exquisite calligraphy, it is a notable achievement for so young a child. So his father evidently thought when he preserved it among his heirlooms, lovingly endorsed with the date and his son's age, all in Latin. In such a genius, born in such a home, and addressed to such a devoted parent, any suggestion of priggishness or undue precocity is unwarranted. Jeremy Bentham was reading serious history and studying Latin at three, playing the violin and speaking French at five. Mozart was composing music, and performing in public, at the same age. These things will happen from time to time, and infant prodigies need not necessarily be conceited in childhood or complete failures in after life.

Wren entered Westminster School as a 'town boy' and remained there until 1646, when he was fourteen years of age. The headmaster was the redoubtable Dr Busby, and it has been suggested that Dean Wren's choice of a school was mainly due to Dr Busby's staunch devotion to the Royalist cause, for the great struggle between King and Parliament had now begun. Hardly anything is known of his son's schooldays, which must have followed the orthodox course, though Westminster had, at that date, a reputation for mathematics and science as well as the inevitable Latin. *Parentalia* relates that 'at the Age of Thirteen, this young Mathematician had invented a new Astronomical Instrument, of general Use', and that he dedicated it to his father in a long Latin inscription. 'About the same time, he invented a Pneumatick Engine; the Description of which, with the Schemes, he thus introduced to his Father' (in another long Latin dedication). . . . 'He contrived also a peculiar Instrument of Use in Gnomonicks, which he explained in a Treatise, intitled Sciotericon Catholicum: the Use and propos'd End of which, was the Solution of this Problem, viz. "On a known Plane, in a known Elevation, to describe such Lines with the expedite turning of Rundles to certain Divisions, as by the Shadow of the Style may shew the equal Hours of the Day".' While Christopher was still at Westminster, his elder sister Susan had married, at the early age of sixteen, one William Holder (1616-98), a young don of Pembroke College, Cambridge, who was destined to play an important part in developing the boy's latent talents and took a prominent part in the foundation of the Royal Society in 1661. Holder received the living of Bletchington, seven miles north of Oxford, in 1642, and in later years instructed the young Christopher in mathematics.

The biographers vary widely in their accounts of his education after he left Westminster in 1646, a date which they all accept. Some of them send him to Wadham College, Oxford, in that year, although he did not graduate B.A. until 1651; others defer his entry at Wadham till 1649, when he was seventeen years of age, which seems more likely. The former date is given in *Parentalia*, and the statement is said to have been initialled by Wren himself just before his death, but he was then a very old man. The latter date is substantiated by the College records, and Sir T. G. Jackson in his history of Wadham College says that he 'entered the College as a Fellow-Commoner on June 25, 1649'. If we accept 1649 as correct, then much of Wren's tuition by Holder may have taken place between 1646 and 1649, and in any case it was so important in developing Wren's intellect that some reference to the family's adventures during the Civil War is needed here to explain how Christopher came to see so much of Holder. The first impact of the war upon them seems to have been the sudden appearance at Windsor of one Captain Fagg, who forced his way into the Deanery and carried off many of the Dean's personal belongings as well as jewels and treasures from the Chapel adjoining. The Wren family, including the Holders, fled to Bristol and remained there until that city surrendered to Fairfax in 1645 after a siege. They then returned to the rectory of East Knoyle, of which Dean Wren still held the living. The Deanery at Windsor was pillaged again in the same year and the living of Great Haseley was taken away from him. The reason for this apparent harshness seems to be that the two Wren brothers were marked men, particularly Matthew, who had treated the Puritans severely in his diocese before the war began and was imprisoned from 1641 to 1660.

The neighbourhood had seen much fighting during the earlier stages of the war, but in 1646 the Dean and his family left East Knoyle for Holder's rectory at Bletchington, as conditions had become less disturbed. Here, one may assume, young Christopher must have spent most of his time from 1646 to 1649; and here must have taken place much of the tuition by Holder that stimulated his active and inquiring mind, for Holder was away at Bristol during the preceding years. In John Aubrey's *Brief Lives*, there is a description of this part of Holder's career, when, in the rectory at Bletchington, 'his hospitality and learning, mixt with great courtesie, easily conciliated the love of all his neighbours to him. The deane came with him thither, and dyed and is buried there. He was very helpfull in the education of his brother-in-law, Mr Christopher Wren (now knighted), a youth of a prodigious inventive witt, and of whom he was as tender as if he had been his own child, who gave him his first instructions in geometrie and arithmetique, and when he was a young scholar at the University of Oxford, was a very necessary and kind friend. The parsonage-house at Bletchington was Mr Christopher Wren's home, and retiring place; here he contemplated, and studied, and found-out a great many curious things in mathematiques. About this house he made severall curious dialls, with his own handes, which are still there to be seen.' He adds that Holder was 'a good poet' . . . 'very musicall' . . . 'hath writt an excellent treatise of musique', and 'has good judgement in painting and drawing'. He was indeed versatile, and in 1678 published a complaint accusing a famous don of robbing him of the credit of teaching a deaf-mute!

Susan Holder also receives favourable mention from Aubrey: 'His vertuose wife . . . is not lesse to be admired, in her sex and station, than her brother Sir Christopher; and (which is rare to be found in a woman) her excellences do not inflate her. Amongst many other guifts she haz a strange sagacity as to curing of wounds, which she does not doe so much by presedents and reciept bookes, as by her own excogitancy, considering the causes, effects and circumstances. His majestie king Charles II, 167–, had hurt his . . . hand, which he instructed his chirurgians to make well; but they ordered him so that they made it much worse, so that it swoll, and pained him up to his shoulder; and pained him so extremely that he could not sleep, and began to be feaverish. [Then someone] told the king what a rare shee-surgeon he had in his house; she was presently sent for at eleven clock at night. She presently made ready a pultisse, and applied it, and gave his majestie sudden ease, and he slept well; next day she dressed him, and . . . perfectly cured him, to the great griefe of all the surgeons, who envie and hate her.'

Part of Wren's time during this mysterious interlude of three years was spent in Oxford and part in London: that much may be inferred from various known facts. A letter in Latin to his father, dated 1647, shows that somehow he had become acquainted with Dr (afterwards Sir) Charles Scarburgh (1616-94), later, physician to Charles II, for whom he was then translating Oughtred's *Clavis Mathematicae*. The boy wrote that Sir Charles was 'most kind to him' and that he lent 'a patient ear to my poor Reasonings'. Other acquaintances of equal calibre were Seth Ward, who preceded Wren as Savilian Professor of Astronomy at Oxford and later became a bishop; John Wilkins, Warden of Wadham College (both men in their thirties); and the Hon Robert Boyle (1627-91) who was rather younger. Wren must have had some charm of manner, as well as great intellectual ability, to enable him to be accepted on equal terms by these older men, among the foremost scientists of a brilliant period, and before he was thirty he joined them in founding the Royal Society. The letter to his father, already mentioned, refers to other early works for Scarburgh, and is here quoted in Miss Milman's translation from the Latin: 'One of these Inventions of mine, a Weather Clock namely, with Revolving Cylinder, by means of which a Record can be kept through the night, he asked me but yesterday to have constructed in Brass at his Expense. The other day I wrote a treatise on Trigonometry which sums up, as I think, by a new method and in a few brief rules, the whole theory of Spherical Trigonometry. An Epitome of this I re-wrote on a brass Disc of about the size of one of King James's Gold Pieces, and having snatched the Tool from the Engraver, I engraved much of it with my own Hand, which Disc Sir Charles had no sooner seen than he insisted upon having a similar one of his own.'

In another letter of the same period to Dr Oughtred, Wren wrote that he was indebted to Dr Scarburgh 'not only for any little skill that I can boast in Mathematics, but for Life itself which, when suffering from recent sickness, I received from him as from the hand of God'. *Parentalia* contains another striking instance of Wren's precocity at this time. 'Mr Christopher Wren was an assistant to the said Dr Scarburgh, in anatomical Preparations and Experiments, especially upon the Muscles of human Bodies, during their Studies at Oxford and elsewhere; and particularly he explained by Models formed on Pasteboards, the Anatomical Administration of all the Muscles of an human Body, as they naturally rise in

Dissection, &c., for the Use of Dr Scarburgh's celebrated Lectures in the public Theatre in Surgeon's Hall. These Models, by credible Report, were deposited in the said Theatre, and destroyed at the Fire of London. Hence came the first Introduction of Geometrical and Mechanical Speculations into Anatomy.' No date is given for this work, but it may well refer to the early period before Wren entered Wadham College.

As previously stated, *Parentalia* gives 1646 as the date for that event: 'In the year 1646, and Fourteenth of his Age, Mr Wren was admitted a Gentleman-Commoner at Wadham College, in the University of Oxford'; but R. B. Gardiner, in *Registers of Wadham College*, states that Wren's 'caution-money' as Fellow-Commoner was received on June 25, 1649, and Sir T. G. Jackson in his history of Wadham College confirms it. Some other writers suggest that the youth may have established an informal connection with the College, or with its dons, at an earlier date. The dates of his graduation as B.A. in 1651 and M.A. in 1653 are not disputed. In the latter year he was elected to a fellowship at All Souls, in itself a significant honour. From 1649 to his appointment in 1657 as Professor of Astronomy at Gresham College in London, it is certain that he was working in Oxford, and that he had not yet made any venture into architecture, so we may consider this period as a definite chapter in his amazing career.

The Civil War was over. Oxford, as the seat of the Court and the headquarters of the Royalist Army during most of the fighting, had sunk to a low ebb; but the 'purge' of its academic staff that had followed the Roundhead victory had been completed, and the newly-appointed dons had already been in office long enough to bring about more settled conditions of study, for they were at least honest men anxious to further the pursuit of learning. Some of the newcomers—including Seth Ward—were friends of Wren's, so the young undergraduate enjoyed a flying start. If many of his contemporaries indulged in 'ragging' or worse, it is inconceivable that this earnest and industrious youth joined them in any such juvenile sports, his nearest approach to relaxation from study being one appearance as an actor in a Greek play. As a fellow-commoner, he dined at the high table, not with the common herd. His social contacts were equally discriminating, the most notable being the weekly gatherings of scientists held in various rooms, and forming the embryo of the future Royal Society. One acquaintance made in this way was Robert Hooke (1635-1703), destined to become one of Wren's closest friends and collaborators, and himself almost as versatile as Christopher himself (see pp. 233-4).

In Evelyn's *Diary*, there are two well-known references to Wren, when Evelyn visited Oxford in 1654. *July* 11 . . . 'After dinner I visited that

miracle of a youth Mr Christopher Wren, nephew of the Bishop of Ely.'
July 13. 'We all din'd at that most obliging and universally curious Dr
Wilkins's, at Wadham College. He was the first who shew'd me the
transparent apiaries, which he had built like castles and palaces . . .
adorn'd with a variety of dials, little statues, vanes, &c. . . . He had also
contriv'd an hollow statue which gave a voice and utter'd words, by a long
concealed pipe that went to its mouth, whilst one speaks through it at a
good distance. He had above in his lodgings and gallery variety of
shadows, dyals, perspectives, and many other artificial, mathematical, and
magical curiosities, a way-wiser, a thermometer, a monstrous magnet,
conic and other sections, a ballance on a demi-circle, most of them of his
owne and that prodigious young scholar Mr Chr. Wren, who presented
me with a piece of white marble, which he has stain'd with a lively red
very deepe, as beautiful as if it had ben natural.'

It must have been about this time that a curious incident occurred to
bring young Christopher Wren face to face with Oliver Cromwell himself. According to *Parentalia*, in the Life of Bishop Matthew Wren: 'A
remarkable Instance . . . should not be passed over in Silence, of his
Magnanimity, Resolution, and Contempt of Adversity; which may convey
a further Idea of his [i.e. the Bishop's] Character. Some Space before the
Decease of Oliver Cromwell, Mr Christopher Wren (only Son of Dr
Christopher Wren and Nephew of the Bishop of Ely) became acquainted
with Mr Claypole, who married the Usurper's favourite Daughter. This
Gentleman being a great Lover of Mathematicks, had conceiv'd a great
Esteem for him, and took all Occasions to cultivate his Friendship, and to
court his Conversation, particularly by frequent Invitations to his House,
and Table; it happened upon one of these Invitations, that Cromwell came
into the Company as they sat at Dinner, and without any Ceremony (as
his usual Way was in his own Family) took his Place; after a little time,
fixing his Eyes on Mr Wren, "Your Uncle (says he) has been long confin'd in the Tower."—"He has so, Sir, but bears his Afflictions with great
Patience and Resignation."—"He may come out if he will."—"Will your
Highness (so he was called) permit me to tell him this from your own
Mouth?"—"Yes, you may." As soon as he could decently retire, he
hasten'd with no little Joy to the Tower, and informed the Bishop of all
the Particulars of this his Interview with Cromwell; upon which his Lordship expressed himself warmly to this Effect.—"That this was not the first
Time he had receiv'd the like Intimation from that Miscreant, but dis-
dain'd the Terms projected for his Enlargement, which were to be, a
mean Acknowledgment of his Favour, and an abject Submission to his

19

detestable Tyranny. That he was determined patiently to tarry the Lord's Leisure, and owe his Deliverance (which he trusted was not far off) to Him only." '

Parentalia contains 'a Catalogue of New Theories, Inventions, Experiments & Mechanick Improvements, exhibited by Mr Wren, at the first Assemblies at Wadham-College in Oxford, for Advancement of Natural and Experimental Knowledge, called then the New Philosophy; Some of which, on the Return of the Publick Tranquillity [i.e. in 1660], were improved and perfected, and with other useful Discoveries, communicated to the Royal-Society'. Previous modern biographers have contented themselves with selecting, from this long list of fifty-three items, those which are most sensational or most obviously bear upon Wren's future career as an architect. I prefer to give the whole list, only abbreviating (not paraphrasing) some of the longer descriptions, because the total is so staggering in its variety and versatility. Many of these inventions are regarded as trivial or even absurd by scientists of today, but their range indicates Wren's chief preoccupations during the years 1649-57.

1. Picture of the Pleiades.
2. Hypothesis of h in Solid.
3. Hypothesis of the Moon's Libration, in Solid.
4. Illumination of the Moon and Planets, in a dark Room.
5. A New Projection Goniscope.
6. New facile exact Ways of Observation.
7. To find whether the Earth moves.
8. The Weather-Wheel.
9. The Libra Expansionis Aëris.
10. Weather-Clock.
11. Perpetual Motion, or Weather-Wheel and Weather-Clock compounded.
12. The Ballance, to weigh without Weights.
13. Strainer of the Breath, to make the same Air serve in Respiration.
14. Artificial Eye, with the Humours truly and dioptically made.
15. The like Eye, made with one Humour only.
16. To write in the Dark.
17. To write double by an Instrument.
18. A Scenographical Instrument, to survey at one Station.
19. A Perspective Box, to survey with it.
20. Several new Ways of graving and etching.
21. Many new and curious Ways of turning.
22. To weave many Ribbons at once with only turning a Wheel.

23. Divers Improvements in the Art of Husbandry.
24. Divers new Engines for raising of Water.
25. A Pavement harder, fairer and cheaper than Marble.
26. To grind Glasses.
27. A Way of Imbroidery for Beds, Hangings, cheap and fair.
28. New Ways of Printing.
29. Pneumatick Engines.
30. New Designs tending to Strength, Convenience, and Beauty in Building.
31. Many new Designs in Sciography.
32. Divers new Musical Instruments.
33. A Speaking Organ, articulating Sounds.
34. New Ways of Sailing.
35. The best Ways for reckoning Time, Way, Longitude and observing at Sea.
36. Probable Ways for making fresh Water at Sea.
37. Fabrick for a Vessel for War.
38. To build in the Sea, Forts, Moles, &c.
39. Inventions for better making and fortifying Havens, for clearing Sands, etc.
40. To stay long under Water.
41. Ways of submarine Navigation.
42. Easier Ways of Whale-fishing.
43. New offensive and defensive Engines.
44. Secure and speedier Ways of attacking Forts than by Approaches and Galleries.
45. New Ways of Intelligence, new Ciphers.
46. Some Inventions in Fortification.
47. To pierce a Rock in Mineing.
48. To purge or vomit, or alter the Mass by Injection into the Blood, by Plaisters, by various Dressings . . .
49. Some Anatomical Experiments.
50. To measure the Basis and Height of a Mountain, only by journeying over it.
51. To measure the straight Distance, by travelling the winding Way
52. A Compass to play in a Coach, or the Hand of the Rider.
53. To perfect Coaches for Ease, Strength, and Lightness, &c.

Wren's scientific work continued long after 1657, indeed long after he turned to architecture, and an attempt to assess its permanent value may be deferred to the end of this chapter. Meanwhile the fact that it was begun during the Commonwealth tempts one to reflect on his attitude to national politics during his student-days. Born as he was of a Tory family devoted to the cause of Church and State, his inherited sympathies must have inclined him to the Cavalier side; but enough has already been written here to prove that the whole bent of his tastes was scientific, and we are often told that science has no frontiers and no politics. He was a delicate, studious youth, diminutive of stature, unlikely to be attracted by any of the swashbuckling appeal of a military career, and probably as insensitive to political enthusiasms as to martial slogans. Several of his biographers indulge in violent diatribes against the fanaticism and iconoclasm of the Puritan Roundheads, coupled with bitter abuse of the arch-villain Cromwell, but there is nothing to prove that Wren himself shared these prejudices; indeed he appears to have numbered several supporters of the Parliamentary party among his cronies at Wadham. Thomas Sprat, one of that gifted company and afterwards historian of the Royal Society, wrote that 'their first purpose was no more than only the satisfaction of breathing a free air and of conversing in quiet with one another without being engaged in the Passions and Madness of that dismal Age'. Wren's outlook was eminently philosophical, but he never ventured into the field of pure speculation, inhibited as he was—one may imagine—by the unquestioning traditional faith of his father and his family.

His appointment in 1657, at the early age of twenty-five, to the Chair of Astronomy at Gresham College, London, is a definite landmark in his progress. This institution formerly occupied Sir Thomas Gresham's palace in Bishopsgate, a pleasant old building with an arcaded courtyard. Founded late in the sixteenth century by the famous merchant and diplomat whose name it bears, the College provided chairs of divinity, astronomy, geometry, music, law, physic and rhetoric. Lectures were delivered weekly in each of these subjects from 1597 onwards. The building has long ceased to exist, but there is a Gresham College in Basinghall Street where lectures are still provided annually in the various subjects prescribed in the original bequest, under the joint auspices of the Gresham Trustees and the Mercers' Company. Wren had to deliver his inaugural address in Latin to an audience of greybeards, learned pundits and civic dignitaries—not to callow undergraduates. It is printed in full, but from his rough draft in English, in *Parentalia*, and is very high-flown in character, with many poetical or purple patches. He begins with an apology: 'Looking round with respectful Awe on this great and eminent Auditory, while here I spy some of the politer Genii of our Age, here some of our Patricians, there many choicely learned in the Mathematical Sciences, and every where those that are more Judges than Auditors; I cannot but, with Juvenile Blushes, betray that which I must apologise for.' The most significant passage of this rather rambling and ambitious effusion is the following: 'Mathematical Demonstrations being built upon the impregnable Foundations of Geometry and Arithmetick, are the only Truths that can sink into the Mind of Man, void of all Uncertainty.' This is a long step from the village rectory.

After Cromwell's death in September 1658, Gresham College was requisitioned and occupied by the army. The weekly lectures were interrupted, and Wren, who had been residing in the College, went to Oxford. His friend Sprat wrote to him shortly afterwards from London to say that the College was in 'a nasty Condition', 'defiled' and full of 'infernal smells'. Reporting a later visit on October 25, he stated that 'a Man with a Gun' stopped him at the gate and told him that there was no admittance. Some time in the following year Wren was able to resume his lectures, and in 1660 the building had been completely cleaned and restored. The chief importance of his work at Gresham College lies in the fact that the galaxy of scientists who had hitherto gathered in Oxford now began to make their attendance at Wren's weekly lecture a convenient substitute. Among them we now meet the names of John Evelyn and other distinguished men who soon afterwards founded the Royal Society. It is remarkable that Ward, Wilkins and Sprat—three prominent figures at these scientific gatherings—all subsequently became bishops.

The Restoration in 1660 was naturally favourable to the fortunes of the Wren family, but it came too late to benefit Christopher's own father, the Dean of Windsor, who had died in 1656. Matthew Wren, the Bishop of Ely, was released from his long imprisonment; and Christopher's cousin Matthew, son of the Bishop, became secretary to Lord Clarendon, the Lord Chancellor. Both these events were to have an influence on Christopher's subsequent architectural career, and his advance henceforth became rapid.

In November 1660, after one of his lectures at Gresham College, where the audience had included many of the scientists already mentioned, 'they withdrew afterwards to Mr Rooke's apartment, where they agreed to form themselves into a Society, and to continue their weekly meetings on Wednesdays at three o'clock, at Mr Rooke's chambers in the Terms and at other times at Mr Balles in the Temple'. After the next lecture, it was announced that the new King was himself interested, and on March 6, 1661, the 'Royal Society' was founded by royal charter. Wren had taken a prominent part in all the steps leading to this result, and indeed drafted a very flowery preamble for the charter, duly printed in *Parentalia*. Two months later he succeeded his friend Seth Ward (appointed to the Deanery of Exeter) as Savilian Professor of Astronomy at Oxford. Wren was the obvious candidate for this post, which he held until 1673, when his architectural practice had grown so large that he was unable to devote proper attention to his academic duties. He was still under thirty when in 1661 Oxford University conferred upon him the degree of D.C.L.; and in the same year he is alleged, in *Parentalia* and most other biographies, to have been awarded 'a like honour' by Cambridge. The *Dictionary of National Biography* describes the degree as 'LL.D.'; but reference to the usually reliable *Alumni Cantabrigienses*, published in 1927, gives a very different statement: 'Wren, Christopher, M.A., 1664, incorporated from Oxford.'

We have now reached the year 1662, in which Wren probably made his first venture into architecture, and we find him resident at Oxford, securely entrenched there but hardly less favourably placed at Cambridge where the powerful influence of his uncle Matthew, Bishop of Ely, was now restored. In London he was already famous, with some standing at Court as well as in intellectual circles, yet he was not thirty years old. At this point, then, before turning to his work as an architect, some consideration must be given to the permanent value of his work as a scientist. Admittedly it continued long after 1662, for he became President of the Royal Society in 1681 and his interest in research never abated; but the circumstances of his crowded life after 1662 prevented him from devoting to it any considerable amount of time.

The list of fifty-three inventions printed on pp. 20-21, long though it is, comprises only those made by Wren in the earlier gatherings at Wadham College, before the Royal Society had been formally constituted in 1661; and it would have to be greatly extended if his later work were to be taken into account. His discoveries indicate the keen spirit of enthusiastic inquiry which inspired all the members of that brilliant throng, and it was a feature of their deliberations that most of their voluntary labours involved team-work. Wren's imaginative mind, his versatility, his youthful willingness, his modesty and his mechanical or manipulative skill, often made him the obvious person to devise apparatus for solving some abstruse problem put to the group. If one analyses the various items in the list quoted, it will be seen that several have an indirect application to the art of architecture and the science of building. Numbers 19 (a Perspective Box), 20 (New Ways of engraving and etching) and 31 (new Designs in Sciography) show evidence of some skill in drawing, as do various diagrams prepared by Wren in early days. Numbers 25 (a Pavement harder than

Marble), 30 (New Designs tending to Strength, etc., in Building), 38 (Building Forts in the Sea), and 39 (Inventions for making and fortifying Havens) show interest in the structural and mechanical aspects of building. The similarity here with the work of Leonardo da Vinci is close. If only as a preparation for Wren's future, we can have no doubt that these preliminary investigations were of value to posterity.

Several other items (e.g. 50, 51) are concerned with mensuration, with ingenious devices for 'writing double' (17) or 'writing in the dark' (16), and with a host of what we should call 'gadgets' for the ordinary affairs of domestic and industrial life; but when we come to fundamental scientific discoveries I must follow the lead of other unscientific biographers and admit with the late W. R. Lethaby, a very wise man, that 'These things are beyond my knowledge, but I know that they represent wonderful progress'. Wren's most important scientific work was in astronomy, and has been assessed by one of his later successors at Gresham College, Professor A. R. Hinks, in a thoughtful essay in *The Wren Bicentenary Volume*. This learned authority points out that, though Wren occupied the Chair of Astronomy in London from 1657 to 1661, and at Oxford from 1661 to 1673, this long tenure of office, sixteen years in all, was interrupted in many ways. Soon after Wren had begun his lectures in London, they were rudely upset by *force majeure* and nobody knows how many he actually delivered. At Oxford, beginning work soon after the Restoration had established more settled conditions, he doubtless started well; but within two years the Vice-Chancellor wrote to Wren's friend Sprat, Secretary of the Royal Society, 'to ask where the Astronomy Professor was, and the Reason of his Absence so long after the beginning of Term'. As we shall see shortly, Wren may have already accepted some sort of post under the Crown as assistant to the Surveyor-General of Works, and though it seems to have been a sinecure for some years, it afforded him an excuse to absent himself frequently from Oxford. In 1665 he went to France (see pp. 38-43), and from 1666 to 1673, when he resigned his chair, he must have been so utterly engrossed in architectural work that he could not possibly have attended to his academic duties properly. Professor Hinks notes, too, that the absence of any published work by Wren is significant, and that much of his ingenious scientific apparatus in the Royal Society's Museum has unfortunately been lost by neglect.

Moreover, Wren was said by his contemporaries to have been a very modest man, at any rate as regards his scientific work; and his invention of 'A Method for the Construction of Solar Eclipses', discovered in 1660, was published some years later by Sir Jonas Moore (1617-79) without any reference to Wren, who heard of it casually at a Royal Society meeting in 1676, when Moore calmly admitted that it was due to Wren. Professor Hinks considers that this was an important point, showing that Wren 'was the first to discover the graphical method of computing eclipses that, with some modifications, due to improved tables, remains by far the most instructive, though not the most numerically accurate way of calculating the circumstances of an eclipse or occultation at a particular place, and is in use today for the graphical prediction of occultations'. Professor Hinks also remarks that a passage in Wren's inaugural lecture at Gresham College in 1657 suggests that he may have anticipated 'the island-universe theory of spiral nebulae today'. It seems incredible that Wren's work as architect of Greenwich Observatory (1675, see p. 214) should not have involved consultation on the equipment, for at that date he knew more about large telescopes and other astronomical instruments than any man in England, but apparently there is no evidence of his share in this important work.

In the very different field of biological science, Professor Sir William Bayliss, also writing in *The Wren Bicentenary Volume*, quotes (without comment) Sprat's guarded statement that Wren was 'the first Author of the Noble Anatomical Experiment of Injecting Liquors into the Veins of Animals. . . . Hence arose many new Experiments, and chiefly that of transfusing Blood, which the [Royal] Society has prosecuted in sundry Instances, that will probably end in extraordinary Success'. This work was carried out in the early gatherings at Wadham College. Professor Bayliss also notes that Wren drew many of the illustrations for Willis's *Cerebri Anatome*; and adds that he was one of the first men to use the microscope, then recently invented, for investigating the structure of insects.

These temperate judgments do not carry us very far in forming an opinion on the permanent value of Wren's scientific work; and even in mathematics—his basic subject—he does not seem to have been an outstanding pioneer or to have made any fundamental discovery. Possibly he was too versatile, and in any case he was overshadowed by the massive genius of Newton. He was certainly an accomplished geometrician, and he might well have achieved eminence in any one of several branches of science, but his special talent appears to have consisted in his ability to apply his knowledge practically. How brilliantly he applied it to architecture will be revealed in subsequent chapters.

II

WREN TURNS TO ARCHITECTURE

1662 — 1666

B EFORE considering the reasons, or perhaps one might say the accidents, that diverted Wren's versatile and inquisitive talents into architecture, we must examine the state of English, and to some extent of European, architecture in 1662. Hardly less important is the vague, indeterminate status of the architect at the same date. England had not wholly accepted the mature Renaissance or 'Italian' style, even in 1662, and examples of that style of design were still relatively few. All through the reign of James I, great mansions continued to be erected in a style which was still partly Gothic, dressed up with the classical Orders and befrilled with ornamental details borrowed in increasing numbers from Italy. Examples are Audley End, Knole in Kent, Hatfield House and Aston Hall, which was not finished till 1635 and is a typical 'Jacobean' design. The marvellous staircase at Christ Church, Oxford, was begun in 1630, in Charles I's reign, and is pure Gothic; while several other examples of that reign, such as St Mary Hall at Oxford (1639-40), are definitely medieval; and the east part of the front quadrangle of Oriel College (1637-42) almost equally so. Smaller domestic buildings all over the country showed the effects of Palladian influence still more slowly.

The introduction of mature Palladian architecture was due solely to one man, Inigo Jones (1573-1653). Nobody has ever questioned that fact. He alone brought full-blown Italian architecture into England. For that reason, his buildings are of outstanding importance; but, though notable, they are comparatively few in number. They comprise the Queen's House at Greenwich (1617-35), the Banqueting House in Whitehall (1619-22), the Water Gate at York Stairs (1626), the church (since rebuilt) and piazza at Covent Garden (1631), possibly Lindsey House in Lincoln's Inn Fields (c. 1640), and certain work at Wilton (1649); but in the last-named building he was associated with John Webb (1611-72), who entered his service as a pupil in 1628 and is now believed to have been largely responsible for the magnificent schemes for the palace at Whitehall and for Greenwich

Hospital (see pp. 173, 200), which at one time were ascribed unhesitatingly to Inigo Jones. Of Jones' authenticated designs, the Queen's House at Greenwich is the most perfect, internally as well as externally, and is akin to the lovely *château* of Maisons near Paris, designed by F. Mansart in 1642-51 (see p. 39). It also resembles the best work of Vignola in Italy.

Inigo Jones, even more than Wren, was a courtier. As a supporter of the monarchy, he was captured at Basing House in 1645, and for some time was out of favour, though it is not certain that he was imprisoned. Undoubtedly he designed many other buildings which have since perished, but by no means so many as have been loosely attributed to him. As with the first introduction of Italian details a century earlier (e.g. at Hampton Court), his novel ideas of design were initially favoured in aristocratic circles, i.e. by the King and the leading noblemen of the day. Jones gained his reputation as a person who had actually studied ancient Roman and modern Italian work on the spot, in Rome itself. Some knowledge of the Orders was common before his time, even before John Shute published *The Chief Groundes of Architecture* in 1563; but Inigo Jones, a skilled scene-painter and theatrical designer, went much further in developing a science of architectural composition and in casting Gothic to the winds. The picturesque gables, the steep roofs and the bold chimneys were thrown overboard, though one must remember that the large windows of the Queen's House originally possessed mullions and small panes.

Andrea Palladio (1518-80), his Italian mentor, had died long before Inigo was able to introduce his principles of design into England; and in Italy, particularly in Rome, his academic style had been largely supplanted by the bold vagaries of the Baroque movement in the hands of such masters as Bernini (see p. 41), Borromini and Rainaldi. As we shall see later, Wren favoured certain aspects of Baroque design as Jones had never done, indeed it is in some of Wren's work of the late seventeenth century, especially his churches, that we can first detect real Baroque influence in England.

John Webb, already mentioned, was Jones' nephew by marriage. He certainly served his master faithfully for many years, and ultimately inherited his practice. So self-effacing was he that the precise responsibility for designing the palace at Whitehall and the Hospital at Greenwich may never be fully known. In most respects he followed his master's lead, but developed some individual character in his later designs. He went into eclipse during the Commonwealth, enjoyed some encouragement at Court immediately after the Restoration, but was grievously disappointed when Wren supplanted him in Royal favour.

English architecture from *c.* 1640 to 1660 was under a cloud: first because of the Civil War, then owing to the Commonwealth. Buildings for the Crown were delayed for obvious reasons, hardly any new churches were erected, and even the meeting-houses of the victorious Independents and Presbyterians did not appear in any numbers until the Toleration Acts permitted their construction a generation afterwards. There was a certain amount of activity at Cambridge, rather less at Oxford, and ordinary folk were not inclined to venture their fortunes in bricks and mortar during this disturbed period.

The status of the architect was still somewhat nebulous, but the introduction of the Renaissance, with its constant insistence upon prescribed rules of design, had resulted in architecture becoming a learned affair, entailing much study of books—mainly foreign. Traditional methods of construction persisted nevertheless, and few of the new manuals of design contained any details of a practical nature, except elaborate roof-trusses—often based upon classical precedent.

Sir Henry Wotton (1568-1639) produced an amusing and delightfully written little book, *Elements of Architecture*, in 1624, largely devoted to classical rules but containing much useful advice which has been freely quoted since his day. John Evelyn, who was one of Wren's closest friends and most influential patrons, as we shall soon see, dabbled in all the fine arts, and indulged in sketching as well as critically observing architecture on his travels abroad. He followed his book on sculpture in 1662 with another on architecture in 1664, copies of which he presented to the King, the Queen Mother and the Lord Chancellor. It was a translation of Fréart's *Parallel* of the Five Orders (1651), based upon the rules of Palladio, to which Evelyn added an introductory 'Account of Architects and Architecture'.

Sir Roger Pratt (1620-84), who became a lawyer after he left Oxford in 1640, studied architecture in Italy to some purpose between 1643 and 1649 and commenced architectural practice *c.* 1650, much earlier than Wren did; but he does not appear to have published any book. The two men's paths crossed frequently in later years. Robert Hooke (1635-1703, see p. 233) had a career closely approximating to Wren's, and ultimately became one of his architectural rivals and collaborators. Proceeding from Westminster School to Oxford, he took part in the gatherings at Wadham College already mentioned, assisted in the foundation of the Royal Society, and later acted as its secretary. His record of scientific research is at least as wide and as miscellaneous as that of Wren, ranging over the field of astronomy, geometry and physics. His conversion to architecture

seems to have been slightly later than Wren's, and we shall encounter him
in Chapter III, when he will appear as author of one of the plans for rebuilding London, and shortly afterwards as Surveyor to the City. Sir John
Denham (1615-69), who was appointed Surveyor-General of His Majesty's
Works at the Restoration in 1660, had a varied career after leaving
Oxford, wrote one successful play and many poems, studied law, and then
undertook sundry diplomatic and courtly commissions for Charles II, but
seems to have had no architectural training or knowledge whatever.

It thus appears that, at the time of the Restoration, architecture was
commonly regarded as a gentlemanly and scholarly profession, if one
could then call it a profession, for which high academic attainment—
whether humanistic or scientific—formed a sufficient preparation, and for
which no apprenticeship or technical skill was required; but John Webb,
trained on what we should consider to be more appropriate lines, was a
formidable exception to this rule.

The stage is now set for Wren's entry on the scene as an architect in
1662. He was then newly appointed as Savilian Professor of Astronomy
at Oxford (cf. p. 24), and still retained a room over the gateway at
Wadham College, but seems to have spent a good deal of his time in
London. It is a question whether his first venture into architecture was as
an actual designer of buildings or as assistant to Sir John Denham, the
Surveyor-General. Some of his biographers (Elmes, Weaver, Webb, the
D.N.B.) give 1661 as the date of the latter appointment; if so, it would
precede his first work as a practising architect, but the evidence is somewhat inconclusive. The town and harbour of Tangier came into British
possession with the marriage in May 1662 of Charles II to Catherine of
Braganza, but the naval expedition to Tangier took place a few months
earlier. It figures frequently in Pepys' diary. At some time in 1661 or 1662,
the King offered Wren a well-paid commission to report upon the works
required at Tangier in military and civil engineering. The following extract from *Parentalia* refers to this incident but gives no date: 'A Commission to survey and direct the Works of the Mole, Harbour and Fortifications of . . . Tangier . . . was at this Time proposed for him (being then
esteemed one of the best Geometricians in Europe) with an ample Salary,
and Promise of other royal Favours, particularly a Dispensation for not
attending the Business of his Professorship, during the Continuance in
his Majesty's Service abroad; and a Reversionary Grant of the Office of
Surveyor-General of the royal Works, on the Decease of Sir John Denham: all of which was signified to him by Letter from Mr Matthew Wren,
Secretary to the Lord Chancellor Hyde. This Employment he had no

Inclination to accept (being not then consistent with his Health), but humbly prayed his Majesty to allow of his Excuse and to command his Duty in England.'

The letter already mentioned (p. 25) from Dr Thomas Sprat, informing Wren of the Vice-Chancellor's displeasure at Wren's continual absence from his professorial chair at Oxford, is worth quoting in full from *Parentalia*, as much for its lively wording as for its real significance. It is dated from Oxford in 1663.

'My dear Sir,

'I must confess I have some little Peek against you—therefore am not much displeased, that I have this Occasion of telling you some ill News. The Vice-Chancellor did yesterday send for me, to inquire where the Professor of Astronomy was, and the Reason for his Absence, so long after the Beginning of the Term—I used all the Arguments I could for your Defence, I told him, that Charles the Second was King of England, Scotland, France and Ireland; that he was by the late Act of Parliament declar'd absolute Monarch in these his Dominions; and that it was this mighty Prince who had confin'd you to London. I endeavour'd to persuade him that the drawing of Lines in Sir Harry Savill's School was not altogether of so great Concernment for the Benefit of Christendom, as the rebuilding of St Paul's, or the fortifying of Tangier: (for I understood those were the great Works, in which that extraordinary Genius of yours was judg'd necessary to be employ'd). All this I urged, but after some Discourse, he told me, that he was not to consider you as Dr Bayley (for so he ow'd you all kindness), but as Vice-Chancellor, and under that Capacity he most terribly told me, that he took it very ill, you had not all this while given him any Account what hinder'd you from the Discharge of your Office. This he bid me tell you, and I do it not very unwillingly, because I see that our Friendships are so closely ty'd together, that the same Thing which was so great a Prejudice to me (my losing your Company all this while here) does also something redound to your Disadvantage. And so, my dear Sir, now my Spite and Spleen is satisfied, I must needs return to my old Temper again, and faithfully assure, that I am with the most violent Zeal and Passion,

'Your most affectionate and devoted Servant,

Tho. Sprat.'

Even if this letter is wrongly dated, and may have been written before the end of 1661, as some biographers have hazarded, it is certain that not later than 1662 Wren had declined the Tangier offer, had already been consulted or was about to be consulted on the structural condition of Old

St Paul's, and had been offered or promised the reversion of the post of Surveyor-General on Sir John Denham's death. There is here no precise evidence that he carried out any duties as Assistant-Surveyor of Works so early as 1661 or indeed at any time before his return from Paris (p. 42) in 1665; we cannot even be sure that he ever occupied such a post.

Turning now to his own buildings, there are only two that can be confidently assigned to this early period: the Sheldonian Theatre at Oxford (Plates IIIa, IIIb) and Pembroke College Chapel at Cambridge (Plate II). *Parentalia* states that the former was 'the first public Performance of the Surveyor in Architecture'; but the Wren Society, with fuller information, considers Pembroke Chapel to be the earlier. His recommendation for the Tangier appointment may have been due to the influence of his friend Evelyn, or to that of his cousin Matthew Wren who conveyed the King's invitation to him. At Pembroke, it is certain that he owed his appointment solely to his uncle Matthew Wren, Bishop of Ely, an *alumnus* of the College. There is nothing discreditable in such a commission: many a young architect has obtained his first work through the kindly interest of an uncle, and has abundantly justified the confidence placed in him. *Parentalia* describes the Bishop's motives for the rebuilding:

'The first Money he receiv'd after his Restitution, he bestow'd on Pembroke-Hall, and to the Honour of Almighty God, to whose Service he had wholly devoted himself; for the Ornament of the University, which he always affected with a fervent and passionate Love; and in a grateful Remembrance of his first Education, which was in that Place receiv'd, and thankfully acknowledg'd, he built that most elegant Chapel there, at the Expence of above five Thousand Pounds, compleatly finish'd, and endow'd it with perpetual Revenues for Repairs. This, however noble and magnificent, is the least of those Monuments he hath left to Posterity.'

In preparing his design, Wren completely ignored the Gothic style of the existing College buildings, erected in 1360 and largely rebuilt or restored since. The walls of Wren's new chapel were of brick 3 feet thick and were plastered externally. The College still possesses an interesting little model of the chapel in mahogany, showing all the timbers of the roof. As the foundation-stone was laid on May 13, 1663, one may assume that this model was made—either by Wren himself or under his directions—some time before the end of 1662. The chapel is a pleasant, scholarly, orthodox, sensible and perhaps unimaginative exercise in Renaissance design, relieved externally by a picturesque little cupola perched on the apex of the gable towards Trumpington Street. There are the inevitable Corinthian pilasters on this gable-end, some carving in the

II   CAMBRIDGE, PEMBROKE COLLEGE CHAPEL, EXTERIOR

IIIa   OXFORD, SHELDONIAN THEATRE   *R.C.H.M.*
EXTERIOR. NORTH SIDE

IIIb   SHELDONIAN THEATRE, INTERIOR
from an engraving by Buckler

tympanum, and niches flanking the large west window. In plan it is rational enough, oblong with a low-pitched roof and ample lighting; but the interior has been altered by the addition of one bay at the back, designed by Sir Gilbert Scott in or about 1883. The organ was added in 1707.

The Sheldonian Theatre is described as follows in *Parentalia*: 'This Theatre, a Work of admirable Contrivance and Magnificence, was the first publick Performance of the Surveyor, in Architecture; which however had been executed in a greater and better Style, with a View to the ancient Roman Grandeur discernable in the Theatre of Marcellus at Rome; but that he was obliged to put a Stop to the Bolder Strokes of his Pencil, & confine the Expence within the Limits of a private Purse. What (among other beautiful and distinguished Parts of this Structure) has been esteemed very observable, is the geometrical Flat-roof; which Dr Plot has particularly described, in his "Natural History of Oxfordshire" as follows ...' (here comes a long description with plans, and detailed elevations of the roof-trusses).

This most important building was entrusted to Wren by Archbishop Sheldon, who had been deprived of his Wardenship of All Souls in 1647, and had remained in obscurity from that date until the Restoration. He became Bishop of London in 1660 and Archbishop of Canterbury in 1663. His munificent venture was inspired by a wish to provide a more seemly meeting-place for the annual Encaenia, which had hitherto taken place in St Mary's Church. Wren exhibited a model of his design to the Royal Society on April 29, 1664, but his work was actually begun in 1663 and completed in 1669. Full accounts for the building have been published by the Wren Society (XIX, 93-4), from which it appears that the total cost (entirely met by Sheldon) amounted to £14,470 11s. 11d., a substantial sum in those days. Evelyn describes a visit to the building in progress, on October 24, 1664: 'The foundation had ben newly laied and the whole design'd by that incomparable genius my worthy friend Dr Christopher Wren, who shewed me the model, not disdaining my advice in some particulars.'

On July 9, 1669, nearly five years later, Evelyn witnessed the opening ceremony: 'In the morning was celebrated the Encenia of the New Theater, so magnificently built by the munificence of Dr Gilbert Sheldon, Abp. of Canterbury, in which was spent £25,000, as Sir Christopher Wren, the architect (as I remember), told me; and yet it was never seene by the benefactor, my Lord Abp. having told me that he never did nor ever would see it. It is in truth a fabrick comparable to any of this kind of former ages. ...' Evelyn then describes in detail the gorgeous ceremonies, lasting

B

33

over two days, which 'drew a world of strangers and other companie to the university from all parts of the nation, and was concluded in the evening with ringing of bells and universal joy and feasting'.

Two of Wren's biographers explain Evelyn's curious statement, that the Archbishop never allowed himself a sight of his great project, by suggesting that he was so industrious and conscientious that he regarded a special trip to Oxford for the purpose as a waste of his valuable time: this is pure hypothesis and seems incredible. Evelyn's figure of £25,000 must be a slip of memory, as the full accounts for the building have been preserved, but it has been quoted by later writers. The Sheldonian Theatre has been respectfully described by many critics and biographers, but none of them has ever applied the word 'beautiful' to it. They all agree that it serves its purpose as efficiently today as when it was new, nearly 300 years ago, and that it possesses admirable acoustic qualities. The *Oxford Almanack* recently pictured its internal appearance at the Encaenia of June 26, 1946, from a painting by Charles Cundall, in which the rich brown woodwork and the great decorated ceiling form a fitting background for the splendid array of scarlet academic gowns. Wren had a functional problem to solve, and he solved it brilliantly. A procession from the Divinity School crossed a quadrangle into the new theatre, and the large galleries were reached by two spacious round-ended staircases flanking the entrance and by six subsidiary staircases ranged round the walls. Thus the arrangements for 'circulation', in the modern phrase, were as efficient as those for the internal orderliness, decorum and splendour of the auditorium. The shape of the building was founded, as *Parentalia* reminds us, on that of the Theatre of Marcellus at Rome (11 B.C.), illustrated in Serlio's book of architecture, the only reliable manual then available in English. The plan was D-shaped, with the spectators seated all round the curve, and the stage on the chord; but the theatre, as usual in all Greek and Roman buildings of the same type, was open to the sky. Wren wished to provide a very large covered auditorium, uninterrupted by columns to support a roof, and was thus faced with the problem of carrying a roof over a clear span of 68 feet between the massive outer walls. This was a task after his own heart, appealing to his scientific ingenuity, and he designed enormous oak trusses to meet the case. The flat ceiling was painted by Robert Streater to represent a *velarium* (awning), such as covered the Colosseum at Rome, but pictures it as if half drawn back by its cords, so that one appears to look through to the sky, against which allegorical figures disport themselves. For the rest, the oak panelling and other accessories are plain but appropriate, though they lack refinement.

34

Externally, the round end towards Broad Street is disappointing; but that is almost unavoidable because of its shape, and that shape was determined by functional requirements. The south front is more satisfactory. Built of stone from Shotover, Burford and Barrington (near Burford), the theatre has a lofty, arcaded and rusticated lower story, with coupled windows between Corinthian pilasters in the upper story. Above this is a bold cornice, and a balustrade ornamented with urns. A large cupola rises above the low-pitched and slated roof. The curved end of the building, towards Broad Street, is enclosed by a tall iron balustrade between stone piers surmounted by busts of ancient philosophers, now somewhat weatherbeaten and unintentionally grotesque. There is more than a hint of the Baroque in this feature. Externally, at any rate, the Sheldonian Theatre shows Wren manfully facing and surmounting a most difficult problem of planning and construction, but clothing it more hesitatingly in the classic garb of the ancients and certainly paying no attention to the 'Oxford Manner' in architecture. It may be added that the stone carving was executed by William Byrde, the wood carving by Richard Clere. The stonework was restored in 1890, 1910 and 1935. The roof-dormers were removed and the central cupola was rebuilt in 1838, the roof repaired in 1900, and the internal woodwork strengthened in 1936-7.

An informative (anonymous) article in the *R.I.B.A. Journal* for 1937 (XLV, 26) describes this last work of restoration, carried out by Mr Fielding Dodd of Oxford. He was not concerned with the roof, but the article states that the roof actually carried, from 1669 to 1713, the enormous weight of the University printing-press, and adds that 'this is an interesting example of Wren's ability to meet the most irrational requests of his clients'. Quoting a statement in the *Oxford Guide* for 1837 that 'in consequence of the roof being in danger of falling, a new one was substituted in 1802', the writer remarks that this could not have been so, as Streater's great painting on the ceiling still remains. A special report on the roof made in 1720 states that it had sagged 11 inches in the middle, owing to the huge load of books stored in it, but was still quite sound.

As for the decorations of the interior, which are rather gaudy, the author of the article observed that they seem to have been little changed: 'the entablature and panelled balustrade of the balcony are painted somewhat crudely to simulate marble, and there is evidence that this dates from the eighteenth century. The organ was brought from elsewhere in 1858, and placed in the minstrels' gallery, where it blocks three windows; the instrument is poor and the case both ugly and inappropriate. During the . . . [early twentieth] . . . century, some new entrances or vomitories into the first or Ladies' Gallery were made', designed by Messrs Smith and Brewer. These were of steel and concrete, faced with oak panelling.

Mr Dodd's work included two new staircases to the upper (or undergraduates') gallery. In the course of his work, he found that all the gallery woodwork was so decayed, as a result of attack by three varieties of beetle, that the galleries were liable to collapse when fully loaded. The columns supporting them were of solid oak, and in fact the whole structure of galleries was designed to be practically self-supporting, independent of the walls, though the back of the upper gallery was carried on stone corbels built into the walls. Mr Dodd substituted an entirely new framework of light steelwork and teak (chosen for its resistance to beetles), and refixed the old panelled gallery-fronts, but the old columns were 'bored and threaded over steel columns—an ingenious if expensive device'.

Only two other designs are ascribed to this early period before 1666. Of these a new block of rooms at Trinity College, Oxford, must have been designed early in 1665, as the letter quoted below proves, but was not built till 1668 and cost about £15,000. It originally had a steep French 'mansard' roof with dormers, but has been much altered in appearance since, sash windows having been substituted for mullioned windows, and an additional story built with a low-pitched roof. The following letter from Wren to Bathurst, President of the College and formerly one of the learned gathering at Wadham College, shows that Wren favoured a three-sided quadrangle with the fourth side left open. The 'Minchin' named in the letter was a carpenter then working on the Sheldonian. The letter is quoted here because it sheds some light on Wren's ideas at this stage. It is dated June 22, 1665.

'My honoured Friend,

'I am convinced with Machiavel, or some other unlucky fellow, 'tis no matter whether I quote true, that the world is generally governed by words. I perceive the name of a quadrangle will carry with it those whom you say may possibly be your benefactors, though it may be much the worst situation for the chambers, and the beauty of the College, and of the particular pile of buildings. If I had skill in enchantment to represent the pile, first in one view, then in another, that the difference might be evidently seen, I should certainly make them of my opinion; or else I will appeal to Mons. Mansard, or Signor Bernini, both which I shall see at Paris within this fortnight. But, to be sober, if any body, as you say, will pay for a quadrangle, there is no dispute to be made; let them have a quadrangle, though a lame one, somewhat like a three-legged table.

'I sent last week to Minchin, to give a full account of the design that was fitted for the grove: and if you resolve upon the other way, of seeing it in the garden [the Fellows' Garden], you have two designs for that also, neither of which do I know at present how to mend. I suppose the first of these two in the books may please you best, that to be set in the garden; I mean the loose paper, which contains a ground plot only, with one bedroom and two studies to each chamber, which Minchin cannot be at a loss in. In this design I intended the stories to be but ten feet high; and though I have not particularly expressed an upright for that, I meant to have used the same that is there glued to the other ground-plot, changing only the height of the stories. If you show this part of the latter to Minchin, I know he will apprehend it. You need not use any apologies to me; for I must beg of you to believe you may command me of things of greater moment, and that I love to serve you, as your most faithful and affectionate

'Friend and servant,

'Christopher Wren.'

It is interesting to note that Wren, although he understood geometry and perspective so well, felt himself unable to supply perspective sketches of his designs, though aware that they were needed in this case.

The charming classical doorway of the north transept at Ely Cathedral resembles Wren's much later doorways at St Mary le Bow, and some of F. Mansart's later work in Paris. A tablet in the nave gives 1662 as the date when certain work was carried out in this part of the cathedral during Matthew Wren's episcopate (1638-67), and tradition has assigned the work to this very early date, thus making it Wren's first architectural commission. Recent opinion, however, inclines to attribute it to the period 1700-2, when Wren certainly supervised the building operations required after the north-west corner of the north transept fell suddenly in 1699. This attribution is supported by the mature and confident character of the design. In 1666, then, he had only completed one building, Pembroke Chapel, and the Sheldonian Theatre was half-way towards completion.

Before Wren had finished either of these buildings, the plague broke out in London. The first cases occurred outside the City, in Drury Lane, towards the end of 1664, and the numbers of dead steadily increased throughout the following spring. By midsummer 1665, as one may read in Defoe's vivid but imaginary *Journal of the Plague Year*, a general exodus of the wealthier classes from London had begun. Turning to the two most famous diaries of this period, we find John Evelyn recording on July 28: 'The contagion still increasing and growing now all about us, I sent my wife and whole family (two or three necessary servants excepted) to my brother's at Wotton, having resolved to stay at my house myselfe and to look after my charge, trusting in the providence and good-nesse of God.' His family returned from the country in February; but it may be recalled that Evelyn's house at Deptford lay south of the river and some distance from the seriously affected areas. Pepys, on the other hand, lived in the City, and was therefore more exposed to risk. On July 1, 1665, he sent his wife and two maids to Woolwich, noting that 'some trouble there is in having the care of a family at home this plague time'. On August 31, at considerable inconvenience, as he had to attend at his office in London daily, he joined them when people were dying at the rate of many thousands a week, but all the household appear to have returned to London on December 4, much earlier than Evelyn's family.

These particulars are given here in an attempt to answer a question often asked: why did Wren suddenly make his one and only visit abroad early in July 1665? Did he go mainly to escape the plague, as has been suggested? If so, he was only following the example of many important persons, and it must be remembered that he was a delicate man. On the other hand, he was not compelled to spend all his time in London: his academic headquarters was at Oxford, and his buildings were rising at Oxford and Cambridge. The Court was oscillating between Oxford and Hampton Court. The visit was apparently planned deliberately some time ahead, and actually occupied six or eight strenuous months. John Evelyn, in a letter to Wren from Deptford on April 4, 1665, wrote: 'I am told by Sr. Jo. Denham that you looke towards France this somer; be assured I will charge you with some addresses to friends of mine there, that shall exceedingly cherish you: and though you will stand in no neede of my recommendations yet I am confident you will not refuse the offer of those civilities which I offer you.' There is every indication that it was a carefully schemed tour of study, and that the subject for study was architecture not science. By 1665, then, Wren had taken the plunge. He had not said good-bye to science, far from it; but henceforth architecture was to be his main occupation.

In view of the prevailing craze for everything Italian, introduced especially by Inigo Jones, it seems strange that Wren, to whom expense cannot have been the first consideration, did not journey to Rome, the Mecca of architects of that day, where Bernini and other famous architects were producing Baroque masterpieces. It may be that, as a delicate man, he shrank from the rigours of extended travel; or he may have grudged the additional time entailed for the journey; but he went to France with the intention, clearly stated in the letter already quoted, of meeting Mansart, Bernini and other leading practitioners in Paris, where Colbert was inviting competitive designs for the completion of the palace of the Louvre. Wren's choice was certainly a wise one, for Paris at that time was alive with architectural activity, and the French architect François Mansart was recognized as the equal of Bernini himself, while Louis Le Vau and others were hardly inferior. Mansart's *château* of Maisons (1642-51), still fortunately preserved, and one of the most lovely buildings of the Renaissance, was finished, and Le Vau's Collège des Quatre Nations (1660-8) was half-built. Wren does not appear to have taken much interest in churches, although several fine domed churches had recently been completed or were then approaching completion, notably the splendid dome of the Val-de-Grâce (completed 1665). Obviously he could not have foreseen in 1665 the wonderful destiny that Fate had in store for him only a year later at St Paul's.

Wren worked diligently during his six or eight months abroad, but it appears to me that some of his biographers are rash in interpreting too literally and technically the statement that he 'surveyed' fourteen or more large country mansions, especially as he adds that he hopes to bring back records 'which I found by some or other ready designed to my Hand, in which I have spent both Labour and some Money'. The last sentence suggests that he purchased a number of engravings to supplement his own —not necessarily exhaustive—observations on the spot.

The only extant description of Wren's visit to Paris is to be found in a letter to an unknown friend, quoted in *Parentalia* and reproduced below. According to the Wren Society (XIII, 40), this unknown friend may have been one Bateman, but not the Bateman of the 'Bateman MS' at Lambeth Palace. It may be added here that Lord St Albans, mentioned at the outset, was a well-known figure at both French and English Courts, a friend of the Queen, and an enlightened patron of architecture who afterwards laid out St James's Square. 'Jermyn Street' recalls his name. The extract from *Parentalia* is as follows:

'In the Year 1665, Mr Wren took a Journey to Paris, where, at that Time all Arts flourish'd in a higher Degree than had ever been known before in France; and where there was a general Congress of the most celebrated Masters in every Profession, encourag'd by Royal Munificence, and the Influence of the great Cardinal Mazarine. How he spent his Time, in that Place, will in Part appear from a short Account he gave by Letter to a particular Friend; wherein he returns Thanks for his Recommendation of him to the Earl of St Albans, who in the Journey, and ever since, had us'd him with all Kindness and Indulgence imaginable, and made good his Character of him, as one of the best Men in the World. He then proceeds

to the following Particulars; I have, says he, busied myself in surveying the most esteem'd Fabricks of Paris, & the Country round; the Louvre
for a while was my daily Object, where no less than a thousand Hands
are constantly employ'd in the Works; some in laying mighty Foundations, some in raising the Stories, Columns, Entablements, &c., with vast
Stones, by great and useful Engines; others in Carving, Inlaying of
Marbles, Plaistering, Painting, Gilding, &c. Which altogether make a
School of Architecture, the best probably, at this Day in Europe. The
College of the four Nations is usually Admir'd, but the Artist hath pur-
posely set it ill-favouredly, that he might shew his Wit in struggling with
an inconvenient Situation.

'An Academy of Painters, Sculptors, Architects and the chief Artificers
of the Louvre, meet every first and last Saturday of the Month. Mons.
Colbert, Superintendant, comes to the Works of the Louvre, every
Wednesday, and, if Business hinders not, Thursday. The Workmen are
paid every Sunday duly. Mons. Abbé Charles introduc'd me to the
Acquaintance of Bernini, who shew'd me his Designs of the Louvre, and
of the King's Statue. Abbé Bruno keeps the curious Rarities of the Duke
of Orleans's Library, well filled with excellent Intaglio's, Medals, Books
of Plants, and Fowls in Miniature. Abbé Burdelo keeps an Academy at his
House for Philosophy every Monday Afternoon.—But I must not think
to describe Paris, and the numerous Observables there, in the Compass of
a short Letter.

'The King's Houses I could not miss; Fontainebleau has a stately Wild-
ness and Vastness suitable to the Desert it stands in. The antique Mass of
the Castle of St Germains, & the Hanging-gardens are delightfully surprising (I mean to any Man of Judgment) for the Pleasures below vanish
away in the Breath that is spent in ascending. The Palace, or if you please,
the Cabinet of Versailles call'd me twice to view it; the Mixtures of Brick,
Stone, blue Tile and Gold make it look like a rich Livery: Not an Inch
within but is crouded with little Curiosities of Ornaments; the Women,
as they make here the Language and Fashions, and meddle with Politicks
and Philosophy, so they sway also in Architecture; Works of Filgrand,
and little Knacks are in great Vogue; but Building certainly ought to have
the Attribute of eternal, and therefore the only Thing uncapable of new
Fashions. The masculine Furniture of Palais Mazarine pleas'd me much
better, where there is a great and noble collection of antique Statues and
Bustos (many of Porphyry), good Basso-relievos; excellent Pictures of
the Great Masters, fine Arras, true Mosaicks, besides Pierres de Rapport
in Compartiments and Pavements; Vases on Porcelain painted by Raphael,

and infinite other Rarities; the best of which now furnish the glorious Appartment of the Queen Mother at the Louvre, which I saw many Times.

'After the incomparable Villas of Vaux and Maisons, I shall but name Ruel, Courances, Chilly, Essoane, St Maur, St Mande, Issy, Meudon, Rincy, Chantilly, Verneul, Lioncour, all of which, & I might add many others, I have survey'd; and that I might not lose the Impressions of them, I shall bring you almost all France in Paper, which I found by some or other ready design'd to my Hand, in which I have spent both Labour and some Money. Bernini's Design of the Louvre I would have given my Skin for, but the old reserv'd Italian gave me but a few minutes view; it was five little Designs in Paper, for which he hath receiv'd as many thousand Pistoles; I had only Time to copy it in my Fancy and Memory; I shall be able by Discourse, and a Crayon, to give you a tolerable Account of it. I have purchased a great deal of *Taille-douce*, that I might give our Country-men Examples of Ornaments and Grotesks, in which the Italians themselves confess the French to excel. I hope I shall give you a very good Account of all the best Artists of France; my Business now is to pry into Trades and Arts, I put myself into all Shapes to humour them; 'tis a Comedy to me, and tho' sometimes expenceful, I am loth yet to leave it.'

He ends with a list of the principal artists then working in Paris, including the architects Bernini, Mansart, Vaux (Le Vau), Gobert and Le Pautre. A postscript adds that 'My Lord Berkley returns to England at Christmas, when I propose to take the opportunity of his Company, and by that Time, to perfect what I have on the Anvil; Observations on the present State of Architecture, Arts, and Manufactures in France'.

Another curious entry in *Parentalia* describes an illness which befell Wren during this tour, underlining the delicacy of his constitution, and also indicating a strange streak of credulity or superstition singularly out of place in so philosophical and scientific a personality. 'When Sir Christopher Wren was in Paris, about 1665, he was taken ill and feverish, made but little Water, and had a Pain in his Reins: He sent for a Physician, who advis'd him to let Blood, thinking he had a Pleurisy; but Bleeding much disagreeing with his Constitution, he would defer it a Day longer: That Night he dreamt he was in a Place where Palm-trees grew (suppose Egypt) and that a Woman in a romantick Habit reach'd him Dates. The next Day he sent for Dates, which cur'd him of the Pain in his Reins.'

The important effect of Wren's studies in France upon his later architecture can be more properly considered in a subsequent chapter of this book (see p. 260). In the meantime, it may be remarked that his fervent admiration of Bernini's grandiose design for the new Louvre seems to most discriminating people today to be singularly uncritical, for modern opinion tends to hold that Paris had a lucky escape when Bernini's terrific and utterly inappropriate façade was rejected. Certainly Wren's taste was catholic, for he studied buildings of two generations of earlier as well as current fashions, and not all architects are as broadminded as that. Probably he was finding his feet, a natural attitude when one remembers that his first venture in architecture had been made less than three years before. Returning to London from Paris, probably before February 1666, he resumed his attendance at meetings of the Royal Society, then much concerned to devise means for preventing any recurrence of the plague, which still lingered on here and there in the suburbs. For some time previously, possibly since 1663, he had been engaged upon the problem of repairing Old St Paul's Cathedral and in May 1666 laid the Commission's Report before the King; but the topic of St Paul's (old and new) is better considered as a whole in a later chapter. This stage of Wren's life closes abruptly with the outbreak of the Great Fire of London on September 2, 1666.

Failing any personal diary of his French tour from Wren himself, the following interesting letter from Edward Browne (1644-1708) to his celebrated father Sir Thomas Browne is illuminating. Edward later became an eminent physician. The third member of the party was Henry Compton (1632-1713), younger son of Spencer Compton, second Earl of Northampton. The letter is dated from Paris, September 1665.

'Three days the last week I was abroad in the country with Dr Wren and Mr Compton. I did not think to see any thinge more at Paris, but was tempted out by so good company. Dr Wren's discourse is very pleasing and satisfactory to mee about all manners of things. I asked him which hee took to bee the greatest work about Paris, he said the Quay, or Key upon the river side, which he demonstrated to me, to be built with so vast expense and such great quantity of materialls, that it exceeded all manner of ways the building of the two greatest pyramids in Egypt. I told him that upon the banks of the river Loire for some miles, there was a wall built of square stone; but because there could not be allowed any thickness proportionall to the Key at Paris, hee did not know how to esteem of that, as not having ever seen it. Wee went the first day to Chantilly, where lives the Prince of Condy, but he was gone out, and so wee mist Abbot Bourdelot (Physician to the Prince) too: Wee saw the Princesse carried in a chair about the gardens, being with child. The house is old built; and belonged formerly to the Duke of Montmorancy, whose statue on horseback in bronze stands before the house; the gardens and waterworks are neat.

'The next day wee went to Liancourt, belonging to the president of Liancourt; the house is built but on two sides, the gate makeing the third, and the fourth layeing open to have a better prospect of the gardens. The waterworks here are in greater numbers than in any place in France, and the water throwne up in pretty shapes, as of a bell turned up or a bell turned downe, out of frog's mouth in a broad thin streame, &c. The mill that serves to rayse the water is the largest I have seen. The president's chaise in which they draw him about the garden, is so well poised upon the wheels, made just like the chaises roulantes that are here so much in the fashion at present, that one may draw it with two fingers. . . . The groves are stately, and cut through in many places into long shady walks. We went from hence to Verneuil, seated upon an high hill, a very neat castel, but furnished with old furniture. The Duke I suppose is still embassador in England; he keeps a pack of English dogs here, and lives in a good hunting country. The house is very finely carved without side. Dr Wren guest that the same man built this which built the Louvre, there being the same faults in one as in the other.' [Both *châteaux*, i.e. Liancourt and Verneuil, are by De Brosse.]

'Wee lye at Senlis this night, a great towne, and a bishop's seat, with three or four good churches in it, and an od kind of hospitall without the towne, where the chambers are built like those of the Carthusians, at some distance one from another. The next day we saw Rinsy, an house belonging to the Dutchesse of Longueville, sister to the Prince of Condé. The gardens and waterworks are not yet finished; the house is small but exceedingly neat, and the modell pleased Dr Wren very much: the chambers are exceedingly well painted, and one roome with an handsome cupola in it is one of the best I have seen. Returning to Paris, the King overtook us in chaise roulante with his Mistress La Valière with him, habited very prettily in a hat and feathers, and a *just aucorps*. He had dined that day with his brother, at a house of his in the country, and had left his company and come away full speed to Paris.'

❧ III ❧

THE GREAT FIRE OF LONDON
AND ITS SEQUEL

1666 — 1669

O<small>N</small> August 27, 1666, John Evelyn records in his diary that he with 'Dr Wren', 'Mr Prat', Mr May, the Bishop of London, the Dean of St Paul's and several others visited Old St Paul's Cathedral 'to survey the generall decays of that ancient and venerable church', and to prepare a report thereon. (This important meeting, together with the events that preceded it, is described in my next chapter where the whole story of the Cathedral, before and after the Fire, is related.) Only six days later, on September 2, Evelyn writes: 'This fatal night about ten, began that deplorable fire neere Fish Streete in London.' On the following afternoon he crossed the river to Bankside, and thence 'beheld the dismal spectacle, the whole Citty in dreadful flames neare the water side; all the houses from the Bridge, all Thames Street, and upwards towards Cheapeside, downe to the Three Cranes, were now consum'd. . . . The fire having continu'd all this night (if I may call that night which was as light as day for ten miles round about, after a dreadfull manner) when conspiring with a fierce Eastern wind in a very drie season; I went on foote to the same place, and saw the whole South part of the Citty burning from Cheapeside to the Thames, and all along Cornehill (for it likewise kindl'd back against the wind as well as forward), Tower Streete, Fen-church Streete, Gracious Streete, and so along to Bainard's Castle, and was now taking hold of St Paule's Church, to which the scaffolds contributed exceedingly. The conflagration was so universal, and the people so astonish'd, that from the beginning, I know not by what despondency or fate, they hardly stirr'd to quench it, so that there was nothing heard or seene but crying out and lamentation, running about like distracted creatures, without at all attempting to save even their goods; such a strange consternation there was upon them; so as it burned both in breadth and length, the Churches, Public Halls, Exchange, Hospitals, Monuments, and ornaments, leaping after a prodigious manner from house to house and streete to streete, at great distances one from the

44

other; for the heate with a long set of faire and warme weather had even ignited the aire and prepar'd the materials to conceive the fire, which devour'd after an incredible manner houses, furniture, and every thing. . . . All the skie was of a fiery aspect, like the top of a burning oven, and the light seene above 40 miles round about for many nights. God grant mine eyes may never behold the like, who now saw above 10,000 houses all in one flame; the noise and cracking and thunder of the impetuous flames, the shreiking of women and children, the hurry of people, the fall of Towers, Houses and Churches, was like an hideous storme, and the aire all about so hot and inflam'd that at the last one was not able to approch it, so that they were forc'd to stand still and let the flames burn on, which they did for neere two miles in length and one in bredth. The clowds also of smoke were dismall and reach'd upon computation neer 56 miles in length. . . .'

September 4. 'The burning still rages, and it was now gotten as far as the Inner Temple; all Fleet Streete, the Old Bailey, Ludgate Hill, Warwick Lane, Newgate, Paules Chaine, Watling Streete, now flaming, and most of it reduc'd to ashes; the stones of Paules flew like granados, the mealting lead running down the streetes in a streame, and the very pavements glowing with fiery rednesse, so as no horse or man was able to tread on them, and the demolition had stopp'd all the passages, so that no help could be applied. The Eastern wind still more impetuously driving the flames forward. Nothing but the Almighty power of God was able to stop them, for vaine was the help of man.'

Next day Evelyn records that the fire was beginning to threaten White-hall, and that there was confusion at Court. He was deputed to take charge of the 'quenching' operations at Fetter Lane, and at last it was decided to blow up a line of buildings in the path of the flames, to the intense anger of the owners and occupiers. However they were spared this drastic remedy. 'It now pleased God by abating the wind, and by the industrie of the people, when almost all was lost, infusing a new spirit into them, that the furie of it began sensibly to abate about noone, so that it came no farther than the Temple Westward, nor than the entrance of Smithfield North: but continu'd all this day and night so impetuous toward Cripple-gate and the Tower as made us all despaire; it also brake out againe in the Temple, but the courage of the multitude persisting, and many houses being blown up, such gaps and desolations were soone made, as with the former three days consumption, the back fire did not so vehemently urge upon the rest as formerly. There was yet no standing neere the burning and glowing ruines by neere a furlongs space.'

On September 7 Evelyn walked from Whitehall through the City to London Bridge 'with extraordinary difficulty, clambering over heaps of yet smoking rubbish, and frequently mistaking where I was. The ground under my feete so hot, that it even burnt the soles of my shoes. . . . At my returne I was infinitely concern'd to find that goodly Church St Paules now a sad ruine, and that beautifull portico (for structure comparable to any in Europe, as not long before repair'd by the late King) now rent in pieces, flakes of vast stone split asunder, and nothing remaining intire but the inscription in the architrave, shewing by whom it was built, which had not one letter of it defac'd. It was astonishing to see what immense stones the heate had in a manner calcin'd, so that all the ornaments, columnes, freezes, capitals, and projectures of massie Portland stone flew off, even to the very roofe, where a sheet of lead covering a great space (no less than 6 akers by measure) was totally mealted. . . . Thus lay in ashes that most venerable Church, one of the most antient pieces of early piety in the Christian world, besides neere 100 more. The lead, yron worke, bells, plates, &c. mealted; the exquisitely wrought Mercers Chapell, the sumptuous Exchange, the august fabriq of Christ Church, all the rest of the Companies Halls, splendid buildings, arches, enteries, all in dust; the fountaines dried up and ruin'd, whilst the very waters remain'd boiling; the voragos of subterranean cellars, wells, and dungeons, formerely warehouses, still burning in stench and dark clowds of smoke, so that in five or six miles traversing about, I did not see one loade of timber unconsum'd, nor many stones but what were calcin'd white as snow. . . .'

September 10. 'I went againe to the ruines, for it was no longer a Citty.'

The reason for quoting so extensively here from Evelyn's *Diary* (though only a small part of his entries is given) and for preferring it to the equally vivid but much more lengthy 'eye-witness' account by Pepys, is explained by his next entry on September 13. 'I presented his Majesty with a survey of the ruines, and a plot [plan] for a new Citty, with a discourse on it; whereupon after dinner his Majesty sent for me into the Queen's bed-chamber, her Majesty and the Duke onely being present; they examin'd each particular, and discours'd on them for neere an houre, seeming to be extreamely pleas'd with what I had so early thought on.'

Evelyn indeed showed remarkable enterprise in making a survey of the ruins and preparing a plan within a few days after the fire had subsided, even before the ashes were cold. From his account it would appear that six days elapsed between the abatement of the fire and the meeting in the Queen's bedroom on September 13; but he may well have submitted his plan some days before that meeting took place. This would appear to be the case from a passage in a long letter that he wrote on September 27 to his friend Sir Samuel Tuke:

'In the meanetime, the King and Parliament are infinitely zealous for the rebuilding of our ruines; & I believe it will universally be the employment of the next Spring: They are now busied with adjusting the claimes of each proprietor, that so they may dispose things for the building after the noblest model: Every body brings in his idea, amongst the rest I presented his Majestie my owne conceptions, with a Discourse annex'd. It was the second that was seene, within 2 dayes after the Conflagration: But Dr Wren had got the start of me. Both of us did coincide so frequently, that his Majestie was not displeas'd with it, & it caus'd divers alterations; and truly there was never a more glorious Phoenix upon Earth, if it do at last emerge out of these cinders, & as the design is layd, with the present fervour of the undertakers.'

Thus we find the modest, delicate and scholarly little figure of Christopher Wren suddenly assuming a new character—that of the energetic and pushful man of action, capable of speedy decisions. He had already been accepted as an expert upon structural matters in the invitation to supervise the works at Tangier, in his task as consultant for the repairs for Old St Paul's, and probably in his commission to design the Sheldonian Theatre; but at Pembroke Chapel he had been selected as an architect pure and simple, by an uncle who had confidence in his powers as a designer. He had also been offered the reversion of Sir John Denham's post as Surveyor-General of His Majesty's Works, though, as we have already seen, there is slender evidence that he ever functioned as Assistant Surveyor, at any rate before 1666. It seems clear that he acted solely on his own initiative, rather than upon any invitation, in presenting his ingenious plan for rebuilding London to the King. Doubtless he was happy in the knowledge that he already stood high in royal favour socially as well as professionally, for Charles II took a keen interest in the doings of the Royal Society.

The direct and immediate result of his enterprise was his appointment jointly with Sir Roger Pratt (whom we have met before), and Hugh May, a senior official of the Office of Works, as the Crown Commissioners for the rebuilding of London, together with three representatives of the City Corporation: Peter Mills, Edward Jerman and Robert Hooke. The last named was already a close friend of Wren, associated in the work of the Royal Society and now Professor of Mathematics at Gresham College. Hooke had also submitted a plan for rebuilding the City. Wren was still Savilian Professor of Astronomy at Oxford, he was still building the

Sheldonian Theatre, he was doing some work for the Royal Society, and at first he must have been so busy with all these extraneous activities that much of the work in London fell upon Pratt, May and Hooke, but eventually he emerged as the principal figure. Nevertheless, the statement in *Parentalia* that, after the Fire, he was appointed 'Surveyor-General and Principal Architect for rebuilding the whole City' is now regarded as quite untrue. He was not appointed Surveyor-General until 1669 (see p. 62); and the King, as Mr Reddaway has recently written in *The Rebuilding of London* (p. 311), 'could only have imposed a Surveyor-General with authority over the rebuilding of the City by an arbitrary exercise of his power. Late in 1667, he attempted to induce the City to appoint its own Lord Mayor to such an office, only to be firmly rebuffed.' Most of Wren's biographers assume too readily that he was the first and only person to envisage a better London, and that but for the stupidity, inefficiency and impatience of the civic authorities, his scheme would have been accepted, with great benefit to posterity. Only a part of this assumption is true.

Long before the Fire occurred, it had been recognized that sweeping changes were required to regulate the spread of population. Rules to prohibit any new buildings just outside the City walls had been made under Elizabeth, James I, Charles I and the Commonwealth—only to be disregarded, in spite of heavy penalties. John Evelyn in his *Fumifugium* (1661), a treatise on smoke abatement, had urged the need for replanning. Charles II in 1665 had expressed his concern to reduce fire-risks and to provide better facilities for traffic by widening the streets. A continuous quay along the Thames had been advocated by Evelyn and others. Schemes for embanking and improving the noisome Fleet River or Fleet Ditch were discussed in James I's reign. The Fire, like Hitler's air-raids, provided an opportunity to realize an ideal which was already taking shape in the minds of far-sighted men of taste. Many of them, notably Evelyn, had seen examples of fine civic planning in Rome; and Wren, even though he did not visit the model town of Richelieu in France, laid out in 1620-35, would be familiar with the dignified Place Royale (1604, now the Place des Vosges) in Paris. Town planning, as we understand it today, had not yet been introduced into England. London, before 1666, was in fact a medieval city of narrow streets and congested alleys, badly paved and drained. Its houses were still mainly of wood, with overhanging fronts and gabled roofs. No town more favourable to the rapid spread of fire could be imagined.

Briefly, the whole area within the City walls was burnt out, except the north-eastern corner, i.e. north of a point on the present 'London Wall' (near the Carpenters' Hall), via the intersection of Gracechurch Street and Bishopsgate, to Tower Hill. Outside the walls, the fire swept westwards as far as a line drawn from the present G.P.O. to Holborn Viaduct, St Andrew's Holborn, Fetter Lane, and the Temple Church to the Thames. Later statisticians computed the destroyed buildings as 13,200 houses, 87 parish churches, 44 halls of the City Companies and many public buildings. The total area laid waste was about 436 acres. The immediate result of the fire was, of course something approaching chaos, and there was complete dislocation of local government, traffic and business. The City Fathers established themselves in Gresham College, and the tens of thousands of 'displaced persons'—taking advantage of the autumn weather—soon began to run up improvised shacks and sheds on the sites of their former dwellings and shops. On September 13 the King issued a proclamation about rebuilding. All new buildings were to be of brick or stone. All main streets were to be wide, so that future fires would not easily spread across them. Narrow lanes were to be abolished. A 'fair key or wharf' was to be built all along the river front. The City Surveyor was instructed to make an immediate survey of the whole area, but meanwhile a new master-plan or lay-out was to be made; and it appears that the King and his advisers believed, at first, that a completely new lay-out was feasible.

The plan made by the City Surveyor, Peter Mills, has vanished; but six others have been preserved, made by Wren, Evelyn, Hooke, Captain Valentine Knight and (two schemes) by one Richard Newcourt, a mapmaker. Of all these, the plans by Wren and Evelyn are the best known and are also considered to be the best submitted. As Evelyn remarked (see p. 47), his plan and Wren's displayed many ideas in common, so they merit comparison here. Both show embankments on either side of a widened and straightened Fleet River. Both treat St Paul's Cathedral as a focal point at the end of converging street vistas. Both have a huge piazza in Fleet Street, half-way between Fleet Bridge (the present Ludgate Circus) and Temple Bar. Wren provides a wide riverside quay all the way from the Tower to the Temple, while Evelyn uses the actual river frontage for a range of public buildings with a street behind them. Evelyn moves the Royal Exchange to the riverside, but Wren leaves it in its old position and makes it the centre of the whole layout. Both have a number of important diagonal streets, Evelyn's chief diagonals being from St Paul's to London Bridge and from St Paul's to Bishopsgate; while Wren provides four diagonal streets radiating from the Royal Exchange to Moorgate, Dowgate Dock, the Custom House and Bishopsgate. He drives a wide straight street from Fleet Bridge via St Paul's direct to Aldgate, another

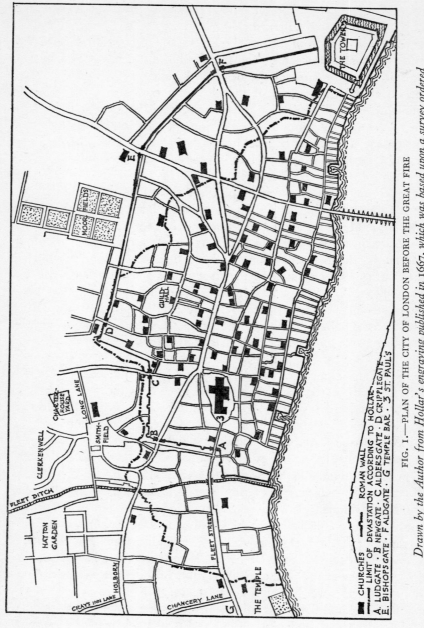

FIG. 1.—PLAN OF THE CITY OF LONDON BEFORE THE GREAT FIRE

Drawn by the Author from Hollar's engraving published in 1667, which was based upon a survey ordered in December 1666 by the City authorities. This plan is therefore much more accurate than Wren's hurried plan illustrated in Fig. 2.

CHURCHES ▬ ROMAN WALL
∙∙∙∙∙∙ LIMIT OF DEVASTATION ACCORDING TO HOLLAR
A. LUDGATE ∙ B NEWGATE ∙ C ALDERSGATE ∙ D CRIPPLEGATE
E. BISHOPSGATE ∙ F ALDGATE ∙ G TEMPLE BAR ∙ 3 ST. PAULS

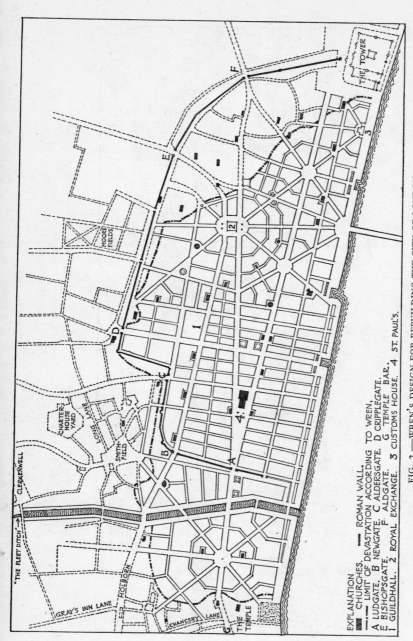

EXPLANATION
▬ CHURCHES.   ▬ ROMAN WALL.
─ ─ LIMIT OF DEVASTATION ACCORDING TO WREN,
A LUDGATE. B NEWGATE. C ALDERSGATE. D CRIPPLEGATE.
E BISHOPSGATE. F ALDGATE. G TEMPLE BAR.
1 GUILDHALL. 2 ROYAL EXCHANGE. 3 CUSTOMS HOUSE. 4 ST. PAUL'S.

FIG. 2.—WREN'S DESIGN FOR REBUILDING THE CITY OF LONDON

Traced by the Author from Wren's design, hastily prepared within a few days of the Great Fire of September 2–7, 1666, on the basis of an inaccurate survey of the City, which he brought up to date by a hurried perambulation of the ruins. Note his proposals for a reduced number of churches, as compared with Fig. 1, and his skilful siting of them for effect.

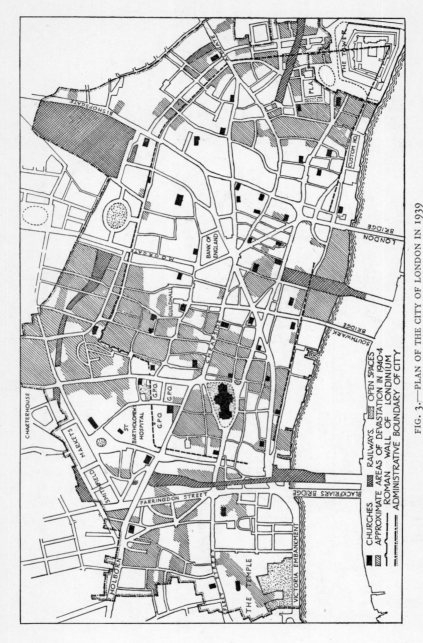

FIG. 3.—PLAN OF THE CITY OF LONDON IN 1939

Drawn by the Author for purposes of comparison with Figs. 1 and 2. It represents the City of London in 1939, with the churches then surviving, the Victorian street-improvements, railways and bridges. Otherwise the pattern of streets has altered little since 1666. The approximate area of devastation during the air-raids of 1940–4 is indicated by hatching.

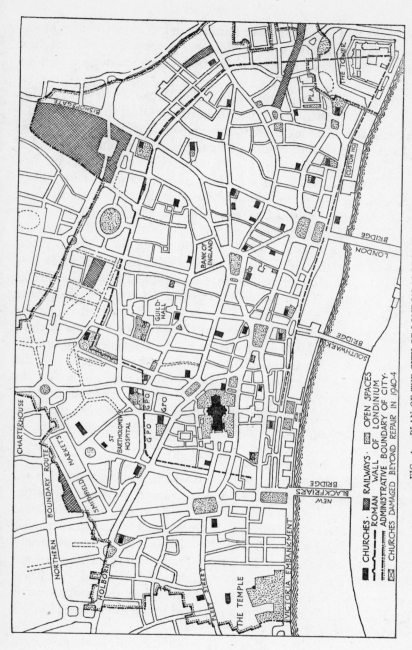

FIG. 4.—PLAN OF THE CITY OF LONDON AS PROPOSED IN 1947

CHURCHES. RAILWAYS. OPEN SPACES
ROMAN WALL OF LONDINIUM
ADMINISTRATIVE BOUNDARY OF CITY.
CHURCHES DAMAGED BEYOND REPAIR IN 1940-4

Drawn by the Author to show the principal recommendations made by Charles Holden and William Holford in their rebuilding scheme published in 1947 for the City authorities. The churches still surviving are shown. The proposed layout should be compared with Wren's design (Fig. 2).

53

from St Paul's to Tower Hill, and a third running due north from Queen-hithe to Moorgate. Evelyn's plan is the more geometrical and theoretical of the two, Wren's the more practical; but both take count of the numerous parish churches.

The Wren Society has published (in Vol. XII) the actual survey made by Wren before preparing his plan, from the original in the All Souls Collection. It shows in single red lines the positions of the former streets, St Paul's and a few other important buildings. Presumably he traced it from existing maps of the City, and then went over the ground on foot while the ruins were still smouldering. Here is the description of his doings from *Parentalia*: 'Dr Wren, immediately after the Fire, took an exact Survey of the whole Area and Confines of the Burning, having traced over, with great Trouble and Hazard, the great Plain of Ashes and Ruins; and designed a Plan or Model of a new City, in which the Deformity and Inconveniences of the old Town were remedied, by the inlarging the Streets and Lanes, and carrying them as near parallel to one another as might be; avoiding, if compatible with greater Conveniences, all acute Angles; by seating all the parochial Churches conspicuous and insular; by forming the most publick Places into large Piazzas, the Centers of eight Ways; by uniting the Halls of the twelve chief Companies, into one regular Square annexed to Guild-hall; by making a commodious Key on the whole Bank of the River, from Blackfriars to the Tower. Moreover, in contriving the general Plan, the following Particulars, were chiefly consider'd and propos'd. The Streets to be of three Magnitudes; the three principal leading straight through the City, and one or two Cross-streets to be at least 90 Feet wide; others 60 Feet; and Lanes about 30 Feet, excluding all narrow dark Alleys.'

Hooke submitted his rival plan to the Royal Society on September 19. The late Lord Mayor was present, and announced the approval of the scheme by the reigning Lord Mayor and his aldermen, 'and their desire that it might be shown to the King, they preferring it very much to that which was drawn up by the City Surveyor'. However, Hooke had already been forestalled by Wren and by Evelyn (both leading members of the Royal Society), if not by others; and though both had risked submitting their designs to the King without having obtained the previous approval of the City Fathers, their rashness was rewarded to the extent that Hooke's plan was not accepted.

Ultimately, none of the competitors was successful. Ideas may have been borrowed from one or another of their designs; but, taken as a whole, the results of all these imaginative projects amounted to little more than the widening and straightening of certain streets. Wren's share in the rebuilding of London, apart from the enormous number of important new buildings actually designed by him and described later in this book, was chiefly confined to advice on technical matters of construction, drainage and minor planning. He was never allowed to function as a town-planner on the grand scale. On October 2, 1666, Dr Oldenburg wrote to the Hon. Robert Boyle: 'The rebuilding of the citty, as to the model, is still very perplext, there appearing three parties in the house of commons about it. Some are for a quite new model, according to Dr Wren's draught; some are for the old, yet to build with bricks; others for a middle way, by building a key, and enlarging some streets, but keeping the old foundations and vaults. I hear, this very day there is a meeting of some of his majesties councill, and others of the nobility, with the leading men of the citty, to conferre about this great work, and to try, whether they can bring it to some issue, before the people, that inhabited London, doe scatter into other parts. The great stresse will be, how to raise mony for carrying on the warre, and to rebuild the citty at the same time.'

After much wrangling in Parliament, the six men appointed by the Crown and the City (see p. 47) were entrusted with the work as 'His Majesty's Commissioners for Rebuilding'; and on October 11 they decided upon the following widths for streets: Quay 100 feet, 'High Streets' 70 feet, 'Some other Streets' 42-50 feet, 'The least Streets' 25-30 feet, 'Alleys, if any' 16 feet. On October 22 specific widths for certain streets were prescribed: Quay 80 feet, Holborn-Aldgate 55 feet, Fleet Street-Tower 50 feet, London Bridge-Bishopsgate 50 feet, St Paul's Churchyard-Cheapside 70 feet with a piazza, Aldersgate-Cheapside-Thames Street 40 feet, Exchange-Thames Street-Moorgate 40 feet, Paternoster Row and Lombard Street both 40 feet, etc.

The work of clearing rubble from the old streets was not finished till December. By that time the new survey was ready for the Commissioners. It was required to show all previous ownerships of sites. Pepys' diary for November 25, 1666, records: 'I spoke with Mr May, who tells me the design of building the City do go on apace, and by his description it will be mighty handsome, and to the satisfaction of the people . . . but I pray God it will not come out too late.'

The Commissioners next proceeded to draw up rules for standard types of houses to be built in the new City, prescribing their height according to the streets in which they stood; and also laying down sensible regulations for the height of rooms (including cellars), thicknesses of walls and scantlings of timber. Arrangements were made concurrently to increase the supply of bricks to meet the huge demand and several new kilns were opened near London. Evelyn was interested in one such venture, while Pepys had a flutter in timber imports.

The City's proposals for widths of streets were bandied to and fro before final approval, the King pressed for the removal of certain street-markets to proper market-places, the height of Fleet Bridge was raised and the gradient of Ludgate Hill eased—all of them commendable improvements; but negotiations were still dragging on between the City freeholders (including the ecclesiastical authorities) and the civic officials about compensation and reinstatement, and no move was made to adopt *in toto* Wren's or any other plan. The whole scheme collapsed for reasons which may be extremely regrettable but were undeniably compelling, as we realize only too well today when another vast scheme for replanning London is painfully struggling towards fulfilment. There are documents in Wren's own writing showing how he strove to adjust small disputes between owners of sites and the surveyors responsible for replanning and rewidening streets, each 'incident' the cause of a law-suit and the basis for compensation. It was the combined effects of legal delays and financial stringency (for the huge sum entailed for compensation was colossal at a time when the 'defence services' were making heavy claims on the Treasury) that finally prevented the adoption of Wren's or any other ideal scheme. For it must be admitted, whether we like it or not, that he and his rivals were planning 'Dream Cities', admirable in conception but impossible of realization under anything short of a prosperous totalitarian régime. Imagine tens of thousands of homeless people, the starving shop-keepers, the harassed merchants, the overworked officials in extemporized offices—and the explanation is simple enough.

Only one thing was saved from the wreck, and even that is now a thing of the past, buried beneath London pavements nearly 200 years ago. Although there had been earlier proposals for widening, straightening, embanking and dredging the muddy 'Fleet River' or 'Fleet Ditch', which runs its short course of five or six miles from Kenwood above Hampstead to the Thames at Blackfriars, it was mainly due to Wren, with the collaboration of Hooke—now City Surveyor—that quays were constructed on either side of the stream, up to Holborn Bridge, in 1671-4. It was intended that sites for warehouses along the new quays should produce rents high enough to pay for the quay-construction and maintenance; but those hopes were never fulfilled, and a century later the river was arched over, and now lies in a sewer beneath New Bridge Street and Farringdon Street. This was the only part of Wren's and Evelyn's plans to be carried out; but there was a brief period, immediately after the Fire, when a part of the projected Thames-side quay was open, from the Tower to London Bridge; and in 1671 a scheme was approved to extend this all the way to the Temple by reclaiming the foreshore for widths varying from 20 to 80 feet in order to produce an even frontage-line; but this scheme too gradually flickered out for the usual reason—want of money—and was abandoned in 1681.

By way of conclusion to this depressing chronicle of failures and facts, it seems necessary to quote the story as given in *Parentalia*, with another reminder that the book in question is an unblushing panegyric of Wren. 'The Practicability of this whole Scheme, without Loss to any Man, or Infringement of any Property, was at that Time demonstrated, and all material Objections fully weigh'd, and answer'd: the only, and, as it happened insurmountable Difficulty remaining, was the obstinate Averseness of great Part of the Citizens to alter their old Properties, and to recede from building their Houses again on their old Ground and Foundations; as also, the Distrust in many, and Unwillingness to give up their Properties, tho' for a Time only, into the Hands of publick Trustees and Commissioners, till they might be dispens'd to them again, with more Advantage to themselves, than otherwise was possible to be effected; for, such a Method was propos'd, that by an equal Distribution of Ground into Buildings, leaving out Churchyards, Gardens, &c. (which were to be removed out of the Town) there would have been sufficient Room both for the Augmentation of the Streets; Disposition of the Churches, Halls, and all publick Buildings; and to have given every Proprietor full Satisfaction; and although few Proprietors should happen to have been seated again directly upon the very same Ground they had possess'd before the Fire, yet no man would have been thrust any considerable Distance from it, but had been placed at least as conveniently, and sometimes more so, as to their own trades than before.'

Before the Fire began, the three Commissioners then appointed by the King to rebuild London—Wren, May and Pratt—were all concerned with the restoration of Old St Paul's; and the still larger task of erecting an entirely new cathedral proceeded abreast of the more general operations just described and of the rebuilding or restoration of the numerous City churches destroyed. Postponing any account of these important doings to later chapters, it remains to mention, at this point, sundry architectural commissions carried out by Wren (mainly outside London) during the period 1666-9.

His chapel at Emmanuel College, Cambridge, is barely mentioned in

Parentalia, but is a most attractive design (Plate IV). The Master of the College, Sancroft, became Dean of St Paul's in 1665 and Archbishop of Canterbury in 1678. He must have been in close contact with Wren in 1665-6 when the restoration, and then the rebuilding, of St Paul's was under discussion. He would also be familiar with Wren's new chapel at Pembroke College, then under construction (see p. 32). The first consultation with Wren must have taken place some time during 1666, for the new Master, John Breton, wrote to Wren on January 25, 1667, that he hoped to receive a promised model of the design as soon as it could be finished, 'but doubt whether we shall be able to lay foundations this year as we did intend', owing to a shortage of coal and the threat of war with Holland. On September 24 he wrote that he was 'much pleased with the Modell of our Chapell'. Evidently this was an elaborate affair, for an entry in the College accounts shows that it was made of oak and cost £13 5s., plus 7s. 8d. for carriage from London.

The existing college buildings then consisted of the remains of a former Dominican Priory which had been converted for collegiate purposes by Ralph Symons, an architect of some repute, late in the sixteenth century, when a chapel and new south block were added, separated from them by a wide open space. Another block of rooms was erected in 1634. Wren's task was to build a new chapel between the existing north and south blocks to form the east side of an open quadrangle, and he did this by means of an arcade with a gallery above, the west end of the chapel forming a central feature of the composition. The arcade is continuous, with thirteen arches in all, of which three form the lower part of the chapel façade. Above them is a corresponding range of thirteen mullioned windows. The gable-end of the chapel has Corinthian pilasters supporting a broken pediment with a central clock, and above it is a very bold cupola or lantern-turret, described by one critic as 'overpowering' and by another as 'ingenious'. The general effect of the composition is distinctly French, and most people find it attractive—a definite advance on the Pembroke Chapel design. Wren originally intended that the walls should be faced with red brick with stone dressings; but eventually they were faced with a thin skin of ashlar masonry. Internally the chapel is elegant and plain, with a fine plaster ceiling modelled by John Grove (also employed at Pembroke), and handsome woodwork (not designed by Wren) which was paid for by Sancroft, who contributed generously to the cost of the building and took a keen interest in its progress. The fine altar-painting by Amigoni was presented in 1734, after Wren's time. The contract for the building was dated February 17, 1668, and by 1672 the walls were finished, the roof fixed, and the plasterers at work. A delay of four years seems then to have occurred, but the internal woodwork was completed and the building consecrated on September 29, 1677. The total cost was £3,972. The stone was obtained from Ketton in Rutland.

Wren's report on the restoration of Salisbury Cathedral (1669) is mentioned by Aubrey in his *Brief Lives*, partly quoted in *Parentalia*, and given in full by the Wren Society (XI, pp. 21-6). He was invited to undertake this work by his old friend Seth Ward (see p. 18), now Bishop of Salisbury. According to Aubrey, 'he was at least a week about it, and a curious discourse it was: it was not above two sheetes'. As a matter of fact, it fills fourteen pages of beautifully neat and distinctive writing, runs to some 4,000 words, and is illustrated by excellent marginal sketches in ink, of joints, bolts, cramps, etc. The actual report is thus too long to quote fully here, but the characteristically pompous description of it from *Parentalia* is of some interest. 'The large and magnificent Cathedral-church of Salisbury discovering manifest Decays, and threatening Ruin, arising partly from the Want of true Judgment in the first Architect, partly from Injuries of Time and Weather, the lofty Spire especially having been much shaken and crackt by some Tempest and Storm of Lightning, required the Skill and Direction of the Surveyor for a speedy Amendment; in order to which, the faults of the Steeple of Necessity claimed the first consideration, because it could not be ruined alone, without drawing with it the Roof and Vaults of the Church. This therefore he took special Care to strengthen, and effectually secure, by braceing with Bandages of Iron wrought by Anchor-smiths, accustomed in great Work for Ships, and these so judiciously placed, and artificially performed, that it continues demonstrably stronger than at the first Erection. He had taken an accurate Survey in the Year 1669, of the whole Structure.' In the course of his long report, Wren commended the general design of the cathedral on artistic grounds, censured its architect for providing inadequate foundations and for not raising them above flood-level, and criticized the unsatisfactory 'poise' of the structure, which he regarded as a common defect in medieval building.

David Laing's Custom House, built in 1814-7 and sadly damaged by bombs in the Second World War, was preceded by Wren's building, described as follows in *Parentalia*: 'The Custom-house for the Port of London, situated on the South-side of Thames Street; was erected in 1668, adorned with an upper and lower Order of Architecture: in the latter are Stone Columns, and Entablement of the Tuscan Order; in the former are Pilasters, Entablature, and five Pediments of the Ionick Order. The West-end is elevated on Columns, forming a Piazza. The length of this Building is 189 Feet, Breadth in the Middle Part 27 Feet, at the West-end, &c, 60 Feet.' The Custom House took many years to build, and was burned down in 1718. An engraving of 1714 by John Harris, regarded as inaccurate in some respects, is reproduced in the Wren Society's Volume XVIII.

In 1668 also, Wren and Hooke submitted designs for new premises for the Royal Society. In a letter from Oxford dated June 7, 1668, to Dr Oldenburg, Secretary of the Society, Wren described a 'scetch' design that he had just handed to 'his honour Henry Howard of Norfolk'. The plan covered a site 100 feet by 30 feet. In the basement was 'a cellar and a fair laboratory', workshops, kitchen and a small larder. On the ground floor was 'a vestibule or passage hall' and a 'library and repository', and 'a parlour for the housekeeper'. A flight of stairs from the vestibule led up to 'the ante chamber of the great Roome'. This last was for meetings, and was 40 feet long and two storeys high, divided from the ante-chamber by a screen so that the two sections might be thrown into one for special occasions, thus making a room 55 feet long. A council room and secretary's office were also placed on this floor. There were two small rooms for the curators on the second floor, and a gallery overlooking the meeting-room. In the attic was a long gallery for experiments, small workshops, other subsidiary rooms, and 'a Cupolo for observations'. Wren suggested that, rather than erect a cheap building, all at once, it would be better to build half of it worthily, and estimated the cost of so doing at £2,000. He offered to have a model made. The Editor of the Wren Society adds that the project was abandoned in 1669. He remarks that the letter 'is of great importance from the possibility that it can be linked with the design, Plate 27 in Volume V, a façade of 90 feet. The plot of ground is given as 100 feet by 30 feet, but the overhang of the great cornice and perhaps passage way or free end space might make up the difference. If the identification can be accepted, it will show that this characteristic Wren work can be dated back to June 1668.' The plate in question shows the façade of a house of about 90 feet frontage, with two important storeys, a semi-basement and an attic. It is well drawn in ink and wash, with the ornamental details of sculpture (cherubs' heads, swags, etc.) skilfully indicated. It is indeed a 'characteristic Wren' design, with two ranges of large mullioned windows leaded in small panes, a fine modillion cornice, a rather steep roof—obviously flat on top—and a dignified projecting central feature with Corinthian pilasters and a curved pediment. Eight wide steps lead up to an imposing entrance doorway.

Wren's work at Trinity College, Oxford, has already been mentioned (see pp. 36-7), but, though his designs were begun in 1665, actual building operations did not commence till 1668. The cost was about £1,500. Two more blocks—western in 1682, southern in 1728—were added later, thus forming a three-sided open 'quadrangle'.

His appointment as Surveyor-General of His Majesty's Works was made in 1669, not in March 1668 as stated in *Parentalia*; for his predecessor, Sir John Denham, was then still alive. It has already been noted (see p. 32) that there is little or no evidence that Wren was appointed Assistant Surveyor in 1661, or at any time previous to 1669. The entry in *Parentalia* is as follows: 'On the 6th of March 1667-8, he receiv'd his Majesty's Warrant under the Privy-seal (in Confirmation of a Deputation from Sir John Denham, Knight of the Bath) to execute the Office of Surveyor-general of the Royal-works: Upon whose Decease in the same Month, his Majesty was pleas'd to grant him Letters Patents, under the Great-seal, to succeed in that Employment.' The fact is that Wren was appointed Deputy Surveyor in March 1669, over the heads of Hugh May and John Webb, both of whom were rival candidates with strong claims for the post. On March 5 Denham wrote to Lord Arlington: 'I find by my patent I have power to make a deputy, during my life; and according to the King's desire, intimated by the Duke of Buckingham, I have appointed Dr Christopher Wren my sole deputy. I desire his Lordship will obtain a warrant for him, he having been already sworn. I know of no verbal deputations, and if Mr May or anybody else pretends thereto, it is without my knowledge or consent.'

It will be remembered that Wren had been offered the reversion of Denham's post so long before as 1661-2 when he declined the Tangier appointment (see p. 30). John Webb (1611-72; see p. 28), a talented and professionally trained architect, had been assisting Denham at Charles II's palace or hospital at Greenwich and had also been offered the reversion of Denham's post, but Denham had opposed it, so that it never passed the Great Seal. Webb urged that he 'cannot now act under Dr Wren, who is by far his inferior, but if joined in the patent with him, will instruct him in the course of the Office of Works, of which he professes ignorance'. Hugh May (1622-84) was made Paymaster of the King's Works in 1660. He, too, was a most competent architect, and had been in charge of the vast overhaul of the royal palaces and buildings that followed the Restoration. He designed many important mansions. It has been aptly suggested that he was the typical first-class Civil Servant like Samuel Pepys, whereas his colleague and Wren's—Sir Roger Pratt—resembled Evelyn in being a gentleman of culture or 'Man of Taste'. The ubiquitous Pepys has something to say of these proceedings. '21 *March* 1669. Met with Mr May, who tells me the story of his being put by Sir John Denham's place, of Surveyor of the King's Works, who, it seems, is lately dead, by the unkindness of the Duke of Buckingham, who hath brought in Dr Wren: though, he tells me, he hath been his servant for twenty years together, in all his wants and dangers, saving him from want of bread by his care and management, and with a promise of having his help in his advancement, and an engagement under his hand for £1000, not yet paid, and yet the Duke of Buckingham is so ungrateful as to put him by, which is an ill thing, though Dr Wren is a worthy man. But he tells me the king is kind to him, and hath promised him a pension of £300 a year out of the Works: which will be more content to him than the place, which under their present wants of money, is a place that disobliges most people, not being able to do what they desire to their Lodgings.'

Sir John Denham was buried in Westminster Abbey on March 23, 1669. On December 15 of that year, the following Warrant was approved 'at the Court of Whitehall': 'The King to the Auditors of Imprest and other Officers, &c. concerned. On Feb. 4 1663, we set down orders relative to the Officers of our Works, granting them certain allowances, but their successors were not to have the same without further Warrant. We now declare that we have made Dr Chris. Wren, Surveyor of our Works, Hugh May, Controller, Phil Packer, Paymaster, and Rich Ryder, Master Carpenter, and they are to have the same allowances as heretofore granted, and a further increase, as expressed in our orders. Endorsed 24th Nov. 1669. This Warrant to be tendered to his Majesty for signature, upon view that the like was done before.' Wren thus added to his already engrossing activities a Crown appointment of great importance. His preferment to Webb and May was probably due to the discernment of the King who, by this time, had come to know him well in various capacities and had formed a high opinion of his ability; but doubtless Wren's friendship with Evelyn —a leading figure at Court—had some influence upon Charles II. Yet, even allowing for the maximum amount of social intrigue and wire-pulling, one may feel quite certain that Wren's own talents were the chief reason for the King's choice, and that Wren himself, however modest he may have been in some ways, lost no opportunity of furthering his own advancement.

Now, at 37 years of age, he was a famous man with an assured income and a brilliant future; and at this stage he married, at the Temple Church, Faith Coghill, then 33 years old, who lived to become Lady Wren when he was knighted in 1673, but died two years later. She bore him two sons: Gilbert, who died in infancy, and Christopher (1675-1747), who followed his father in architectural practice and collected the material for *Parentalia*. But for the younger Christopher's filial piety, we should not know as much as we do about his distinguished sire; unfortunately *Parentalia* is singularly deficient in human interest and tells us nothing of what was probably a very happy married life, presumably spent in Wren's official residence in Scotland Yard. We may assume that he had known his bride for many years, as she was the daughter of Sir John Coghill of Bletchington in Oxfordshire, the village in which Holder had his rectory, where, as we have seen, Wren spent so many of his youthful years. By a lucky chance, however, one of his love-letters to her has been preserved; and though it has been so often quoted by his various biographers that it may now be considered hackneyed, it must be given here because it gives a rare picture of the more intimate side of Wren's character. Apparently she must have dropped her watch into the sea and entrusted it to her betrothed for repair. He returned it to her with this delightful missive:

'Madam,—The artificer having never before mett with a drowned Watch, like an ignorant physician has been soe long about the cure that he hath made me very unquiet that your commands should be soe long deferred; however, I have sent the Watch at last and envie the felicity of it, that it should be soe neer your Side, and soe often enjoy your Eye, and be consulted by you how your Time shall passe while you employ your Hand in your excellent Workes.

'But have a care of it, for I put such a Spell into it that every Beating of the Ballance will tell you 'tis the Pulse of my Heart which labours as much to serve you, and more Trewly than the Watch; for the Watch, I believe, will sometimes lie, and sometimes perhaps be idle and unwilling to goe, having received soe much injury by being drenched in that briny Bath, that I dispair it should ever be a Trew Servant to you more.

'But as for me (unless you drown me too in my Teares) you may be confident that I shall never cease to be—Your most affectionate, humble servant,

'Christopher Wren.'

IV

DESIGNING
ST PAUL'S CATHEDRAL
1666 — 1675

THE date of Wren's first connection with St Paul's is uncertain, but is suggested by Dr Sprat's letter about the Tangier appointment (see p. 31), written about 1662; yet Wren's name is not mentioned in the list of notabilities forming the Commission of April 18, 1663, though Sir John Denham (Surveyor-General) and Thomas Chicheley (Master of the Ordnance) are named. After Sancroft's appointment as Dean of St Paul's in 1664, a report on the old cathedral was issued on May 3, 1665—signed by Denham, John Webb (see p. 28) and Edward Marshall—but again there is no mention of Wren, and Mr (afterwards Sir) Roger Pratt was the next 'expert' whose advice was taken. It was not until May 1, 1666, just before the Great Fire, that Wren issued a report, signed with his own name.

Old St Paul's must have been a magnificent building in its prime, with its lofty spire and its massive bulk dominating the medieval city studded with lesser towers and spires. Nothing of its glory now remains save some foundations of the cloister and chapter-house, but the splendid set of drawings by Benjamin Ferrey, exhibited in the Trophy Room, and other restorations by A. E. Henderson, enable us to picture it as it was. It stood near the middle of the little hill that rose some 50 feet above sea-level between the two ancient and now buried streams, the Fleet and the Walbrook. Tradition ascribes its foundation to the year A.D. 604, when St Augustine consecrated Mellitus as Bishop of London, according to Bede's *Ecclesiastical History* (II, iii); but there is mention of a much earlier Bishop of London, Restitutus, at the Council of Arles in A.D. 314. Bede adds that King Ethelbert, upon his conversion by Mellitus, 'built the church of St Paul in the City of London', but, if he did, no trace of it remains. That church, or a successor to it, was burnt and rebuilt in 962, and again in 1086 or 1087. The Norman bishop Maurice began rebuilding it in 1087; and that rebuilding, which continued for two centuries and more, formed the bulk of the great cathedral as Wren would know it in boyhood. Within fifty

IV CAMBRIDGE, EMMANUEL COLLEGE CHAPEL, EXTERIOR, FROM WREN'S DRAWING

V   OLD ST PAUL'S, WITH WREN'S CUPOLA, AND THE 'CASING' BY
INIGO JONES

years of its beginning, the new church was seriously damaged by fire. Most of it was finished, however, by 1240, including the tower and spire; but a new choir was built in 1258-1314, a new steeple in 1315 and a new south cloister in 1332. In its final form, by the middle of the fourteenth century, it was an enormous building, larger than any European cathedral except St Peter's (Rome), Milan and Seville, with a floor-area of nearly 82,000 square feet. It was bigger than any cathedral in England, and measured nearly 600 feet in length. The exact height of its lofty tower and spire is disputed, estimates varying from *c.* 220 feet to more than 260 feet for the tower and another 200 feet or more for the spire; but Stow gives the total height as 520 feet! Nave and choir were each twelve bays in length. The architectural style ranged, as one would expect, from late 'Norman' to late 'Decorated'. The general effect to our tolerant eyes would have been most impressive; but Wren, Evelyn and their sophisticated contemporaries regarded it as barbaric, rude and uncivilized. It had already been shorn of some of its glory before their time. 'Paul's Walk', as the nave was commonly called, had been since the fifteenth century a place of public resort and a sort of promenade for the riff-raff and the fashion of the town. Shakespeare so pictures it in *Henry the Fourth* and Evelyn described it as 'a den of thieves'. The splendid spire was destroyed by fire in 1561, and the chapter-house seriously damaged. There was a good deal of violence and iconoclasm in the cathedral during the Reformation years.

One way and another, it was in a sad state of disrepair and neglect when Inigo Jones was first consulted about it in 1620, but he did not begin its restoration till February 1634. This work lasted for some nine or ten years, when it was interrupted by the Civil War. He had then cased most of the building, except the steeple, with ashlar masonry at a cost of about £100,000, including the new portico described below (Plate V). All this work was greatly admired by his contemporaries, as appears from the following reference in John Webb's *Stone-Heng Restored*, published in 1655: 'Mr Jones, who was sole Architect . . . reduced the Body of it, from the Steeple to the West-end, into that Order and Uniformity we now behold; and by adding that magnificent Portico there, hath contracted the Envy of all Christendom upon our Nation, for a Piece of Architecture, not to be paralleled in these last Ages of the World.' Webb was, as has been mentioned already, Inigo Jones's pupil and admirer; but the discerning Evelyn is hardly less eulogistic when he calls it 'that beautifull portico (for structure comparable to any in Europe . . .)'. Sir Roger Pratt is equally laudatory, and traces the origin of its various details to specific monuments of ancient Rome. Wren regarded it as 'an intire and excellent Piece' which 'gave great Reputation to the Work in the first Repairs, and occasion'd fair Contributions': in other words, it had a good publicity value. Critics of today are less appreciative. Mr Gotch writes thus of it in his *Inigo Jones*: 'The design is of quite an ordinary description; the old traceried windows were replaced by large round-headed openings surmounted by a cornice; the buttresses gave way to shallow pilasters prolonged upwards to carry a ball; over the large windows were circular openings surrounded by an architrave. Against the south end of the transept he placed two tall, plain buttresses of large projection, reduced at the top by means of a curve to a size sufficient to support a square pinnacle.' Because the eastern part of the building remained unaltered, 'the play of fancy in the Gothic work, its delicacies of light and shade, its mixture of plain surfaces and intricate detail, were brought into harsh contrast with the severity and even, if one may say so, the clumsiness of some of the Classic work'. That judgment is supported by reference to Hollar's view of the south front, published in 1658. The same artist's view of the west front shows the new octastyle Corinthian portico which added 40 feet to the already great length of the cathedral. Mr Gotch accepts this as 'in itself a noble design', but adds that 'it had very little relation to the internal disposition of the building'. He might have gone further, and stated frankly that it was, like Jones's casing of the church itself, utterly incongruous with the Gothic building.

At one period during the Civil War, the nave served as a stable or cavalry barracks for the Parliamentary Army, and, during the Protectorate, the state of the cathedral grew steadily worse. Apart from a renewal of neglect and decay, 'Paul's Walk' became once more a public mart and a fashionable or notorious promenade. This was the state of affairs when Wren appeared upon the scene; and now we may refer again to the filial if sometimes unreliable pages of *Parentalia*: 'Upon the happy Restoration of King Charles II, it was determin'd to proceed in the Repairs of the old cathedral Church, which had been interrupted by the Great Rebellion; and Dr Wren was order'd to prepare proper Designs for that Purpose; his Predecessor Mr Inigo Jones had put the Quire, of a more modern Gothick Style . . . than the rest of the Fabrick, into very good Repair; he had proceeded to case great Part of the Outside with Portland-stone; had rebuilt the North and South-fronts; and also the West-front, with the Addition of a very graceful Portico of the Corinthian Order, built of large Portland-stone. The great Tower remained to be new cased Inside and Outside; and the whole Inside from the Choir to the West-door to be new cased, and reformed in some Measure. The Vaulting wanted much to be amended. . . . The first Business Dr Wren enter'd upon, previous to the forming Designs for the general Repairs, was to take an accurate Survey of the whole Structure, even to Inches; in the Prosecution of which, he was astonish'd to find how negligent the first Builders had been.'

On May 1, 1666, he handed to the Commissioners his report, which is of such interest and importance that I quote it here in full:

'Among the many Proposals that may be made to your Lordships concerning the Repairs of St Pauls some may possibly aim at too great Magnificence, which neither the Disposition nor Extent of this Age will probably bring to a Period. Others again may fall so low, as to think of piecing up the old fabrick, here with Stone, there with Brick & covering all faults with a coat of plaster leaving it still to the next Posterity as a further object of Charity. I suppose your Lordships may think fitt to take the middle way & to neglect nothing that may answer to a decent uniform Beauty or durable firmness in the fabrick & suitable to the Expense already laid out on the outside especially since it is a pile as much for ornament as use.

'For all the occasion either of a Quire, Consistory, Chapter House, Library, Court of Arches & preaching Auditory might have been supplied in less Room with less Expence & yet more Beauty: but then it had wanted of that Grandeur which exceeds all little Curiosity: this being an effect of Witt only, the other a monument of power & mighty zeal in our Ancestors to publick Works in those Times when the City contained neither a 5th part of the people nor a 10th part of the Wealth it now boasts of, I shall presume to enumerate as well the Defects of Comliness as of Firmness that the one may be reconciled with the other in restitution. And yet I should not propose any thing of meer Beauty to be added but where there is necessity of rebuilding & when it will be neer the same thing to perform it well as ill.

'First, it is evident by the Ruin of the Roof, that the Work was both ill-design'd and ill-Built from the Beginning; ill-design'd, because the Architect gave not Butment enough to counterpoise, and resist the Weight of the Roof from spreading the Walls; for, the Eye alone will discover to any Man, that those Pillars as vast as they are, even eleven Foot diameter, are bent outwards at least six Inches from their first position; which being done on both Sides, it necessarily follows that the whole Roof must first open in large and wide Cracks along by the Walls and Windows, and lastly drop down between the yielding Pillars. This bending of the Pillars was facilitated by their ill Building; for, they are only cased without, and that with small Stones, not one greater than a Man's Burden; but within is nothing but a Core of small Rubbish-stone, and much Mortar, which easily crushes and yields to the Weight; and this outward Coat of Freestone is so much torn with Age, and the Neglect of the Roof that there are few Stones to be found that are not moulder'd and Flaw'd away with the Salt-peter that is in them; an incurable disease, which perpetually throws off whatever Coat of Plaister is laid on it, and therefore not to be palliated.

'From hence I infer, that as the Outside of the Church was new flagg'd with Stone of larger size than before, so ought the Inside also; and in doing this it will be as easy to perform it, after a good Roman manner, as to follow the Gothick Rudeness of the old Design; and that, without placing the Face of the new Work in any Part many Inches farther out or in, than the Superficies of the old Work; or adding to the Expense that would arise were it perform'd the worse Way.

'This also may safely be affirmed not only by an Architect taking his measures from the precept & example of the Ancients, but by a Geometrician (this part being liable to a Demonstration that the Roof is and ever was too heavy for its Butment). And so any part of the old Roof now peeced will still but occasion further Ruine and the 2nd Ruine will much sooner follow than the first, since it is easier to force a thing already declining. It must so be either a timber roof plaistered (which in such Buildings where a little soak of wether is not presently discovered or remedied will soon decay) or else a thin & light shell of stone very geometrically proportioned to the strength of the Butment. The Roof may be brick if it be plaistered with Stucco which is a harder plaster that will it fall off with the Dripp of a few Winters, & which to this Day remains firm in many ancient Roman Buildings.

'The Middle Part is most defective both in Beauty and Firmness, without and within; for, the Tower leans manifestly by the settling of one of the ancient Pillars that supported it. Four new Arches were, therefore, of later Years, incorporated with the old ones, which hath straighten'd and hinder'd both the room, and the clear thorough View of the Nave, in that Part, where it had been more graceful to have been rather wider than the rest. The excessive Length of Building is no otherwise commendable, but because it yields a pleasing perspective by the continu'd optical diminution of the Columns; and, if it be cut off by Columns ranging within their fellows, the Grace that would be acquired by the Length is totally lost.

'Besides this Deformity of the Tower itself within there are others neer about it for the next Intercolumn in the Nave or Body of the Church is much less than all the Rest. Also the N & S wings have Isles only on the West Side, the other being originally shut up for the Consistory. Lastly the Intercolumn of Spaces between the Pillars of the Quire next adjoyning to the Tower are Very Unequal. Again on the outside of the Tower the

Buttresses that have been erected one on the back of another to secure 3 corners on the inclining sides (for the 4th wants a Buttress) are so irregular that upon the whole matter it must be concluded that the Tower from top to Bottom and the adjacent parts are such a heap of deformities that no Judicious Architect will think it corrigible by any Expense that can be laid out upon new dressing it, but that it will still remain unworthy the Rest of the Work, infirm and tottering: and for these Reasons (as I conjecture) was formerly resolved to be taken down.

'I cannot propose a better remedy than by cutting off the inner corners of the Cross, to reduce this middle part into a spacious Dome or Rotundo, with a cupola, or hemispherical roof, and upon the Cupola (for the outward ornament) a lantern with a spiring top, to rise proportionably, though not to that unnecessary height of the former Spire of Timber and Lead burnt by Lightening. By this Means the Deformities of the unequal Intercolumnations will be taken away, the Church, which is much too narrow for the heighth, render'd spacious in the Middle, which may be a very proper Place for a vast Auditory: the Outward appearance of the Church will seem to swell in the Middle by degrees, from a large Basis, rising from a Rotundo bearing a Cupola, and then ending in a Lantern: and this with incomparable more Grace in the Remoter aspect, than it is possible for the lean shaft of a Steeple to afford. Nor if it be rightly order'd, will the expence be much more than that of investing the Tower and Corners yet unfinish'd, with new Stone, and adding the old Steeple anew, the lead of which will be sufficient for a Cupola; and the same quantity of Ashler makes the corners outward, that would make them inward as they now are; And the Materials of the old Corners of the Ailes will be Filling Stone for the new Work; for I should not persuade the Tower to be pull'd down at first, but the new work to be built round it, partly because the expectations of Persons are to be kept up; for, many Unbelievers would bewail the loss of old Paul's Steeple, and despond if they did not see a hopefull Successor rise in its stead; and chiefly because it would save a great quantity of Scaffolding Poles; the scaffolds which are needful being fix'd from the old to the new work; and when the Tholus or inward Vault is to be laid, the Tower taken down to that Height will rest the centers of the Vault with great Convenience, and facilitate the planting of Engines for raising the Stones; and, after all is finish'd and settl'd, the Tower that is left may be taken clear away from within. All which can only from the Designs be perfectly understood. And for the Encouragement and Satisfaction of Benefactors that comprehend not readily Designs and Draughts on Paper, as well as for the inferior Artificers clearer Intelligence of their business, it will be requisite that a large and Exact Model be made; which will also have this use, that if the Work should be interrupted, or retarded, Posterity may proceed where the work was left off, pursuing still the same Design.

'And as the Portico built by Inigo Jones, being an intire and excellent Piece, gave great Reputation to the Work in the first Repairs, and occasion'd fair Contributions; so to begin now with the Dome may probably Prove the best Advice, being an absolute Piece of itself, and what will most likely be finished in our Time; will make by far the most splendid appearance; may be of Present use for the Auditory, will make up all the outward repairs perfect and become an Ornament to His Majesty's most excellent reign, to the Church of England, and to this great City, which it is pity in the Opinion of our Neighbours, should no longer continue the most unadorn'd of her Bigness in the world.

'In the meanwhile till a good quantity of Stone be provided, things of less expense but no less consequence ought to be regarded, Such as fixing again all the cramps that the Roof hath been spoiled off, covering all Timber from Weather, taking down the falling Roofs, searching the Vaults beneath, & securing them. And before the foundation be digged for the Dome, the Arches on which the Tower stands must be secured after a peculiar manner to be represented in the Designes.

'I shall crave leave to subjoin, that if there be use of Stucco, I have great Hopes, from some Experience already had, that there are English Materials to be brought by Sea at an easy Rate, that will afford as good Plaister as is any where to be found in the World; and that with the Mixture of cheaper Ingredients than Marble-meal, which was the old, and is now the Modern Way of Italy.

'The Proposer also (considering that high Buildings grow more and more expensefull as they rise, by reason of the Time and Labour spent in raising the Materials) takes this Occasion to acquaint your Lordships, that having had the Opportunity of seeing several Structures of greater Expence than this, while they were in raising conducted by the best Artists, Italian and French; and having had daily Conference with them, and observing their Engines and Methods, he promoted this geometrical Part of Architecture yet farther, and thinks the raising of Materials may yet be more facilitated, so as to save in lofty Fabricks, a very considerable part of the Time, and Labourers Hire.'

This forcible report was accompanied by a remarkable set of drawings, now in the collection at All Souls College, Oxford, and reproduced in the Wren Society's Volume I. They are signed by Wren, dated 1666, and are admirably drawn in Indian ink with some suggestion of relief by means of wash. The scheme consists in building a large new 'Rotundo' or dome on four massive piers at the crossing in the old church, in place of the existing tower. The dome itself has a circular plinth at the level of the main roof-ridge of the nave, then a colonnade of single Corinthian columns with tall rectangular windows between them. Above the entablature there is a wide stone band decorated with swags, then a rather steep fluted lead-covered dome, and above it an iron balustrade. The stone lantern has Doric pilasters, then a concave feature, and then an enormous pineapple, 68 feet high, terminating in a ball and cross. The whole dome rises from four tall arches between the main piers. The interior order of the crossing and the nave arcade has Corinthian pilasters, but the choir remains Gothic and unaltered. The design is far inferior to Wren's favourite 'Rejected' Design or to the building as ultimately erected; indeed the whole scheme is some-what amateur and the pineapple is its worst feature (Plate V.)

Some four months later, on August 27, 1666 (five days before the Great Fire began), Wren met the Commissioners to discuss his rather startling proposals on the site. Among those present was John Evelyn, who describes the gathering in his *Diary*: 'I went to St Paule's Church, where with Dr Wren, Mr Prat, Mr May, Mr Thos. Chichley, Mr Slingsby, the Bishop of London, the Deane of St Paule's [Sancroft] and several expert workmen, we went about to survey the generall decays of that ancient and venerable church, and to set down in writing the particulars of what was fit to be don, with the charge thereof, giving our opinion from article to article. Finding the maine building to recede outwards, it was the opinion of Mr Chichley and Mr Prat[1] that it had ben so built *ab origine* for an effect in perspective, in regard of the height; but I was, with Dr Wren, quite of another judgment, and so we entered it; we plumb'd the uprights in severall places. When we came to the steeple, it was deliberated whether it were not well enough to repair it onely on its old foundation, with reservation to the 4 pillars; this Mr Chichley and Mr Prat were also for, but we totaly rejected it, and persisted that it requir'd a new founda-tion, not onely in reguard of the necessitie, but for that the shape of what stood was very meane, and we had a mind to build it with a noble cupola, a forme of church-building not as yet known in England, but of wonder-full grace: for this purpose we offer'd to bring in a plan and estimate, which, after much contest, was at last assented to, and that we should nominate a Committee of able workemen to examine the present

[1] It is known that Sir Roger Pratt had hopes of rebuilding St Paul's himself. (See G. Webb's *Wren*, p. 56.)

foundation. This concluded, we drew all up in writing, and so went with my Lord Bishop to the Deanes.'

The tale of the Fire has been briefly told in a previous chapter (pp. 44-46), where mention was made of the damage sustained by Old St Paul's. The story from that date until Wren's final design obtained the King's approval in 1675 is involved, but its stages may be followed in contemporary documents, most of which have been published by the Wren Society. Wren made another visit to the ruins on October 4, 1666, in company with May, Pratt, Hooke, Mills and Jarman; and some time between then and the following February wrote another report on the state of Old St Paul's after the Fire:

'What Time and Weather had left entire in the old, and Art in the new repair'd parts of the great Pile of S. Pauls, the late Calamities of the Fire hath so weakened and defac'd that it now appeares like some Antique Ruine of 2000 years continuance; and to repaire it sufficiently will be like the mending of the Argo-navis, scarce anything will at last be left of the old. The first Decaies of it were great from severall Causes. First, from the original Building itself. For it was not well shap'd or design'd for the firm bearing of its owne Vault, how massy soever the Walls seem'd to be (as I formerly show'd in another Paper) nor were the Materialls good; for it seem'd to have been built out of the Stone of some other antient Ruines, the Walls being of 2 severall sorts of Freestone, and those small; and the Coar within was Raggestone, cast in rough with Mortar and Putty, which is not a durable way of Building, unless there had been that peculiar sort of Banding with some thorowe Courses, which is necessary in this kind of Filling Work, but was omitted in this Fabrick. This Accusation belongs chiefly to the West, North, and South Parts. The Quire was of later and better worke, not inferiour to most Gothick Fabricks of that Age. The Tower, though it had the effects of an ill manner of building, yet it was more carefully Banded and cramped with much Iron.

'A second reason of the Decaies, which appeared before the last Fire, was in probabilitie the former Fire, which consum'd the whole Roof in the Reign of Q. Elizabeth. The fall of Timber then upon the Vault, was certainly one maine cause of the Cracks which appear'd in the Vault, and of the spreading out of the Walls above 10 inches, in some places, from their true Perpendicular, as it now appears more manifestly. The giving out of the Walls was endeavoured to be corrected by the Artist of the last Repaires [Inigo Jones], who plac'd his new case of Portland Stone truely perpendicular, and if he had proceeded with casing it within, the whole had been tolerably corrected. But now, even the New work is gone away from its Perpendicular, allso by this second fall of the Roofe in this last Fire. This is most manifest in the North West Isle.

'The second Ruines are they that have put the Restauration past Remedy, the effect of which I shall briefly enumerate:

'First, the Portick is totally depriv'd of that excellent beauty and strength which Time alone and Weather could have no more overthrown than the naturall Rocks, so great and good were the materials and so skilfully were they lay'd after a true Roman manner. But so impatient is the Portland Stone of fire, that many Tonns of Stone are scaled off and the Columns flaw'd quite through.

'Next, the South West corner of one of the vast Pillars of the body of the Church, with all it supported, is fallen. All along the body of the Church the Pillars are more given out than they were before the Fire, and more flaw'd towards the bottome by the burning of the Goods belowe and the Timber fallen.

'This further spreading of the Pillars within hath also carried out the Walls of the Isles, and reduc'd the circular Ribbs of the Vaults of the Isles to be of a Form which to the eye appears distorted, and compress'd, especially in the North West Isle of the Body of the Church.

'The Tower, and the parts next about it, have suffered the least by reason that the Walls, lying in form of a Cross, give a firm and immoveable Buttment each to the other, and they stand still in their position and support their Vaults, which shews manifestly that the fall of the Timber alone could not break the Vaults, unless where the same concussion had force enough to make the Walls allso give out.

'And this is the reason of the great Desolacion which appears in the new Quire, for there the falling Vaults, in spite of all the small Buttresses, hath broken them short or deslocated the stouter of them, and, over throwing the North Walls and Pillars and consequently the Vaults of the North East Isle, hath broken open the Vaults of St Faith's (though those were of very great strength), but irresistible in the force of so many 1000 Tonns, augmented by the height of the Fall.

'Having shown in part the deplorable Condicioun of our Patient, we are to consult the Cure if possibly Art may effect it. And herein we must imitate the Physitian, who, when he finds a totall decay of Nature, bends his skill to a Palliation, to give Respite for a better settlement of the Estate of the Patient. The question is then Where best to begin this kind of practise, that is to make a Quire for present use.

'It will worst of all be effected in the New Quire, for there the Walls and Pillars, being fallen, it will cost a large sume to restore them to their former Height, and, before this can be effected, the very substruction and Repaire of St Faith's will cost so much that I shall but fright this Age with the Computacion of that which is to be done in the Darke, before anything will appear for the Use desired.

'The old Quire seems to some a convenient Place and that which will be the most easily affected, because the Vault there lookes firme or easily reparable as far as to the Place where was once the Old Pulpit. But the Designe will not be without very materiall Objections. First, the place is very short, and the little between the stone Skreen and the Breach is only capable of a little Quire, not of an Auditory.

'And if the Auditory be made without, yet, Secondly, all the adjacent places are under the Ruines of a fallen Tower, which every day throws off smaller Scales, and in Frosts will yield such showers of the outside Stones (if no greater parts come downe with the Tempests) that the new Roofs (yet to be made) will be broken if no further mischiefs ensue. Thirdly, you are to make such a dismall Procession through the Ruines to come thither that the very passage will be a Penance. Fourthly, this cannot be effected without considerable expense of making of particion walls to the topp to sever this part on every side from the Ruines, and covering with Timber and Lead these 4 short parts of the Cross next the Tower, and covering the Tower also, that is, if you make Room for the Auditory as well as the Quire, the Quire itself being very little.

'These waies being found inconvenient and expensefull, either of taking out a part, where the old Quire was, or where the new Quire is, with the parts west, north, and south next the Tower as far as the Vaults stand; it remains that we seek it in the Body of the Church. And this is that which I should humbly advise as the properest and cheapest way of making a sufficient Quire and Auditory after this manner.

'I would take the Lesser North and South doors for the Entrances and leaving two Intercolumnations Eastward and 3 or 4 Westward, I would there make particion Walls of the fallen stone upon the place. The last part above the Doores may be contriv'd into a Quire, the West into an Auditory. I would lay a Timber Roof as low as the botoms of the upper Windows with a flat fretted Ceiling. The Lead saved out of the burning will more than cover it. Of Iron and Pavement there is several for all Uses. The Roof lying low, will not appear above the Walls, and since we cannot mende this great Ruine we will not disfigure it, but that it shall have its full motive to work, if possible, upon this or the next Ages; and yet within it shall have all convenience and Light (by turning the second storey of arches into Windows) and a beauty desirable to the next two

74

Centuries of years, and yet prove so cheap that between three and four thousand pounds shall effect it in one summer.

'And having with this ease obtained a present Cathedrall, there will be time to consider of a more durable and noble Fabrick, to be made in the Tower and Eastern parts of the Church, when the minds of men, now contracted to many Objects of necessary charge, shall by God's blessing be more widened, after a happy Restoration, both of the Buildings and Wealth of the City and Nation. In the meanewhile to derive, if not a streame, yet some little drills[1] of Charitie this way, or at least to preserve that already obtained from being diverted, it may not prove ill advised to seem to begin something of this new Fabrick. But I confesse this cannot well be put in Execution without taking downe all that part of the Ruines which whether it be yet seasonable to do, wee must leave to our Superiours.'

Within a year after Wren had presented this bold and remarkable scheme of restoration to the authorities, the need for providing some temporary facilities for worship in the ruined building had become urgent, and on January 15, 1668, the Commission ordered the formation of a temporary choir at the *west* end, but Wren's name is not mentioned. 'Whereas the dreadful calamity of Fire . . . hath fallen . . . so heavy upon the Cathedrall Church of St Paul, and so far disturbed, and set back the method of its repaires, that we cannot, as the state of affairs now is, hope suddenly to proceed in that great work as was intended. It being thought necessary in the mean tyme (till it shall please God to bless us with a more favourable juncture for doing something more lasting and magnificent), that some parte of that venerable pile be forthwith restored to its religious use, where it may be done with the least expense of tyme and treasure; and it being also apparent that the whole east parte of that Cathedrall is under greater desolation than the rest . . .; the restoration of which . . . will both take up more tyme and cost far more money than the whole work intended to serve the present necessity will require: It was this day ordered, that a Choir and Auditory for present use be forthwith set out, repaired, and finished (if it may be) in the course of the next summer, in the body of the Church between the West end and the second pillars above the little North and South dores . . . and that the whole management of this Work bee left to the care of' [seven persons, mostly bishops] 'and the Dean and Chapter of the said Cathedrall Church . . . to be by them pursued and finished with all convenient speed, in such method, by and with the assistance of such artists, officers, and workmen, as they shall think fitt to consult and employ therein.'

[1] 'Drills' in Wren Society's Volume, but 'rills' seems to me more probable. M. S. B.

Then followed some months during which workmen were busily engaged in clearing rubble from the cathedral, and shoring up such portions as were dangerous. On April 25, 1668, Dean Sancroft wrote to Wren:

'Sir, as he said of old, *Prudentia est quaedam divinatio*, so Science (at the Height you are Master of it) is prophetic too. What you whisper'd in my Ear at your last coming hither, is now come to pass. Our Work at the West-end of St Paul's is fallen about our Ears. Your quick Eye discern'd the Walls and Pillars gone off from their Perpendiculars, and I believe other Defects too, which are now expos'd to every common Observer.

'About a Week since, we being at Work about the third Pillar from the West-end on the South-side, which we had new cased with Stone, where it was most defective, almost up to the Chapitre, a great Weight falling from the high Wall, so disabled the Vaulting of the Side-aile by it, that it threaten'd a sudden Ruin, so visibly, that the Workmen presently remov'd; and the next night the whole Pillar fell, and carry'd Scaffolds and all to the very Ground.

'The second Pillar (which you know is bigger than the rest) stands now alone, with an enormous Weight on the Top of it; which we cannot hope should stand long, and yet we dare not venture to take it down.

'This Breach has discover'd to all that look on it, two great Defects in Inigo Jones's Work; one, that his new case of Stone in the upper Walls (massy as it is) was not set upon the upright of the Pillars, but upon the core of the Groins of the vaulting: the other, that there were no Keystones at all to tie it to the old Work; and all this being very heavy with the Roman Ornaments on the Top of it, and being already so far gone outward, cannot possibly stand long. In fine, it is the Opinion of all Men, that we can proceed no farther at the West-end. What we are to do next is the present Deliberation, in which you are so absolutely and indispensably necessary to us, that we can do nothing, resolve on nothing without you.

''Tis therefore, that in my Lord of Canterbury's Name, and by his Order (already, as I suppose, intimated to you by the Dean of Christ-Church), we most earnestly desire your Presence and Assistance with all possible Speed.

'You will think fit, I know, to bring with you those excellent Draughts and Designs you formerly favour'd us with; and in the mean Time, till we enjoy you here, consider what to advise, that may be for the Satisfaction of his Majesty, and the Whole Nation; an Obligation so great and so publick, that it must be acknowledg'd by better Hands than those of—

'Your very affectionate Friend, and Servant,

'W. Sancroft.'

Then comes another interval, during which argument continued as to the respective merits of restoration and rebuilding. On July 2, another letter from Sancroft to Wren hints that some immediate action is contemplated: 'The Designs of such a Quire at least, as may be a congruous Part of a greater and more magnificent Work to follow.'

On July 25 came a Royal Warrant, authorizing the preliminary operations for the building of the new choir:

'Whereas upon strict Survey and Examination of the Ruines of the Cathedrall Church of St Paul, London, by knowing and experienced Artists it is found that the Walls now standing are in all Parts so decayed by the late Fire, that they are judged altogether insufficient for bearing another Roof or any new Work. It is therefore our express Will and Pleasure that immediate care be had for taking downe the Walls, and clearing the ground to the Foundation of the East End, the old Quire, and the Tower in such Manner as shall be judged sufficient to make room for a new Quire, of a faire and decent Fabrick, neare or upon the old Foundations; and also that Care be taken of the Cornishes, Ashlers and such parts of the Former towards the West, as shall be deem'd usefull for the new Fabrick, lest they be spoil'd by the Fall of more of the Walls which seeme to threaten immediate Ruine. And for so doing this shall be your Warrant.'

A news-letter of July 21, 1668, states that 'several "artists" have been consulted', and that the estimated cost of a new choir is £40,000. For five years from July 1668, there is an almost complete break in the story, due in some degree at least to financial stringency, for funds did not yet justify any substantial rebuilding project at St Paul's. An entry in the cathedral accounts for September 1, 1669, as to the purchase of gunpowder from Oxford, shows that demolition was then in progress, and indeed it continued till 1674. *Parentalia* gives some description of the procedure: 'Scaffolding was rais'd for Search of the Walls, and cutting the Remainder of the unmelted Lead from the high Roof, and other parts of the Church. In which Employment, as also in digging up the melted Lead, clearing the Rubbish, taking down the Remainder of the vaulted Roof and Walls, with the greatest Part of the Tower-steeple, digging up the Floors, sorting the Stone, and carrying it to several Places . . . & building new offices for the Work, no less than two Years were spent. The pulling down of the Walls, being about 80 Feet high, and 5 Feet thick, was a great and troublesome Work: the Men stood above, and work'd them down with Pickaxes, whilst Labourers below moved away the Materials that fell, and dispersed them into Heaps: the want of Room made this Way slow, and dangerous, and some Men lost their Lives; the Heaps grew steep and large; and yet this was to be done before the Masons could begin to lay the Foundations.' It is then explained that most of the rubble, which was Kentish Rag, was sold to the City for street-paving; and that Wren had to carry his sight-lines, for his survey, over and around the great mounds of rubble. 'Thus he proceeded, gaining every day more Room, till he came to the middle Tower that bore the Steeple; the Remains of the Tower being near 200 Feet high, the Labourers were afraid to work above, thereupon he concluded to facilitate this Work by the Use of Gunpowder.' Wren used 18 lb. of gunpowder to remove the north-west pillar of the tower; and, as the explosion also brought down two arches of the adjoining arcade, the total weight of stone dislodged by this single explosion was 3,000 tons, thus effecting an immense saving in dangerous manual work. As he had to leave London soon afterwards, he left the exploding of the next 'mine', as he called it, to his deputy, who carried it out carelessly, with the result that one lump of stone flew into the room of a neighbouring house where some women were working, and caused much public alarm. So 'he was importun'd to use no more Powder, and was so directed also by his Superiors; tho' with due Caution it might have been executed without Hazard, and sav'd much Time and Money. He then turn'd his Thoughts to another Method; to gain Time, prevent much Expence, and the endangering of Men's Lives; and that was, to make an Experiment of that ancient Engine in War, the Battering-ram.' He used a ram of wood, about 40 feet long, iron-tipped, with fifteen men on each side of it.

Meanwhile he was busy in preparing designs for an entirely new cathedral. For the sake of clearness here, the design of May 1666, already described (pp. 67-71), will be called the 'Pre-Fire design'; and the next in order the 'New Model', which was being made in the summer of 1670, as appears from references in the Cathedral Accounts. A news-letter of November 10, 1672, mentions it as 'a most curious Model' made by Wren to the orders of the King. On November 2, 1672, Hooke records in his diary that he saw it, and that it had been already approved by his Majesty. In the Wren Society's Volume XIII, a somewhat battered wooden model, now exhibited in the Trophy Room at St Paul's, is identified with this 'New Model' and is fully illustrated and described. This 'New Model' design of 1670-2 was conceived on a much smaller scale than those which followed it, and is presumed to have had at its western end a spacious domed vestibule, within which rose a flight of steps giving access to the interior above burial vaults; and with entrances to the vestibule on north, south and west. (All this portion is missing on the model.) The interior of the church is a simple open rectangle without aisles, more like the Protestant 'meeting-house plan' favoured by Nonconformists in their earlier buildings than the orthodox Gothic cathedral plan, but with one unusual feature. The space beneath the wide galleries on north and south was not open to the body of the church but was occupied by covered colonnades open to the churchyard, thus forming a circulation-passage round the central mass of burial vaults and replacing the public space provided by Inigo Jones's portico at the west end of Old St Paul's. The internal arcades on the line of the gallery-fronts probably carried a continuous barrel-vault, as at St James's Piccadilly (see p. 129). Modest as the scheme was, it must be remembered that a very large new cathedral was not then regarded as 'practical politics'; but, in thus subordinating his aspirations to practical requirements, Wren did lay himself open to criticism.

This must have been the model seen in July 1673 by Sir Roger Pratt, when he recorded in his *Diary* his 'Objections against the Model of St Paul's standing in the Convocation House there as its now designed by Dr Renne, July 12, 1673, according as it offered it selfe to me upon the shorte and confused vewe of ¼ of an hour onely. . . . *Planta*. First as to the forme of it. Its wholly different from that of all the cathedrals of the whole Worlde besides, this being one long continued body only; all others besides, in the form of a Cross either more or lesse. 2ndly, That the two side aisles are wholly excluded from the Nave of the Church and turned into uselesse Porticos without, instead of adding a spacious gracefulnesse to the Church within. 3rdly. In setting the Cupola at the west end of the Church instead of over the middle of the cross aisles, and then separating the whole diameter of this Cupola from the Nave of the Church, as I remember, which hath most causelessly and ungracefully shortened it. 4thly. Making several Porticos all of the same fashion at the western ende of the Church whereas there seemeth to be no necessary use of any more than one.

'*The upright*. As to this I had scarce time to vewe it, and so can say but little to it, but see that since (as I remember) there is a double Portico, as it were one over the other, the lowermost looking from the Church, the uppermost into it, whither all the side lights of the Nave come not through that upper Portico which, if so, then how dark and ungraceful will the Nave be. 2ndly. How ungracefully and weakly do the Lucarnes stand which are over the Portico of the East end &c. *Vide* with what basement the Church raised. What ornament of the windows to Porticos &c. Ten windows, as I remember, make the whole length of the Church, the Architects in such case usually make an odd one. That which I

observed in the Cupola was that the Pillars stood two thick, and consequently the Windows between much too crowded and too plain; being
without all ornament: and that there were no Lucarnes in the Arch of it,
and contrary to all custom, which must needes darken it.'

Parentalia has this to say about the model: 'The Surveyor was at first
directed to contrive a Fabrick of moderate Bulk, but of good proportion;
a convenient Quire, with a Vestibule, and Porticoes, and a Dome conspicuous above the Houses. A long Body with Ailes was thought impertinent, our Religion not using Processions. It was to be vaulted underneath for Burials, that the Pavement might be preserved. A Model in
Wood was made of this Church, which tho' not so large, would have been
beautiful, and very fit for our Way of Worship; being also a convenient
Auditory . . . and by the help of the Vestibule, it was capable of any grand
Ceremony. It had Porticoes on the outside, which might prevent Dis-
turbance within. This was applauded by Persons of good Understanding,
as containing all that was necessary for the Church of a Metropolis; of a
beautiful Figure, and of an Expence that reasonably might have been compass'd; but being contriv'd in the Roman Stile, was not so well understood
& relished by others, who thought it deviated too much from the old
Gothick Form of cathedral Churches, which they had been used to see
and admire in this Country. Others observed it was not stately enough,
and contended, that for the Honour of the Nation, and City of
London, it ought not to be exceeded in Magnificence, by any Church in
Europe.'

Records prove that in September 1673 Wren had begun work on the
so-called 'Great Model', his third completed design (Plate VI); and on
November 12 of the same year it was approved by the King in a very
lengthy document appointing a huge number of Commissioners and containing the following important paragraph: 'We have caused several
Designs to that Purpose to be prepared by Dr Christopher Wren, Surveyor-General of all our Works and Buildings, which We have seen, and
one of which We do more especially approve, and have commanded a
Model thereof to be made after so large and exact a Manner, that it may
remain as a perpetual and unchangeable Rule and Direction for the Conduct of the whole Work.' Yet this splendid conception has come to be
known as the 'Rejected Design', because it did not please the Duke of
York or the ecclesiastics, and was superseded by another design within
two years.

The 'Great Model' well deserves its name, for it is probably the largest,
most elaborate, and most highly finished example of architectural model-

VI   ST PAUL'S CATHEDRAL: THE 'GREAT MODEL'

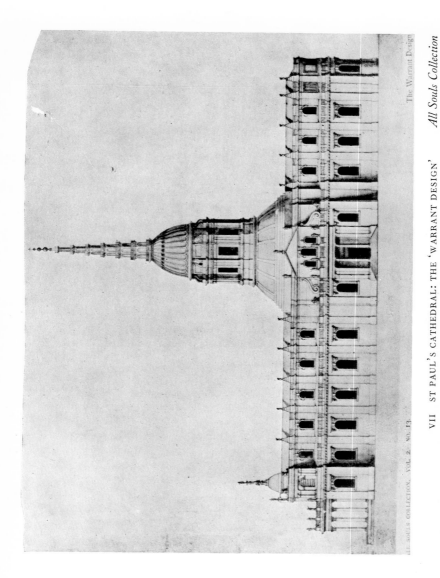

The Warrant Design

VII   ST PAUL'S CATHEDRAL: THE 'WARRANT DESIGN'   *All Souls Collection*

making ever constructed. It is now displayed in the Trophy Room at St Paul's. It is made of oak to the scale of ½ inch to 1 foot, measures about 20 feet in length, and shows all the carving, gilding and other ornamental work. As it is raised on a stand about 5 feet high, visitors can go inside it to examine the interior, which is electrically illuminated. The original cost in 1673 was *c*. £600, equivalent to perhaps ten times as much today. This 'Great Model' or 'Rejected Design' was Wren's own favourite. Again quoting *Parentalia*:

'After this, in order to find what might satisfy the World, the Surveyor drew several Sketches meerly for Discourse-sake, and observing the Generality were for Grandeur, he endeavour'd to gratify the Taste of the Connoiseurs and Criticks with something coloss and beautiful, with a Design antique & well studied, conformable to the best Stile of the Greek and Roman Architecture. Some Persons of Distinction, skill'd in Antiquity and Architecture, express'd themselves much pleased with the Design, and wished to see it in a Model. The Surveyor comply'd with their Desires as well as his own and made a very curious large Model in Wood, accurately wrought, and carv'd with all its proper Ornaments, consisting of one Order only, the Corinthian (as at St Peter's in Rome) ... The Surveyor in private Conversation, always seem'd to set a higher value on this Design, than any he had made before or since . . . but as yet nothing could be fully resolv'd upon; the Chapter, and some others of the Clergy thought the Model not enough of a Cathedral-fashion; to instance particularly, in that the Quire was design'd circular.'

Wren is said to have actually wept when this design was finally rejected, and we can sympathize with his feelings, for it is a noble conception, entirely logical, and no critics of importance have ever denied its splendour or its beauty. It shows a thorough understanding of Roman or Renaissance principles and a masterly confidence. It has been described as a 'Greek cross plan': more precisely it is a square of about 320 feet, with the four angles cut off on a quadrant described from the points of the square. There are no aisles, the fine central dome being surrounded by an ambulatory with lesser domes. There is something Baroque about the whole effect, alike in the plan, the impressive interior, and the splendid grouping. To this symmetrical block Wren added a large marthex with a second dome, and an octastyle Corinthian portico facing Ludgate Hill, thus repeating Inigo Jones's portico of forty years earlier, which, as has been mentioned already, was greatly admired. Wren's western portico seems hardly in keeping with the rest of the scheme, but the narthex did produce the effect of a nave, in the absence of the usual plan of nave, transepts and choir.

Wren ignored this ecclesiastical tradition of planning as completely as he had discarded Gothic tradition throughout his design: it was, indeed, to be a building in 'the good Roman manner'. It was, moreover, an essentially 'Protestant' design intended to provide a spacious auditorium for preaching rather than facilities for ritual processions, in spite of its obvious inspiration from 'papist' Rome. Finally, it was above everything a glorification of the dome as an external and internal feature. That particular dome would have been slightly larger in diameter and much less in height than that of the existing cathedral,[1] and the church—even including the narthex—would have been somewhat less in length.[2] In certain respects the design is akin to that of the famous church of S. Maria della Salute at Venice, begun in 1631 but not finished till 1680. The model dome, if inferior to the masterpiece actually built, shows a great advance upon Wren's amateurish 'Pre-Fire Design'; and in fact is far superior to the 'Warrant Design' which followed it and was approved in 1675 (see below). The exterior of the 'Great Model' has a lofty podium and plinth, a single order of Corinthian pilasters, and a tall attic stage above the entablature.

Yet even among modern admirers of the design, as well as among its clerical critics at the time when it faced their attacks, there are some who recognize its shortcomings from the point of view of accepted Anglican ritual. Wren had assumed, perhaps too readily, that preaching was the chief function of cathedral services, and that the current discouraging of religious processions was likely to remain permanent. He also underestimated the strong clerical predilection for the traditional long choir. By risking these assumptions, he was able to secure a view of the dome (but not of the altar) from all parts of the interior; whereas any lengthening of the arms of the cross would fail to provide such a view, as one can realize on entering St Paul's today from the west door. Miss Milman, as befits a daughter of the Deanery, observes in her life of Wren (p. 118) that 'the fact that the High Altar would have been invisible to all but a fraction of the congregation is a fault for which no vistas right or left would have atoned'.

The addition of the narthex proved inadequate as a sop to the clergy, and the debate dragged on before the Commission. Funds were now beginning to accumulate as the new tax on coal took effect, one-quarter

[1] Diameter of dome: model 120 feet; existing cathedral 112 feet. Height of dome: model 180 feet; existing cathedral 281 feet; 363 feet to top of cross.

[2] Length of church overall: model *c.* 490 feet; existing cathedral 513 feet. Breadth of church overall: model *c.* 320 feet; existing cathedral 248 feet.

of the proceeds being allotted to St Paul's and the residue to the City parish-churches. The need to make a decision and start rebuilding was becoming urgent. At this point let *Parentalia* take up the tale:

'The Surveyor then turned his Thoughts to a Cathedral-form (as they called it) but so rectified, as to reconcile, as near as possible, the Gothick to a better Manner of Architecture; with a Cupola, and above that, instead of a Lantern, a lofty Spire, and long Porticoes. King Charles approved these Designs, & that there might be no further Interruption, the Warrant . . . was issued.' It was dated May 14, 1675, and runs as follows: 'Whereas We have been informed that a Portion of the Imposition laid on Coals, which by Act of Parliament is appointed and set apart for the rebuilding of the cathedral Church of St Paul, in our capital City of London, doth at present amount to a considerable Sum, which, though not proportionable to the Greatness of the Work, is notwithstanding sufficient to begin the same; and, with all the Materials, and other Assistances, which may probably be expected, will put a new Quire in great Forwardness; and whereas among divers Designs which have been presented to Us, We have particularly pitched upon one, as well because We found it very artificial, proper, and useful; as because it was so ordered that it might be built and finished by Parts: We do therefore by these Presents, signify Our Royal Approbation of the said Design, beginning with the East-end, or Quire, and accomplishing the same with the present Stock of Money, and such Supplies as may probably accrue, according to the Tenor of the Commission to you directed; and, for so doing, this shall be your Warrant.' It will be noticed that one argument advanced in favour of this new design is that it can be built by instalments, whereas Wren's 'Great Model' certainly could not unless the erection of the narthex were to be deferred, and that expedient would hardly appeal to the clergy.

Modern critical opinion on this so-called 'Warrant Design'—Wren's third project for an entirely new cathedral, or fourth if one includes his 'Pre-Fire Design'—is uniformly unfavourable; and no wonder! The conception is so feeble, so bizarre, whether compared with the cathedral as we see it today or with the 'Great Model', that some of his biographers have tried to explain it away as a hoax, as the result of a fit of bad temper or of overstrain—a rather poor joke thrown at the King under mental stress, in the hope that its very absurdity would ensure its rejection. It is suggested that, still smarting under the discarding of his pet 'Great Model' scheme, he submitted this 'Warrant Design' to Charles in order to prove how ridiculous were the requirements of the clergy (and the Duke of

York) when set out on paper. But Wren was not given to jokes or hoaxes —his whole career disproves that idea, and he was a very hard-working and indeed overworked man. Unfortunate as are some features of the 'Warrant Design' (Plate VII), the elaboration of the drawings suggests a most careful and cold-blooded consideration of the problem, certainly nothing to indicate a passing fit of spleen. In plan, the design does not differ materially from that of the present building. In course of building, Wren slightly altered the subdivision of the nave into bays, shortened the two transepts by one bay each, and added the two western chapels with the rooms over. The glaring faults of the 'Warrant Design' are to be found in the dome and the West front. The former is utterly unworthy of the creator of the 'Great Model' or the present dome. Its whole outline, from its awkward springing from its base in the form of a convex roof, up through the drum which lacks horizontal emphasis, to the ugly 'minaret' or 'telescope' (two appropriate terms used by critics) which forms a lantern and which Wren subsequently adopted more successfully at St Bride's (see p. 119) is lamentable. The west front is evidently a re-miniscence of Inigo Jones, with a decastyle Corinthian portico, a pedi-mented gable above flanked by two enormous and clumsy Baroque scrolls, and two feeble western towers.

This, then, was the design approved by the Royal Warrant of May 14, 1675. Again quoting *Parentalia*: 'From that Time, the Surveyor resolved to make no more Models, or publickly expose his Drawings, which (as he had found by Experience) did but lose Time, and subjected his Business many Times to incompetent Judges. By these Means, at last, the Scheme of the present mighty Structure (different in some Manner from the former, & preferable in his Majesty's own Judgment, upon After-thoughts) was no sooner concluded on, and order'd by his Majesty, but begun and prosecuted by his Surveyor, with Vigour, in the Year 1675. And the King was pleas'd to allow him the Liberty in the Prosecution of his Work, to make some Variations, rather ornamental, than essential, as from Time to Time he should see proper; and to leave the Whole to his Management.'

No time was lost after approval had been given to the 'Warrant Design', and the foundation-stone was duly laid on June 21, 1675; but there is some doubt about this important event. Elmes (p. 353), quoting as his authority Clutterbuck's *History of Hertfordshire* (I, 168, published in 1815), states that the stone was laid by Wren himself, assisted by his master-mason Thomas Strong. Sir Reginald Blomfield, in his *Short History of Renaissance Architecture in England* (1900, p. 129), says that 'the first stone of St Paul's was laid in 1675 by Henchman, Bishop of London, who died in the same year'; but does not cite any authority. *Parentalia* mentions the year, 1675, but nothing else; and the Wren Society's exhaustive volumes are no more informative. The Cathedral Accounts, published in those volumes, mention no formal ceremony.

V

ST PAUL'S CATHEDRAL
AFTER 1675

HERE are two alternative methods of writing the life of Wren: in strictly chronological order, or under the heads of his various buildings. Some of his previous biographers have adopted the former method, others the latter. In this book I have contrived to observe chronological sequence up to 1669 or thereabouts, but from that date onwards up to 1714, when he retired from practice, the task seems to me impossible. Abreast of his multifarious duties as Surveyor-General of His Majesty's Works—involving great palaces and important public buildings as well as innumerable minor commissions—he was engaged simultaneously on St Paul's Cathedral, more than fifty City churches, a certain number of houses, and many academic buildings at Oxford and Cambridge. He continued his active scientific interests and his connection with the Royal Society, he became a Member of Parliament, and—though we know little about it—there is something to be said of his social and domestic life apart from architecture. Yet, after 1669 or a little earlier, his career is so completely identified with his buildings that it seems kinder to the reader to treat them separately rather than to attempt to follow their progress simultaneously in a chronological sequence and a factual jumble. In adopting this method, however, it is necessary to emphasize the enormous volume of work that was passing through his hands from 1669 to 1710, after which he began to relax his efforts, for he was then an old man.

The building of St Paul's, definitely started in 1675 as we have seen, is popularly assumed to have been completed in 1710, when he attended a meeting of the Commission officially for the last time, but that date is open to question. According to *Parentalia*, the construction of the cathedral was finished in 1710 when Wren's son Christopher laid the topmost stone of the lantern in position; but the Editors of the Wren Society's Volumes point out (Vol. XIV, p. ix) that the masons' bill for the lantern and the painters' bill for painting the copper work and gilding on the west towers and lantern were paid in December 1708, while the masons were employed mainly in cleaning-down, paving and minor works during 1709-10. The Building Accounts of the cathedral contain no references to any formal ceremony of formal completion, so the Editors conclude that unless some other (unknown) record exists, the younger Christopher's 'memory was confused when he wrote his account in *Parentalia*'. It may be added that a good deal of decorative work remained to be done inside the cathedral after 1710 and that the final payment to Sir James Thornhill for painting the inner dome was not made till 1721. Moreover, Wren *did* attend two later meetings of the New Commission, in July 1715, though these were only 'courtesy attendances'. Thus we may accept 1710 as the date when his main work was virtually completed, though not in any precise sense. Even then, however, the story does not end, for sordid disputes about his designs and his fees continued for some time after 1710, as will be explained later; and it will be necessary to include in this chapter a brief account of the later changes—both structural and decorative—made in the building up to the present day, in so far as they affect his original scheme, for better or for worse. The Chapter House, the Deanery and the Canons' Houses in Amen Court—all designed by Wren—will also be described at the end of the chapter.

Whatever may be the exact date assumed for the completion of his work at St Paul's, it certainly extended over some thirty-five years after the foundation-stone had been laid; and throughout that period he must have devoted an enormous amount of time to supervising the progress of construction, to checking accounts, to attending meetings, and above all to modifying his original designs and preparing elaborate detail drawings. It is not the least among the many debts that we owe to the Wren Society that so many of those drawings are now easily available to any student in their published volumes. They prove to us that Wren, amateur of architecture as he had been in 1663, was capable of adjusting his designs and improving them as time elapsed, never regarding them as crystallized or unalterable. That in itself is a testimony to his greatness, the more so when we remember the colossal amount of other work that engrossed him simultaneously with St Paul's. It would be interesting to discover to what extent his designs for the dome were based upon the science of structural mechanics as we know it today. His published drawings do not appear to include any graphical or other calculations of thrusts, yet he must surely have embraced some knowledge of mechanics in his considerable scientific repertoire. It is difficult to believe that it was entirely empirical, intuitive or 'guesswork', or even mere geometrical deduction. One of his rough

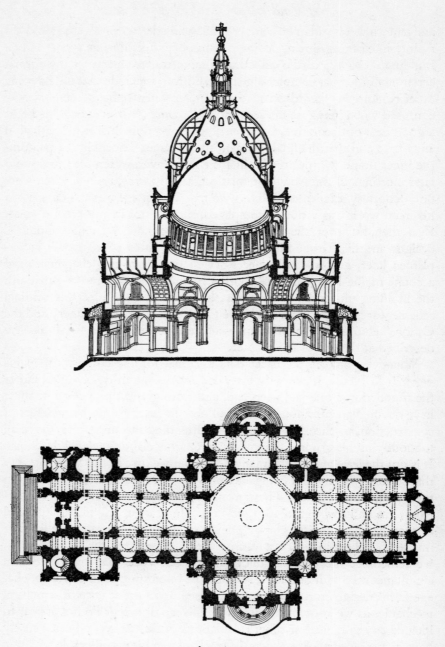

FIGS. 5 AND 6.—ST PAUL'S CATHEDRAL: PLAN AND SECTION

sketch-sections of the dome suggests that he understood and was adopting Galileo's theory of the catenary curve, discovered early in the seventeenth century.

On the other hand, he was as ingenious, as practical and as painstaking as we should expect. From the outset, the condition and nature of the site was a worry to him. According to *Parentalia*: 'The Graves of several Ages and Fashions in strata, or Layers of Earth one above another, particularly at the North-side of Paul's, manifestly shew'd a great Antiquity from the British and Roman Times, by the Means whereof the Ground had been raised; but upon searching for the natural Ground beneath these Graves, the Surveyor observed that the Foundation of the old Church stood upon a Layer of very close and hard Pot-earth and concluded that the same Ground which had borne so weighty a Building, might reasonably be trusted again. However, he had the Curiosity to search further and accordingly dug Wells in several Places, and discern'd this hard Pot-earth to be on the North-side of the Churchyard about six Feet thick, and more, but thinner and thinner towards the South, till it was upon the declining of the Hill scarce Four Feet: still he searched lower and found nothing but dry Sand, mix'd sometimes unequally, but loose, so that it would run through the Fingers. He went on till he came to Water and Sand mix'd with Periwincles and other Sea-shells; these were about the Level of Low-water Mark. He continued boreing till he came to hard Beach, and still under that, till he came to the natural hard Clay, which lies under the City, and Country, and Thames also far and wide. By these Shells it was evident the Sea had been where now the Hill is, on which St Paul's stands. . . .

'In the Progress of the work of the Foundations, the Surveyor met with an unexpected Difficulty; he began to lay the Foundations from the West-end, and had proceeded successfully through the Dome to the East-end, where the Brick-earth Bottom was yet very good; but as he went on to the North-east Corner, which was the last, and where nothing was expected to interrupt, he fell, in prosecuting the Design, upon a Pit, where all the Pot-earth had been robb'd by the Potters of old Time. . . . It was no little Perplexity to fall into this Pit at last; He wanted but six or seven Feet to compleat the Design, and this fell in the very Angle North-east; he knew very well, that under the Layer of Pot-earth, there was no other good Ground to be found till he came to the Low-water Mark of the Thames, at least forty Feet lower: his Artificers propos'd to him to pile, which he refus'd. . . . He therefore sunk a Pit of about eighteen Feet square, wharfing up the Sand with Timber, till he came forty Feet lower, into Water and Sea-shells, where there was a firm Sea-beach. . . . He bored through the Beach till he came to the original Clay; being then satisfied, he began from the Beach a square Peer of solid good Masonry, ten Feet square, till he came within fifteen Feet of the present Ground, then he turned a short Arch under Ground to the former Foundation, which was broken off by the untoward Accident of the Pit. Thus this North-east Coin of the Quire stands firm, and, no doubt, will stand.' It is strange that when Mr (afterwards Sir) Mervyn Macartney, the Surveyor to the cathedral, sank nine boreholes at this point in 1914, he found no trace of Wren's stone foundation, but did reach the London Clay at 40 feet.

According to Dugdale's account, great care was exercised in carrying out the work, as well as great energy, 'so that by the beginning of April anno 1685 the walls of the quire with the side isles thereto containing one hundred and seventy feet and in breadth one hundred and twenty foot, with the great arched vaults beneath, were finished. As also two stately porticoes North and South opposite to each other and the huge and massive pillars of the Dome . . . brought to the same height, the work being totally wrought of large Portland stone.' The west end of Old St Paul's was not entirely demolished till 1686. On December 2, 1697, the choir was formally dedicated on the occasion of a thanksgiving service for the Peace of Ryswick. Evelyn writes thus on December 5, 1697: 'Was the first Sonday, S. Paules has had service performed in it since it was burnt in 1666, which I myselfe saw, and now was likewise my selfe there, the Quire being compleatly finished, and the Organ esteemed the best in Europe. I think 40 stops. . . . In the afternoon preached Dr Sherlocke the Deane, but the presse of people was so greate that I durst not venture.' The fact that the morning-prayer chapel (St Dunstan's Chapel) was completed by 1699 seems to indicate that the work at the west end was then nearly finished.

Even in March 1696, however, Wren was facing trouble with serious settlements of the great piers carrying the dome, and for two months from September 1709 repairs were undertaken. Further repair was carried out in 1716 and 1722. It appears that he had built some of the piers on the foundations of Old St Paul's, and that, had he based them instead on the London Clay, the immense amount of restoration required in the present century might have been avoided. He relied too confidently upon the thin stratum of 'pot-earth' which, in the end, proved inadequate. Other causes of subsequent failure are to be found in the design of the piers and arches supporting the dome, but these are too highly technical for description here. It must be mentioned, nevertheless, that Wren, in his use of iron cramps to strengthen his masonry, did not practise what he preached; for whereas he wrote that 'in cramping of stones no iron should lye within nine inches of the air', in fact iron was freely used within 2 or 3 inches of the surface, and had so corroded even before 1831, when Penrose surveyed the fabric, that it had spalled and fractured the masonry in all parts of the building. Besides these structural defects, for which Wren must be held responsible, he could not have foreseen other causes of subsequent damage. such as the construction of underground railways and sewers, draining off the porous soil above the London Clay; and for the effects of these he must be exonerated. None of his biographers seems to have pointed out that the responsibility for such an immense undertaking was a 'full-time job' for any man, even for a man of great ability and energy; whereas Wren was carrying out so much other work on a large scale during those thirty-five years that, conscientious as he was, St Paul's cannot have occupied more than a share of his working hours. In the later stages of its building, he is said to have been raised in a basket up to the dome to view the progress, for he was then very old.

His duties are defined in a document printed by the Wren Society (XIII, 34): 'Sir C. Wren, Surveyor-Generall, who draws all the Designes of the Building, hath the universall care thereof, gives all directions to workmen and other Officers, examines all accounts, agrees for the prices of workmanship and materials, &c. His salary is £200 per annum.' On March 4, 1697, that salary was halved 'until the said Church should be finished; thereby the better to encourage him to finish the same work with the utmost diligence and expedition'. This drastic step led to further troubles, described on a subsequent page (see p. 94).

Besides certain deputies and administrative officers, most of the chief craftsmen of the day were employed at St Paul's. Much information about their work, status and pay is obtainable from the Building Accounts of the cathedral, reprinted in Volumes XIII-XV of the Wren Society; but some description of the leading artists is given in Chapter XIII of this book. Examination of the Minute Books also throws some light on the human side of the actual progress of the building. Thus on March 23, 1697, the Commissioners resolved: 'That Mr Dean of St Paul's be desired to con-sider of some methods to prevent the boys from playing in the Church, who dayly resort thither in great numbers, and do many times harm to the Building'. A week later, the Minutes record that 'Mr Dean of St Paul's, being at the last Committee desired to consider of some means to prevent the boys from playing in the Church, did offer his opinion that the Clark of the Cheque should be employed to keep them out of the work, he having very little other bussiness in regard of very few laborers are now at work'.

In September 1692, Wren complained about the 'ill behaviour of Rd. Warden, a Gate-keeper in the Works', who was summoned before the Committee for reprimand. Numerous cases of pilfering materials are recorded. There were several instances of fatal accidents to workmen, mostly incurred during the demolition of Old St Paul's. In most cases, payments were made to the men's widows as compensation, and funeral expenses were also paid. There were numerous non-fatal injuries, of which the following is a typical example: '7 July 1692. Upon the Petition of John Hoy setting forth that he hath been a laborer in St Paul's about 23 years and that he was lately very much hurt by a great Stone falling upon him, whereby he was disabled for 20 weeks and paid to his Chirurgeon £3-10-0, and praying the Commissioners Charity for his reliefe; and also upon Sir Chr. Wren's commendation of him to have been a very skillful laborer in the taking downe of old Ruines both at St Paul's and other Churches in London, it was ordered that £10 be given him for the losse of his time and for paying the Chirurgeon.'

Another example, though it occurred after Wren's retirement, is worth quoting: '24 March 1718. That the summe of £5 be paid to 2 men belonging to the Plummer, who were employed in repairing and sodering the Leads of the Dome for 14 weeks, viz, between the 15th of July 1717 and 9th of November following for an addition of 3s. per week to their usual wages in consideration of the sickness they suffered in the very hot weather by working so high, and that the same be paid to them in proportion to the time they were severally sick.'

One minor incident during the rebuilding, sentimental rather than architectural in significance, is related in *Parentalia*: 'In the beginning of the new Works of St Paul's, an Incident was taken notice of by some People as a memorable Omen, when the Surveyor in Person had set out upon the Place, the Dimensions of the great Dome, and fixed upon the Centre; a common Labourer was ordered to bring a flat Stone from the Heaps of Rubbish (such as should first come to Hand) to be laid for a Mark and Direction to the Masons; the Stone which was immediately brought & laid down for the Purpose, happened to be a Piece of a Gravestone, with nothing remaining of the Inscription but this single Word in large Capitals, RESURGAM.' Comment is needless.

Wren wisely encouraged the use of Portland stone at St Paul's, as in the City churches and his other buildings. He did much to develop the quarries at Portland, but great difficulties of supply and transport were encountered. Some of these were due to the capture of hoys by privateers during the war years, others by a landslide which destroyed many of the piers and quays at Portland, others again by the 'Islanders' who objected to the Royal Warrant for quarrying as they preferred to work the stone themselves. These difficulties accounted to some extent for later failures at St Paul's. Burford stone was used fairly plentifully as a substitute, but failed externally, and was largely replaced by Portland stone during the surveyorship of Robert Mylne (1762-1811). For the piers of the dome, a thin casing of Portland stone was used, the core being of rubble, available in large quantities from the old building. This method of construction, essentially medieval, was doubtless favoured by the master-masons, Marshall and Strong, who had been trained in this tradition. Lastly, Wren may have felt the need to take full advantage of Charles II's real, but possible transient, enthusiasm for the building scheme; and so may have decided to take risks by rushing it forward with the materials ready to hand. He relied implicitly upon the strength of the mortar he used. As it happens, it was very good mortar, but its use could not atone for defects in structural design, and before the end of the century Wren was engaged in the difficult process of removing the worst parts of the split stone facing and replacing it with new masonry. It is odd to learn that the north and south pediments, the statues, and the recessed walls of the west portico were painted, presumably as a precaution against damp.

The use of brickwork was limited to the inner dome, the cone (Fig. 5), the buttresses, reversed arches and vaulting of the crypt. Marble was obtained from Ireland, Wales, Denmark, Sweden, Belgium and Purbeck. Most of it was used for paving, but there was a marble choir-screen, since removed. A great deal of wrought ironwork was supplied, apart from the magnificent screens by Tijou. Double-leaf gold was employed on the ball and cross, and on the terminal features (pineapples) of the western towers. Much of the lead was recovered from the old cathedral and melted down. It is now generally agreed that Wren intended the windows to be glazed with clear, not stained, glass. Some of the timber members required were very large: 47 feet long and increasing from 13 or 14 inches square at the smaller end to a much bigger base. They were eventually obtained from the Duke of Newcastle's estate at Welbeck Abbey. The joiners at St Paul's were mainly employed in preparing models, templets and setting-out boards for the masons: one of them, Charles Hopson, was promoted to be 'Purveyor of the Works' and was knighted.

The cost of the new cathedral has been estimated by the Rev Arthur Dimock in his *Handbook for St Paul's* (1907, p. 74) as £846,214 12s. 6d.

up to the date of Wren's death in 1723. This includes the sum of £736,752 2s. 3d. as given in *Parentalia*, plus preliminary items, purchase of houses, and interest on loans. The Editors of the Wren Society (Vol. XIII, 11) consider that £750,000 is a fair estimate of its cost *as a building*. The amount received from coal-dues, according to Dimock, was £810,181 18s. 2d., and from subscriptions, etc., £68,341 14s. 1d. As the cathedral was some thirty-five years a-building, the annual outgoings, meticulously recorded in the accounts, thus averaged rather more than £21,000 per annum.

The Wren Society has reproduced in its Volume XIV a large number of contemporary engravings of St Paul's, with the very interesting information that these, or many of them, were made and published at the expense of the Commissioners with a view to obtaining contributions for the Building Fund as well as to satisfying public curiosity in the appearance of the finished cathedral. The accounts show that the copper plates, the engravings and the paper were all paid for by the Commissioners, and it is believed that the prints were actually struck off at the cathedral works.

In 1710, the question of paying the deferred half of his salary since 1697 (see p. 91) was raised by Wren himself in a pathetic petition to Queen Anne, as follows: 'The most humble petition of Sir Christopher Wren sheweth: That there being a Clause in an Act of Parliament which suspends a moiety of your petitioner's salary at St Paul's till the building be finished, and being obstructed in his measures for completing the same by the arbitrary proceedings of some of the Commissioners of that fabric; your petitioner most humbly beseeches your Majesty to interpose your Royal Authority so as that he may be suffered to finish the said building in such manner and offer such designs as shall be approved by your Majesty, or such persons as your Majesty shall think fit to appoint for that purpose.' This was dated February 13, 1710, and it will be noted that the church was then virtually finished (cf. p. 87).

The appeal was duly laid before the Commissioners on April 30, and six days later they issued a lengthy reply, full of innuendoes against Wren's competence and of justification of their own attitude. It makes sorry reading after the completion of one of the greatest buildings in the world, especially as the two main points of difference between Wren and themselves clearly concerned the material (cast iron instead of wrought iron) of an iron railing, and the conduct of Richard Jenings or Jennings— one of Wren's favourite craftsmen—who was alleged to have been trafficking in materials belonging to the cathedral. On the first point, Wren was undoubtedly in the right; as to Jenings, now Master-Carpenter, he was dismissed from the cathedral works on April 14, 1711, but Wren nevertheless saw that he was allowed to complete his contract for the Chapter House (1712-4, see p. 107).

Wren, having failed to obtain redress from the Commissioners, next appealed to the Archbishop of Canterbury and the Bishop of London in a long letter dated January 25, 1711: 'May it please your Lordships, That I humbly lay before you the state of the suspension of a moiety of my salary (as Surveyor of S. Paul's Cathedral) by a Clause in an Act of Parliament, which is thus: The design of the Parliament in granting the coal duty for the said cathedral at that time being to have the building completed with all possible speed, they did, to encourage and oblige the Surveyor's diligence in carrying on the work, suspend half of his allowance, till all should be done. Whereby I humbly conceive it may be justly from thence be implied that they thought the building, and everything belonging to it, was wholly under my management and direction, and that it was in my power to hasten or protract it. How far it has been so your Lordships know; as also how far I have been limited and restrained. However it has pleased God so to bless my sincere endeavours, as that I have brought the building to a conclusion, so far as is in my power, and I think nothing can be said now to remain unperfected, but the iron fence round the Church, and painting the Cupola, the directing of which is taken out of my hands, and therefore I hope that I am neither answerable for them, nor that the said suspending clause can, or ought to, affect me any further on that account. As for painting the cupola, your Lordships know it has been long under consideration: that I have no further power left me concerning it, and that it is not resolved in what manner to do it, or whether at all. And as for the iron fence it is so remarkable and fresh in my memory, by whose influence and importunity it was wrested from me, and the doing it carried in a way that I may venture to say will ever be condemned. I have just this to observe further, that your lordships had no hand in it: and consequently ought not to share in the blame that may attend it.

'This, then, being the case, and nothing left that I think can keep the said clause of suspension any longer in force against me, I most humbly pray your lordships to grant your warrant for paying me what is due to me on that article, which was £1300 last Michaelmas. And if for the future my advice and assistance be required in anything about the said cathedral, I will be ready to give the same, and to leave the consideration of it to your lordships. . . .'

Wren's case was then laid before the Attorney-General, who ruled on

January 30, 1711, that the Commissioners were not empowered to pay Wren's deferred salary as Parliament had laid down that it was not to be paid till the cathedral was completely finished. But as Wren rightly held that the structure was then entirely finished, except for certain decorative details that had been taken out of his hands, he made a third appeal in February 1711, this time to Parliament itself, in terms as dignified as those of his second petition; and on this occasion, as he himself recorded later, 'that Honorable and August Assembly so considered his case and were so well satisfied with the Justice and Reasonableness of it, as to declare the Church to be finished as far as was required to be done and performed by him as Surveyor-General. And it was accordingly enacted, that the suspended Salary should be paid him on or before the 25th of December 1711.'

Unfortunately, this happy decision was by no means the end of Wren's troubles at St Paul's, although he had now almost concluded his work there. In April 1712 a pamphlet appeared bearing the catchpenny title, *Frauds and Abuses at St Paul's*, ostensibly inspired by a desire to secure for the rebuilding of the church of St Mary Woolnoth certain funds required for completing the internal fittings of the cathedral, but including a bitter attack on the poor old man for various alleged irregularities, notably his defence of the supposedly peccant Jenings. The authorship of this scurrilous tract, which contains forty-two pages of splenetic abuse, is now ascribed to Dr Francis Hare, who afterwards became Dean of St Paul's and, later still, Bishop of Chichester. He was a member of the Commission for rebuilding St Paul's, from 1707 to 1711, but was abroad for part of that time and attended comparatively few meetings. As an expert pamphleteer, he was probably instigated to this attack by other jealous members of the Commission. Wren was stung into a sharp rejoinder. Altogether, six pamphlets were published in the course of this controversy in 1712-3, all anonymous. Three of them defended Wren, one supported the originator of the sordid squabble, and the remaining two, already mentioned, were written by Wren and Hare respectively. Copies may be studied at the Soane Museum and the R.I.B.A. Library, but the whole incident is so unedifying and unjustified that further description of it here is superfluous. Wren emerged from it with his character untarnished, nothing having been proved against his integrity or his professional competence.

On October 15, 1717, a newly-appointed body of Commissioners wrote a letter to him insisting that his cathedral could not be considered complete without a crowning balustrade of stone, giving him a fortnight to

VIII   ST PAUL'S CATHEDRAL; EXTERIOR FROM S.E.   R.C.H.M.

IX   ST PAUL'S CATHEDRAL; EXTERIOR OF DOME   *R.C.H.M.*

furnish any objections or comments. He replied on October 28 in terms which were dignified but sharp. He began by stating why he never designed a balustrade, and why it was superfluous, adding that 'Ladies think nothing well without an edging'. He also defined his objections to the use of vases as parapet ornaments, for if he were to make them big enough to suit the scale of the church, he 'would fall into the crime of false bearing, which artizans of the lowest rank will have sense to condemn'. He concluded: 'My opinion therefore is to have statues erected on the four pediments only which will be most proper, noble and sufficient ornament to the whole fabric, and was never omitted in the best ancient Greek and Roman architecture: the principles of which throughout all my schemes of this colossal structure, I have religiously endeavoured to follow: and if I glory it is in the singular mercy of God, who has enabled me to begin and finish a great work so conformable to the ancient model.' Wren had now been dismissed from his post, and only entered St Paul's as a privileged visitor.

Before turning to a brief consideration of his masterpiece as a design, it is necessary to complete its history up to the present date so far as subsequent changes have modified or altered that design. After the repairs to the structural masonry in 1709, 1716 and 1722, already mentioned, there is no record of any serious anxiety until 1831. In that year a proposal was made to lay a sewer along the south side of the cathedral from Ludgate Hill to Cannon Street. The then Surveyor, C. R. Cockerell, reinforced by the advice of Robert Smirke and George Rennie, warned the authorities that this scheme would inevitably weaken the foundations of the south transept, already cracking, and reminded them that—as Wren had stated long before (p. 89)—the foundations rested on a thin layer of pot-earth, beneath which was a thick stratum of sand. As a result of this protest, the sewer was diverted to Carter Lane. In 1890, owing to some anxiety about the stability of the cathedral, further burials in the western part of the crypt were forbidden. The next scare occurred in 1906, when a proposal very similar to that of 1831 was made for a low-level sewer, and a contract was actually let for it before the newly-appointed Surveyor, Mervyn Macartney, was able to examine the fabric thoroughly. As a result of his new Advisory Committee's interim report on March 16, 1907, the LCC agreed to divert the sewer to Upper Thames Street. In 1911 came a scheme to construct an underground tramway tunnel running north to south towards a new 'St Paul's Bridge'. This tunnel, close to the east end of the cathedral, was abandoned after strong protests in the Press. In the same year the Central London Railway Bill authorized a tube railway

70 feet below the cathedral floor, running along Newgate Street, with a still larger tube for the station, all close to St Paul's. The Surveyor pointed out the familiar facts about the successive layers of pot-earth and sand on which the foundations of the great church rested, and forecast damage to the structure, but the railway was eventually constructed.

Apart from these underground risks, it had long been apparent that substantial settlements had already occurred in the building, due to defects in the design and to the corrosion of the iron cramps. The dome had been accurately measured in 1878, and again under the Surveyorships of Somers Clarke (1897-1906) and Macartney (1906-31); but the latter, in an article in the *R.I.B.A. Journal* of November 1907 (XV, 71), wrote of the foundations that 'in no case have these shown signs of insufficiency, nor has any organic weakness been discovered in the structure itself. . . . All observations tend to prove that the danger to the cathedral comes from subterranean or atmospheric weakness.' Nevertheless, an appeal for £70,000 for repairs had to be made in 1914.

In 1921, when new excavations in the vicinity were threatened, Macartney called in Sir Francis Fox, an eminent engineer, who took a grave view of the situation. A committee was formed to recommend and undertake repairs. An appeal for £100,000 was made early in 1922, after their first report had been issued, and that large amount was already nearly spent when, on January 7, 1925, the District Surveyor for the City suddenly served a 'Dangerous Structures Notice' (under the London Building Acts) on the Dean and Chapter in respect of St Paul's dome. On the very next day an appeal for funds was made in *The Times*, and the country was so panic-stricken that the sum asked for was subscribed within a fortnight. When the fund was closed, on August 26, £250,000 had been received.

An elaborate programme of conservation was undertaken immediately, and lasted over five years. The cathedral was reopened on June 25, 1930, at an impressive service attended by the King and Queen. Briefly summarized, the work of repair was as follows. The piers of the dome were drilled, the dust was blown out, then indented bars of stainless steel were inserted, and liquid cement ('grout') was forced in under high pressure. The amount thus injected was, however, so relatively small (not more than 5 per cent) that Wren's masonry was proved to have been much better than typical medieval work. Diagonal ties, also of stainless steel, were inserted in the base of the peristyle, in order to relieve the brick buttresses of some of the thrust from the dome, and two steel girdles or chains of stainless steel were fixed round the drum of the dome to supersede Wren's heavy iron chain. Other tie-rods were fixed at gallery level.

Interesting models showing this procedure are now exhibited in the Trophy Room. Besides the operations just described, and many others too numerous and technical to mention here, a most elaborate series of tests and measurements was made, with highly sensitive instruments, some of which still remain in position to record automatically all movements and all changes of temperature. When all was done, the architects responsible claimed that: 'The underlying principles of the present work have been to fortify the building where weak without marring its beauty or interfering with the historical value of Wren's craftsmanship, and to pass it on to future generations leaving no scars or disfigurements of the last few years.'

Nine years later the Second World War began, and on September 12, 1940, St Paul's suffered its first attack. A heavy delayed-action bomb fell in the roadway near the south-west tower, burying itself 27 feet deep in the ground. A bomb-disposal squad under Lieutenant Davies dug a tunnel down to it, and transported it, at imminent risk to themselves, to Hackney Marshes, where it was exploded, making a crater 100 feet across. This miraculous escape was followed a month later by a direct hit in the early morning of October 10. On that occasion a bomb penetrated the outer roof of the choir, but, fortunately, hit one of the massive brick transverse arches, exploding between the vault and the outer roof. As a result, a huge amount of debris crashed into the choir below, destroying the high altar and damaging the ornate marble reredos. If, however, the bomb had penetrated one of the saucer-domes and had fallen direct into the choir, the damage would have been far more serious and would have ruined the portion of Wren's choir-stalls that had not been removed to a place of safety.

There were innumerable incendiaries, many of which were extinguished by the devoted volunteer-members of 'Paul's Watch' (mostly architects). Two more 'incidents', in the euphemistic jargon of the day, occurred in the terrible raids of December 29, 1940, and April 16, 1941. On the former night, all Paternoster Row and the adjoining streets went up in flames. As *The Times* wrote afterwards: 'None who saw it will ever forget their emotions on the night when London was burning and the dome seemed to ride the sea of fire like a great ship lifting above smoke and flame the inviolable ensign of the golden cross.' One more ordeal was to come, on April 16, 1941, when a heavy bomb crashed through the saucer-dome of the north transept and exploded on the floor beneath. The resultant debris broke through the vaulted floor into the crypt and great damage was done. The glass of the windows was shattered and the iron frames twisted out of shape. Monuments were injured, and the marble portico inside the north door, bearing the famous inscription to Wren and formerly part of the choir-screen, was destroyed. On that awful night, the Keeper of the Muniments, who was patrolling the precincts in a lull between the attacks, discovered a huge unexploded bomb, 8 feet long, in the north-east corner of the churchyard. This was removed within four hours by the heroic efforts of a naval officer and a squad of helpers; but, if it had exploded, much of the cathedral would have been wrecked.

Apart from these grievous wounds, which it has taken years to heal, many changes, mostly detrimental, were made to Wren's cathedral during the second half of the nineteenth century; and other alterations have taken place since. In 1853, an ornate polychrome marble memorial pulpit under the dome was erected from the designs of the Surveyor, Penrose; it is entirely out of harmony with Wren's work, and is more or less in early Italian Renaissance style. Between 1858 and 1872, the whole arrangement of the choir was altered. The magnificent organ-case by Wren formerly stood on a screen across the entrance to the choir. In 1858 this screen was removed and the organ re-erected in the north-east arch of the choir with the keyboard at floor-level. In 1870-2 the instrument was completely rebuilt as a divided organ on both sides of the choir. The floor of the choir was raised by several steps, and the choir-stalls, which had formerly been 'returned' under the screen, were straightened out to form a single line on either side. Sundry stained-glass windows were inserted, though Wren, as I have said, is believed to have relied entirely on clear glass for lighting.

The huge and bombastic pink marble reredos, designed by Thomas Garner, was installed in 1888, thereby blocking the view of the apse and spoiling Wren's design. The elaborate mosaics by Sir William Richmond, begun in 1891, though theoretically fulfilling Wren's intention of having mosaics, are generally considered to be out of character with the Late-Renaissance style of the building, being somewhat Byzantine in treatment. Alfred Stevens' great monument to the Duke of Wellington was moved in 1892 to the nave, where it seems to me to interrupt the noble rhythm of Wren's arcade. The splendid bronze candelabra were placed near the west door in 1899.

During the present century, the chief additions—none of them clashing with Wren's scheme—have been the Chapel of St Michael and St George, dedicated in 1906; the Kitchener Memorial Chapel (1925) under the north-west tower; and St Paul's Cross (1910) in the churchyard, designed by Sir Reginald Blomfield. One beneficial result of the bomb-damage has been the recent decision of the Dean and Chapter to restore the choir in some degree to Wren's original intention. The floor is to be lowered to its former level and repaved with black and white marble. The pink reredos is to be removed, and replaced by an elegant Baroque *baldacchino* or *ciborium* above the high altar, standing at the entrance to the apse. In the Trophy Room is a wooden model with twisted columns (illustrated in the Wren Society's Volume XIII, plate xxvii), showing that Wren always intended a *baldacchino* of this type to be erected, allowing a clear view through it into the apse. The design now approved, and also shown in a beautiful model now (1952) exhibited in the Trophy Room, appears to meet the case admirably and to be perfectly in scale with the interior as a whole. It is the work of Messrs Godfrey Allen (Surveyor to the Cathedral) and S. E. Dykes Bower (consultant architect).

This chapter must inevitably include some criticism and eulogy of Wren's masterpiece, however presumptuous the attempt may seem to the reader. Fortunately for the critic, there are few 'Men of Taste' today who would deny the transcendent merits of Wren's design as a whole. No longer is it necessary, as it was a century ago, to apologize for any cathedral that is not Gothic. Ruskin's description of the Renaissance as 'a foul torrent' is now obsolete, and Lethaby's dictum that Renaissance buildings constitute 'the architecture of boredom' hardly applies to St Paul's, which surely has a romance all its own. Even in Wren's lifetime, however, some critics had made themselves heard, among them Lord Burlington, who considered that Wren's new portico was far inferior to its predecessor designed by Inigo Jones, and observed that 'the Jews, who recalled the First, wept when they saw the Second, Temple'. Burlington gave material support to his opinion by employing Flitcroft as draughtsman and Hulsbergh as engraver to prepare a print of the earlier portico and publishing it after Wren's work was complete. *Parentalia* contains a lengthy defence of Wren's design in general, concerned mainly with aesthetic matters but also explaining the structural principles of the dome.

A century later, James Fergusson, in his *History of the Modern Styles of Architecture* (1862), devotes several pages to a detailed criticism of St Paul's, concluding that 'whether seen from a distance or near, it is, externally at least, one of the grandest and most beautiful churches of Europe', though he regards Wren as 'more of an engineer than an architect'. Nevertheless, he has several sharp comments upon the plan and the internal design: these strictures will be considered here, with others, in their due place.

More recent writers on English Renaissance architecture are uniformly appreciative of Wren's design as a whole. Sir Reginald Blomfield, most learned and forthright of them all, leaves us in no doubt. In his study of the period published in 1897, he observes of St Paul's that 'leaving St Peter's out of account, as differing both in scale and intention, the result is unquestionably the finest church in Europe produced by any architect of the Renaissance. . . . The most conspicuous characteristic [of Wren's design] is its magnificent sanity. In this, Wren avoided that excessive multiplication of parts which had been the weak point in all his previous attempts. . . . Wren, like all great architects, had an extraordinary aptitude for bringing his work along in the actual process of building.' Sir Thomas Jackson (1922) remarks that 'from every point of view the dome of St Paul's is well seen, its outline is perfect, and its beauty is unrivalled. Not less successful is the design of the western towers.' Mr A. S. G. Butler (destined later to serve in 'Paul's Watch') wrote in 1926, in his book *The Substance of Architecture*, that we enjoy St Paul's dome 'not only for the charm of its outline, but as well for its suggestion of mountainous rigidity and grandeur, its look of a supreme and culminating summit guarding London with a fat maternal benignity'. Mr Sacheverell Sitwell (1945) writes: 'There can be no hesitation in the opinion that St Paul's is the most magnificent building of the Renaissance. . . . It stands over the City of London and its merchandise. It presides over this meeting of the four corners of the earth. . . . The twin *campanili* of St Paul's are fantastically elaborate in invention. The porch or frontispiece is rich and magnificent in its light and shadow. The north and south doors advance their pillars in a hemicycle. We may walk all round St Paul's and look at it from every angle, and its fugal structure is for ever moving. . . . The interior of St Paul's is Protestant, instantly, and from the entrance . . . St Paul's is the most entire and unanimous of the great buildings.'

Very different is the view taken by that delightful impressionist Mr E. V. Lucas in his *Wanderer in London* (1906): 'Of St Paul's Cathedral I find it very difficult to write. Within, it is to me the least genial of all cathedrals, the least kindly. It has neither tenderness nor mystery. . . . It is simply so much noble masonry without sympathy. Wren, of course, had no religion: one sees that in every church he built. . . . His churches are churches for a business man, and a successful one at that: not for a penitent, not for a perplexed or troubled soul, not for an emotional sufferer. Poor people look out of place in them. Wren's churches are for prosperity. . . . As it is, St Paul's is a desert: nothing is done for you, and its lighting is almost commercial. The dominant impression it conveys is of vastness: one emerges with no hush on one's soul. . . . St Paul's best appeal, true appeal, is external. It has no religious significance for me: it is the artistic culmination of London city, it is the symbol of London.'

Among Wren's recent biographers, Mr Geoffrey Webb (1937) considers the 'exterior features' of St Paul's, including the western towers, to be 'among the finest Baroque designs in Europe'; an opinion which would have aroused furious dissent fifty years ago when the term 'Baroque' was synonymous with everything that was most despicable in architecture. Miss Milman, bred in the Deanery of St Paul's, does not find the cathedral irreligious: she speaks of 'poignant impressions' and a feeling of 'tenderness and awe'; but, writing in 1908, she naturally does not once use the word 'Baroque' in her long description of the church: at that date it was regarded as a term of abuse. Fifteen years later (1923), Sir Lawrence Weaver describes St Paul's as 'the apogee of English Baroque'. He also considers it 'incomparable as a piece of architecture, and prodigiously English'.

Turning now to a more detailed examination of specific points of the design, no critics of repute seem to disparage the general siting, grouping and massing. Wren was fully conscious that the site was cramped, especially on the west and north-west, but he was limited by private ownerships of properties round the churchyard which could only be bought out on equitable terms by Act of Parliament. Then, as now, financial reasons prevented an ideal setting for his masterpiece. In the unavoidable circumstances, he did his best, but his best has since been ruined by the erection of tall buildings all round the cathedral, notably Faraday House in our own day which has completely spoiled the view from Bankside across the river, where an inscription on the bombed pumping-station of the London Hydraulic Company records: '1907. The house formerly on this site was frequented by Sir Christopher Wren; thence he watched the building of St Paul's Cathedral.' (The statement is repeated in the official guide to the Borough of Southwark, p. 12.) In the various schemes prepared after the Second World War for the replanning of the City of London, much thought was properly given to providing improved points of view for its largest, most beautiful and most famous building—alike from the Thames, from Ludgate Hill, and from the east and north. As a result of the bombing, new prospects have been opened from Cheapside on the north, but long before that occurred, lovers of St Paul's had discovered a fine view of the great dome at a time when certain sites were vacant at the south end of Aldersgate Street. Another impressive view of the dome from the south is obtainable from the corner of Godliman Street. At the time of writing (1952), when many vital decisions have still to be made, it seems certain that substantial changes east of the cathedral will improve the prospect

FIG. 7.—ST PAUL'S CATHEDRAL FROM THE NORTH, AS SEEN IN 1942

from that side: it is probable that a wide opening on the south will afford a good view from the river and that there will be something of an axial vista on the north, but the general line of Ludgate Hill is unlikely to be altered. It is not yet clear whether a formal piazza will ultimately supersede the present somewhat irregular shape of the courtyard; or, if so, whether it will be oblong or elliptical, the only two possible alternatives.

Unfavourable criticism of the external appearance of the dome seems to be completely lacking, as one would expect: it is a masterpiece. Wren undoubtedly profited by study of recognized manuals of classical design, Italian and French, as well as by first-hand study of certain famous domes in Paris, and some account of his sources of inspiration is given in Chapter XIV (p. 260); but the chief point to emphasize here is that his dome, as actually built, shows an enormous advance upon his preliminary designs described in my previous chapter. It is hardly necessary to repeat here the familiar argument, stated by every writer on his work, that for visual effect the outer dome had to be much loftier than the inner one. A single dome, splitting the difference between the optimum heights externally and internally, would have been too low to dominate the group externally, yet would have appeared as a dark funnel from below, as does Vanbrugh's dome at Castle Howard. To carry the tremendous weight of the stone lantern, itself an essential feature in the design as a whole, Wren erected a tall cone two bricks in thickness, thus relieving both inner and outer

X   ST PAUL'S CATHEDRAL; INTERIOR LOOKING EAST   *R.C.H.M.*

XI ST PAUL'S CATHEDRAL; INTERIOR LOOKING WEST   R.C.H.M.

domes of this heavy duty. It has been suggested (Wren Society Volume XVI, p. 10) that Wren was aware of the brick cone used in the medieval Baptistery at Pisa, possibly described to him by Evelyn or some other traveller; or, alternatively, that Kentish brick oast-houses may have given him the idea. On the structural design of the piers carrying the dome, something has been said already (see p. 90).

One common criticism of the external design of St Paul's is that the lofty screen-walls round the cathedral are superfluous shams, carried up far above the roofs of the aisles for mere effect, and, moreover, involving the use of two tiers of coupled pilasters. Pugin said that one-half of St Paul's was built to hide the other half! Fergusson holds that Wren should have frankly accepted 'the medieval arrangement of clerestory and side aisles', the outer walls of the side aisles being then much lower than the clerestory. Modern critics generally consider that his solution is defensible as a means of creating the desired effect of monumental mass and height; and that, in fact, the high screen walls do serve a functional purpose in providing additional counterpoise to outward thrusts of vaults and dome. As to the use of two tiers of orders, Wren states in *Parentalia* that, having decided upon Portland stone as the most suitable material, he found that blocks of that stone more than 4 feet in diameter were unobtainable. He therefore resorted to two superimposed orders instead of one large one. He adds that these coupled pilasters act as buttresses, citing as a precedent the Temple of Peace illustrated in Serlio's book, as well as other examples from the work of such acknowledged masters as Bramante, Raphael and Michelangelo; and, in his own day, from the new Louvre at Paris. Inevitably the use of two tiers of orders on the portico of the west front led to some criticism, alike in his lifetime and subsequently; but, in the end, expert opinion has become reconciled to this expedient, now so much a part of our first impression of St Paul's from Ludgate Hill. The two western towers are among the highest flights of Wren's genius in design—immeasurably superior to the jejune efforts in his drawings prepared at a late stage in the cathedral's progress, and are quite definitely Baroque in style.

Internally, Fergusson finds fault with the plan, as involving the separation of 'two moderate-sized apartments' (nave and choir), almost identical in size, by a third 'apartment' (the space under the dome), more than double the width and double the height of either. It is true that one cannot see the dome properly from the west door, and that Wren—determined to have his great dome—took that risk. It was a compromise between his ideal and the 'Latin cross plan' imposed upon him by his employers. Fergusson also regards the octagonal plan of the dome-space as 'a radical defect', criticizes the 'perfectly useless attic 12 feet high' between the entablature of the main arcade and the spring of the vault above, and considers the vault itself, with its saucer-domes, as 'singularly confused and inartistic'. He regards the interior design of St Paul's as inferior to that of St Peter's at Rome or the Panthéon at Paris. Later critics are less dogmatic, and are inclined to swallow the fact of the undeniable compromise just mentioned in view of the magnificence of the total interior effect. The saucer-domes do not appear to them, or to me, to deserve the censure Fergusson awards to them, and the height of the attic stage is a disputable question of taste. When the proposed new *baldacchino* (cf. p. 100) has been erected, we shall be able to judge better of the internal effect that Wren hoped to produce.

Parentalia informs us that he wished to adorn the interior of the dome with mosaics, and we know that he disapproved of Thornhill's scheme of monochrome painting; but we can only surmise what would be his feelings if he could see the mosaics and other decorative additions carried out during the nineteenth century. This is not a guidebook to the cathedral, and specific description of its manifold beauties cannot be included here; but among the outstanding features may be mentioned the wood-carvings of the stalls and organ-case, the magnificent Baroque wood screens of the north and south chapels at the west end, the geometrical staircase under the south-west tower, the elegant curved porticoes on north and south, the 'Dean's Door', the decorations of the Lord Mayor's Vestry, the Library, and the Trophy Room upstairs, and the splendid ironwork by Tijou. Whether by personal magnetism or unerring judgment, Wren contrived to obtain from his multitude of craftsmen a standard of workmanship that has never been surpassed in all the history of our national architecture. Of those master-craftsmen, and of his relations with them, something will be said later in this book (see Chapter XIII). It is enough to add here that, among the critics, amateur or professional, who have seen fit to disparage certain aspects of his design in general, none seems to be able to find fault with the decorative details which make St Paul's a museum of all the crafts connected with architecture.

Three buildings erected by Wren for the Dean and Chapter under the shadow of St Paul's must be treated as a postscript to this account of the cathedral. In the charming little backwater known as Amen Close, with gateways and garden, is a group of three Canons' Houses built at a cost of £3,039 in 1670-3. (Illustrated in Wren Society Vol. XIII.) Externally they show his work at its plainest, with brick walls, sash and casement windows, dormers, steep roofs tiled and slated, and no ornament except wrought-iron torch-extinguishers at the entrances. In front, they are two storeys high with basement and attics; at the back they are three storeys high. There have been slight external alterations since they were erected, and many more internally. Nos. 1 and 3 have fine original staircases and contain some good original panelling. The houses miraculously escaped destruction in the air-raids of 1940, when the creeping fires reached close to them on three sides.

The Deanery, in Dean's Court, which also escaped with relatively slight damage, is one of the best examples of Wren's domestic design, and was built by him for his old friend Dean Sancroft in 1670-3 at a total cost of £3,993. It is of two storeys, plus a basement and attics, with brick walls and a hipped roof covered with tiles. The frontage is about 64 feet, and there are seven sash-windows in each storey, with dormers above. Two small additions at the back have not materially altered the appearance of the house. The east (or entrance) front is crowned by a bold modillion cornice. There is a very fine doorway on this front, with a moulded hood supported on carved trusses; and an imposing flight of steps, resting on an arch, leads up to the door. Internally there are two fine original staircases, original panelling in four ground-floor rooms, and some panelling upstairs. The house is illustrated in Wren Society Vol. XIII.

The Chapter House in St Paul's Churchyard, north of the cathedral, was completely gutted in an air-raid on December 29, 1940. Begun by Wren in 1712, it may be regarded as his last architectural design. It is plain, dignified and solid. The walls are of brick, with rubbed brick dressings and stone quoins. A tall parapet masks the roof. There are three storeys and a basement. Each storey has a range of seven windows facing the cathedral, and there are twin entrance doorways on this side with pedimented heads. Altogether, it forms another fine example of Wren's domestic design, though very unlike the Deanery. It is illustrated in Wren Society Vol. XIV.

VI

WREN'S CITY CHURCHES

1670—1700

I N Chapter III, reference was made to the destruction of a large number of City churches in the Great Fire of 1666. It is now necessary to
describe in detail Wren's work in rebuilding or restoring fifty-one of
these churches, which was carried out simultaneously with his work
on St Paul's Cathedral, dealt with in Chapters IV and V, and with a great
deal of other building to be described in subsequent chapters.

As stated on p. 46, John Evelyn recorded on September 7 that 'near 100'
churches had been destroyed, but that figure was exaggerated: the actual
number was eighty-seven, out of a total of 108 or 109, twenty-one or
twenty-two[1] having survived. This total of 108 pre-Fire churches is considerably less than it had been some five centuries earlier, when William
Fitzstephen (d. 1190) wrote that in his day there were thirteen conventual
churches and 126 parochial churches, making 139 in all. Peter of Blois
gives the number of parish churches, at about the same time, as 120; and
Fabyan, writing in 1516, states that the figure was then 113. Even that
allowance of churches within a square mile seems excessive, but it may be
recalled that, in the Middle Ages, Norwich had sixty, Lincoln forty-nine
and York forty-one. At the time of the Great Fire, London's numerous
churches were closely packed together, some of them actually contiguous,
and most of them comparatively small and of no great architectural importance. St Faith was in the crypt of St Paul's, St Gregory was attached
to the west front of the old cathedral. The most notable were All Hallows
Barking, St Giles Cripplegate, St Dunstan in the East, St Stephen Walbrook, St Mary Aldermary, St Mary le Bow and—outside the Walls—
St Bride and St Sepulchre. Of these, the two first-named survived the
Fire, and St Sepulchre was only partially destroyed. (It may be added that,
when the Second World War began, the twenty-one surviving pre-Fire
churches had been reduced to ten in number, including three monastic
foundations; and that of these three were gutted and one completely

[1] According to various methods of reckoning.

destroyed in the air-raids of 1940-1.) With only one-fifth of the churches remaining after the Fire, it was inevitable that a state of something like chaos ensued in parochial life. The wretched inhabitants who had lost their homes were camping in improvised shacks, and the streets were blocked with heaps of rubble. Emergency measures were quickly put in hand. The Grocers' and Stationers' Companies put their halls at the disposal of neighbouring parish clergy for Sunday services. At St Michael Wood Street a temporary roof was fixed on the surviving stone walls: similar efforts were made unsuccessfully at St Mildred, Bread Street and at St Mary Magdalen on Fish Street Hill. St Sepulchre Holborn was quickly repaired pending permanent restoration.

On being appointed to design and direct the work of rebuilding, Wren's first task was to recommend how many of the old churches should be restored or replaced. It was evident that the previous number was excessive, and that some reduction would be an advantage, but obviously any scheme of amalgamation of parishes would lead to violent protest. They would lose their identity (and one remembers what happened when cavalry regiments had to be amalgamated and mechanized in our own day!). His first proposal, intended to avoid these local squabbles, was to place the patronage of all the churches with the Lord Mayor and Corporation of the City; and then to reduce the number of parishes from 108 or 109 to thirty-nine by amalgamating the smallest in area. This would have resulted in fewer but finer churches. His scheme, together with his figure of thirty-nine parishes, was in fact embodied in the First Rebuilding Act which became law in 1667; but it never became really operative because of the bitter opposition of the powerful interests affected. One reason for its failure was the omission to specify the thirty-nine new parishes, the final choice being left to the Archbishop of Canterbury and the Bishop of London. As soon as lists were prepared, protest-meetings followed all over the City; and ultimately it was resolved, in the Second Rebuilding Act of 1670, to rebuild fifty-one churches in all. It is certain now that this number was far too large.

During the four years that elapsed while these unseemly wrangles occurred, burials continued to take place in the deserted churchyards, which became the resort of thieves and other undesirables. Thefts of church plate and even of lead from church roofs were reported. The ecclesiastical authorities then had the happy thought of requisitioning eight Dissenting meeting-houses from which Nonconformist congregations had been evicted by an Order in Council of June 15, 1670, but this militant Christian action was insufficient to satisfy the urgent needs of the

Established Church, many of the meeting-houses being mere rooms. The last of them—the Moravian Chapel in Fetter Lane—was completely destroyed in the Second World War.

The next step was the provision of ten so-called 'tabernacles' or temporary halls for worship at an estimated average cost of £150 each, by order of the Archbishop. The sum of £1,500 for this purpose was derived from the recently imposed coal-tax (cf. p. 82), and was voted in October 1670. The cost varied greatly in different parishes, rising from £50 in one case to £265 in another. Ultimately the total number was increased to thirty. These 'tabernacles' were constructed of timber on a brick base, and provided with very simple fittings and furniture. The contemptuous term 'tin tabernacle', often applied to modern temporary church buildings—whether Anglican or Nonconformist—constructed of corrugated iron, apparently had its origin in these improvised halls of 1670.

In that year, four years after the Fire, a beginning was made at last with the erection of the fifty-one churches now authorized under Wren's direction and his general design. Thirty-three of the fifty-one served two (old) parishes each, and St Mary le Bow served three. Most of them were built on new foundations, but at least five were erected largely or partly on old walls, notably St Mary le Bow and St Vedast among those still surviving. Funds were mainly obtained from the coal-tax of 1667, which had permitted Parliament to collect for ten years (from June 24, 1667) 1s. per 'chaldron' or ton upon all coal brought into the Port of London. The Second Rebuilding Act trebled the amount of this levy, which had proved quite inadequate, from May 1, 1670, and also continued the consolidated duties for 10¼ years after the expiry of the original term. Three-quarters of the new duty was allotted to the City churches (with a proviso that a quarter of that sum might be spent on St Paul's) and the remaining quarter was assigned to the City for street improvements, etc. Naturally, the receipts from this tax fluctuated according to the weather, becoming substantial in a hard winter and dwindling in the summer months. War risks also affected supplies by sea, and, during the third Dutch war, *c.* 1672, coal shipments arrived in convoy.

The total amount expended on the City churches from this source amounted to £265,467 3s. 0d. between 1670 and 1687, and about £53,000 between 1687 and 1700. During the latter period, only one-fifth of the coal tax was allocated to them, the remainder being given to St Paul's. The most expensive churches were St Lawrence Jewry (£11,870 1s. 9d.); Christ Church, Newgate (£11,778 9s. 6d.); and St Bride, Fleet Street (£11,430 1s. 9d.). The cheapest was St Vedast (£1,853 15s. 6d.), where old foundations and walls were utilized, but five others were erected at a cost between £2,000 and £3,000 each. In addition to these sums provided out of public funds, a considerable amount was contributed privately for many churches. Thus one donor gave £5,000 to St Mary Aldermary, and another gave £2,000 to St Mary le Bow, where private subscriptions amounted to £2,385 towards a total expenditure of £8,071 18s. 1d. The various officials employed to supervise the buildings were paid by 'piece-work', but Wren himself was paid a salary of £100 a year for thirty years. His chief assistant or deputy was Robert Hooke, like him a scientist by training (cf. pp. 233-6), who had likewise turned to architecture comparatively late in life. (Outside London, Hooke built a small country church at Willen in Buckinghamshire.)

There are some amusing entries in the accounts of the churches showing how grateful the parisioners were to Wren for the personal interest he took in their buildings: for example, the churchwardens' accounts for St Stephen Walbrook record that they gave a dinner costing nine guineas in his honour on March 7, 1673; then a bonus for him to give to 'his Lady' to encourage and hasten the rebuilding; another dinner six years later when the church was completed, together with another gift (of £10) to Lady Wren; and a hogshead of claret costing £9 10s. in 1681. Even the small church of St Michael, Wood Street, managed to treat Wren to a dinner which cost the parishioners fifteen guineas, during the rebuilding, and another when the work was finished. The churchwardens of St Peter, Cornhill, gave him five guineas 'as a gratuity for his paines in the furtherance of a Tabernacle for this parish'.

The work of building commenced in earnest during 1670, when seventeen churches were begun. These were completed by 1678, when two others had also been repaired, five more were far advanced, and a further six had been started. By 1683, twenty-five were actually in use, seventeen nearly finished, three just begun, and six more not yet raised above foundation-level. Thus the inscription on the Monument, recording that London was rebuilt in three years, is disproved. The relatively slow start was partly due to the tardy and uncertain yield of the coal-tax, partly to obstruction by unwillingly united parishes, but partly also to the City authorities' deliberate wish to discourage precipitate action. In February 1671 the City 'Chamber' (Treasury) was closed to deposits by parishes for future rebuilding, on the grounds that 'the number of Churches in hand are as many as are Suitable, to the Time, Mony, and Materialls, requisite to the orderly Finishing of them'. Materials, in this case, practically meant stone, all of which had to be brought by sea and mainly from

Portland (cf. p. 92). The churchwardens in most parishes did all they could to salvage old materials, but the amount so obtained was trifling compared with what was needed.

Before proceeding to any general or detailed account and criticism of Wren's churches, it seems desirable at this point to state how many of them still remain for the reader to see, and how the others have perished. *Parentalia* (pp. 309-18) gives 'A Catalogue, short Description, and general Dimensions, of Fifty-one parochial Churches of the City of London, erected according to the Designs, and under the Care and Conduct, of Sir Christopher Wren, in lieu of those which were burnt and demolish'd by the Great Fire in the Year 1666, together with other Churches built and repair'd'. (This last item includes the three large churches of St James Piccadilly, St Clement Danes and St Andrew Holborn, described in Chapter VII, pp. 128-130). Of Wren's fifty-one churches as enumerated in *Parentalia*, the following had ceased to exist before 1939:

Rebuilt since Wren's day:

1.	St Mary Woolnoth	1716-27
2.	St Dunstan in the East (except tower)	1817-8

Demolished before 1939:

3.	St Christopher le Stocks	1781
4.	St Michael, Crooked Lane	1831
5.	St Benet Fink	1844
6.	St Bartholomew Exchange	1850
7.	St Benet Gracechurch	1867
8.	St Mary Somerset (except tower)	1867
9.	St Mildred Poultry	1872
10.	St Antholin, Budge Row	1875
11.	St Michael Queenhithe	1876
12.	St Dionis Backchurch	1878
13.	All Hallows, Bread Street	1878
14.	St Matthew, Friday Street	1884
15.	St Mary Magdalen, Old Fish Street	1886
16.	St Olave, Old Jewry (except tower)	1888
17.	All Hallows the Great	1894
18.	St Michael, Wood Street	1896
19.	St Michael Bassishaw	1900
20.	St George, Botolph Lane	1904
21.	All Hallows, Lombard Street	1938

(Tower, etc., removed to Twickenham)

There being twenty-one churches in the above list, the total number of

XII   LONDON, ST MARY ALDERMARY; INTERIOR   *R.C.H.M.*

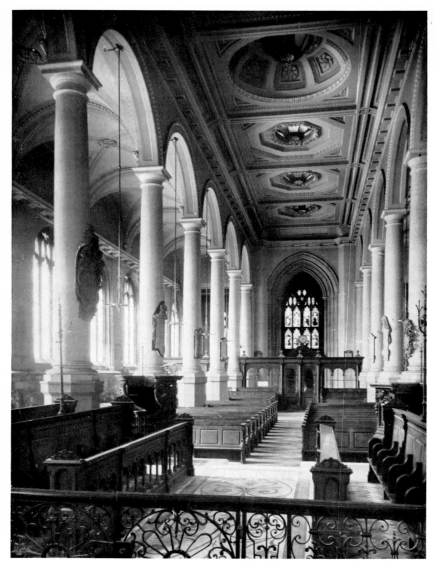

XIII   LONDON, ST SEPULCHRE, HOLBORN; INTERIOR   *N.B.R.*

XIVb   LONDON, ST MICHAEL CORNHILL; TOWER

E. J. Farner

XIVa   LONDON, ST DUNSTAN IN THE EAST; STEEPLE

xva   LONDON, ST MARY LE BOW; STEEPLE
b   ST BRIDE, FLEET STREET; STEEPLE

Wren's churches surviving in 1939 was thirty, plus the towers of three more. It will be noticed that the number of churches deliberately demolished between 1867 and 1900 is thirteen. Most of them, admittedly, were small and several were plain in design, but some were beautiful, and their loss is irreparable. Their destruction was defended on grounds of ecclesiastical expediency, the population having moved out of the City and the churches being hardly used—even on Sundays; but whether the clerical authorities were justified or not in the nineteenth century, Wren was certainly justified in 1667 when he advised the reduction in number of the City parishes to thirty-nine. Of the thirty churches rebuilt or restored by Wren and still surviving in 1939, the following were so hopelessly damaged in the air-raids of 1940-1 that no attempt is to be made to rebuild them and their sites are to be sold:

22. St Alban, Wood Street
23. St Andrew by the Wardrobe
24. St Mary Aldermanbury
25. St Mildred, Bread Street
26. St Stephen, Coleman Street
27. St Swithin, London Stone

The loss of St Mildred, Bread Street, is particularly deplorable because, although small, it was lavishly decorated, and preserved, more perfectly than any other church in the City, its original appearance as Wren designed it. Of the remaining twenty-four Wren churches, the following were gutted or very seriously damaged but are to be restored for various uses:

28. St Augustine, Watling Street
29. Christ Church, Newgate Street
30. St Bride, Fleet Street
31. St Mary le Bow
32. St Nicholas Cole Abbey
33. St Stephen Walbrook
34. St Lawrence Jewry
35. St Michael Paternoster Royal
36. St Vedast, Foster Lane

This group includes most of Wren's largest City churches, some with galleries; and many of the beautiful fittings and decorations were destroyed. Less serious damage was sustained in the following four churches:

37. St Anne and St Agnes
38. St James Garlickhithe
39. St Magnus the Martyr
40. St Mary Abchurch

We are thus left with only eleven churches by Wren which escaped unhurt or with negligible damage. They are:

41. St Clement Eastcheap
42. St Edmund King and Martyr
43. St Margaret Lothbury
44. St Margaret Pattens
45. St Martin Ludgate
46. St Mary Aldermary
47. St Mary at Hill
48. St Michael Cornhill
49. St Peter Cornhill
50. St Sepulchre, Holborn
51. St Benet, Paul's Wharf (Thames Street)

The proposals of the London Diocesan Reorganization Committee for the future of all the churches in the City, including Wren's thirty churches (Nos. 22-51 above), were placed before a Chapter of the City clergy in the summer of 1949. They recommended that six of Wren's churches which had been irreparably damaged (Nos. 22-7 above) should be demolished and their sites sold; that two other seriously damaged churches—St Augustine, Watling Street, and Christ Church, Newgate Street, together with St Dunstan in the East, of which only the tower is by Wren—should be restored for 'special or institutional work'; and that the remaining twenty-four Wren buildings should become either 'parish' or 'ward' churches, restored as necessary. In several cases—e.g. St Bride, St Mary le Bow, St Stephen Walbrook—the amount of restoration needed would be substantial and very costly. The pre-war number of forty-six parish churches was to be reduced to fifteen, of which eight would have been Wren churches. The twenty-one 'ward churches' (including fifteen by Wren) would have an extra-parochial status, and would 'become particularly associated with the life of the wards in which they were situated, and thus the link between the church and the civic life of the City would be fostered'.

Admirers of Wren's work grudge the disappearance of any of his churches, but every honest person must sympathize with those responsible for the affairs of the Church of England in the difficult decision thrust upon them by the cruel ravages of war, at a time not only of acute financial stringency for the nation as a whole but also of real anxiety for the best disposal of church funds when a poorly-paid clergy has every claim for consideration. This summary of recent events thus shows that only twenty-four of Wren's City churches, out of the original fifty-one, are likely to remain, while several of those will be without many of their most beautiful decorative features. Moreover, two of the twenty-four—St Sepulchre and St Mary Aldermary—were only repaired or restored by Wren, so that they cannot be regarded as typical of his characteristic planning and design.

In attempting any description or criticism of Wren's City churches, one has to avoid two things: indiscriminate praise of everything he did, on the one hand; disregard of the difficulties which he encountered, on the other. At the same time, his designs and his methods must not be judged by the social circumstances and spiritual needs of our day, as the Victorians were too apt to judge them when the ecclesiologists and John Ruskin fulminated against 'the foul torrent' of the Renaissance. Wren came, as we have seen, from a High Church family imbued with Erastian ideas of Church and State; but he himself, at Oxford and in London, maintained a typical scientist's attitude of aloofness to all political and sectarian questions. He mixed freely with Puritans and dissidents in the gatherings at Wadham, and he challenged the dogmatism of the clergy when he was planning St Paul's. From the Reformation to 1666, very few parish churches had been erected anywhere in England, and Wren felt free to face his tremendous problem with an entirely open mind, regardless of medieval precedent.

His attitude towards church planning is stated quite clearly in the long letter or memorandum that he wrote *c.* 1710, near the end of his career, and is of such importance that it is quoted later in full on pp. 135-7. He speaks therein of 'our reformed religion' and of 'the minister', not 'the priest'. The chief point in planning, he argues, is to ensure that all can see and hear the preacher of the Gospel, and galleries must be provided if necessary to ensure this rather than a lengthening of the church beyond a convenient distance for hearing. None of his churches has a deep chancel, in fact most of them have hardly any chancel proper, a space for the altar being screened off or railed off in certain cases. There are no ambulatories for processions and no arrangements for any elaborate ritual at the altar. Some of his interiors have been described as dark, gloomy, dusky; but they were not so when Wren built them. High surrounding buildings have suffocated them and diminished their light; enthusiastic but misguided Victorian church-milliners have obscured what light remains with incongruous stained-glass windows.

Miss Milman, striving to reconcile her admiration for Wren with her own clerical upbringing, analyses the religious impressions created in her mind by his church interiors, which, she writes, 'combine to produce a mood of complacency inconsistent with missionary zeal or much searching of conscience. Churchmen of that later seventeenth century practised a reserved devotion, and were as little prone to consider the critical issue of their own tenets as to deem them inconsistent with a clinging to creature comfort. Of comfort, too, their appreciation was consciously the keener for memories fresh in their minds of misery wrought by the fanaticism which they deplored as "enthusiasm" and shunned as an infectious distemper of the soul. Spirituality was at a low ebb, and rampant Erastianism finds expression in the lion and unicorn which flank the Decalogue. . . . There is no suggestion of mystery in these City churches: no dim aisles lure the soul to speculate upon things unseen, no majestic altar elevation typifies arduous access to the Most High: the mood indeed is rather calm than ecstasy. . . . Devotion here would scarcely disturb a prosperous trader's conception of the world as a pleasant place in which an honest man can await without fretful impatience the coming of the next. . . . On the other hand, we find here displayed no trace of the Puritan contempt for the dignity of the Sacraments. . . . The sanctuaries of these churches are carefully enclosed against profanation; the most elaborate carving is that of the altar-piece, while the font of precious marble lavishly adorned is reverently covered.'

Mr E. V. Lucas, in *A Wanderer in London*, regards these churches as 'a monument to the obsolete', but echoes Miss Milman's views in one respect: 'Comfort, ecclesiastical comfort, is the note of the City church. It reflects the mind of the comfortable citizen for whom it was built, who liked things plain but good, and, though he did not want so far to misbehave as to think of religion as a cheerful topic, was still averse from Calvinistic gloom.'

Mr Sacheverell Sitwell, in the course of a eulogy of Wren's City churches, observes that the charming little brick exterior of St Benet, Paul's Wharf (XVII), recalls 'a Quaker or Moravian meeting-house'; and, in fact, the interiors, as well as the exteriors, of the Congregational and Presbyterian 'chapels' erected at this period, when the Toleration Act had permitted Nonconformists to build again, are in a simpler and more economical version of Wren's style. Examples are to be seen at Norwich Old Meeting (1693); Friar Street Chapel, Ipswich (1700); Churchgate Street Chapel at Bury St Edmunds (1711); Mary Street Chapel at Taunton (1721); Underbank Chapel at Stannington, Yorks (1742); Lyme Regis Congregational Chapel (1750-5); and elsewhere.[1] Except in the case

[1] See my book *Puritan Architecture*, pp. 23-36.

of the more prosperous congregations, however, the Nonconformist chapels lacked the fine decoration of Wren's churches, for they were entirely dependent upon the offerings of the faithful and had no coal-tax to support them. Although they were nearly all aisleless and oblong in form, like most of Wren's churches, they had the pulpit in the middle of one of the longer sides, and galleries on the remaining three—an ideal arrangement for preaching—with the communion-table in front of the pulpit; whereas Wren placed the altar at the end, on one of the shorter sides, but not invariably at the east end, for he was sufficiently unorthodox to ignore orientation if he obtained a better arrangement thereby. He never used side-galleries if he could avoid them, though he found it necessary to provide them in the case of the larger churches.

The chief difficulties facing Wren in his herculean task were caused by overwork, cramped sites, shortage of material and obstruction by clerics with medieval prejudices. His personal output throughout the period 1667-1700 was prodigious, for it included St Paul's Cathedral and a host of other important buildings to be described in later chapters, as well as his manifold duties as Surveyor-General. In 1669 he must have been working upon designs for at least seventeen churches simultaneously, besides St Paul's. He was in general administrative charge of them all, but it is not known how far he was responsible for the design of interior finish or fittings, about which the individual vestries had much to say. Some of the details are coarse in execution, and of this Wren must have been aware, for he had seen much fine craftsmanship when he visited the workshops of the Louvre in 1665. He was opportunist as well as practical by nature, always ready to make the best of circumstances, and relying implicitly on sound commonsense to solve his problems. In the end, his individuality was stamped upon every building, and nowhere else in the world were there so many churches designed and erected by one man in a single city. Robert Hooke acted as his lieutenant, and drew up many of the contracts and agreements with the various building craftsmen, referring the accounts to Wren for approval. His diary records frequent visits to churches in course of construction, sometimes alone, sometimes in company with Wren.

The sites of the churches were, for the most part, cramped and inadequate. Wren showed great ingenuity in planning the buildings so as to obtain the maximum accommodation and internal effect. Many sites were surrounded at the outset on three sides by houses and shops, so that external emphasis had to be concentrated on a tower or steeple rising above the roofs; but, since his day, encroachments have been permitted, in several instances, destroying the effect still further; and many spires are buried or hidden among tall modern buildings, much as the view of St Paul's has been obscured from the river by Faraday House. Costly nineteenth-century churches in New York have suffered the same fate.

Reference has already been made (p. 92-3) to the difficulty of obtaining suitable and sufficient materials, especially Portland stone: this was a source of continual worry to Wren, who did much to develop the quarries at Portland. Lastly, he had to contend with the obstinate attachment of many church people to the familiar forms and accessories of the old Gothic churches, and in some of his designs he made earnest but not always successful attempts at compromise. When all else failed, he used to take his drawings to King Charles, his faithful friend and patron, for the readily given endorsement 'With His Majestie's Approbation', and thus many of his difficulties were smoothed away. His record as a Royalist doubtless stood him in good stead in such emergencies, but the King also had the highest opinion of his technical and artistic abilities.

According to *Parentalia* (p. 268), Wren's instructions or proposals for rebuilding were as follows: 'The Churches to be design'd according to the best Forms for Capacity and Hearing, adorn'd with useful Porticos, and lofty Towers and Steeples, in the greater Parishes. All Church-yards . . . to be placed out of the Town.' Most of the larger churches—Christ Church, St Bride and the three described in Chapter VII—were placed outside the City walls, in districts then regarded as suburban.

The intention of the spires, steeples and towers is clear enough: to mark out the church above the huddle of surrounding roofs; possibly also to form a cluster or constellation of white points around, and acting as a foil to, the great dark dome of St Paul's. It has been observed that the ultimate effect is no less than 'a symphony in stone'; and, up to modern times, that was a reasonable claim. It is in these towers and spires, above all, that the fecundity of Wren's imagination is most apparent, reaching in the later examples to the fantasies of Continental Baroque.

Writers on Wren's churches like to classify them either according to their towers and steeples; or according to their planning and internal arrangements. External grouping only comes into question in the few cases where island sites were available. From Wren's own sketches in the All Souls collection and elsewhere, we learn that the spires as actually built differed greatly from the preliminary studies, and that the change was almost always for the better: the design for St Mary le Bow is a case in point. Of Wren's forty-nine churches—after excluding St Mary Woolnoth (repaired by Wren and since rebuilt) and St Sepulchre which retains its medieval tower—eleven had plain square towers terminating in a parapet or balustrade, and in some cases decorated with finials. Only three of the eleven have survived, viz. St Clement Eastcheap, St Olave Jewry and St Mary Somerset. The latter two are the only portions of the two churches now standing, the rest of the buildings having been demolished during the nineteenth century. There is nothing much to be said about this group of square towers which, especially if decorated with finials, produce a somewhat Gothic effect and would therefore doubtless please pious parishioners. The next group comprises six towers with modest bell-turrets of lead: of these only two remain, at St Anne and St Agnes, and at St Mary at Hill. We now come to a slightly more elaborate type, having a belfry or lantern raised on a dome or pyramid or steps. There were eight examples of this type, of which only three have survived: St Benet, Paul's Wharf, a most attractive design; St James Garlickhithe; and St Stephen Walbrook. The last two may be reckoned as steeples, though of no great height, and recall Baroque examples from Italy.

Coming next to built-up spires or steeples of stone, in diminishing stages, we have four of Wren's finest designs, all of which are standing. They are at St Mary le Bow (XVa), St Bride (XVb), St Vedast, Foster Lane, and Christ Church, Newgate Street. Generally speaking, Wren's spires are later than the churches to which they are attached, and some were built many years afterwards. Most writers on his work have succumbed to the temptation to name their favourite among all this array of fantasy, and all the four spires just named have had their backers; but the most popular pair are the largest and finest, viz. those of St Bride and St Mary le Bow. The former is considered by Sir Reginald Blomfield to be more 'monotonous' than the latter, yet he regards it as 'the stronger' [in design] of the two, and sees in it an indication that, as Wren's artistic taste developed, he renounced the rather amateur ideas of design that he had acquired in France for the more powerful and 'strenuous' architecture of Inigo Jones. The spire of St Bride, on the other hand, is an exotic, and it is a matter for profound thankfulness that it stands where it does, and not—as it so nearly did—on the top of the great dome of St Paul's (cf. p. 84). More than one critic finds a Jacobean quality in the steeple of St Mary le Bow.

Of the next group of three, which had towers with true spires, only one remains, at St Margaret Pattens. It is entirely Gothic in form, although the spire rises from a square tower crowned with a balustrade having tall finials at the angles. The spire of St Antholin, deliberately demolished in 1875, was a lovely thing, and one of Wren's best.

Then come two square towers with concave or trumpet-shaped spires covered with lead, very original in design and somewhat Baroque in character. These are at St Edmund the King and Martyr, and at St Nicholas Cole Abbey, two churches which fortunately survived the Second World War.

The largest group comprises nine churches with built-up spires covered with lead and mostly concave in form. Five have perished, but the following remain: St Mary Abchurch, St Margaret Lothbury, St Martin Ludgate and St Peter Cornhill. Of this quartette, St Martin's is the most successful, and is indeed one of Wren's most imaginative and graceful designs, with a touch of Austrian Baroque about it. Apart from its intrinsic beauty, it is a familiar object in the view of St Paul's from Ludgate Hill, and serves as a foil or satellite to the great dome and the magnificent western towers of the cathedral.

The tower of St Magnus the Martyr near London Bridge, now dwarfed by Adelaide House and other tall buildings adjoining it, was one of Wren's latest and best designs, erected twenty years after the church itself. The lower part of the steeple is octagonal, then comes a steep lead dome, and from it rises a graceful spirelet. Here again, Baroque influence is apparent; and this steeple stands in a category of its own.

Lastly comes a small group of four Gothic towers, all in stone, and of these the smallest was destroyed in the Second World War. The survivors are at St Mary Aldermary, St Michael Cornhill and St Dunstan in the East. The two former are completely Perpendicular Gothic in style with prominent octagonal angle-turrets culminating in lofty pinnacles. St Mary Aldermary contains a good deal of medieval work, including the lower part of the tower, and Wren evidently felt bound to maintain as much of the original fabric as practicable—indeed it was a condition of a handsome bequest made to the church that it should be rebuilt as nearly as possible in its old form (XII). The tower of St Michael Cornhill (XIVb) was not finished till 1721, when Wren was nearly ninety years of age; and he is supposed to have had Magdalen Tower at Oxford in mind when he designed it, but in many ways it differs from that famous masterpiece. The lofty, striking and elegant spire of St Dunstan in the East (XIVa), 1698, is said to have been inspired by the old (pre-Fire) tower of St Mary le Bow, but certainly has a close kinship with that of St Nicholas (the cathedral) at Newcastle, *c.* 1445, and with others in Scotland. The remainder of the church, which was partly destroyed in the Great Fire of 1666, was rebuilt in 1817-8 and badly damaged by bombs in 1940. Under close scrutiny, these three Gothic towers display coarse detail and unsympathetic handling, picturesque as they are in general outline; but Wren never

XVI   LONDON, ST LAWRENCE JEWRY; EXTERIOR   *R.C.H.M.*

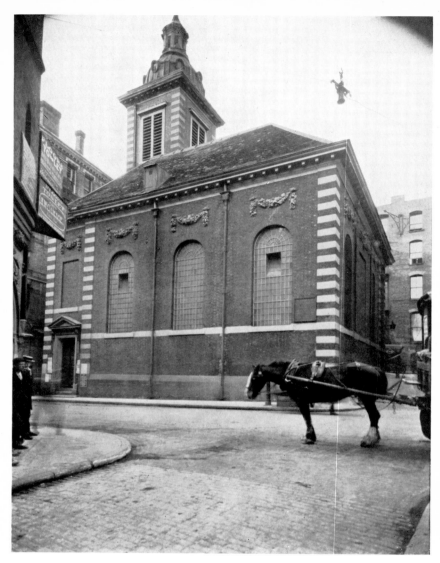

XVII   LONDON, ST BENET, PAUL'S WHARF; EXTERIOR   *R.C.H.M.*

pretended to appreciate our medieval architecture, as he made clear in various pronouncements (see pp. 142-7).

Earlier in this chapter, some reference has been made to the planning of Wren's City churches and to the principles which actuated him in this task, especially to the need for providing optimum conditions for hearing and seeing the preacher. It would be exaggeration to state that he attached less importance to the dignity of the altar, but he did not favour a long or 'deep' chancel: in fact, most of his churches have no chancel, but only a railed-off sanctuary. Owing to the extremely cramped nature of the available sites, the desired accommodation could only be obtained by studiously compact planning; and in the larger churches galleries were needed to provide the necessary number of seats. Several of the smaller sites were oblongs of about 60 by 40 feet, or were about 50 feet square; others were small irregular polygons. No standard type of plan could be adopted, and every site presented a separate complicated problem. Entrances might have to be on north, south or west; or sometimes on two sides. Island sites were almost unobtainable. The tower, prescribed for most churches, often had a porch beneath; and a vestry was required, though this was often a tiny room.

After excluding St Mary Woolnoth and St Dunstan in the East (both rebuilt since his time), Wren's City churches have been classified, according to their plans, in five groups: (i) plain rectangular rooms; (ii) plain rooms with one aisle; (iii) 'nave' and two aisles; (iv) rectangular but with an internal cruciform arrangement of pillars; (v) other domed interiors.

The first group was originally a large one, comprising fourteen churches, but only three are now standing: St Edmund the King, St Nicholas Cole Abbey and St Michael Paternoster Royal. The loss of so many of these plain little churches is regrettable, for they showed great ingenuity in planning. St Edmund has a rectangular auditorium or 'nave' about 60 by 40 feet, and a distinct chancel. The other two are about the same size, but without a chancel and with a small western gallery over the vestibule. These churches may be described, without offence, as of the 'meeting-house type', being simple oblong chambers.

The next group, in which a single aisle has been added, comprised seven churches, and fortunately six of them still survive, viz. St Benet Paul's Wharf (Fig. 13), St Clement Eastcheap, St Lawrence Jewry, St Margaret Lothbury, St Margaret Pattens (Fig. 14) and St Vedast, but St Lawrence— formerly one of the most richly decorated—has been gutted, as has St Vedast. The addition of the aisle was presumably made to obtain additional seating in a side-gallery rather than for 'mere' effect, and because the shape

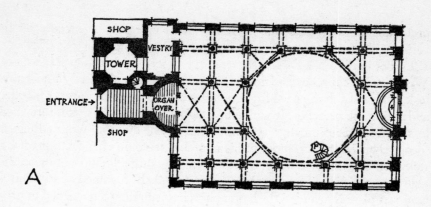

A

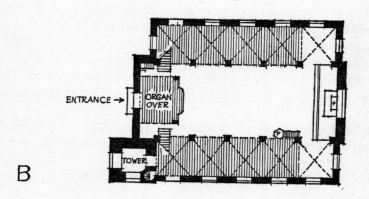

B

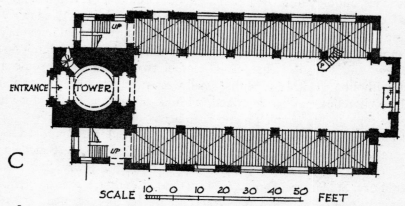

SCALE 10 0 10 20 30 40 50 FEET

FIGS. 8-10.—PLANS OF THREE LARGE CITY CHURCHES: 8 (A) ST STEPHEN, WALBROOK;
9 (B) ST ANDREW BY THE WARDROBE; 10 (C) ST BRIDE, FLEET STREET.
Shaded portions indicate galleries above.

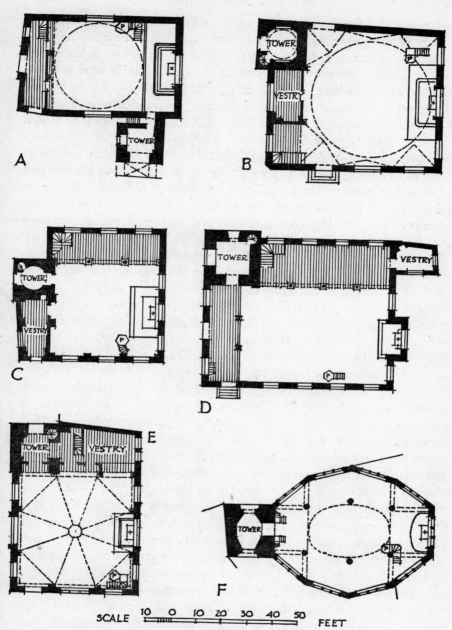

FIGS. 11–16.—PLANS OF SIX SMALLER CITY CHURCHES: 11 (A) ST MILDRED, BREAD STREET; 12 (B) ST MARY ABCHURCH; 13 (C) ST BENET, PAUL'S WHARF; 14 (D) ST MARGARET PATTENS; 15 (E) ST SWITHIN; 16 (F) ST BENET FINK.
Shaded portions indicate galleries above.

of the site permitted it. At any rate, a side-gallery was provided in each case.

The third group had north and south aisles, and originally included seventeen churches, but seven of these have perished. Of the remaining ten, St Mary Aldermary (XII) and St Sepulchre (XIII) were restored Gothic churches where the medieval plan was retained, and eight may be described as 'basilican' churches of Roman Renaissance type. They are Christ Church Newgate, St Bride (Fig. 10, XXI) and St Mary le Bow; and the smaller churches of St Augustine Watling Street, St James Garlickhithe, St Magnus, St Michael Cornhill and St Peter Cornhill; several of these have been gutted. All except St James, St Magnus, St Michael and St Peter had north and south galleries, but those of St Mary le Bow were removed as part of a drastic scheme of internal alteration during the nineteenth century. This church, unlike most of the others, never had a western gallery owing to its unusual plan.

From the fourth group, churches rectangular on plan but with a cruciform arrangement of internal pillars, four churches remain out of the original five. They are St Anne and St Agnes, St Mary at Hill, St Martin Ludgate and St Stephen Walbrook. Each of the first three has a 'nave' or auditorium of oblong or square form, with sides measuring from 50 to 70 feet, and in this auditorium an inner oblong or square space formed by four pillars. The central space at St Anne and St Agnes and at St Martin is covered by intersecting barrel-vaults, at St Mary by a dome, all in plaster. The interior of St Stephen (Fig. 8, XVIII) is far more elaborate and is generally admitted to be one of Wren's most successful designs, though it measures only 83 by 60 feet. Here a beautifully decorated dome of 42 feet diameter is centrally placed in the 'nave', supported on twelve Corinthian pillars in groups of three each; and here, for once, galleries were avoided and every artifice was used to produce a splendid effect, for this is the Lord Mayor's parish church.[1] It has often been stated that Wren was experimenting in these domed churches (and especially at St Stephen), with domical planning, with a view to his great task at St Paul's; and, though precise evidence is lacking, it may be noted that he did not design domes in any of the later churches, so that there is some ground for the supposition. Be this as it may, the effect at St Stephen is masterly, the appearance of a cruciform church being produced by means of pillars and clever vaulted ceilings, although the 'nave' is an oblong apartment without any recesses. The same effect is produced, less spectacularly, in the three other churches mentioned above.

[1] Wren intended to provide a porch and loggia on the north side of the church. (See article by J. Summerson in *RIBA Journal*, Vol. LIX, pp. 126-9.)

The fifth and last group comprises five small churches, of which only one, St Mary Abchurch (Fig. 12, XIXb), has survived, but it suffered damage in 1940. It has a quasi-elliptical dome of *c.* 43 ft. diameter set on pendentives and arches over a rectangular space 53 by 55 ft. The result is singularly impressive. Two of the four destroyed churches in this group—St Antholin and St Benet Fink (Fig. 16)—were among the most remarkable of all Wren's work, and it is lamentable that they were deliberately demolished in 1875 and 1844 respectively. In size they were almost identical, the length of the polygonal 'nave' in each case being about 63 feet, and in shape each was approximately elliptical on plan, the former being a quasi-octagon and the latter a decagon; but whereas St Antholin had an elliptical central dome carried on eight columns, a dome of similar shape at St Benet Fink was supported by six columns. These geometrical forms were determined by the awkward shape of the two sites, making the usual oblong 'nave' impracticable without a heavy sacrifice of space; so Wren made a virtue of necessity and turned his profound knowledge of geometry to good account. St Mildred, Bread Street (Fig. 11, XIXa), was another precious example that has gone in the air-raids. It has already been mentioned (p. 113) as the least altered of all Wren's City churches before the war, but now it has been so utterly ruined that it is to be completely demolished and its site sold. It had a plaster saucer-dome of *c.* 34 feet diameter, centrally placed over an oblong space 59 by 37 feet, and had a small western gallery.

The churches where side-galleries were used have already been named (p. 121). In many others where there were pillars but no side-galleries, the walls had a panelled dado, and the pedestals of the columns were made the same height as the dado and were panelled to match it. This method had the advantage of reducing the columns to a convenient height and diameter for fairly close spacing. At St Bride (1680), the gallery-front cut clumsily across the coupled Doric columns half-way up their height, but at Christ Church, Newgate (XX), 1687, Wren solved this problem by providing a tall pedestal up to gallery-level and starting his Corinthian columns from that point. He also adopted this improved device at St Andrew by the Wardrobe (1692) and at St Mary le Bow, but there the galleries have been removed, as previously mentioned.

The typical Wren church was amply lighted by round-headed windows glazed with clear glass in fairly small panes. The plasterwork usually included much enriched moulding and modelled fruit and flowers. The woodwork was of oak, with profuse carving in limewood and lavishly enriched mouldings. The sense of comfort commented upon by several critics was enhanced by the general use of oak pews with fairly high panelled sides and hinged doors. The removal of these pews during the nineteenth century did much to alter and spoil the original appearance of the church interiors. A considerable amount of furniture has survived from Wren's day, though far more was lost in the air-raids of 1940-1. There are fine pulpits at St Benet Paul's Wharf, St Clement Eastcheap, St James Garlickhithe, St Magnus, St Margaret Lothbury, St Mary Abchurch, St Mary le Bow and St Stephen Walbrook. (Some of these were saved by being stored elsewhere during the raids.) St Peter Cornhill has a splendid chancel-screen. There are notable altar-tables at St Benet Paul's Wharf, St Mary Abchurch and St Stephen Walbrook; and altar-pieces at the same three churches, also at St James Garlickhithe, St Margaret Lothbury and St Martin Ludgate. Well-designed fonts have survived at Christ Church Newgate, St Anne and St Agnes, St Margaret Lothbury, St Margaret Pattens, St Mary Abchurch, St Mary Aldermary and St Stephen Walbrook. St Lawrence Jewry has lost its beautiful vestry. The pulpit, font, organ-case and altar-piece from All Hallows Lombard Street were transferred to the new church of All Hallows, Twickenham, in 1938.

Where organs were installed in Wren's churches, they were usually placed in a western gallery and had magnificently carved cases. Up to 1708, organs are known to have been provided in twelve churches, but four of these have been demolished or rebuilt. The remaining eight were at St Bride, Christ Church, St Clement Eastcheap, St James Garlickhithe, St Lawrence Jewry, St Martin Ludgate and St Mary at Hill. St Bride, St Lawrence Jewry and Christ Church were gutted in 1940-1, and all three organ-cases perished in the flames. The number of organs in Wren's churches had risen to about twenty by 1732, and a few more were added during the remainder of the eighteenth century. The two chief rival builders were Harris and 'Father' Smith or Schmidt, but the fine organs at St Benet Fink (now in Malmesbury Abbey) and St Magnus were built by Abraham Jordan. Wren's drawings at All Souls include at least two designs for organ-cases (see Wren Society Vol. IX, Plates 41, 42), but these are inferior to many of those mentioned above, the finest of all having been at St Lawrence Jewry.

As they stand today, the handful of Wren's City churches which still preserve many of their original features after the disastrous air-raids of 1940-1 have nearly all been altered for the worse by Victorian 'restorers' imbued with dogmatic medieval views. Most of the comfortable pews have been replaced by quasi-Gothic seats, and thus the whole proportion of the interior design has been altered, for the panelling of pews and dadoes formed a strong dark horizontal line from which rose the columns and pilasters, if any such were used. The height of several of the pulpits has been reduced—an even more unpardonable offence—and some of their sounding boards have been removed. Seats in the sanctuary have been re-arranged to provide for a more elaborate ritual at the altar. The whole bright and cheerful effect of the ample lighting through clear glass windows has been obscured by the insertion of pseudo-Gothic stained-glass windows, often of deplorable design. The plain walls have been 'decorated' with incongruous mural paintings of feeble quality, organ-pipes have been tricked out with coloured patterns, and texts in Gothic characters have been painted here and there. Brass gas-standards or electric-light fittings of inappropriate character have been installed. Altar-pieces have been mangled through Victorian piety. All this vandalism dates from the ecclesiological fervour of the mid-nineteenth century, when one of the prime objects of its devotees was to make Wren's churches look as different as possible from the 'meeting-houses' to which they were so closely akin; and then in turn the owners of the old Nonconformist meeting-houses followed suit and 'went Gothic' too.

Apart from the towers, there is little to be said about the exteriors of Wren's churches, for few of them presented important façades to the street, and hardly any stood on island sites. Of the latter, St Lawrence Jewry has the most impressive exterior, on a prominent site (XVI); St Bride and Christ Church Newgate can be seen to advantage; and the delightful little brick church of St Benet Paul's Wharf has already been mentioned (XVII). Most of Wren's other churches were faced with stone towards the street. The façades of St Mary le Bow and of St Martin Ludgate are both admirably designed, but they really form part of the composition dominated by their central feature, the tower and steeple.

VII

WREN'S OTHER CHURCHES AND
HIS VIEWS ON CHURCH-PLANNING

APART from the City churches rebuilt or restored by Wren after the
Great Fire and paid for out of the coal tax, as described in the last
chapter, three other London churches and one chapel-of-ease—
all gutted in the air-raids of the Second World War—were designed by him, as well as some more churches outside the London area.[1]

St Andrew's Holborn is sometimes classified among his City churches,
and does in fact lie within the present boundaries of the City, in the ward
of Farringdon Without; but it escaped the Fire, and its rebuilding in 1686-7
became necessary because the old fifteenth century church was ruinous.
The expenditure amounted to about £9,000. Wren retained the three lower
stages of the square medieval tower but refaced them with Portland stone
in 1704, when he added an upper stage. Considerable internal alterations
were made in 1872. It is a large rectangular church, 91 by 64 feet, with
north and south aisles, a shallow sanctuary flanked by small vestries, galleries over the aisles with vaulted ceilings above, an elliptical barrel-vault
over the main space, vestibules on either side of the western tower containing staircases leading to the galleries and the organ. The Corinthian
pillars supporting the vaulted ceiling rose at the height of the gallery front
from square bases or pedestals. The church was one of Wren's larger and
plainer designs, but contained notable plasterwork and many fine wood
fittings including communion rails, reading-desks and pulpit. All these,
and many other beautiful examples of craftsmanship, were destroyed in
an air-raid on April 16, 1941.

St James's, Piccadilly (XXII), was designed by Wren for Henry
Jermyn, Earl of St Albans, who has been mentioned in this book in connection with Wren's visit to Paris in 1665 (cf. p. 39). The church was
consecrated in 1684. Its dedication was a compliment to King James II, not
a particularly saintly person. The principal vestry was added a few years

[1] Recently discovered drawings prove that he also designed the church of St Anne,
Soho, consecrated in 1686, and gutted during an air-raid in 1940. The tower was
added in 1800. (See article by J. Summerson in *RIBA Journal*, Vol. LIX, pp. 126-9.)

ST STEPHEN WALBROOK.

XVIII   LONDON, ST STEPHEN, WALBROOK
from an engraving of 1735

XIXa LONDON: ST MILDRED, BREAD STREET; INTERIOR   *R.C.H.M.*

XIXb LONDON: ST MARY ABCHURCH; INTERIOR   *R.C.H.M.*

XX LONDON: CHRIST CHURCH, NEWGATE STREET; INTERIOR

XXI LONDON: ST BRIDE, FLEET STREET; INTERIOR

R.C.H.M.

XXII   LONDON: ST JAMES, PICCADILLY; INTERIOR   *R.C.H.M.*

XXIII   LONDON: ST CLEMENT DANES; INTERIOR   *R.C.H.M.*

later, and the spire towards the end of the eighteenth century. Drastic alterations were made in 1856, when the original staircases were removed and the two vestibules added at the west end. In an air-raid on October 14, 1940, the spire and roof were destroyed together with the Victorian rectory and gateway; but fortunately most of the internal fittings were saved, including the splendid organ-cases, the altar-piece and the font—all displaying fine carvings by Grinling Gibbons in wood and marble. The design of this church is of special interest because Wren himself regarded it as a successful effort to provide a very large number of seats at the comparatively low cost of £8,500 (cf. p. 110). He wrote of it that it had 'no walls of a second order, nor lanterns nor buttresses, but the whole roof rests upon the pillars as do the galleries—the cheapest of any form that I could invent'. The plan is of the simplest form, with no division between nave and chancel, and the 'sanctuary' is barely a yard deep. Including the two aisles, the interior measures about 88 by 62 feet. There are galleries on north, south and west, with the organ at the west end. As at St Andrew's Holborn, the Corinthian pillars supporting the barrel-vaulted ceiling spring from the top of the gallery-front, with square pedestals or bases beneath. For the rest, a contemporary description may be quoted to show how the church was regarded at the time of its consecration: 'The Beauty of the Church consists chiefly, 1st in its Roof within divided into Pannels of Crocket and Fret-work, and the twelve Columns that support it, and in the Cornice. 2ndly. In the Galleries with neat fronts on North, South and West. 3rdly. In the Door-cases especially that fronting Jermyn-street which has enrichments. 4thly. In the Windows, especially two at the East-end, the upper Order a Venetian Window, adorned with two Columns and two Pilasters of the Composite Order and the lower Corinthian. The Wainscot round the Church 10 Ft. high is well painted. Pews and Pulpit neat and of Wainscot. The Font has a curious large Marble Bason. . . . The Altar-Piece is very curious and spacious, consisting of fine Bolection Pannels, with Entablature of Cedar with a large Compass Pediment, under which is very admirable carved work, being a Pelican feeding its young between 2 Doves. Also a noble Festoon, with exceeding large Fruit of several kinds, fine leaves, &c, all very neatly done in Lime-wood. The enclosure with strong and graceful Rail and Banister of white marble, artfully carved, and the Foot-pace within of marble. A pretty Organ the gift of the Queen in the Year 1691.' It is interesting to note that the galleries, which Wren himself disliked (p. 117) and only inserted when the need for accommodation made them unavoidable, are here mentioned as contributing to the beauty of the church!

St Clement Danes (XXIII), the famous church in the Strand, was built in 1680-2 from designs by Wren, who—as at St Andrew's Holborn—incorporated a medieval west tower in his plan, but it was so completely cased in new stonework as to be invisible; and the picturesque stone spire was added in 1719 by James Gibbs, Wren's disciple. This church, which John Evelyn considered to be 'pretty built and contrived', was bombed on three separate occasions in 1940-1 and altogether gutted. The original cost was nearly £7,800—to be precise, £7,798 19s. 11½d. (Wren Society Vol. X, p. 111). It is a fairly large building and was most lavishly decorated internally. Its prominent island site allows it to be viewed from all sides, unlike most of Wren's City churches, so its exterior is treated with considerable dignity, but there is no superfluity of ornament on the austere elevations with their bold cornice and deep parapet. The plan includes some features in common with the two other large churches just described —a rectangular nave or auditorium with north and south aisles, measuring 73 by 63 feet in all; square vestibules on either side of a western tower and containing staircases; galleries on north, south and west, with a fine organ (1690) in the western gallery; Corinthian columns rising from the gallery-front to carry a barrel-vaulted roof, and square pedestals or bases beneath them. The eastern end of the church, however, differs profoundly from most of Wren's churches in having a semi-circular chancel terminating in a smaller semi-circular apse. This feature was doubtless planned with a view to external as well as internal effect, but the double curves are not happy. The plaster decorations of the ceilings were exuberantly rich, and many of the beautiful fittings, now so lamentably destroyed, were also very ornate. Here again, a contemporary description of the building seems worth quotation: 'The Fabrick is of Stone, strong and beautiful, of the Corinthian Order, with a Tower, and the late Addition thereon of an ornamental Steeple. The East-ends both of the Church and Chancel are Eliptical. The Roof is camerated, supported with Corinthian Columns, and enrich'd with Fretwork. On the South, facing the Strand, is a spacious circular Portico of six Ionic Pillars. It is a very neat Ornamental Church, both in and outsides, for the latter, you have at the East-end a circular Pediment and Shield with the Anchor. A Cornish round the Church, the Windows are adorned with Cherubims on the Key-stones, the Arches with Enrichments and the Battlements, and other proper places, with Vases. It is not less ornamental within. The Roof is Camerated, supported with neat wooden Columns, of the Corinthian Order, the Roof and Arches plentifully enrich'd with Fretwork, especially that of the Choir, with Cherubims, Palm-branches, Shields, &c, and 6 Pilasters painted blue and the capitals &c gilt standing above the Wainscot. The Queen's Arms in Fretwork and painted. Well Wainscotted and the Pillars cased up to the Galleries which extend on North, West and South sides, having handsome Bolection Work in the Fronts. Oak Pulpit, curiously enrich'd and carved with Cherubims, Cupids, Palm-branches, Festoons, fine finniering, &c. Well Pewed and has 3 oak inner Doorcases. Oak carved Altar-piece of the Tuscan Order with 2 Columns, Entablature and arched Pediment, under which are 3 Cherubims in relievo.'

Less familiar than these important churches is a chapel-of-ease in Hatton Garden, built by Wren in 1687 and converted into a charity school in 1696, when plaster figures of a boy and girl in uniforms were added to the façade. Fortunately these had been removed to safety when the building was altogether destroyed, except the outer walls, during an air-raid. The present state of the forlorn ruins, known as St Andrew's Parochial Schools, shows that hardly anything of Wren's original interior arrangements can have been in existence when the calamity occurred, and even the exterior has been greatly altered by the substitution of a hipped roof with dormers, and by the removal of the previous cornice and lantern, presumably of wood. It was, however, an excellent façade design in brick, characteristic of Wren's more restrained and economical style of building. An old print reproduced by the Wren Society (Vol. XVIII, Plate X) recalls its former appearance.

Outside London, Wren built three churches of some importance. St Mary's at Ingestre, near Stafford (XXIVa, XXIVb), was erected by him in 1673-6 for Walter Chetwynd, MP, FRS, who lived in the adjoining Ingestre Hall, a fine Elizabethan mansion since destroyed by fire and rebuilt. Wren had close contacts with Chetwynd as a result of their mutual interest in the Royal Society. When the church was consecrated in 1677, Chetwynd provided 'a splendid Dinner at the house for the Nobilitie, Clergy and Gentry, both men and women, of the whole county in a manner, which came in that day to see the solemnity performed'. Moreover, 'a Piece of Plate double Guilt' was given to the Bishop and the Dean who preached. A description of the building was also published, somewhat flowery in style, which stated that it was 'in the form of a Parish-church, not great, but uniform and elegant: the outer walls being of squared freestone with a well proportion'd Tower at the West end, of the same: adorned round the top with rail and balister, and flowerpots at each corner. The Chancell within paved throughout with black and white marble, the Windows illustrated with Armes and matches of the Chetwynds in painted glass: and the Ceilings with the same in Fretwork; the side-walls beautifyed with funeral Monuments of the Family, curiously carved in white marble: and the whole vaulted underneath for a dormitory for it, wither all the bodies belonging to it were removed out of the old Church, and decently deposited. The Navis or body of the Church separated from the Chancell with an elegant skreen of Flanders Oak, garnisht with the Kings Armes, and great variety of other curious carvings at the South corner whereof stands the Pulpit, made of the same wood, adorned in like manner with carved work, and the Ironwork about it curiously painted and guilt. The Seats are also made of the same Oak, all of equal height and goodness throughout the whole Church, the lord himself not sitting himself in a finer Seat (only somewhat larger) than the meanest of his Tenants; so humble is this truly Wise man, in the midst of all this magnificence. Near the entrance on the left hand, stands a curious Font all of white marble, the whole Church too being ceiled with the finest Plaister, garnisht also with deep and noble Fretwork.'

In cold fact, it is a comparatively small building, consisting of a 'nave' about 40 feet square, plus a chancel of medium size and a western tower, slightly battered, with a circular porch beneath it. The nave proper is narrow, with side aisles, the arcade between nave and aisles having remarkable piers composed of four three-quarter round Doric columns clustered together, quite in Gothic fashion. Over the chancel is a barrel-vaulted ceiling. Although the internal walls are plain enough, the pulpit, font and chancel-screen exhibit the high standard of ornate craftsmanship typical of Wren's City churches, and the whole effect of the interior is beautiful in its simplicity, dignity and restraint.

All Saints' Church, in the middle of the town of Northampton (XXV), adjoins the Sessions House, and the two buildings were designed as a harmonious group of great distinction, probably though not certainly by Wren, in 1675-8. The Editors of the Wren Society's Volumes (Vol. XIX, p. 58) conclude that, though the authorship is not proved, 'it is natural to suppose that Sir C. Wren was consulted, and there are two facts that seem more than coincidences': viz. that the plan (of the church) closely corresponds to that of St Mary-at-Hill; and that the plan of the west portico, 100 feet wide, resembles that of Old St Paul's, though it is Ionic and not Corinthian. 'It is clear that the details and proportions of the church are not up to the Wren standard. The Ionic columns supporting the dome are very clumsy, and the two scales of proportion in the windows are ill related.' The original church had been destroyed by fire in 1675. An organ and organ-gallery at the west end were added in 1700, the other galleries in 1710 and 1714. Subsequent restorations took place in 1865 and 1888.

The old tower, late Gothic in style, was incorporated in Wren's rebuilding, but the cupola over the centre of the church is characteristic of his work. It is a large church, measuring approximately 73 by 69 feet internally, plus a chancel 33 by 24 feet. (For excellent illustrations see the Wren Society's Vol. XIX.)

At Farley in Wiltshire, near Salisbury, Wren designed between 1680 and 1690 a 'hospital', consisting of a church and almshouses (XXVI), for his friend Sir Stephen Fox, the Paymaster-General, with whom he had been closely associated at Chelsea Hospital (see p. 195). The church was intended to serve as a chapel-of-ease for the locality as well as for the inmates of the hospital. The original contract was for £1,200, including the almshouses, but this sum was considerably exceeded. A drastic restoration in 1875 altered the appearance of the little church. The plan of the building is very simple, consisting of a 'nave' or central space 47 by 28 feet, with transeptal chapels on north and south, a tower on the west, and a chancel 21 feet square on the east. The exterior is very plain, with brick walls and stone dressings. The tower is square, crowned by a balustrade and with stone vases at the angles. Internally there are no arches or pillars, and the ceiling is barrel-vaulted, but that feature may not be original. It is a pleasant little building, worthy of Wren.

The parish church of All Saints at Isleworth in Middlesex has a stone Gothic tower of the late fifteenth century and a modern chancel. The nave is commonly attributed to Wren, and was included in a list of his works by Wyatt Papworth, the learned Editor of the *Dictionary of Architecture* (1853-92); but the Wren Society offers no opinion on the point. The 'Middlesex' volume of the Historical Monuments Commission states (p. 84) that 'the nave was rebuilt in 1706-7 and is said to have been in part designed by Sir Christopher Wren'. It measures 84 by 54 feet including the north and south aisles, over which are galleries approached by staircases at the west end. Doric columns rising from the top of the gallery-front support an elliptical barrel-vault of plaster, and rest upon square brick piers beneath the gallery. In that respect, the design is characteristic of Wren. The brick walls, with round-headed windows, are also typical of his style. The interior was not particularly beautiful, but one can only regret that the building was gutted in an air-raid during the Second World War.

In addition to the eight churches described above, to which Greenwich Parish Church should perhaps be added, it is possible that Wren was concerned in the rebuilding of the large and handsome church of St Mary at Warwick (Fig. 17, Plate XXVII), of which the western half and the

FIG. 17.—ST MARY'S, WARWICK
Attributed to Wren

tower were destroyed by fire in 1694. In the All Souls collection of Wren
drawings at Oxford, there are several which are listed by his son Christopher in *Parentalia* (p. 342) as: 'Designs for the Parochial Church of St
Mary at Warwick, after the Fire of the Town in 1694, not executed. Ortho-
graphy of the Tower of the Parochial Church of St Mary at Warwick,
erected after an unsuccessful Attempt in Execution of a defective prior
Design by other Hands.' The Editors of the Wren Society's Volumes
(Vol. X, pp. 127-8) mention a theory that these designs may have been
made *c.* 1691, *before* the fire and with a view to repairs. The 'other Hands',
whose 'unsuccessful Attempt' failed, were those of one Sir William Wilson, a wealthy builder, who is the other possible author of the present remarkable quasi-Gothic tower and nave, an odd but not altogether un-
pleasing concoction. The poet Gray, a competent antiquary, writing in

1754, ascribed it unhesitatingly to Wren; a guidebook of 1757 as positively attributed it to Wilson.

Mr Marcus Whiffen in a recent book on *Stuart and Georgian Churches* (1948) confidently attributes the design of the rebuilt tower and nave to Wilson (whom he describes as a 'master-architect' who also built a school at Appleby and possibly a small church in Cornwall), but he gives no documentary evidence though he is aware of the attribution to Wren. (Further information about Sir William Wilson and his other buildings is given on pp. 237-8 of the present work.)

It was, however, a case of church restoration rather than church design; and, as such, may be grouped with the extensive works of repair and restoration that he carried out on the spire of Chichester Cathedral in 1684 and as Director of the Works at Westminster Abbey from 1697 to the time of his death. Neither commission can be regarded as church planning, and further reference to them is therefore postponed to a later occasion (see pp. 139-49); but an appropriate conclusion to the present chapter is furnished by the lengthy letter or memorandum that he wrote to 'a Friend' in 1710 or slightly later, summing up the fruits of his long and varied experience of designing churches of all shapes and sizes, often on extremely inconvenient sites. The identity of 'a Friend' appears to be still unknown, but some writers assume that he must have been, as Wren was himself, one of the Commissioners appointed by Queen Anne in 1711 to build fifty new churches in London and Westminster. That pious aspiration was never fulfilled: only eight had been completed by 1730, but nevertheless their architects must have benefited greatly from Wren's sound advice. His letter, printed in *Parentalia* (pp. 318-21), is too long to quote here in full, but the following extracts from it will enable the reader to comprehend the opinions at which he had arrived towards the close of his busy life.

'Since Providence, in great Mercy, has protracted my Age, to the finishing the cathedral Church of St Paul, and the parochial Churches of London, in lieu of those demolished by the Fire . . . and being now constituted one of the Commissioners for Building, pursuant to the late Act, Fifty more Churches in London and Westminster: I shall presume to communicate briefly my Sentiments, after long Experience. . . .

'1. First, I conceive the Churches should be built, not where vacant Ground may be cheapest purchased in the Extremities of the Suburbs, but among the thicker Inhabitants, for convenience of the better sort, although the Site of them should cost more. . . .

'2. I could wish that all Burials in Churches might be disallowed, which is not only unwholesome, but the Pavements can never be kept even, nor

Pews upright: and if the Churchyard be close about the Church, this is also inconvenient, because the Ground being continually raised by the Graves, occasions, in Time, a Descent by Steps into the Church, which renders it damp, and the Walls green, as appears evidently in all old Churches.

'3. It will be enquired, where then shall be the Burials? I answer, in Cemeteries seated in the Outskirts of the Town . . . half a Mile, or more, distant from the Church', each of about two acres in area, 'decently planted with Yew-trees', and each serving four parishes. 'In these places beautiful Monuments may be erected; but yet the Dimensions should be regulated by an Architect, and not left to the fancy of every Mason; for thus the Rich, with large Marble Tombs, would shoulder out the Poor; when a Pyramid, or good Bust, or statue on a proper Pedestal, will take up little Room . . . and will be properer than Figures lying on Marble Beds.

'4. As to the Situation of the Churches, I should propose they be brought as forward as possible into the larger and more open Streets, not in obscure Lanes, nor where Coaches will be much obstructed in the Passage. Nor are we, I think, too nicely to observe East or West, in the Position, unless it falls out properly: Such Fronts as shall happen to lie most open in View should be adorn'd with Porticos, both for Beauty and Convenience; which together with handsome Spires, or Lanterns, rising in good Proportion above the neighbouring Houses (of which I have given several Examples in the City of different Forms) may be of sufficient Ornament of the Town, without a great Expence for enriching the outward Walls of the Churches, in which Plainness and Duration ought principally if not wholly to be studied. When a Parish is divided, I suppose it may be thought sufficient, if the Mother-church has a Tower large enough for a good Ring of Bells, and the other Churches smaller Towers for two or three Bells; because great Towers, & lofty Steeples, are sometimes more than half the Charge of the Church.'

5. Dealing next with the question of materials, he says that good bricks are scarce, though sound London bricks last longer in London than any stone; that Portland or Roche Abbey stones are the best, though expensive; that marble is too costly except for altarpieces; that oak is the best timber for roof-carpentry, failing that, 'good yellow deal. . . . Our tiles are ill-made, and our slate not good. . . . Lead is certainly the best and lightest Covering, and being of our own Growth and Manufacture, and lasting, if properly laid, for many hundred Years, is, without question, the most preferable; though I will not deny but an excellent Tile may be made to be very durable; our artisans are not yet instructed in it. . . .'

XXIVa   INGESTRE CHURCH, STAFFORDSHIRE; EXTERIOR

XXIVb   INGESTRE CHURCH
STAFFORDSHIRE; INTERIOR

XXV   NORTHAMPTON, ALL SAINTS CHURCH; INTERIOR   *N.B.R.*

XXVI   FARLEY CHURCH, WILTSHIRE; EXTERIOR

XXVII ST MARY'S CHURCH, WARWICK; INTERIOR

6. On the important question of accommodation, he argues that, on a basis of relating church attendance to population, each of these new churches should accommodate about 2,000 persons. 'The Churches must therefore be large; but still in our reformed Religion, it should seem vain to make a Parish-church larger, than that all who are present can both hear and see. The Romanists, indeed may build larger Churches, it is enough if they hear the Murmur of the Mass, and see the Elevation of the Host, but ours are to be fitted for Auditories. I can hardly think it practicable to make a single Room so capacious as to hold above 2,000 Persons, and all to hear the Service, and both to hear distinctly, and see the Preacher. I endeavour'd to effect this, in building the Parish-church of St James's, Westminster, which, I presume, is the most capacious, with these Qualifications, that hath yet been built; and yet at a solemn Time, when the Church was much crowded, I could not discern from a Gallery that 2,000 were present. In this Church I mention, though very broad and the middle Nave arched up, yet there are no Walls of a second Order, nor Lanterns, nor Buttresses, but the whole Roof rests upon the Pillars, as do also the Galleries; I think it may be found beautiful and convenient, & as such, the cheapest of any Form I could invent.

'7. Concerning the placing of the Pulpit, I shall observe. . . . A moderate Voice may be heard 50 Feet distant from the Preacher, 30 Feet on each Side, and 20 behind the Pulpit, and not this, unless the Pronunciation be distinct and equal, without losing the Voice at the last Word of the sentence, which is commonly emphatical, and if obscur'd spoils the whole Sense. A French Man is heard further than an English Preacher, because he raises his Voice, and not sinks his last Words: I mention this as an insufferable Fault in the Pronunciation of some of our otherwise excellent Preachers which School-masters might correct in the young, as a vicious Pronunciation, and not as the Roman Orators spoke; For the principal Verb is in Latin usually the last Word, and if that be lost, what becomes of the Sentence?

'8. By what I have said, it may be thought reasonable, that the new Church should be at least 60 Feet broad, and 90 Feet long, besides a Chancel at one End, and the Bellfry and Portico at the other. These Proportions may be varied, but to build more Room, than that every Person may conveniently hear and see, is to create Noise and Confusion. A Church should not be so fill'd with Pews, but that the Poor may have room enough to stand and sit in the Alleys, for to them equally is the Gospel preach'd. It were to be wish'd there were to be no Pews, but Benches; but there is no stemming the Tide of Profit, & the advantage of

Pew-keepers; especially too since by Pews, in the Chapels of Ease, the Minister is chiefly supported.'

The remainder of Wren's letter gives hints for the acquisition of church-sites in London, and suggests a basis for compensation where existing buildings have to be demolished, based upon his own experience in St Paul's Churchyard.

VIII

WESTMINSTER ABBEY

1697 — 1722

WHEN Wren was appointed Surveyor to Westminster Abbey in 1697 (according to the Historical Monuments Commission) or 1698 (according to the Wren Society), he had already had considerable experience in restoring medieval buildings. The method of treatment adopted, rightly or wrongly, in the present book has entailed a description of some of these in preceding chapters, viz. Salisbury Cathedral spire (p. 59) among his early works; Old St Paul's before the Fire (pp. 66-71), and after the Fire (pp. 72-6); sundry City churches (pp. 108-127); and St Mary's, Warwick (pp. 133-5). He had also completed 'Tom Tower' at Oxford (1681-2, pp. 155-6) and had carried out some work at Windsor Castle (pp. 164-7), of which he became surveyor in 1684.

In 1694 he is stated by Elmes (1823) and some other biographers to have restored the spire of Chichester Cathedral, but this work is not mentioned in *Parentalia* or in the index of the Wren Society's twenty volumes. It cannot, however, be ignored here, because Elmes himself repaired and reinstated Wren's work in 1813-4, so writes from first-hand knowledge of its nature. The tower and spire collapsed suddenly in 1861, and were completely rebuilt by Sir Gilbert Scott in 1866, so that no vestige of Wren's ingenious handiwork now survives. According to Elmes (p. 520), Wren 'took down and rebuilt the upper part of the spire . . . and fixed therein a pendulum stage to counteract the effects of the south and south-westerly gales of wind, which act with considerable power against it, and had forced it from its perpendicularity'. Elmes prints a section showing 'the situation and dimensions of this curious and useful piece of machinery. To the finial is fastened a strong metal ring, and to that is suspended a large piece of yellow fir-timber, 80 feet long and 13 inches square; the masonry of the spire, being from 9 inches to 6 inches thick, diminishing as it rises. The pendulum is loaded with iron, adding all its weight to the finial, and has two stout solid oak floors, the lower one smaller by about 3 inches, and the upper one by about $2\frac{1}{4}$ inches, than the octagonal masonry which

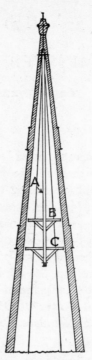

FIG. 18.—SECTION OF CHICHESTER CATHEDRAL SPIRE SHOWING WREN'S 'PENDULUM'
(A) 80-FT. PENDULUM; (B, C) FLOORS

surrounds it. The effect in a storm is surprising and satisfactory. While the wind blows high against the vane and spire, the pendulum floor touches on the lee side, and its aperture is double on the windward; at the cessation, it oscillates slightly, and terminates in a perpendicular. The rest of the spire is quite clear of scaffolding. This contrivance is doubtless one of the most ingenious and appropriate of its great inventor's applications.'

In 1682 Wren reported that the Temple Church was 'ruinous for want of repaire'. He estimated the cost of providing new internal fittings, repairs and paving at £1,400. The new woodwork, finished in 1683, included a pulpit with sounding-board (afterwards installed at Christ Church, Newgate Street), pews, panelling, altar-rails, a fine altar-piece (now in the Bowes Museum at Barnard Castle) and a splendid organ-case. The carving was done by William Emmett. It appears that the buttresses of the nave were 'classicized' at the same time and a classic cornice added. The whole of Wren's work, including the organ-case, was swept away in 1840, when a drastic 'restoration' of the building took place. In June 1952 it was announced that the Benchers of the Inner and Middle Temple had agreed to repurchase and reinstate the altar-piece bought from their predecessors in 1840 by John Bowes.

Thus, when Wren undertook his new duties at Westminster, he had already handled a large amount of difficult repairs to Gothic buildings, involving a study of medieval architecture by means of personal observation rather than from books—indeed, no such books existed in his day. He had also formed his own opinions on the nature of Gothic, and his views will be summarized later in this chapter. The scope and extent of his work at Westminster Abbey has now been determined with some accuracy by scholarly research, but widespread misunderstandings attribute to him many features of the Abbey for which he was not responsible, especially the two western towers. It is hardly exaggerating to say that not a single stone of Wren's considerable work of restoration is visible on the exterior of the church today, for the Reigate and Burford stone that he used has had to be replaced in its turn.

His appointment was related to a decision taken by Parliament in 1698 to devote a part of the coal duty (cf. pp. 82, 94) to refacing the external masonry of the Abbey which had grievously disintegrated as a result of London smoke. (Repairs continued for nearly fifty years, long after Wren's death, and in that half-century almost all the medieval stone was replaced. The scheme did not include Henry VII's Chapel, which was entirely, and rather clumsily, refaced by Wyatt in 1807-22.) This appointment brought Wren once more into touch with Dr Thomas Sprat, who had become Dean of Westminster in 1683, and, as we have seen (pp. 22, 23, 31), was a friend of long standing, even back to the old Wadham days. Work began on the south side of the nave and proceeded westwards.

In 1713, when Wren was eighty years of age, he addressed to Dr Sprat, now Bishop of Rochester, a 'Memorial' or report for the benefit of his successors, describing the work that he had already completed, and outlining also the projects which, in his opinion, were essential to complete the whole scheme of restoration. As in the case of his report on parish churches (pp. 135-8), this document is the fruit of long experience and deep thought by a very learned man: it therefore has a claim for fairly extensive quotation here.

'When I had the Honour to attend your Lordship to congratulate your Episcopal Dignity, and pay that Respect which particularly concerned myself as employed in the chief Direction of the Works and Repairs of the Collegiate-church of St Peter in Westminster; you was pleased to give me this seasonable Admonition, that I should consider my advanced Age;

and as I had already made fair Steps in the Reparation of that ancient and ruinous Structure, you thought it very requisite for the Publick Service, I should leave a Memorial of what I had done; and what my Thoughts were for carrying on the Works for the future.

'In order to describe what I have already done, I should first give a State of the Fabrick as I found it; which being the Work of 500 Years, or more, through several Ages and Kings Reigns, it will come in my Way to consider the Modes of Building in those Times, and what Light Records may afford us; such as at present I am able to collect, give me leave to discourse a little upon.' (Wren then traces this history of the Abbey and its building progress from the legendary site of a pagan temple, discussing the origin and principles of Gothic architecture, and certain defects in its structural design and execution, especially in regard to vaulting and buttressing.)

'But that which is most to be lamented, is the unhappy Choice of the Materials, the Stone is decayed four Inches deep, and falls off perpetually in great Scales. I find, after the Conquest, all our Artists were fetched from Normandy; they loved to work in their own Caen-stone, which is more beautiful than durable. This was found expensive to bring hither, so they thought Rygate-stone in Surrey, the nearest like their own, being a Stone that would saw and work like Wood, but not durable, as is manifest; and they used this for the Ashlar of the whole Fabrick, which is now disfigur'd in the highest Degree: this Stone takes in Water, which, being frozen, scales off, whereas good Stone gathers a Crust, and defends itself, as many of our English Free-stones do.' (He then mentions the unfortunate choice of chestnut timber for some parts of the roof, although excellent English oak was available.)

'All this is said, the better, in the next Place, to represent to your Lordship what has been done, and is wanting still to be carried on, as Time and Money is allowed to make a substantial and durable Repair.

'First in Repair of the Stone-work, what is done shews itself: beginning from the East-window, we have cut out all the ragged Ashlar, & invested it with a better Stone, out of Oxfordshire, down the River, from the Quarries about Burford. We have amended and secured the Buttresses in the Cloister-garden, as to the greatest Part; and we proceed to finish that side; the Chapels on the South-side are done, and most of the Arch-buttresses all along as we proceeded. We have not done much on the North-side, for these Reasons' (briefly, that houses had encroached right up to the walls, with outbuildings which prevented the erection of ladders and scaffolding for repairs).

'And now, in further Pursuance of your Lordship's Directions, I shall distinctly set down, what yet remains to finish the necessary Repairs for Ages to come.' (He then enumerates various urgent repairs of masonry and timber, remarking that he has said nothing of Henry VII's Chapel, 'a nice embroidered work', but that it 'is so eaten up by our Weather, that it begs for some Compassion'; and he commends it to the attention of the Queen, 'as it is the regal Sepulture'.) 'Of the necessary Repairs of the Outward Stone Work, one third Part is already compleated. The most dangerous Part of the Vaulting over the Quire now in Hand will be finished in a few Months, but the Roof over it cannot be opened till Summer. The Repairs of the Stone Work, with all the Chapels, Arch-buttresses, Windows, and Mouldings of the North-side are yet to be done, excepting Part of the North-cross Aile: a great Part of the Expence will be in the North-front, and the great Rose Window there, which being very ruinous, was patched up for the present to prevent further Ruin, some Years since, before I was concerned, but must now be new done: I have prepared a proper Design for it.' (He then describes repairs urgently needed to the timber and leadwork of the roofs.)

Up to this point, it will be noticed, Wren has confined his observations to works of repair and replacement. He has said nothing of additions to be made to the fabric of the Abbey which would materially alter its existing appearance, internally or externally; but in his next paragraphs he makes important proposals for a new steeple, a new west front and a new front for the north transept.

'And now having given a summary Account of what will perfect the meer Repairs, let me add what I wish might be done to render those Parts with proper Aspect, which were left abruptly imperfect by the last Builders, when the Monastery was dissolved by King Henry the Eighth. The West-front is very requisite to be finished, because the two Towers are not of equal Height, and too low for the Bells, which hang so much lower than the Roof, that they are not heard so far as they should be: the great West-window is also too feeble, & the Gabel-end of the Roof over it, is but Weather-boards painted. The original Intention was plainly to have had a Steeple, the Beginnings of which appear on the Corners of the Cross, but left off before it rose so high as the Ridge of the Roof.'

This steeple, he explains, would entail considerable strengthening of the supporting piers beneath, as they had already bent inward, but he had considered this problem and had represented it 'in a Model'. He continues that he had made a design for a steeple 'which will not be very expensive but light, and still in the Gothick form, and of a Style with the rest of the

Structure, which I would strictly adhere to, throughout the whole Intention: to deviate from the whole Form, would be to run into a disagreeable Mixture, which no Person of a good Taste could relish. I have varied a little from the usual Form, in giving twelve Sides to the Spire instead of eight, for Reasons to be discerned upon the Model. . . .'

The proposed steeple was never built, but Wren prepared two designs: one dated 1715 for a very ingenious dome (illustrated in Wren Society Vol. XI, Plate IV) and another dated 1722 (*ibid.*, Plate V) for an exotic cupola, very steep in outline and not unlike the curious example at Bayeux Cathedral, which is an octagonal Gothic cupola of the fourteenth to sixteenth centuries. Wren surrounded the base of his cupola with a ring of Gothic pinnacles, and capped it with an ornamental *flèche*, again resembling that at Bayeux. It was a picturesque design (XXVIIIa), but would perhaps have looked out of place in London. An oil-painting recently presented to the Abbey, and believed to have been executed *c.* 1734-40, depicts the church from the north, with Wren's cupola duly indicated, and two very tall western towers crowned with spires. An engraving dated 1737 and reproduced by the Wren Society (Vol. XI, Plate VI) shows a lofty central spire, like that of Salisbury, over the crossing, ascribing the credit to Wren; but that design must have been due either to Hawksmoor, who became Surveyor to the Abbey in 1725, or to John James, who succeeded him in 1736. Records and accounts of 1724, just after Wren's death, prove that he was not responsible for the squat central tower that exists today, which appears to be entirely modern.

Returning to his report, Wren's next paragraph describes his proposals for the west front: 'Something must be done to strengthen the West-window, which is crazy; the Pediment is only boarded, but ought undoubtedly to be of Stone. I have given such a design, as I conceive may be suitable for this Part: the Jerusalem-Chamber is built against it, and the Access from Tothill-street is not very graceful.' An engraving of the north front by Hollar, made in 1654, shows that the western towers then terminated abruptly at the level of the roof-ridge. They had no roofs or parapets or pinnacles, and were obviously intended to be raised higher, but this work cannot be ascribed to Wren, for in 1736, more than twelve years after his death, the author of *A New View of London* wrote that: 'There is a rumour that the Dean and Chapter still design to raise the towers.' Professor Lethaby also stated categorically that the completion of the western towers was not Wren's work. The north-west tower was raised by Hawksmoor and James between 1734 and 1739, the other by James after 1739. There is a record that Hawksmoor submitted a drawing of a 'rough section

a

b

XXVIIIa LONDON, WESTMINSTER ABBEY; THE PROPOSED CUPOLA FROM A DRAWING BY WREN

b LONDON, WESTMINSTER ABBEY; NORTH TRANSEPT FROM WREN'S DRAWING

XXIX   CAMBRIDGE, TRINITY COLLEGE LIBRARY; EXTERIOR

and idea' in 1724. The evidence, taken as a whole, seems conclusive: Wren did not design the towers.

Coming next to his work on the front of the north transept, it is interesting to note that Hollar's engraving of 1654 shows the 'galilee' or projecting 'Solomon's Porch' added by Richard II and demolished *c.* 1662, but does not show the row of houses which in Wren's time obstructed the north front of the Abbey on both sides of the transept. Those houses, clearly depicted in the oil-painting of *c.* 1734-40 already mentioned, are referred to in the following further extract from Wren's report of 1713: 'The principal Entrance is from King-street, and I believe always will continue so, but at present, there is little Encouragement to begin to make this North-front magnificent in the Manner I have designed, whilst it is so much incumbered with private Tenements, which obscure and smoke the Fabrick, not without danger fireing it. The great North-window had been formerly in danger of Ruin, but was upheld, and stopt up, for the present, with Plaister. It will be most necessary to rebuild this with Portland-stone, to answer the South-rose-window, which was well rebuilt about forty years since; the Stair-cases at the Corners must now be new Ashlar'd, and Pyramids set upon them conformable to the old-Style, to make the Whole of a Piece. I have therefore made a Design in order to restore it to its proper shape first intended, but which was indiscreetly tamper'd with some years since, by patching on a little Dorick Passage before the great Window, & cropping off the Pyramids, and covering the Stair-cases with very improper Roofs of Timber and Lead, which can never agree with any other part of the Design.'

It will be seen from this quotation that Wren was reinstating, to the best of his ability, the appearance of the north transept as it had been prior to restorations carried out not long before his day. The 'pyramids' to which he refers, or 'pinnacles' as we should call them, are the chief features of difference in the interesting pair of comparative drawings in ink and wash, preserved in the Abbey collections and reproduced as Plates II and III in the Wren Society's Volume XI, showing the north front before and after alteration. His 'staircases at the corners' are, of course, angle-turrets, which he has crowned with pinnacles, and he has also added another tall pinnacle on the apex of the gable where Hollar's engraving shows only a small finial. The design was approved in 1719 and carried out forthwith. Lethaby, with his usual felicitous phrasing, writes of this restoration that 'the smile of the old work shone, as it were, through an ungraceful veil, and the whole front still preserved a certain lightness and spring'. Yet, though naïve and picturesque, it *was* somewhat ungraceful, so that when Sir

Gilbert Scott took it in hand in 1875, he, and J. L. Pearson who followed him in 1884, remodelled it in a more orthodox form which has aroused almost universal condemnation. Scott's work ceased above the triple portal—everything above that level was carried out by Pearson. Comparing Wren's drawing (XXVIIIb) with a modern photograph, one finds that the general silhouette has been preserved save for the omission of Wren's pinnacle over the gable, and that change is justified. The design of the rose-window is completely different, the niches and details of the buttresses are different, and steep gables have been added over the three portals. The pinnacles crowning the angle-turrets are more austere and not quite so tall as in Wren's design. On the other hand, Scott claimed that he had devoted twenty-five years of research to the history of the Abbey, after he was appointed Surveyor in 1849, before he touched the north transept front; and in a study of his work published in 1908 in the *Architectural Review* I quoted a statement by Mr J. Oldrid Scott, Sir Gilbert's son, that every detail of the front was based upon existing evidence.

Criticism of Wren's work at Westminster must be restricted to the parts of the building for which he was actually responsible, and critics should bear in mind that his careful and scientific treatment probably saved the Abbey in his day; just as Sir Gilbert Scott, in spite of all his faults, saved the Chapter House two centuries later. The final paragraph of Wren's report of 1713 reads as follows: 'For all these new Additions I have prepared perfect Draughts & Models, such as I conceive may agree with the original Scheme of the old Architect, without any modern Mixtures to shew my own Inventions; in like manner as I have among the Parochial Churches of London given some few Examples (where I was oblig'd to deviate from a better Style) which appear not ungraceful, but ornamental, to the East part of the City; and it is to be hoped, by the publick Care, the West part also, in good Time, will be as well adorned; and surely by nothing more properly than a lofty Spire, and Western-towers to West-minster-Abbey.'

In all this work Wren was assisted by William Dickinson, who died early in 1725 at the age of 54. Dickinson's name appears in the building accounts of St Paul's Cathedral in 1696, when he was paid 10s. a day as assistant to Oliver, Wren's deputy, for measuring the builders' work. It seems probable that Wren transferred him to the Abbey when repairs began there in 1698, and that Dickinson had made a careful study of Gothic architecture. It was he who initialled and dated the design of the Gothic tower of St Michael's Cornhill, one of Wren's best works, in 1721. The Editors of the Wren Society (Vol. VII, p. 9) go so far as to suggest that 'with Wren, Dickinson may be regarded as one of the earliest Gothic revivalists, or, better perhaps, as a continuator of the never entirely dead Gothic tradition'. Certainly his touch in Gothic design was more sensitive than that of Hawksmoor. Dickinson actually worked as Surveyor to the Abbey from 1722, when he succeeded Wren, up to his own death in 1725, when he was followed by Hawksmoor.

Wren's views on Gothic architecture can be inferred from the extracts given above; also from various references in his reports on Old St Paul's, e.g. where he compares 'the good Roman manner' with 'the Gothick rudeness of the old Design' (p. 68); and in his earlier report of 1667 upon Salisbury spire, where he speaks of the 'better and Roman Art of Architecture'. This rather contemptuous attitude reflected not only his low opinion of medieval construction as unscientific, but also the prevailing opinion among cultivated men of his own day. 'Gothic' was frankly and intentionally a nickname, possibly first used in Italian by Palladio at the end of the sixteenth century, certainly employed by Evelyn to describe a church at Haarlem in 1641. Sir Kenneth Clark has taken the trouble to count the number of times that Evelyn uses the term—variously spelt 'Gotiq', 'Gotick', 'Gottick' and finally 'Gothic'—in his *Diary*. He makes the total at least twenty-five. By the time that Wren was launched into architecture, about 1663, 'Gothick' was a fashionable term among *cognoscenti*, and Gothic architecture was as completely ot of fashion. In the nineteenth century, or a little earlier, the pendulum swung the other way, and everything Gothic—good or bad—became sacrosanct. (In the first half of the twentieth century, we have seen 'Baroque' similarly transformed from a term of abuse to the name of a style or cult favoured by intellectuals.)

Many instances of the unreliability of *Parentalia* have already been noted here, and perhaps it is unfair to accept blindly this as a statement of Wren's opinion of Gothic: 'The Goths and Vandals, having demolished the Greek and Roman architecture, introduced in its stead a certain fantastical and licentious manner of building which we have since called modern or Gothic—of the greatest industry and expressive carving, full of fret and lamentable imagery, sparing neither pains nor cost.' That was doubtless the view of the author of *Parentalia* in 1750, and of most men of his time; but was it the view of Sir Christopher himself in say 1665, only twenty-five years after the Gothic fan-vaulting of the staircase at Christ Church, Oxford, was erected? On the whole, I am inclined to think that it was.[1] Yet he was much less ruthless in handling old buildings than

[1] In a letter of 1661, he refers to 'Gothicism' as 'enmity to the progress of learning'.

is commonly supposed, and he was prepared to supply designs which he regarded as Gothic when clients or circumstances so required, as at 'Tom Tower' at Oxford, and at some of his City churches. There was no system of architectural training then in vogue compelling every entrant to the profession to make a study of the historical styles, Gothic included, such as is in force today, though less rigorously than in our fathers' time; besides, Wren never had any architectural training. Evelyn and Defoe and Celia Fiennes all preferred 'the good Roman manner', and Wren was a child of his day.

His attempt at a history of the building of Westminster Abbey, in his report of 1713, may seem rather childish according to modern standards, but it was a creditable effort in the circumstances of the time, and it contains some passages, ascribing the origin of Gothic architecture to the 'Saracens', which are completely in accord with modern scholarship and far ahead of some Victorian ideas: 'This we now call the Gothick Manner of Architecture (so the Italians called what was not after the Roman Style) tho' the Goths were rather Destroyers than Builders; I think it should with more Reason be called the Saracen Style; for those People wanted neither Arts nor Learning; and after we in the West had lost both, we borrowed again from them, out of their Arabick Books, what they with great Diligence had translated from the Greeks. They were Zealots in their Religion, and where-ever they conquered (which was with amazing Rapidity) erected Mosques and Caravansara's in Haste; which obliged them to fall into another Way of Building; for they built their Mosques round, disliking the Christian Form of a Cross, the old Quarries whence the ancients took their Blocks of Marble for whole Columns and Architraves, were neglected, and they thought both impertinent. Their Carriage was by Camels, therefore their Buildings were fitted for small Stones, and Columns of their own Fancy, consisting of many Pieces; and their Arches were pointed without Key-stones, which they thought too heavy. The Reasons were the same in our Northern Climates, abounding in Free-stone, but wanting Marble. The Crusado gave us an Idea of this Form. . . .'

As a postscript to this chapter, mention may be made here of two works by Wren intended for Westminster Abbey, neither of which was carried out. In 1695 he designed a monument to Queen Mary II, to be placed in the south aisle of Henry VII's Chapel. His remarkable drawing (reproduced as frontispiece to the Wren Society's Vol. V) is in the All Souls collection, and was made jointly with Grinling Gibbons. It is as flamboyantly Baroque as anything ever conceived in England, with clouds, cherubs, sun-rays, lively figures and twisted 'barley sugar' columns wreathed with garlands of gilt bronze. In 1711 he prepared alternative designs for a large new dormitory for Westminster School, within the Abbey precinct. His drawings show a three-storey building of seventeen bays, crowned by a balustrade—all very massive, academic and severe. Further variations were made, probably by Dickinson and Hawksmoor, and one scheme of 1721 is endorsed '5th design'. All these were superseded, however, by designs submitted by Lord Burlington, who is now considered to have been solely responsible for the present building, his first independent work as an architect. The whole story is related and fully illustrated in the Wren Society's Vol. XI; but when the Dormitory was reopened in June 1950, having been seriously bombed during the Second World War, its authorship was ascribed in the royal speech, in *The Times*, and elsewhere, to Wren without question.

IX

WREN'S LATER BUILDINGS
AT OXFORD AND CAMBRIDGE

REN'S first works in architecture were at Oxford and Cambridge, partly by reason of family influence at Cambridge and partly because of his own close academic connection with Oxford. His chapels at Pembroke College (pp. 32-3) and Emmanuel College (pp. 57-9) at Cambridge, his Sheldonian Theatre (pp. 33-6) and his buildings for Trinity College (pp. 36-7) at Oxford have already been described. It was only natural that both universities should wish to obtain his services for designing other buildings even after he had become Surveyor-General of His Majesty's Works in 1669. His increased prestige doubtless encouraged them in their ambitions to employ the foremost architect of the day, but the enormous amount of work that he was carrying out in the period 1670-1700 made it impossible for him to give close personal supervision to buildings fifty miles from London, and much of the execution was therefore delegated to local assistants. Their share in the operations was thus considerable, and the available evidence of responsibility is insufficient, in many cases, to enable us to know with any certainty where Wren was actually concerned and where the credit must be ascribed to others.

An example is the river-front or west front of Clare College, Cambridge, built in 1669-76. The complete rebuilding of this college, where the older buildings had become ruinous, was begun in 1635. The east and south sides of the quadrangle had been finished by 1642, and the west front had just been begun, when the Civil War interrupted the work. It was resumed in 1669, when the inner side of the west front was built to harmonize with the rest of the new quadrangle, but the other side, towards the river (or, as it is now commonly called, 'The Backs'), was erected in a completely different style, with Doric pilasters on the lower two storeys and Ionic pilasters extending through the upper two storeys. Above these was a balustrade, behind which was a row of dormers lighting the attics. The windows originally had mullions, transoms and leaded glazing, but were replaced by sash-windows in 1715, the sills of those on the ground and first floor being lowered in 1815. Tradition ascribes the authorship of the design to Robert Grumbold, 'Freemason', and he certainly carried it out as builder; but the Editors of the Wren Society suggest (Vol. V, p. 7) that the character of the façade makes it possible, at least, that it 'owes a good deal to Wren'. It is indeed a most attractive composition, although considerably altered by the successive changes made to the windows, as just described.

At St John's College, Cambridge, almost exactly the same sequence of events took place at the same time, and the same builder was employed. The first court was erected at the beginning of the sixteenth century, the second court at the end, and the north side of the third court in 1624. The remaining two sides of the third court—the west side, facing the river, and the south side—were built in 1669-71 by Robert Grumbold. Here again, the character of the design suggests the hand of Wren, but there is some attempt to harmonize the new additions with the older buildings adjoining them, especially in the windows and parapets. Wren sometimes made such concessions, but in doing so rendered his own work more difficult to identify; and in this instance, where qualities of picturesqueness are manifest, documentary evidence is still lacking. The so-called 'Wren Bridge' at St John's is a much later work, and Wren certainly prepared sketch-designs for it in 1697, sending them to the Master, but it was not built (by Robert Grumbold) till 1709-12. It cost £799 19s. 3d., a substantial sum in those days. The scheme included, however, the magnificent stone gate-piers and iron gates close to the south-west angle of the college. It is, perhaps, the most beautiful bridge in Cambridge, reminiscent in some ways of examples that Wren would have seen in Paris in 1665. Probably the actual erection was supervised by Hawksmoor.

Yet another building in Cambridge that is freely attributed to Wren without conclusive documentary evidence is Bishop's Hostel at Trinity College, erected in 1669-71. It stands at the corner of Trinity Lane and Trinity Hall Lane, and is detached from the great complex of older buildings of the college, but has since been surrounded by the extensive additions made by Wilkins in 1823-5, and by Sir Arthur Blomfield in 1878. The site had originally been occupied by Garret Hostel and Ovyng's Inn, the buildings of which had become ruinous when it was decided to demolish them in 1662. Dr John Hackett, Bishop of Lichfield and Coventry, formerly a Scholar and Fellow of the college, bequeathed the sum of £1,200 for the erection of a new hostel, hence its present name. It is a simple dignified brick building with two projecting wings, two storeys high plus attics with dormers in the steep hipped roofs, and massive chimneys.

The windows have mullions and transoms. There is a deep coved cornice. The central feature has Ionic pilasters flanking the entrance doorway. The absence of ornament gives the design a domestic rather than an institutional character. In every respect, the building is characteristic of Wren's style, and his authorship is the more likely because the work was carried out by Robert Minchin of Bletchington in Oxfordshire, who had acted as carpenter at the Sheldonian Theatre (p. 36), and had then been employed by Wren at Trinity College, Oxford (p. 37). Whatever hand Wren may have had in the design, it is probable that he was, at the least, consulted in the matter.

Another echo, or result, of the Sheldonian Theatre commission may be found in the scheme initiated in 1674 or 1675 by Dr Isaac Barrow, Master of Trinity College, Cambridge, to provide a Senate House. Hitherto the University Church of Great St Mary had accommodated academic functions, with the same disadvantages that had prevailed at Oxford before the Sheldonian Theatre was erected a few years earlier. It was a natural and justifiable rivalry. Barrow, exiled as a Royalist during the Civil War, became Professor of Mathematics at Cambridge in 1663, and would obviously find Wren a man after his own heart. He knew him well, and had a high opinion of his mathematical attainments. The list of Wren's works in *Parentalia* includes: 'Plans, Elevation and Section of a Theatre, or Commencement-house, with a Library annexed, according to an Intention, for the university of Cambridge, about the Year 1678, but not executed.' This date is, however, like so many 'facts' in *Parentalia*, now known to be inaccurate, for Robert Hooke's *Diary* contains a reference to the 'theatre' at Cambridge as early as March 1675. Wren's first design (illustrated in the Wren Society's Vol. V, Plates XIII, XIV) is in the All Souls collection. The site is now occupied by the Old University Library built from Stephen Wright's designs in 1755-8 (and since remodelled for other University purposes in 1936), south of the present Senate House by James Gibbs (1722-30) and immediately opposite Great St Mary's Church. It was intended that the new building should be axially placed in relation to a recently opened avenue, the 'Bishop's Walk', and united at the back, towards King's Parade, with an older quadrangle. The lower part of Wren's projected building consisted of an open cloister. The Library was upstairs, and measured about 130 by 23 feet internally. The Senate Chamber was large and lofty with a barrel-vaulted ceiling. Externally the group was not one of Wren's happiest compositions. The turrets over the four staircases to the Senate Chamber resembled castors, and the whole façade was lacking in imagination.

XXX CAMBRIDGE, TRINITY COLLEGE LIBRARY; INTERIOR

N.B.R.

XXXI   OXFORD, OLD ASHMOLEAN MUSEUM; EXTERIOR   *R.C.H.M.*

XXXII   OXFORD, 'TOM TOWER'   R.C.H.M

XXXIII   OXFORD, TRINITY COLLEGE CHAPEL; INTERIOR   *N.B.R.*

However, according to the *Life* of Barrow's successor, Dr John North, 'sage caution prevailed, and the matter, at that time, was wholly laid aside. Dr Barrow was piqued at this pusillanimity, and declared that he would go straight to his college and lay out the foundations of a building to enlarge his back court, and close it with a stately Library, which should be more magnificent and costly than what he had proposed to them. . . . And he was as good as his word; for that very afternoon he, with his gardeners and servants, staked out the very foundation upon which the building now stands.'

Thus, while Wren's design for the Senate House must be added to his considerable list of professional disappointments already mentioned in this book, he did ultimately produce, in his fine new Library for Trinity College, one of his major works. Yet, even for this commission, he prepared a scheme which was rejected before he achieved finality. This first project may be dated 1675 at the latest, for actual building began in the following year. He followed Palladian precedent, using the famous Villa Rotonda as his model and designing a dome on a square base, with a hexastyle Ionic portico on the east side. The diameter of the dome was 65 feet, and its height from the floor 90 feet, dimensions roughly corresponding with those of the rejected Mausoleum at Windsor (p. 218). It was imposing enough, antique in its splendidly monumental character, but not conceived with any idea of connecting it with Nevile's Court, then closed by a wall on the side towards the new site.

Soon after Wren had made these first drawings, it was decided to extend Nevile's Court further westwards towards the river and to make the new library form the west side of the Court, continuing a cloister beneath it and providing access to it from the first floor of the new wing. This decision not only involved an entirely new design, but also influenced certain features of that design, as we shall see. Externally, the (east) front towards Nevile's Court is very different from the (west) front towards the river (XXIX). The composition of the former façade shows an attempt to harmonize the Library with the three-storey buildings of Nevile's Court, which are far lower than the two-storey block of the Library. Wren adopted two tiers of classical Orders on this front, using engaged columns, Doric below and Ionic above, with a balustrade above which almost hides the roof. Between the columns are large round-headed windows illuminating the Library, and beneath them are the arches of a cloister, higher than the adjoining arches of the north and south arcades of the quadrangle and with their tympana (upper parts) solid, to conceal the Library floor, which is level with the imposts of the arches, and not—as would be normal practice—

above the level of their crowns. This curious expedient (also adopted by Wren at Hampton Court, less happily, but for a similar reason) was explained in an undated letter which he wrote to, presumably, Dr Barrow: 'I have given the appearance of arches as the Order required fair and lofty: but I have layd the floor of the Library upon the impostes, which answar to the pillars in the cloister and the levels of the old floores, and have filled the arches with relieves of stone, of which I have seen the effect abroad in good buildings,[1] and I assure you where porches are lowe with flat ceilings is infinitely more gracefull than lowe arches would be and is much more open and pleasant, nor need the mason feare the performance because the Arch discharges the weight, and I shall direct him in a firme manner of executing the designe. By this contrivance the windows of the Library rise high and give place for the deskes against the walls, and being high may be afforded to be large, and being wide may have stone mullions.'

Critics differ as to the merits of this façade, some finding it satisfactory; others objecting to the subterfuge just described and to the clumsy relation of its horizontal lines to the north and south sides of the Court. Ironically enough, the connection between the Library floor and the adjoining buildings was never made, so Wren's ingenuity was fruitlessly applied in this case! The west front or river-front has also impressed some critics and repelled others, who regard it as disappointing and monotonous. Wren seems never to have foreseen that 'The Backs' (of the colleges) would come to be regarded as the most delightful feature of Cambridge, and certainly his treatment of the river-front is austere, consisting in the omission of the Orders on both storeys and of the arches in the lower storey. As for the interior of the Library, a single splendid room 150 by 38 feet (XXX), no critic seems disposed to find fault with that, satisfying as it does functional requirements as well as aesthetic needs. It is divided into carrels or bays by projecting bookcases, beautifully carved by Grinling Gibbons. Today it is clear to us that Wren, although he carried out this great building gratis in token of friendship for Dr Barrow, took great pains with the details of furnishing and decoration. Robert Grumbold, who was directing the work, was constantly journeying up to London to consult Wren on matters of detail, and to obtain detail-drawings and instructions. Much of the decorative work, in fact, was done in London workshops and sent down to Cambridge, but many of the craftsmen on the site were already known to Wren. Except some of the bookcases and fittings, the work was finished by the end of 1690. According to Atkinson and Clark's *Cambridge* (1897), the portico on the east side of

[1] E.g. at the Hôtel de Beauvais, Paris (1656), which Wren must have seen.

Nevile's Court (facing the Library), added in 1682, 'was probably designed by Sir C. Wren'; but it has also been ascribed to Grumbold.

Of buildings attributed to Wren at Oxford, some at least cannot be ascribed to him with absolute confidence. One of them is the Old Ashmolean Museum in Broad Street (XXXI), erected in 1679-83. Elmes accepts it unhesitatingly as Wren's work but gives no confirmatory evidence, Sir Reginald Blomfield rejects it, the Wren Society apparently ignores it, but the Historical Monuments Commission's volume on *Oxford City*, published in 1939, concludes that 'apart from its general excellence, the evidence is against the ascription'. Messrs Belcher and Macartney, in their great work *Later Renaissance Architecture in England* (1901), attribute the fine doorway to Wren, the rest to an architect or master-mason, Thomas Wood, whose name appears upon an old engraving. It is a very small building measuring only 35 by 62 feet. The longer side, or flank, towards Broad Street, has two tiers of stone-mullioned windows capped with pediments and is in no way remarkable; but the entrance-front, small as it is, might conceivably have been designed by Wren in an exuberant mood. It was planned as a museum, and its appearance suggests an institution, not a domestic building. The doorway is approached up a flight of ten steps, beneath an imposing portal with coupled Corinthian columns supporting a broken entablature and a curved pediment. Above this stage is a tall mullioned window, with stone panels carved with festoons of foliage on either side, and a raking pediment above with carved heraldry in the tympanum. Rather French in effect, it is one of the most striking buildings in Oxford, and it would be pleasant to be able to add it to Wren's formidable catalogue of masterpieces. At the back is a handsome oak staircase. The building now serves as a Museum of the History of Science. There is a modern stained-glass window (1927) commemorating Wren's work as Professor of Astronomy and President of the Royal Society, not as an architect. Among the exhibits upstairs is the mechanism of a clock (No. 193) from Wadham College, 'believed to have been designed by Wren'.

Close to the Old Ashmolean lies the Bodleian, where Wren is known to have inserted the north doorway of the Divinity School in 1669. Some thirty years later (*c.* 1700-2), he strengthened that building, and enlarged the buttresses projecting into the garden of Exeter College. *Parentalia* mentions 'proposals for the Repairs of the Publick-library and Schools at Oxford, with Drawings annexed; imparted to Dr. Gregory. Now in the Bodleyan Library.'

The same authority (p. 342) also refers to 'the Campanile, or Bell-tower, over the Gate, in the Front and principal Access to the great Quadrangle-court of Christ-church, Oxon., in the Gothick style; begun on the old Foundation (laid by Cardinal Wolsey) in June 1681, and finished November 1682'. Here at 'Tom Tower', there is no doubt at all that Wren was the architect concerned, and that the master-mason employed was Christopher Kempster of Burford, who had acted in a like capacity on the Market House at Abingdon (1678-81, pp. 216-7), and previously had worked at St Paul's Cathedral. Wren's employer at Christ Church was Dr John Fell, Dean and subsequently Bishop of Oxford. When Wren appeared upon the scene, the work had been stopped just as Wolsey left it after he fell into disgrace in 1529. The half-finished turrets on each side of the great gateway were covered with makeshift roofs of lead, and though the archway itself was complete, the porch had not yet been vaulted and remained open to the sky. It is not known how Wolsey intended to finish the tower: perhaps it would have been a massive and lofty structure like Lupton's Tower at Eton. Wren was instructed to complete it in the 'Gothick manner'; and although he did so in a highly unorthodox way, the result is among his most successful efforts to work in an idiom foreign to his own taste (XXXII). In the previous chapter I have examined his attitude to Gothic architecture, as indicated by his work at Westminster and elsewhere, and as expressed in his scanty writings. At Christ Church he seems to have made the ogee his guiding form, and he applied it generously all over his design. The window over the portal has an ogee arch of slightly un-Gothic type, the remarkable octagonal cupola has an ogee dome and windows with ogival heads, and the turrets are similarly crowned. The transitional stage containing the clock, between the square base and the octagon, has canted angles with yet more ogees above them. The result is an orgy of ogees, but comically picturesque. Most remarkable of all, Wren provided stone Gothic vaulting over the gateway, decorated with heraldry in colour and altogether medieval in spirit; yet one must remember that the noble fan-vaulting over the porch of Christ Church Hall had been completed only forty years before. For the rest, 'Tom Tower' was refaced just before the First World War, it has had a whole book written about it, and it contains the huge bell—'Great Tom'—which once hung in the magnificent abbey of Osney, long since demolished. Ever since it was installed here in 1684, that bell has rung its 101 strokes at five minutes past nine in the evening. Wren was asked to provide an observatory in the tower but he wisely declined to do so (p. 215).

The chapel of Trinity College, one of the most beautiful in Oxford

(XXXIII), was rebuilt, after a fire, in 1691-4, possibly from Wren's designs, possibly from Dean Aldrich's, or it may have been due to collaboration between them. The Historical Monuments Commission says that it was probably designed by Aldrich in consultation with Wren, and the Editors of the Wren Society's Volumes (Vol. V, pp. 15-6) do not accept Aldrich as sole author. The tradition which ascribes it to him is based entirely on the facts that Aldrich was a friend of Bathurst, President of Trinity, and that he subsequently displayed some architectural ability in designing All Saints Church in Oxford in 1707. On the other hand, it seems unlikely that Bathurst, as head of a college, should invoke the aid of the head of a rival college, Aldrich being then Dean of Christ Church. A letter from Bathurst, at Oxford, to Wren in London, dated February 25, 1692, shows that Wren was consulted, but makes no mention of Aldrich:

'Worthy Sir,

'When I sent Mr. Phips [probably the builder] to wait on you with a scheme of our new building, he told me how kindly you was pleased to express your remembrance of me [from the old Wadham days], and that you would send me your thoughts concerning our designe; and particularly of the pinnacles, which as they were superadded to our first draught, so, I must confess, I would be well content to have omitted with your approbation. The season for our falling to work againe will now speedily come on; which makes me the more hasten to entreat from you the trouble of two or three lines in relation to the promise, whereby you will farther oblige

   'Sir, your old friend, and ever faithfull servant,

           'R. Bathurst.'

It appears from this letter that some person other than Wren had already prepared a design for Bathurst: Aldrich is not ruled out. Wren replied from his London office at Scotland Yard within a week:

'Sir,

'I am extremely glad to hear of your good health, and, what is more, that you are vigorous and active, and employed in building. I considered the designe you sent me of your chapel, which in the maine is very well, and I believe your worke is too far advanced to admitt of any advice: however, I have sent my thoughts which will be of use to the mason to form his mouldings. He will find two sorts of cornice; he may use either. I did not well comprehend how the tower would have good bearing upon that side where the stairs rise. I have ventured upon a change of the staire, to leave the wall next the porch of sufficient scantling to bear that part which rises above the roofes adjoining. There is noe necessity for pinnacles; and those expressed in the printed designe are much too slender. I have given another way to the rayle and baluster, which will admit of a vase that will stand properly above the pilaster.

'Sir, I wish you success, and health, and long life, with all the affection that is due from,

'Your obliged, faithful friend, and humble servant,

'Chr. Wren.'

'P.S. A little deal box, with a drawing in it, is sent by Thomas Moore, Oxford Carrier.'

This correspondent does not clear up the mystery in the least. Wren had done architectural work for Trinity College in 1665 (see pp. 36-7), and the chapel shows all the characteristics of his taste in design. It is relatively small, 68½ by 27½ feet. The stone walls are faced externally with ashlar, and have Corinthian pilasters on a high stylobate. Above the cornice is a balustrade ornamented with vases. The exterior is a correct and competent exercise in the Palladian style. Internally, the simple oblong room is a triumph: due not so much to its admirable proportions as to the beauty and lavishness of its decorations in carved wood and modelled plaster, including some of the finest work of Grinling Gibbons. Even at Hampton Court, or in the City churches before the Second World War, there is no interior so splendidly arrayed, and nothing more typical of the craftsmanship favoured by Wren. Here one sees the late Renaissance at its best in England.

The Library of Queen's College, Oxford (XXXIV), is another masterpiece to which it is unfortunately necessary to append a question mark. We do know that it was built in 1692-5, and that Nicholas Hawksmoor, Wren's pupil and assistant, was concerned in its erection. The rebuilding of the college had been begun in 1672, and most of the work was undoubtedly done by Hawksmoor, but some critics have suggested that the whole scheme was inspired by Wren. The Editors of the Wren Society (Vol. V, pp. 24-5) consider that the design of the Library, at least, was made by Wren about 1682, though not carried out till 1693-5, and possibly modified in execution by Hawksmoor. Externally the building is faced with ashlar. The principal (east) front is eleven bays wide, with a pediment supported on Corinthian pilasters over the central three bays. The windows on each of the two storeys are large and round-headed, but those on the lower storey were formerly open arches. Internally, the Library upstairs is a really magnificent room, 123 by 30 feet and very lofty. It is slightly smaller than Wren's other great library, at Trinity College, Cambridge; but resembles it in many respects: its splendid lighting, its division into carrels or alcoves, its bookcases superbly carved by Grinling Gibbons, and its fine plaster ceiling. The prevailing brown tint of the woodwork harmonizes admirably with the mellow bookbindings and the rich hues of the Persian rugs on the floor. Whether actually designed by Wren or not, it is indeed worthy of his genius, and the attribution to him seems justified.

Finally, there is a drawing by Wren in the All Souls Collection which is reproduced in the Wren Society's Vol. XII, Plate XXX, and is described by the Editors as 'possibly an idea for the Clarendon Press on a different site than the Broad'. It shows an imposing façade with a frontage of 195 feet, and a central Doric portico 50 feet wide. This constitutes one more puzzle for the student of Wren's work, but is only one among many dozens. His output was phenomenal.

X

ROYAL HOUSES

COMPARABLE in importance with Wren's work at St Paul's and the City churches were his numerous designs, executed or projected, for palatial residences for the Crown. Of these, Hampton Court is the most celebrated, but Kensington Palace is also notable, and substantial alterations were made at St James's Palace. The great palaces of Whitehall and Winchester, as well as the King's House at Newmarket, have long since been demolished. The vast scheme for remodelling Windsor Castle never came into being. As for Greenwich, although Charles II, one of Wren's most constant and devoted patrons, spent a huge sum in rebuilding the old Palace there between 1662 and 1669, the work was designed and supervised by John Webb; and when Wren was appointed architect in 1695, it was to remodel the whole building as a hospital, so that a description of his doings there is postponed to the next chapter, on 'Royal Hospitals'.

After Wren became Surveyor-General in 1669, it was many years before he was entrusted with the design of a palace on the grand scale (except the abortive scheme for Whitehall mentioned on p. 172, about which little is known). Webb was busy at Greenwich, as mentioned above, and Hugh May remained in charge at Windsor from 1673 until his death in 1684, when Wren succeeded him. His first commission of any note on royal residences seems to have been in connection with the King's House at Newmarket. Building had begun there in 1668 under one Samuel, about whose precise status there is some doubt. John Evelyn's *Diary* contains the following entry for July 22, 1670: 'So passing through Newmarket, we alighted to see his Majesty's house there, now new building; the arches of the cellars beneath are well turn'd by Mr Samuel the architect, the rest meane enough and hardly fit for a hunting house. Many of the roomes above had the chimnies plac'd in the angles and corners, a mode now introduc'd by his Majesty which I do at no hand approve of. I predict it will spoile many noble houses and roomes if follow'd. It does onely well in very small and trifling roomes but takes from the state of greater. Besides this house is placed in a very dirty streete, without any court or avenue, like a common one, whereas it might, and ought to have ben built at

XXXIV   OXFORD, QUEEN'S COLLEGE LIBRARY; INTERIOR

XXXV   KENSINGTON PALACE; ENTRANCE FRONT

R.C.H.M.

either end of the towne, upon the very carpet where the sports are celebrated; but it being the purchase of an old wretched house of my Lord
Thomond's, his Majesty was persuaded to set it on that foundation,
although the most improper imaginable for a house of sport and pleasure.'

Remembering that Evelyn was not only a most discriminating critic of
architecture but also one of Wren's oldest and closest friends, it seems
strange that he should name Samuel if Wren was, in fact, responsible. The
suggestion made by the Wren Society (Vol. XIX, p. xiii), that Samuel
may have been placed there by Wren, is possible, and may help to identify
him with a master-bricklayer named Samuel mentioned several times by
Hooke in his *Diary* as having been employed by him: on the other hand,
one Samuel applied for the post of City Architect; and Lord Arlington's
house of Euston, near Newmarket, has also been attributed to him, as well
as the original Eaton Hall near Chester, demolished in the nineteenth
century. On October 3, 1674, Hooke notes that he has heard a story of
'Sir Chr. Wren's disfavour with the King'. Possibly this may refer to an
anecdote later repeated in the Rev M. Noble's *Biographical Dictionary*
(pub. 1806, iii, 327) that Charles complained of the lowness of the rooms
at Newmarket, and Wren, who was of diminutive stature, replied that he
thought that they were high enough. The King, himself over six feet tall,
then 'lowered himself to Wren's height and strutted about the room, repeating: "Ay, Ay, Sir Christopher, I think they are high enough." '

Charles spent a great deal of money, as well as a good deal of time, at
Newmarket; but his life there was rudely interrupted by an unforeseen
event described in Evelyn's *Diary* under the date September 23, 1683:
'There was this day a collection for rebuilding Newmarket, consum'd by
an accidental fire, which removing his Majesty thence sooner than was intended, put by the assassinates, who were disappointed of their rendezvous
and expectation [the so-called Rye House Plot] by a wonderfull providence. This made the King more earnest to render Winchester the seate
of his autumnal field diversions for the future, designing a palace there,
where the antient castle stood; infinitely indeede preferable to New-market
for prospects, air, pleasure, and provisions. The Surveior [Wren] has
already begun the foundation for a palace, estimated to cost £35,000, and
his Majesty is purchasing ground about it to make a parke, &c.'

It remains uncertain how far Wren was responsible for designing the
King's House at Newmarket, of which no vestige remains; but ample information is available about his work at Winchester though the palace
there has also been demolished in more recent times. Charles II's expenditure upon building and finishing his various palaces had been prodigal

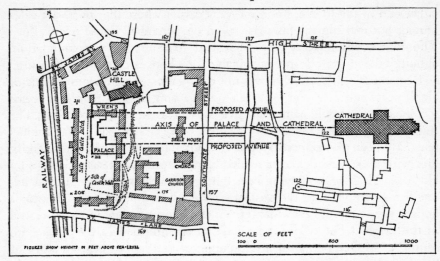

FIG. 19.—PLAN SHOWING RELATION OF WREN'S WINCHESTER PALACE (DESTROYED 1894)
TO THE CATHEDRAL AND TO EXISTING STREETS AND BUILDINGS

enough hitherto, albeit little of the work had passed through Wren's hands; and when the King began to toy with a new scheme at Winchester, in or about the year 1682, being then fifty-two years of age, his extravagant ambition assumed that his long career of debauchery would not affect his splendid health and that he might expect to occupy the vast building that he now projected. As we shall see, he died before it was finished.

Wren must have received his instructions some time in 1682, and it may be significant that the King and the Duke of York were voted the Freedom of the City of Winchester on September 1 in that year. At any rate, the foundation-stone of the palace was laid on March 23, 1683. The old castle that formerly occupied the site had been partially demolished during the Civil War, but some ruins were certainly standing in 1651. When the King's intentions became known, the mayor and corporation formally and tactfully handed over to him all their rights—if any—to the site. It is generally, and perhaps rightly, assumed that Charles wished to emulate the glories of Versailles, possibly stimulated by the fact that his mistress of the moment—the 'Duchess of Portsmouth'—who had been sent over to England from France with the specific object of capturing Charles' easy affections for the benefit of her native country, had created a fashion for all things French at his Court, as Evelyn's *Diary* proves. Such of Wren's designs as survive do indicate that the plan of the new palace resembles that of Versailles as Le Vau left it before J. H. Mansart began his immense extensions in 1676. Moreover, Wren projected a scheme of monumental layout hitherto unknown in England and obviously inspired by French precedent. The new palace was so planned that a great avenue connected the axial line of the building with the west front of the cathedral down in the valley, a magnificent idea.

Evelyn, visiting the house on September 16, 1685, mentions the 'incomparable prospect' from the site. *Parentalia* (1750) quotes Camden's *Britannia* to the effect that 'there was particularly intended a large Cupola, 30 Feet above the Roof, which would have been seen a great Way to the Sea; and also a regular Street of handsome Houses, leading in a direct Line down the Hill, from the Front of the Palace to the West-gate of the Cathedral; for which, & for the Parks, the Ground was procured'. *Parentalia* adds that preparations were also made 'for proper Plantations, a necessary Ornament for that open Situation. The Surveyor [Wren] had projected also to have brought from the Downs a River through the Park, which would have formed a Cascade of 30 Feet Fall.'

From *A Journey Through England* (1722), we learn that the palace itself was 'to have a Terrass round it as at Windsor and the Ground laid out for a Garden, very spacious with a Park marked out of eight Miles Circumference, and that Park to open into a Forest of twenty Miles Circumference, without either Hedge or Ditch'. A description is given of the building. 'It will be the finest Palace in England when finished and inferior to few abroad. It fronts the City to the East by a noble area between two Wings. . . . The stair-case carries up to the great Guard-hall from whence you enter into sixteen spacious Rooms in each Wing, nine of which make a Suite to the End of each Wing. There are also two entries under the Middle of each Wing to the North and South, above which are to be two Cupolas; and the Front to the West extends 326 Feet, in the Middle of which is another Gate, with a Cupola to be also over it. Under the great Apartment, on each side from the ground, is a Chapel, on the Left for the King and another on the Right for the Queen; and behind the Chapel are two Courts, finely piazza'd to give Light to the inward Rooms.'

In general appearance the building was more palatial and less domestic than, say, Chelsea Hospital, for the roof was concealed behind a balustraded parapet. The walls were of red brick with stone dressings. The height of all the principal rooms was 14 feet, but the chapels were two storeys high. Of the three cupolas, the central one was so lofty that 'from thence you might see the men of war riding at Spithead. This was to please the king, who loveth the fleet of England.' The quotation is from a letter written on October 24, 1738, by the second Earl of Oxford, who also remarks upon the very fine situation and the facilities for sport. He observes that 'the plan or design was made by Sir Christopher Wren, and I believe is better than ever he executed because in this he was left to himself by the King'—a most discerning criticism.

The carcass of the building was completed and roofed in when the King died suddenly, after a very short illness, on February 6, 1685. James II visited Winchester in the following September, but nothing seems to have been done, and in 1722 'five Marble Pillars sent by the Dukes of Tuscany for supporting the Portico of the great Stair-case' were still lying about. In 1738, according to the Earl of Oxford's letter already quoted, they lay there for many years in their cases till 'the late Duke of Bolton begged them from the King, and they were granted to him and he carried away above three hundred waggon loads of marble to his house at Hackwood, and there they remain still boxed up, never put up, or ever seen by mortal eye'. He also tells us that 'Queen Anne and Prince George went over the house . . . but the Queen liked Windsor much better'. After her accession, she asked for a survey to be made and an estimate of the cost required to complete it for her husband's occupation, but no action appears to have been taken either by her or her successor. *Parentalia* (1750) remarks: 'Whether his Majesty [George II], or the Prince, when they please to make a Circuit through their Dominions, may not think it worth while to finish so noble a Structure, Time will discover.' On the contrary, during the second half of the eighteenth century, the great bare house served to accommodate large numbers of French prisoners-of-war, as many as 5,000 on one occasion in 1756. In 1796 it was converted into barracks for 2,000 soldiers, including officers, the existing three stories being made into four. These alterations, carried out by the army, doubtless ruined Wren's design; but in 1894 a serious fire destroyed the whole pile, and entirely new barracks were begun in 1899. In these, still existing, hardly any fragments of Wren's original palace have been incorporated—at most some architectural features in stone—so that it is true to say that nothing now remains of one of his most successful and magnificent buildings. It was perhaps his greatest disappointment.

Although Wren had been appointed Surveyor-General in 1669, the extensive building operations at Windsor Castle continued to be carried on from 1673 by Hugh May until his death on February 24, 1684, when Wren took charge. These works had included the erection of the large block on the north of the Castle which includes most of the State Apartments, splendidly decorated with carvings by Gibbons and Phillipps and with ceilings painted by Verrio, but the architecture of the building is mediocre in quality. Besides this major item, a large amount of refacing had been executed on the towers and other parts, terraces had been formed along the east and south fronts in continuation of that on the north, and 240 young elms had been planted to make the beginnings of the 'Long Walk' in the Great Park. When Wren was appointed 'Comptroller of the Works in the Castle of Windsor' in 1684, all these schemes had been completed except sundry decorative details.

His first work seems to have been the erection of a Guard House, ordered by James II. The building account for this, amounting to £774 14*s*. 10*d*., exists at the Public Record Office, certified by Wren, who submitted a claim for four days 'riding charges' on this commission in the following January. Other documents include a claim from Verrio the painter for work in 'the Queen's Round Closet' and 'Henry VIII's Chapel', amounting to £2,000 for work already finished. Wren approved this, commenting on the item for the Queen's Closet that 'Her Majestie having changed the 1st Designe for this wch. is fuller of Figures; though £300 is demanded yet I hope I do not undervalew it at £250'. He remarks that these payments are additional to Verrio's regular salary.

On September 27, 1693, Wren approved a claim for £204 13*s*. 11*d*. from Robert Streeter, 'their Majesties Sergeant-painter', with this illuminating postscript: 'I humbly crave leave to Represent that the Revenue is noe way capable to pay it, the same being eaten out with Pensions, soe that the Remainder is not sufficient to keep the Castle in Lead and Glass, which is humbly left to yor Lps. consideration.' In 1692 we find him reporting to the Duke of Norfolk ('Earl Marshall of England and Constable of the Castle of Windsor') on the Castle Ditch, saying that he has had a survey made showing all existing tenancies of sites thereon, and naming a vacant site which might be granted to an applicant, one Arnold Thompson. 'Neither will it hinder the proposition of Joyning the 2 Tarraces if their Majesties shall at any time think fitt to prosecute the said Design provided the Ground be sett out as the Map represents it.'

Wren's actual work at Windsor was confined to these minor routine duties, but in 1698 he produced for King William a grandiose scheme for remodelling the Castle, which never reached fruition. This project is illustrated in six drawings from the All Souls Collection. Some of them were reproduced in Wyatville and Poynter's book on Windsor Castle, published in 1841, but their true significance had escaped the attention of Wren's various biographers until they were again reproduced much more fully in the Eighth Volume of the Wren Society in 1931, after their rediscovery at All Souls. Of the six drawings, the first two are elaborate

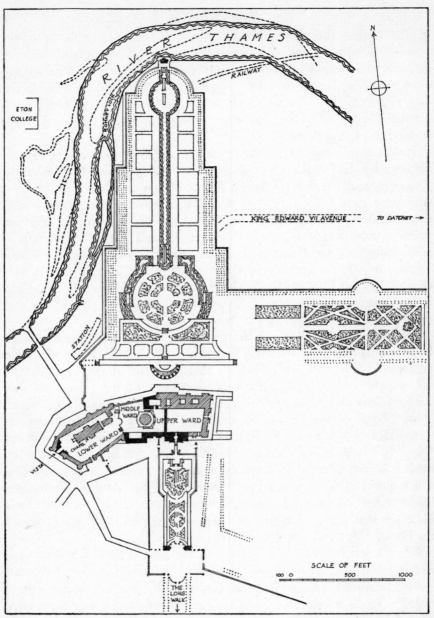

Labels within the plan:

RIVER THAMES

RAILWAY

ETON COLLEGE

N

KING EDWARD VII AVENUE — — — — TO DATCHET →

STATION

MIDDLE WARD

UPPER WARD

CHAPEL

LOWER WARD

VISTA

THE LONG WALK

SCALE OF FEET
100 0 ... 500 ... 1000

FIG. 20.—PLAN OF WINDSOR CASTLE BASED UPON WREN'S DRAWING OF 1698 IN THE BODLEIAN LIBRARY

Modern landmarks have been added in dotted lines, including the present course of the river, and Romney Lock. Wren's scheme was never carried out. Buildings existing in his day are hatched. Proposed new buildings are shown in black, with a projected vista of St George's Chapel from High Street.

lay-out plans, depicting a most ambitious scheme extending far to the north and south of the Castle, and involving the demolition of most of the south side of the Upper Ward in order to make room for an imposing range of new royal apartments, 200 feet wide, with a great central gateway aligned through a new Italian garden on to the Long Walk. New or remodelled wings doubled the width of this south front (Fig. 20).

On the north of the Upper Ward, Hugh May's comparatively new block containing Charles II's State Apartments remained intact, with most of its medieval surroundings, but from its centre an axial line (*not* continuous with that on the south) was projected through a series of stately terraces, parterres and ornamental canals to the bend of the river near Romney Lock. Excluding the Long Walk itself, this vast lay-out stretched for nearly a mile from south to north. Another line of parterres ran eastwards from near the present 'Broad Water' in the direction of the present Victoria Bridge.

The Middle Ward was also to be formalized, and the Keep (the 'Round Tower') was to be approached from the Upper Ward by an immense double flight of steps flanked by two monumental gateways. In the Lower Ward, the quaint Horseshoe Cloister was to be cleared away, and an opening made in the outer walls between the Bell Tower and the Garter Tower, giving an axial view, from Thames Street, of the west end of St George's Chapel, which would then be freed of all obstructions.

Wren's designs for the elevations of the new south block were uncompromisingly Italian in character, and, though domes and Orders were excluded, made no concession whatever to the medieval setting. He evidently appreciated St George's Chapel sufficiently to wish to isolate it and to provide a vista of it from the town, but in other respects his proposed treatment of the Castle was somewhat ruthless, and we may be thankful that his scheme was never carried out.

Under Queen Anne, heavy arrears of necessary repairs to the Castle were undertaken by Wren, £40,000 being spent in this way during 1702-10. The decoration of the State Apartments was completed by the painting of the Great Staircase by Sir James Thornhill, and the double steps were made in the middle of the South Terrace. In 1711 Wren designed a charming formal garden north of the Castle for the Queen, who died before it could be completed. The fine coloured plan of this garden is preserved in the Soane Museum, and illustrated in the Wren Society's Vol. VIII, Plate XVI.

Wren was concerned in sundry additions and alterations to St James's Palace—where, incidentally, his second marriage took place in 1676—

but documentary evidence relating to them is so slender, and the building has been so much transformed since his day, that any precise description of his work there is impossible. The original palace, a rambling and picturesque Tudor house, was erected by Henry VIII on the site of the medieval Hospital of St James, dissolved in 1532. It was planned round four courts, but one of these has ceased to exist, and another has been altered out of recognition. A disastrous fire in 1809 destroyed all the southeastern part of the group, including some of the best portions of the Tudor building, and also the 'French Chapel' designed by Inigo Jones for the Infanta in 1623. Charles II liked St James's Park, and added some fields to it in 1667, but the Palace was occupied by James Duke of York for some years after the Restoration, and Mary of Modena decided to move in there in 1688. It was just before that date, in 1686, that Wren's name first appears as certifying an account for alterations to the Council Chamber, then a comparatively small room. Very little building seems to have been done between 1686 and 1702, when Queen Anne ordered alterations immediately after her accession. An estimate signed jointly by Wren and Vanbrugh on July 3, 1702, comprises various items in the Council Chamber, Drawing Room and Chapel. It was accompanied by the following cautious and amusing letter to the Lord High Treasurer:

'May it please your Lordship,

'This Estimate is as neer as (in the best of our opinions) the works herein particularly named may amount to, but it must be considered that it is all but peeceing old and new and noe person can know all the consequences which appear necessary in pulling down, and wch. could not be foreseen; it must also be considered that while work is in hand, new commands doe often arise, but upon the whole matter, if your Lordship please to provide a reasonable weekly allowance, Wee suppose Wee may be able, one thing with another, to bring this matter within the aforesaid summe; wch. is humbly submitted,

(Signed) Chr. Wren
J. Vanbrook
Benj. Jackson
Mathew Banckes.'

Office of her Majesty's Workes.
July the 3rd, 1702.

The discreet words 'new commands doe often arise' are significant, showing that the Queen, if not such a tartar as her crony the Duchess of Marlborough (see pp. 228-9), was regarded as a potentially 'difficult' client; and the endorsement on the estimate shows that she was a determined woman: 'Read to the Queen 8 July 1702. Her Ma'ty has put a stop to the Works she intented.'

However, some alternative scheme must have been prepared and approved very quickly, for she is recorded to have visited 'Her Building' in October. Various alterations were certainly authorized by Wren during the next few years, and the absence of Vanbrugh's name on the documents suggests that he had fallen out of favour. Under George I, he regained his old position, and the Kitchen Block seems to have been built by him for the then Prince of Wales. The only substantial part of the Palace which can be confidently attributed to Wren (or to Wren and Vanbrugh) is the range of rooms facing the park and containing the following State Apartments: Drawing Room, Throne Room and Council Chamber. (The Boudoir at the west end and Queen Anne's Room at the east end are later additions.) Internally these fine rooms have been so much altered and repaired that it is impossible to say how much of their Renaissance decoration is original. Externally, the walls are of stock bricks with battlements of rather clumsy type. There are very tall sash-windows to the first floor rooms comprising the State Apartments. The later additions at each end exactly match the older work. Wren attended board meetings at the Palace up to April 7, 1718, after which date his name appears no longer on the minutes. He probably had something to do with the design and erection of the Banqueting Room.

In default of more exact information about his architectural work at the Palace, it is interesting to see how trivial were some of the duties imposed upon him in his capacity as Surveyor-General. Thus in 1690 there was some correspondence between the Treasury and one 'John Webb, keeper of their Majesties fish and fowl in St James' Park'. Webb petitioned that 'their Majesties Granary in the sd. Parke, being gon to decay and rendred useless for want of repair', Sir Christopher should be asked to see to it. Wren replied with an estimate of £10 within ten days. About the same time came another petition from James Frontin, 'Yeoman of their Majesties Ice-houses', which 'are soe farre decayed & become defective that they are of no use'. This too was referred to Wren, who submitted full estimates within three weeks. Then Webb reappeared with a claim for birdseed: 'The Bill of Extraordinary Charges for Oates, Meale, Hempseed, &c, for keeping their Majesty's Fowle'; but apparently suggested to the Treasury that this was not a matter for an architect and that some financial expert should deal with it. In 1693 the New River Company sent in a bill to the Treasury for 2¼ years of arrears of rent for water supplied to St James's Palace: it was endorsed 'Refer to Sir C. Wren', who replied seven weeks later approving the claim. In the same year, a plumber named John Cock applied for payment of a bill for £22 6s. 10d. for work done at the

Palace, but on this occasion Wren took nine months to certify the claim
as correct. These examples, which might be multiplied a thousand-fold, are
cited as typical of the trifling items of business inflicted upon one of the
greatest brains in history, though naturally Wren would delegate most of
the routine work to subordinates.

Another specimen emanates from an official acting under direct instructions from Queen Mary II. Wren submitted his estimate six days later.
'Sr.   St James, Octo'r. 1694

'The Queen haveing taken notice of a heap of Rubbish very obnoxious
and inconvenient lying against the wall under the Library of St James
House . . . her Majestie hathe commanded me to signifie her Pleasure to
you that Speedy Order be given for removeing the said heap of Rubbish
from thence unto ye Pitts neer their Majesties Ice-house in the said Parke,
where the same will be of use toward levelling that Ground.' The writer
then mentions necessary repairs to some railings and the need for a new
gate, 'the old being so rotten and decayed that it cannot be shutt . . . '.

'I have nothing more at present but to assure you that I am, Sir,
                                         'Your most humble Servant,
                                                        'Bathe.'

On December 3, 1695, Wren was consulted, apparently in his capacity
as Surveyor-General, by the fourth Earl of Suffolk, about the great mansion of Audley End in Essex, erected in 1603-16 by the first Earl at a reputed cost of £190,000, an enormous sum in those days. The fourth Earl,
who resided at Audley End, complained that the mansion was in a dilapi-
dated condition and asked that it should be surveyed and repaired immediately. He said that high winds had made the chimneys dangerous,
'great stones falling from them daily', that one of the pillars in the cloister
was liable to collapse with the rooms over it, that a bridge was unsafe,
and that the stables and barn needed attention. Wren replied fully, ten days
later, that 'when this house was purchased by King Charles, an estimate
was given of the Charge of Repaires, amounting to abt. £10,000; for little
had been done to it from the first foundation. . . . For this an allowance
of £500 p.ann. was settled upon the wood farme. While this continued,
halfe the house was new leaded, and the Roofe substantially repaired, and
many Stacks of Chimneys new built, and diverse of the necessary defects
amended.' The allowance of £500 had ceased in 1688, and now Wren
estimated the cost of necessary repairs at £2,830. There is no mention of
this work in *Parentalia*, or by any of Wren's biographers except Elmes
(pp. 478-9), and the *West Essex* volume of the Historical Monuments
Commission does not refer to it, or to Wren. From another source it

appears that much of the mansion had become ruinous and had to be pulled down, either in 1700 or 1749, leaving only the main block. Audley End is mentioned here as one more 'palace' that belonged, for a time at least, to the Crown; and as an example of Wren's prompt procedure in dealing with the royal houses.

The most notable of all the designs that he prepared for these stately homes was his scheme for rebuilding Whitehall in 1698. It entails a rather long and complicated story. Whitehall Palace in the mid-sixteenth century covered the whole ground from the present Great Scotland Yard (*not* New Scotland Yard) on the north to the present Richmond Terrace on the south, both inclusive; and from the Cockpit (now the garden of 10 Downing Street) on the west, in St James's Park, to the old river-bank on the east. It covered the site of the present War Office, Horse Guards, Treasury, Foreign Office and many other buildings. 'Whitehall' itself ran south from Charing Cross as it does today, but was a broad cul-de-sac, not a thoroughfare, and terminated at the Tudor 'Holbein Gate'. It was continued as a narrow alley, 'The Street', to another gateway at its southern end. The river-bank, before the construction of the present Embankment, was then much further west, and the river itself was far more used for transit than it is now because there was no bridge across it except London Bridge. Though it included the considerable open spaces known as the Privy Garden and the Bowling Green, as well as several courts and two 'Scotland Yards', this area contained some 2,000 rooms in a vast congeries of unrelated Tudor buildings, mainly of brick, even after Inigo Jones had erected in 1619-22 the splendid stone Banqueting House that was to form the nucleus and first instalment of a new palace. This building was greatly admired by Wren and his contemporaries, for it has been well described as 'the finest classical work north of the Alps'. Sorbière, author of *A Voyage to England*, came to London in 1665, and was specially pleased with the Banqueting House, which, he says, 'looks very stately, because the rest of the Palace is ill built, and nothing but a heap of Houses, erected at divers times and of different Models, which they made Contiguous in the best Manner they could for the Residence of the Court; Which yet makes it a more Commodious Habitation than the Louvre, for it contains above Two Thousand Rooms, and that between a Fine Park and a Noble River, so that 'tis admirably well situated for the Conveniency of Walking and of going about Business into the City'.

During the Civil War, no real change was made, and the first mention of Charles II's ambitions is to be founded in Evelyn's *Diary* for October 27, 1664: 'Being casually in the privy gallery at Whitehall, his Majesty

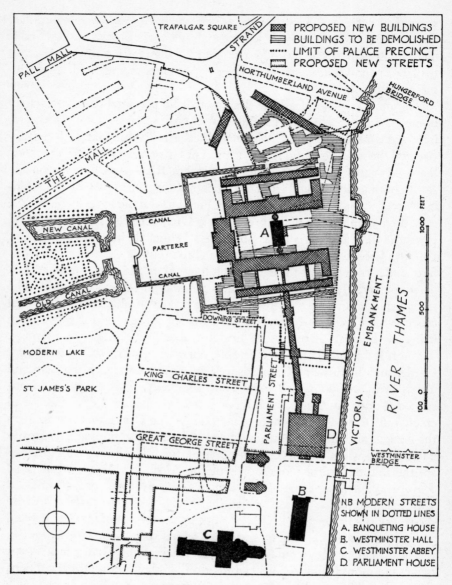

FIG. 21.—WREN'S LAY-OUT FOR WHITEHALL PALACE, 1698

gave me thanks before divers lords and noblemen for my book of *Architecture* and for my *Silva*. . . . He then caus'd me to follow him alone to one of the windows, and asked me if I had any paper about me unwritten, and a crayon; I presented him with both, and then laying it on the window-stool, he with his own hands, design'd to me the plot for the future building of Whitehall, together with the roomes of state, and other particulars.' No trace of this royal sketch-plan has ever been found, and no exact date can be assigned to the first design that Wren made for rebuilding the palace. *Parentalia* states that he made three drawings for it, but the date of them is unknown and the Editors of the Wren Society hesitate between 1664 and 1669 in dating the only two that have survived, in the All Souls Collection (illustrated as Plates X and XI in the Wren Society's Vol. VII). Indeed, the uncertainty is such that the second drawing, Plate XI, is captioned 'alternatively 1685 for James II'. If one must infer that Wren had in mind Charles II's ideas as revealed to Evelyn, it may also be assumed that he wished to follow Inigo Jones's lead. The first drawing shows part of an elevation, not very Roman and not very attractive, including a pedimented portico with Ionic columns below and Corinthian above. The second, presumably an alternative, depicts an enormous façade decorated with similar features. Either scheme would have involved the destruction of the Holbein Gate (which, in fact, survived until 1759). Neither of these alternatives, which may be described here, jointly, as his 'first' design, was ever carried out.

Wren's second design was made for James II and was actually built between May 1685 and November 1686, a remarkable achievement. It consisted of a new wing about 300 feet long running east from the Holbein Gate—which was left intact—to the Stone Gallery near the river-front. At the west end, next to the Holbein Gate, was a chapel, and half-way along the wing, projecting northwards into 'Pebble Court' behind the Banqueting House, was a new Council Chamber and a 'great stone staircase'. The cost of the block was about £35,000, nearly as much as Charles' new palace at Winchester. The whole wing was completely destroyed in the great fire of 1698 (see below), and our only knowledge of its appearance is derived from a beautiful bird's-eye view made, probably, by Knieff, soon after its erection (reproduced in the Wren Society's Vol. VII, Plate VII). From this, it is clear that the building was three storeys high plus attics, with brick walls crowned by a large wooden modillion cornice. On the principal floor was the Privy Gallery, overlooking the Privy Garden on the south. The chapel had a ceiling painted by Verrio and a marble altar-piece by Grinling Gibbons and Quellin. Evelyn's description is characteristically terse and accurate: '18 October 1685. The King was now building all that range from East to West by the Court and Garden to the Streete, and making a new Chapel for the Queen, whose lodgings were to be in this new building, as also a new Council Chamber and offices next the South end of the Banquetting House.' A technical point that he omitted, of much interest to architectural historians, is that most of the 269 windows in this wing were sashes 'with very good lines and brass pullies'. Thus the introduction of sliding sashes into England is proved to have occurred before William II's accession, and, though the idea may have come from Holland, was not primarily due to 'Dutch William'.

Another entry in Evelyn's *Diary* notes the reintroduction of Roman Catholic worship in the chapel: '29 December 1686. I went to hear the musiq of the Italians in the New Chapel, now first opened publickly at White-hall for the Popish service. Nothing can be finer then the magnificent marble work and architecture at the end, where are four statues . . . in white marble, the work of Mr Gibbons, with all the carving and pillars of exquisite art and greate cost.' After describing the ritual, he concludes: 'I could not have believ'd I should ever have seene such things in the King of England's Palace, after it had pleas'd God to enlighten this Nation.' In 1687 the chapel was enlarged by the addition of a transept. Part of the altar-piece is now preserved in Burnham Church, Somerset.

On April 10, 1691, Evelyn records: 'This night a sudden and terrible fire burnt down all the buildings in the stone gallery at White-hall to the water-side, beginning at the apartment of the late Dutchesse of Portsmouth (which had ben pull'd down and rebuilt no less than 3 times to please her), and consuming other lodgings of such lewd creatures, who debauch'd both K.Cha.2, and others, and were his destruction.'

Wren's next work at Whitehall, probably towards the end of 1697, was the design of a new drawing-room with a terrace on the riverside; but all his new wing of 1685-6 was destroyed by another fire on January 2, 1698, the effect of which is laconically summarized by Evelyn: 'Whitehall burnt, nothing but walls and ruins left.' This is not quite correct: the Banqueting House, if damaged, was not destroyed.

Immediately after this catastrophe, Wren set to work designing a scheme for rebuilding the whole palace on a colossal scale. This fact is remarkable, indeed almost inexplicable, because the King is stated to have frequently expressed a dislike of Whitehall as a residence—having Windsor, Hampton Court, Kensington and St James available as alternatives; moreover, Queen Mary, who had been the moving spirit in these royal adventures, was dead. In spite of these apparently unfavourable circumstances, Wren produced a plan which exceeded in magnitude even his previous efforts at Windsor and Winchester. One hesitates to regard him as a megalo-maniac, but the common estimate of his character by some biographers as 'modest' seems to me to be falsified by these colossal imaginings—for imaginings many of them remained.

Turning from Evelyn to another diarist of the period, Narcissus Luttrell (1657-1732), we find the following entries in his *Diary of Events*: '20 January 1698. Sir Chr. Wren has taken a survey of the ruins of Whitehall and measured the ground, in order to rebuild the same: his Majestie designs to make it a noble Palace, which by computation may be finished in 4 years. . . . 5 March 1698. About 200 labourers are daily employed at Whitehall to clear down the rubbish from the Banquetting House in order to fit up for a chapel, and his Majestie has given directions to Sir Chr. Wren to erect a range of buildings at the end of the Banquetting House, next to the Privy Garden, to contain a Council Chamber and 5 lodgings for his own use, but the rest will be omitted till Parliament provides for the same.'

It appears from engravings of 1713 and later that some sort of brick structure was erected in the position described by Luttrell, but no substantial measure of rebuilding took place, and Wren's design remained on paper. This, his third, project for rebuilding Whitehall Palace (Fig. 21) is illustrated on several drawings in the All Souls Collection (reproduced as Plates I-VI in the Wren Society's Vol. VIII). The whole design is focused upon Inigo Jones's Banqueting House as a centre-piece. On the east side, towards the river, a colossal portico, quite 100 feet high, is added to the façade. This procedure is unlike Wren, and suggests an inappropriate and misguided attempt to introduce Baroque splendour, possibly to please the King or even to emulate Bernini's design for the Louvre (p. 42). At all events, one may be thankful that it was never carried out. At either end of the Banqueting House, Wren proposed domed vestibules, again bombastic and open to criticism. North and south of the vast court in which the Banqueting House stood were immense hollow wings with outer frontages of about 320 feet to Charing Cross and to the Privy Garden respectively. Towards the river, the great court was open, but on the west side, towards the park, there was a huge central block on a colossal scale, with its axial line prolonged through parterres and ornamental gardens with canals, all the way to Buckingham House. A formal approach through a triangular piazza from Charing Cross was contrived by the demolition of property round Scotland Yard and Spring Gardens, thus providing a view of the somewhat austere north front, four storeys high with 189 windows!

Yet this huge group of buildings, measuring some 350 feet square, was not the sum total of the scheme. Much further south, and approximately where the forecourt of *New* Scotland Yard (police headquarters) is now situated, Wren planned a large square Parliament House aligned with the old Westminster Hall, still standing today. Between the two buildings he envisaged a broad street running east and west on the line of the modern New Bridge Street, with two small buildings flanking its west end. Possibly these were to be churches, like the pair flanking the Corso in the Piazza del Popolo at Rome. The Parliament House was to be connected with the new Palace by a wide and immensely long colonnade. Westminster Abbey was to be secluded in a 'precinct'. It must have been great fun for Wren, busy man though he was, to plan this great dream-palace regardless of expense, yet nothing came of it. Nevertheless he proceeded almost at once, or even simultaneously, to design another alternative scheme for the palace itself, presumably leaving the other lay-out unaltered.

This fourth design for Whitehall is represented on drawings in the All Souls Collection (Wren Society's Vol. VIII, Plates VII-X), and is chiefly notable in that the main new east-west axis does not pass through the centre of the Banqueting House, as in the third scheme; but through a new central feature on the south of which a replica of the Banqueting House is placed. Between this feature and each of the twin blocks thus provided is a domed structure, and similar domes between each of the twin blocks and the outer blocks forming the ends of the façade. Thus the sequence of the west front from north to south runs as follows: outer block, dome, Old Banqueting House, dome, central feature, dome, replica, dome, outer block. Towards the river, there is a great open court as in the third design. This fourth design had its faults, but the idea of duplicating the Banqueting House was adopted by Sir Charles Barry in 1859 when he was preparing a lay-out for new Government offices, though in that case he placed the replica north of the old building.

The next royal dwelling to be taken in hand by Wren was the house at Kensington which Sir Heneage Finch, afterwards first Earl of Nottingham, had bought from his younger brother, and appears to have subsequently rebuilt. It must therefore have been nearly new when it was purchased for the Crown some time in 1689. According to an entry in Luttrell's *Diary* for June 18, 1689: 'The King hath bought the Earl of Nottingham's house at Kensington for 18,000 guineas, and designs it for his seat in the winter, being near Whitehall.' The sum mentioned seems very large, as the house was relatively small, but doubtless the transaction included a considerable area of surrounding land.

XXXVI   KENSINGTON PALACE; QUEEN'S GALLERY

XXXVII   KENSINGTON PALACE; QUEEN'S STAIRCASE   *R.C.H.M.*

R.C.H.M.

XXXVIII   KENSINGTON PALACE, THE ORANGERY; EXTERIOR

XXXIX   KENSINGTON PALACE, THE ORANGERY; INTERIOR

R.C.H.M.

Alterations and additions began very speedily, contracts for carpentry and brickwork being signed on July 3. King William and his Queen appear to have been impatient folk, for the King demanded great urgency in the work; partly because he hated to dine in public, as tradition required at Whitehall. According to the Editors of the Wren Society (Vol. VII, p. 135), Wren, in this instance as at Hampton Court, 'took great risks, for he had adopted a method of running up the outer walls in brickwork while forming the interior merely with trussed timber partitions, on which he balanced the chimney-breasts and heavy brick stacks'. This fact explains an accident recorded by Luttrell on November 7, 1689, caused perhaps by raising new foundations on an old brick vault: 'The additional buildings to the King's house at Kensington, being newly covered with lead, fell down on a sudden, and hurt several people and killed some, the Queen was herself there but little before.'

She wrote to the King in December as follows: 'I was so unsettled at Holland House I could not do as I would. This made me go often to Kensington to hasten the Worckmen and I was too impatient to be at that place, imagining to find more ease there. This I often reproved myself for and at last it pleased God to shew me the uncertainty of all things below: for part of the house which was new built fell down. The same accident happened at Hampton Court. All this, as much as it was the fault of the Worckmen, humanly speacking, yet shewed me plainly the hand of God was in it, and I was truly humbled.'

Yet apparently the Court went into residence at Kensington on December 24, 1689, and two months later Evelyn has this entry in his *Diary*: '25 February 1690: I went to Kensington, which King William had bought of Lord Nottingham and altered, but was yet a patched building, but with the garden however it is a very sweet villa, having to it the Park and a straight new way through the Park.'

The King went off to Ireland on June 4, and his wife described the progress of building in her letters to him during his absence: July 26-August 5, 1690. 'I have bin this morning at Kensington for tho I did believe you would not be willing to stay at Whitehall yet I confesse what you write me would make me in a milion of fears specially since I must needs confess my faults. I have not bin pressing enough till it was too late, the outside of the house is the fideling work wch. takes up more time than one can imagin and while the schafolds are up the windows must be boarded up but as sone as yt is done your own apartment may be furnisht and tho can not possible be ready yet awhile, I have found out a way if you please, wch. is that I may make use Lord Portland's & hee ly in some of the other roomes, we may ly in your chamber & if I go throw the councel roome down or els dresse there & I suppose your busines will bring you often to town so ye may take such times to see company heer . . . our being there will certainly forward the work.'

August 2-12, 1690. 'I have bin at Kensington for some hours quiet, tomorrow being the first sunday of the month & have made use of Lord Portland's closet as I told you in my last I woud, the house would have been ready by teusday night & I hope will be in better order now, at least it shall not be my fault if 'tis not.'

August 13-23, 1690. 'I have been this day at Kensington, which looks really very well, at least to a poor body like me, who have been so long condemned to this place [Whitehall], and see nothing but water and walls.'

In these very human and artless letters, Queen Mary—who was then 28 years old—figures as the loving wife and shows youthful impatience to occupy her new home, but she died only four years later, in December 1694. Nevertheless, building did continue on a considerable scale though the whole of Wren's scheme was never accomplished. The last instalment of his work, the large block forming the eastern portion of the south front, was begun in 1695 and completed in 1696, as the following extract from Evelyn's *Diary* shows: '23 April 1696. I went to see the King's house at Kensington. It is very noble tho' not great. The Gallery furnished with the best pictures. A great collection of porcelaine, and a pretty private library.'

Wren's work at Kensington (excluding the Orangery, a later addition of 1704-5, and 'the Alcove', which are described on p. 180) has been surrounded and partially obliterated by extensive subsequent alterations and additions, but consists of the following portions still surviving: the south range of the Clock Court; the west range of the Clock Court including the portico completed in 1690; Queen Mary's Gallery running north from the main block, completed in 1691; the large block forming the eastern part of the south front as mentioned above, including the King's Gallery; and the King's Grand Staircase behind it (Fig. 22). Wren's building at the east end of the Clock Court was rebuilt for George I by William Kent in 1718-26, and in this portion are several of the State Apartments now open to visitors, including the King's Privy Chamber, the King's Drawing Room and the Cupola Room. The extensive remaining parts of the Palace are mainly of much later date, and are not accessible to ordinary visitors.

Externally, Wren's work is characterized by an attractive domestic reticence, approaching the picturesque in the quaint cupola and gateway of the

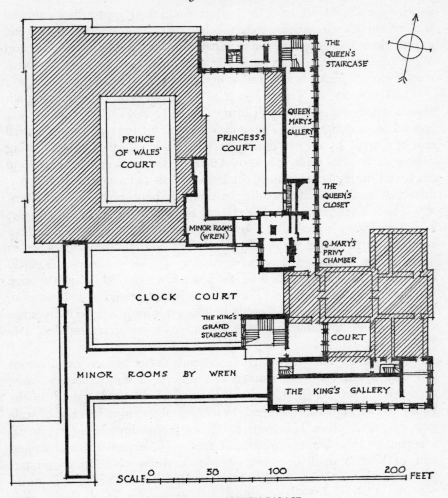

FIG. 22.—KENSINGTON PALACE

Plan of Second Floor (State Apartments). The portion hatched indicates buildings added or remodelled after Wren's time.

Clock Court, and achieving the splendid in the fine exterior of the King's Gallery building with its bold cornice, its central attic crowned with vases, and its rhythmical range of sash-windows. Much rubbed brickwork is used, and some stone in dressings. Internally the finest rooms are the King's Gallery (96 by $21\frac{1}{2}$ feet), Queen Mary's Gallery (84 by $21\frac{1}{2}$ feet), Queen Mary's Privy Chamber,[1] and the two great staircases. With their simple

[1] Damaged by incendiary bombs on October 14, 1940.

panelling, their handsome chimney-pieces and their appropriate contents in the form of furniture and pictures, they make a more intimate aesthetic appeal than the gorgeous State Apartments of Hampton Court and Windsor. The King's Staircase has an iron balustrade by Tijou; whereas the Queen's Staircase is a charming design in oak (XXXVII).

The Orangery, or 'Green-house' as it is described in the building accounts, about 100 yards north of the Palace (XXXVIII, XXXIX), was erected from designs by Wren and Vanbrugh in 1704-5. The estimated cost of £2,599 5s. 1d. was greatly exceeded, the bill for brickwork being double the original price. It is known that the design was much altered and improved during construction, the influence of Vanbrugh being discernible. It is a really beautiful building, measuring about 170 by 30 feet externally. The main room or gallery, 112 by 23 feet internally, has a central apse; and at each end is a circular room with niches and attached Corinthian columns on the walls. Externally, the walls, columns and arches are of brick, the projecting portions being rusticated. The fine cornice is partly of wood, and the slated roof is of low pitch. On the south front is a range of enormous sash-windows. The interior is as splendid as it is tasteful. Naturally and properly, this noble building has long formed a favourite subject for detailed measurement by students, as an example of late Renaissance architecture at its best.

The so-called 'Alcove', which now stands rather forlornly and incongruously in the Fountain Garden at the head of the Serpentine, once occupied a more appropriate site at the end of the garden south of the Palace for which it was designed. In its present situation it is out of scale as well as out of place. This seems to be the structure for which £555 7s. 9d. was paid to John Smoute, mason, in 1706-7. There is another charming relic of Wren's work in a small garden-pavilion with Doric columns (illustrated in the Wren Society's Vol. XII, Plate XLVIII). It is a pity that the old formal garden south of the Palace, for which these architectural accessories were provided, has not been maintained in something like its original form.

In 1942 it was discovered, from a duplicate copy unearthed in the Royal Library at Windsor, that a hitherto unidentified plan in the All Souls Collection (reproduced in the Wren Society's Vol. XII, Plate XVII) was a design for the rebuilding of Kensington Palace on a far grander scale. The date must have been between 1715 and 1718. The style of the design points clearly to Vanbrugh as the author, but it must have been submitted to Wren for approval before he was dismissed from his post as Surveyor-General. Nearly everything except the King's Gallery was to be demolished, and a large rectangular block was to replace the old palace, with its axis on the centre of the Round Pond towards the east. In the opposite direction, on the west side, was to be a colossal group of stables and offices with a concave front, on the same axis. The façade of this latter group was to be 680 feet, thus exceeding the greatest dimension of any mansion in England, Stowe coming next with *c.* 500 feet frontage. This enormous project, like so many of its kind and period, never matured. Kensington Gardens and the Serpentine were laid out by Charles Bridgman in 1730-3.

Hampton Court (Fig. 23) is not only the most famous of Wren's great royal houses but is the only one that enables us to judge of his ideas of monumental palace-design, although in fact his work there is a mere fragment, modified and altered, of his original scheme of rebuilding. The immense Tudor palace of Hampton Court was begun by Cardinal Wolsey in 1514 when that ambitious prelate was forty years of age and already held an archbishopric, five bishoprics, an abbacy and sundry offices of profit. His normal household consisted of 500 persons, but beds were always kept ready for 280 guests, as twice that number were entertained on occasion. After Wolsey's fall in 1529, King Henry VIII took possession of the palace, rebuilt the Great Hall on a still more magnificent scale, and made numerous additions, including the Tennis Court.

This work was completed *c.* 1540, and thereafter very little building took place until the Restoration, though all the sovereigns of England from Henry VIII to Charles I lived there frequently. Cromwell followed their example, but after his death in 1659 a strong party in the House of Commons favoured the sale of this with the other royal palaces, and were only appeased by a resolution that it would be 'very convenient for the retirement of those that were employed in public affairs, when they should be indisposed in the summer season'. This ingenious proposal, in the form of a Bill, was rejected after a second reading in 1660. The Palace then passed into the hands of General Monk, who relinquished it in return for a handsome sum down as compensation, together with the post of custodian and steward for life, an appointment confirmed by Charles II after the Restoration a few months later. The new King soon put in hand various works of repair and extension. Hugh May (cf. pp. 164-7) figures in this work as 'Paymaster', and about £8,000 was spent on repairs in the eighteen months ended October 1662. To some extent this outlay was due to the King's decision to spend his honeymoon at Hampton Court with Catherine of Braganza. A new guard-house was also erected— apparently the first instalment of the 'Barracks' on the left as one approaches the Palace—and the stables on the Green were reconditioned.

But the most important work carried out by Charles II was the construction of the great canal known as the 'Long Water', 150 feet wide, starting from the centre of the old East Front, and extending eastward for over three-quarters of a mile, together with the avenue flanking it, and two other avenues radiating from the same point. Charles had spent the years of his exile in France and Holland, the influence of those countries being evident in the design of his work at Hampton Court. Evelyn visited the Palace during the royal honeymoon. Of the building, he says that it is 'as noble and uniforme a pile, and as capacious as any Gotiq architecture can have made it'. After describing the furniture, he speaks of 'the park, formerly a flat naked piece of ground, now planted with sweete rows of lime trees; and the canall for water now neere perfected; also the hare park. In the garden is a rich and noble fountaine, with syrens, statues, &c, cast in copper by Fanelli, but no plenty of water. The cradle-walk of hornebeame in the garden is, for the perplexed twining of the trees, very observable. There is a parterre which they call Paradise, in which there is a pretty banquetting-house set over a cave or cellar. All these gardens might be exceedingly improved, as being too narrow for such a palace.' (The fountain here mentioned, by Fanelli, is the so-called 'Diana Fountain', now standing in the centre of the 'Great Basin', in Bushy Park, whither it was moved by Wren.)

After 1662, Charles II seldom visited Hampton Court, except for a brief space during the Plague Year, and never lived there during the latter part of his reign. As for James II, it is doubtful if he ever spent a night there; but William and Mary visited it ten days after their coronation, and fell in love with it at sight. A fortnight or so later, they came again for a more prolonged inspection, and within another month Wren had actually begun building (early April 1689). This remarkably speedy start did not, of course, involve the great 'Wren Block' that we now see, still less the enormous scheme for replacing the whole of the Tudor palace, but was confined to the remodelling of the 'Water Gallery', demolished a few years after the Queen's early death in 1694. Wren was evidently hustled by the Queen, who, in 1689, was an extremely lively and energetic young woman of only 27, with a perfect passion for building. The very first morning after her arrival at Whitehall on February 13, according to Evelyn, 'she rose early, and in her undresse, as it was reported, before her women were up, went from roome to roome, to see the convenience of Whitehall'. So also, directly she arrived at Hampton Court, the spiteful but probably accurate pen of the Duchess of Marlborough records that she began 'looking into every closet and conveniency, and turning up the quilts upon the bed, as people do when they come into an inn'. She superintended the gardening with equal zest, and introduced many rare plants from abroad. Her new quarters, luxuriously decorated by Grinling Gibbons and other noted craftsmen, included a white marble bath, 'made very fine, suited either to hot or cold bathing, as the season should invite'. Sash windows (cf. p. 174) were also substituted for Tudor casements with mullions and leaded lights. *Parentalia* (p. 326) states that 'the Queen, upon observing the pleasant Situation of the Palace, proposed a proper improvement with Building and Gardening, & pleased herself from time to time, in examining and surveying the Drawings, Contrivances and whole Progress of the Works, and to give thereon her own Judgment, which was exquisite; for there were few Arts or Sciences in which her Majesty had not only an elegant Taste, but a Knowledge much superior to any of her Sex, in that, or (it may be) any former Age.... The Surveyor [Wren] had many opportunities of a free Conversation with her Majesty, not only on the subject of Architecture, but other Branches of Mathematicks, and useful Learning.'

King William, who hated the pomp and ceremony of Whitehall as we have seen, favoured Hampton Court because the air there suited his health and reminded him of his native Holland, and also because he could live a simple life there and indulge his favourite pastime of coursing in the park. His share in hustling Wren with plans and estimates was almost as active as the Queen's, and they must have been a difficult pair of clients, impatient and exacting. Sarah Churchill describes William as 'indeed, so ill-natured, and so little polished by education, that neither in great things nor in small had he the manners of a gentleman'. He attended in person at a meeting of the Board of Works on May 4, 1689, when Wren submitted an estimate for alterations at Hampton Court.

In a matter of three months, at the outside, from Wren's first encounter with this formidable couple, he must have prepared the tremendous scheme for replacing the whole Tudor palace (except the Great Hall) with an enormous Renaissance building, comparable in size with the Louvre and with his own great projects for Whitehall, Winchester and Windsor already described. A number of drawings for this scheme, mainly by his own hand, are preserved in the Soane Museum and the All Souls Collection and have been reproduced by the Wren Society, Vol. IV, Plates 1-14. The sketches for the first lay-out are tentative and incomplete in some respects, but they enable one to obtain a fairly clear idea of the whole scheme in relation to the existing Tudor palace, the Long Water and Charles II's avenues. Wren based his conception upon two controlling

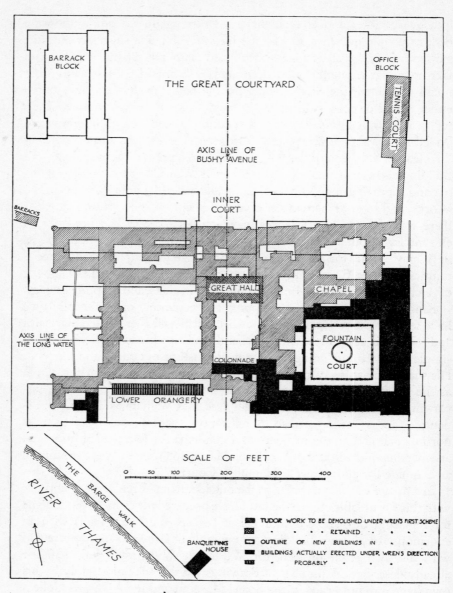

BARRACK
BLOCK

THE GREAT COURTYARD

OFFICE
BLOCK

TENNIS COURT

AXIS LINE OF
BUSHY AVENUE

BARRACKS

INNER
COURT

GREAT HALL

CHAPEL

AXIS LINE OF
THE LONG WATER

FOUNTAIN
COURT

COLONNADE

LOWER ORANGERY

SCALE OF FEET

0   50   100   200   300   400

THE BARGE WALK

RIVER THAMES

BANQUETING
HOUSE

TUDOR WORK TO BE DEMOLISHED UNDER WREN'S FIRST SCHEME
    "   "   "   RETAINED   "   "   "
OUTLINE OF NEW BUILDINGS IN
BUILDINGS ACTUALLY ERECTED UNDER WREN'S DIRECTION
    "   "   PROBABLY   "   "   "

FIG. 23.—WREN'S LAY-OUT FOR HAMPTON COURT PALACE

184

XL. HAMPTON COURT PALACE; SOUTH FRONT

R.C.H.M.

XLI   HAMPTON COURT PALACE; SOUTH AND EAST FRONTS

axial lines, one running east-west from the centre of the then existing east front on the line of the Long Water, the other running north-south, at right angles to it, through the centre of the Great Hall, which he had decided, or had been instructed, to preserve. Every other part of the vast Tudor palace was to be demolished, and we do not know whether he contemplated any external alteration to the Great Hall to bring it into harmony with an otherwise Renaissance design. The north-south axis was to be continued right across Bushy Park, with a flanking avenue (the present 'Chestnut Avenue'), and a huge circular basin having the 'Diana Fountain', a much earlier work, as its centre-piece. On the east side, towards the Home Park, there was to be a semi-circular formal garden (the present 'Fountain Garden') centred upon the middle of the new east front, coincident with the centre of the Tudor east front; this project entailed the shortening of the Long Water by several hundred feet, and the construction of other canals round the perimeter of the hemicycle. Of all this colossal scheme, only the Chestnut Avenue and Great Basin in Bushy Park, the Fountain Garden on the east, and sundry other gardening works with their embellishments, were ever carried out.

Continuing the description of Wren's proposed new buildings, we find from his plans that they covered an area about 780 feet square, whereas the present 'Wren Block' (or 'William and Mary Block') measures only 315 by 300 feet, and the whole existing Palace—the Wren Block included—about 700 by 370 feet, excluding the various outbuildings in the Wilderness and the Barracks on the west. The present Wren Block is considerably smaller than the corresponding hollow feature forming the south-east portion of the projected new palace, and the present Fountain Court is proportionately smaller in size. The principal entrance was to continue to be from the west, as in Tudor times and as it is today, but one large courtyard on that side—the 'Entrance Court'—was to cover the whole space then and now occupied by the Moat, the Base Court, the Clock Court and the two intervening blocks of buildings. At the east end of this great forecourt, Wren placed the 'Grand Front', as it is called on his sketches, through which one would look under an open ground-storey along the line of the already existing canal, the Long Water. Wren's elevation of this front (Wren Society, Vol. IV, Plate IIa) carries a note that through the 'midlmost' of the five openings is a 'thorow vista ... looking down the Canall'; and all five openings would give a vista into the Home Park, across the hemicycle of formal gardens which still exists and is shown on his first design. This east-west axial line now terminates, as it did in Charles II's day, at the east front of the Palace, and is not carried through the Fountain Court, the axis of which lies about 20 feet further south. That curious discrepancy, which must strike visitors as singular when they leave the Fountain Court to return through the Tudor Palace, is due to the reduced size of the Wren Block as actually built.

The central part of the 'Grand Front' rose to about 70 feet in height, the remainder to about 50 feet. Above the open stage just mentioned was the principal floor containing the State Apartments, and a single Corinthian Order covered these two storeys. A tall attic crowned the five central bays, and in the middle Wren provided a dome of unusual and disagreeable form. North and south of the 'Entrance Court' were two large blocks extending eastwards to a point about 120 feet short of the 'Grand Front'. This gap, or intervening space, was filled on the north by the Tudor Great Hall but was left open towards the river on the south, thus providing a view of the side of the Great Hall from that side of the Palace.

From the north, one approached the new palace along the projected avenue through Bushy Park (shown on Wren's first designs), traversed a huge 'Great Courtyard' with a 'Barracks Court' on the right and an 'Offices Court' on the left, then an 'Inner Court', and finally reached the north entrance through some sort of semi-circular colonnade, masking the lower part of the north side of the Tudor Great Hall, which closed the north-south vista. The whole scheme was magnificent, a worthy and probably intentional rival of Versailles, but it inevitably entailed the destruction of all the Tudor Palace except the Great Hall, and even that might have suffered some external change. Yet, though we have lost the chance of a monumental building on a scale unrivalled in England, we have saved one of our finest relics of Tudor architecture, rich in craftsmanship and redolent of a splendid period of our history. The annals of Hampton Court in the sixteenth century are unsurpassed in dramatic incident and gorgeous background, linked at every point with the handsome rooms where Cardinal Wolsey entertained like a prince and where Henry VIII pursued his sports, his feasts and his amours.

Wren's first design just described, a second design or modification of the first (reproduced in Wren Society Vol. IV, Plate 13), and the various projects resulting in the present 'Wren Block', must all have been prepared at great speed, for building materials were being ordered in June 1689 (three months after Wren had received his first instructions), and actual construction of foundations commenced in the following month. Though Wren, now a famous and very busy man, must have delegated a good deal of his work to others, it seems to be agreed that these various Hampton Court designs are the work of his own hands. The failure of his first project must be attributed to its cost, the Treasury being unable to meet the ambitious demands of the new King and Queen. The 'Wren Block' as we now see it is a compromise, and, if the Queen had lived a little longer, would probably have formed the first instalment of an entirely new palace. At all events, its erection was pressed forward with great and, as it happened, dangerous urgency to appease her impatience, for, in December 1689, an accident occurred in which at least two workmen were killed and others injured. This came only a month after the similar disaster at Kensington (see p. 177), and must be ascribed to Wren's possibly tactful but certainly rash desire to humour his exigent royal clients, for there seems to be little doubt that in both cases he adopted methods of hasty construction that he would not have used in normal circumstances.

Mr A. T. Bolton, Editor of the Wren Society's Volumes, made a careful examination of the structure in an attempt to discover the actual position, details and cause of the occurrence (Vol. IV, pp. 72-4). He came to the conclusion that a wall or pier gave way somewhere inside the central part of the south wing, and that one of the great roof-trusses over this portion collapsed as a result, carrying with it a part of the floor over the State Apartments. He discovered that the apparently thick brick walls between these rooms are, in reality, mostly constructed of timber framing, which carries some of the heavy brick angle-fireplaces. Perhaps the massive timber trusses of the roof were placed in position before the brickwork had set properly. At any rate, the accident caused a considerable commotion, and Wren, together with the Comptroller, William Talman, had to face a very critical court of inquiry. On that occasion, Talman gave evidence against Wren, accusing him of negligence; and for the remainder of their association at Hampton Court, lasting over many years, he figured as Wren's evil genius. Although inferior in talent to Wren, he was an architect of some standing, and had designed Chatsworth in 1681. His status as Comptroller of the Works at Hampton Court is curious, for the accounts show that he drew 'riding charges' at a higher rate than Wren, and he seems to have been in a position to thwart Wren at every point. The ultimate result of the inquiry appears to have been favourable to Wren, the work continued apace, and the new block was well advanced when Queen Mary died suddenly at the end of 1694, but she never occupied the State Apartments provided for her at such vast expense. Possibly to avoid a public funeral with a consequent risk of scandal, the two dead workmen were hurriedly buried beneath the new Fountain Court. When two adult bodies were discovered in this strange position on November 2, 1871, it was thought at first that they must have been the forgotten victims of some romantic plot long ago, but now they are identified with the disaster of 1689. As for the charge of negligence on Wren's part, the records of his 'riding charges', for which he was allowed 4s. 10d. *per diem*, show that he was paid for 308 days during the two years ended March 31, 1691, and for 438 days during the ensuing three years. This fact implies that he averaged three days a week at Hampton Court throughout the five years when the 'Wren Block' was under construction, a remarkably creditable performance for a tremendously busy man.

After Queen Mary's death, the work of completing the new block seems to have languished, but it continued half-heartedly. During the next two years, there are large payments to Tijou the smith for decorative ironwork on the new staircases as well as in the gardens, to Gabriel Cibber for carving reliefs on the great stone tympanum, and to many others. In or about December 1693, Wren estimated the total cost of completing the block at £35,515; on April 28, 1699, at only £6,800. This latter figure was furnished to the King, who had decided to expedite the completion of the block, and referred only to the King's five rooms, thus excluding those originally intended for the Queen, and all the others. The actual sum paid for this work, in the end, was £7,092 19s. 0½d., a relatively slight variation; but that amount excluded substantial payments to Verrio the painter, i.e. £400 for the King's Bedchamber, and £1,800 for the King's Staircase with the little Dressing Room adjoining the Bedroom. The completion of the Communication Gallery was also undertaken in 1699, and in that year 400 men were engaged on constructing or decorating the palace and its gardens. The work out-of-doors included the Broad Walk, 2,300 feet long; the 'Chestnut Avenue' in Bushy Park with its 732 limes and 274 chestnuts at a cost of only £4,300; and much work in the Wilderness and Privy Garden: all under the direction of the Royal Gardener, George London, in collaboration with Henry Wise, who also laid out the gardens of Blenheim and Chatsworth. London was paid £200 per annum, but was also appointed 'a Page of the Backstairs' to Queen Mary! Up to 1696, it was estimated that the total cost of the Palace to date had been £131,788 10s. 11d., but very large amounts were paid out long after that date, £10,715 being expended on the gardens in 1700 alone.

Two items are worth quoting, from the mass of surviving documents relating to Wren's connection with all this work. On April 28, 1699, Talman wrote to him as follows: 'I thought it would not be unwelcome to you to heare of our proceedings at Hampton Court. The 5 Roomes are almost finished, the great stone Staires is done, and the ironwork put up; the Gallery for the Cartoones of Raphell is so forward that I shall fix up the pictures in a week; the Kings Great Bed-chamber and two Closetts are in hand that his Majestie will find I have made use of my time, for it proves a greater work than I expected, and I hope it will be to his Majesties satisfaction. Wee are making a Road of 60 ft. broad through the Middle Park and a Bason of 400 ft. diameter in the middle of the circle of trees, which will be very noble; we have abundance of our projects (if his Majestie will like them) by severall noble Lords that wee here call the Critiques.'

On January 9, 1699, Captain Moore, 'Keeper of his Majesty's Tennis Courts', wrote the following letter to the Treasury:

'May it please Your Lordps.

'His Majestie having commanded Sir Xpher Wren to make an Estimate of the repairs of Hampton Court Tennis Court in the state it now is & report the same to Your Honors, and Sir Xtopher having accordingly given in his Report with mending the brick paving and making it useful it will amount to £200. But Sir Xpher has declared his being unacquainted with Tennis Play has consulted mee (who have the honor to be Master of his Majesties Tennis Courts) and desire mee to give him my Estimate which accordingly I have done, viz. a Stone fflor with out which no ball can give a true bound, a boarding ceiling altogether necessary not only for Play but preservation of the Roof, Curtain rodds, rings, hooks &c. A Penthouse frame for Netts. Plaster of Paris, blacking & figuring which will for the Court only in the whole amount to £365. The lodgings at each end of the Court, the one being the King's Apartment, the other for the Players are much out of repair and will cost £160 to make them good. The totall for the Court & Lodgings will come to £525, which I conceive will be the utmost.

'I am

'My Lords,

'Yr Lps Most humble Servant

'Horatio Moore.'

It is interesting to note that, in spite of this expert opinion, their Lordships declined to spend more than £200, and gave orders for a brick floor.

It has been stated that in 1695 Wren, who was then Grand Master of Freemasons, initiated the King into the mysteries of that craft[1]; but their relations had not been invariably harmonious during their frequent contacts at Hampton Court, and William was apt to be dictatorial on technical questions and in matters of taste. According to *Parentalia* (p. 326), he accepted the blame for having forced Wren to alter his design for the Fountain Court: 'King William was pleased to excuse the Surveyor [Wren]

[1] See, however, pp. 275-6.

for not raising the Cloysters under the Apartments higher; which were executed in that Manner according to his express Orders'; but, as will be explained shortly, that statement is not entirely convincing.

The King was killed by a fall from his horse in the Park of Hampton Court on March 8, 1702, when the interiors of the 'Wren Block' were still incomplete. An inquiry made at that date shows that the estimated amount required to complete the Palace and its surroundings was £38,082 17s. 5¼d. (Palace £19,558 15s. 4d., Gardens £18,263 12s. 5¼d., Mews £160 9s. 5d.). The mention of halfpennies and even farthings in these meticulous accounts is characteristic of that spendthrift age, but none the less amusing. By way of contrast, it may be mentioned that for four magnificent carved marble 'vauzes' or 'urnes', Cibber and Pierce were paid nearly £1,500. If one multiplies that sum by, say, ten to obtain corresponding money values of today (1952), one obtains some idea of the lavishness with which the splendid rooms and gardens of Hampton Court were embellished. (Instances of large payments to other craftsmen, e.g. Grinling Gibbons, Tijou and Verrio, are given in Chapter XIII.)

Queen Anne does not seem to have cared much for Hampton Court, relations with her sister Mary not having been particularly happy there; but work continued throughout her reign, and also under George I. From 1702 up to December 10, 1717, when Wren attended a meeting of the Board of Works for the last time, he had some concern with the buildings, and since 1706 he had been living at the Old Court House on the Green in order to be close at hand (cf. p. 229); but during this later period Vanbrugh was associated with him and it seems likely that the heavy style of the decorations reveals Vanbrugh's hand. On June 12, 1716, it was resolved that 'all woodden mantels in the New or Old Building be taken out, and supplied with Iron Barrs, or Brick Arches, and that all Deal or wooden Chimney-pieces be taken down and Portland or Ffreestone Chimney-pieces be put up instead, and very broad Portland Slabbs laid to preserve the floors, and all hearths repaired where wanting for preservation of the Palace from fire'. Queen Anne made some minor changes, and one of her first acts after her accession was to root up much of the box-edging which 'Dutch William' had introduced from Holland too prodigally into the parterres.

It now remains to describe briefly Wren's various additions and alterations to the buildings of Hampton Court. Externally, the immense south and east façades of the main 'Wren Block', over 60 feet high and over 300 feet long, look even larger than they actually are, because of the small scale of their elements. The sky-line is almost aggressively severe, unrelieved by any features except the plain chimneys standing well back from the face of the wall. The colossal Order of the first design (see p. 186), carried through two storeys, is here reduced in height by subdivision of the front into four stages, of which the basement forms a pedestal or plinth for the Corinthian columns and pilasters (serving a purely decorative purpose), and the tall attic forms the fourth stage. The use of circular windows in most of the rooms of the first or principal floor is attractive externally, but difficult to justify on functional grounds. An unusual feature is the varying division of sashes into panes on the several floors, i.e. although the widths of the sashes are uniform on three floors, the windows have five panes in their width on the lowest floor, four on the principal floor, six in the attic storey; but the three central windows on the east side have only three panes. The suggestion has been made that this differentiation was adopted to provide a better view of the Fountain Garden and the Long Water; but in any case it jars upon the critical sense of architects accustomed to some uniformity of fenestration, and it is a question whether it is defensible. Another criticism relates to the awkward diagonal slicing of two windows by the pediment on the east front, where, it might be urged, those windows should have been omitted altogether. Except for such doubtful mannerisms, expedients or defects, the general effect of the Wren Block is universally agreed to be magnificent: more homely than the bombastic splendours of Versailles and therefore more in keeping with the King's simple tastes, but far more colourful because of the masterly use of fine red brickwork in conjunction with Portland stone. Sculpture is employed with discretion and restraint, concentrated at points of interest, and is admirable in execution.

On three sides of Fountain Court, the interior façades echo the design of the exterior, but the lowest storey consists of an arcade in which there are secondary segmental arches concealing the floor-level of the State Apartments above. Alternatively, Wren might have blocked up the tympana of the arcade by a slab masking a flat ceiling, as he did years before at Trinity College, Cambridge (p. 153); and the anecdote of King William's interference in this matter (pp. 189-90) may have arisen from a proposal by Wren to raise the floor of the State Apartments to a higher level, above the crown of the arches, so that the existing treatment represents a compromise on Wren's part. It remains an ingenious rather than a beautiful solution, and, when the King accepted responsibility for it, he may have realized that he had compelled an aesthetic blunder to be made. The fourth, or west, side of the Court is only two storeys high, consisting of a 'Communication Gallery' above the arcade, continuing the line of windows of the State Apartments and cleverly providing a partial screen to the picturesque jumble of Tudor battlements and chimneys behind it.

Internally, the range of State Apartments consists of a double row of intercommunicating rooms without independent corridors. This is an inconvenient plan, militating against privacy and domestic comfort. In the following century, architects contrived more practical as well as more imposing arrangements. Yet none of them ever produced more beautiful rooms than these State Apartments, taken individually, with their wealth of fine craftsmanship, which here at Hampton Court attained a level that has never been surpassed in this country. The Soane Museum possesses twenty-seven designs for chimney-pieces and several designs for doorcases and entablatures, drawn by Wren but with the elaborate ornament added very boldly by Grinling Gibbons, an accomplished draughtsman. (Illustrated in Wren Society's Vol. IV, Plates 27-43.) These drawings show how closely Wren was concerned with all the decorative details, and how intimately he worked in collaboration with his master-carver. If there is nothing at Hampton Court so gorgeous as the Hall of Mirrors at Versailles, that grandiose palace has nothing so excellent as these more homely galleries and saloons where the genius of Wren presided over the achievements of a galaxy of great artists. Moreover, in spite of the Italian origin of the Renaissance, this work is as triumphantly English as Versailles is French.

Outside the main block, Wren erected a colonnade of coupled Ionic columns, rather widely spaced with a balustrade above the entablature, on the south side of the Clock Court, as an entrance to the State Apartments. He remodelled the Tudor chapel, providing a half-floor resting on oak pillars to serve as a royal pew, and inserted a fine altar-piece. He also extended the Barracks block further westwards, and built a new Banqueting House (not open to visitors today) on the river bank. He must have had a controlling hand in the general plan of the gardens and in their embellishment with lead statues, marble 'vauzes' and 'urnes', and above all with the splendid iron screens and gates by Jean Tijou. Nowhere in England has the combination of fine architecture with fine garden-design been more successfully achieved than at Hampton Court, though admittedly Charles II had done something to prepare the way before Wren's advent.

Today some forty-five privileged pensioners and nominees of the Crown occupy suites in the immense rabbit-warren of rooms remaining from Tudor times and in some of the buildings added by Wren. Residence at Hampton Court is an appropriate and delightful sequel to a long career of public service, and it is pleasant to know that this haven of peace escaped almost scot-free in the air-raids of the Second World War.

XLII   HAMPTON COURT PALACE; FOUNTAIN COURT

R.C.H.M.

R.C.H.M.

XLIII   HAMPTON COURT PALACE; THE CARTOON GALLERY

XLIV   HAMPTON COURT PALACE; OVERMANTEL IN THE SECOND PRESENCE
CHAMBER

XLV   HAMPTON COURT PALACE; IRON GATES IN THE FOUNTAIN GARDEN

XI

ROYAL HOSPITALS

U P to a generation or so ago, biographers of Wren connected his name with three Royal Hospitals: Kilmainham, Chelsea and Greenwich. Today, however, reliable historians have eliminated the first of the trio. A scheme for a hospital for the army in Ireland was first suggested in 1675 and approved by King Charles II in 1679, a Building Committee was appointed in February 1680, the foundation-stone was laid on April 29, 1680, and the Hospital, to accommodate 300 pensioners, was completed in 1696 at a total cost of £23,559. The attribution to Wren rests upon a very ambiguous statement in a description of the Hospital published in 1711, that 'orders were issued to HM Surveyor of Buildings (whom they thought most proper to advise in that behalf) requiring that he do with all convenient speed view the lands of Kilmainham near Dublin'. At that time, Wren was Surveyor-General, but there is no known record of any visit by him to Ireland, or any mention of the work in *Parentalia*. But there was such an official as 'H.M. Surveyor of Buildings for Ireland', then Sir William Robinson, and it is to him that modern scholarship ascribes Kilmainham Hospital. Apparently the only documentary ground for attributing it to Wren rests in the reference to the 'Surveyor', just quoted, yet Papworth in his *Dictionary of Architecture* included it in his list of Wren's buildings, and he has been followed not only by Miss Milman (1908) but also by Professor A. E. Richardson in the *Wren Bicentenary Volume* (1923). The last-named writer, an authority on the period, considers that the Hospital is entirely characteristic of Wren's genius (except the tower, an addition of 1707), and indeed describes it as one of his 'most consistent designs', displaying a monumental lay-out of terraces and subsidiary buildings. Knowing how busy Wren was at that date, Professor Richardson suggests that 'it can be deduced that Wren furnished the ground-plans and elevations, and entrusted the execution of the work to local supervision'; but that 'the beauty of the finish is such as could only have resulted from accurate drawings and descriptions'. Kilmainham Hospital still stands much as it was built, except that the walls were roughcasted and the sash windows Gothicized at the beginning of the nineteenth century, and it is—like Groombridge

Place and many other buildings (cf. p. 231)—very similar to Wren's work, but in view of the evidence it must be ruled out.

With its exclusion, another legend disappears, that Wren's experience at Kilmainham was useful to him in planning Chelsea Hospital. It may well be that the foundation of the Hospital in Dublin suggested to the King that there was need for a similar institution in England. It is equally probable that the enormous 'Hôtel Royal des Invalides' in Paris, founded in 1670, inspired the venture, for rivalry between Louis XIV and Charles II was, as previously noted, very keen. Evelyn's *Diary* gives a far more complete story than *Parentalia* (p. 327) of its genesis. On two occasions during 1665 Evelyn visited 'Chelsey College' to see the prisoners-of-war then quartered there, and on September 24, 1667, records its presentation to the Royal Society. On September 14, 1681, he notes: 'Din'd with Sir Stephen Fox, who propos'd to me the purchasing of Chelsey College, which his Majesty had some time since given to our Society, and would now purchase it againe to build an Hospital or Infirmary for Souldiers there, in which he desired my assistance as one of the Council of the R. Society.' Hitherto, the flamboyant ladies of Charles II's court have been excluded, as far as possible, from this book; but it does seem necessary here to relate a story of Nell Gwyn. The tale runs that when the King impulsively offered to present the site of the College for a new Hospital, he suddenly remembered that he had already promised it as a *douceur* to that frail charmer, and exclaimed: 'Odso, 'tis true I have already given that land to Nell here.' She promptly replied: 'Have you so, Charles? Then I will return it to you again for this purpose.' The story sounds apocryphal, though anything of the sort was possible with Charles II; but a sceptical visitor is startled to find, on entering the Great Hall of the Hospital, that Nell Gwyn's name heads the 'List of Benefactors' inscribed at one end of the Hall, while at the other end is a copy of her portrait by Lely—as large as life—installed there not so long ago and illuminated at night! The respectable Evelyn does not mention this anecdote of Nell.[1] On January 27, 1682, he outlines detailed proposals for the finance, government and accommodation of the new Hospital: 'This evening Sir Ste. Fox acquainted me againe with his Majestys resolution of proceeding in the erection of a Royal Hospital for emerited souldiers on that spot of ground which the Royal Society had sold to his Majesty for £1300, and that he would settle £5000 *per ann.* on it, and build to the value of £20,000 for the reliefe and reception of 4 companies, viz. 400 men to be

---

[1] In his new book, *The Royal Hospital, Chelsea*, published in 1950, Capt C. G. T. Dean discounts the whole story.

as in a colledge or monasterie. I was therefore desir'd by Sir Stephen (who had not onely the whole managing of this, but was, as I perceiv'd, himselfe to be a grand benefactor, as well it became him who had gotten so vast an estate by the souldiers) to assist him, and consult what method to cast it in, as to the government. So in his study we arranged the governor, chaplaine, steward, housekeeper, chirurgeon, cook, butler, gardener, porter and other officers, with their several salaries and entertainments. I would needes have a Library, and mention'd several bookes, since some souldiers might possibly be studious when they were at leisure to recollect. Thus we made the first calculations, and set downe our thoughts to be consider'd and digested better, to shew his Majesty and the Archbishop. He also engag'd me to consider of what laws and orders were fit for the government, which was to be in every respect as strict as in any religious convent.' Within four months, the first plan had been prepared. '25 May 1682. I was desir'd by Sir Ste. Fox and Sir Christopher Wren to accompany them to Lambeth, with the plot and designe of the College to be built at Chelsey, to have the Abp.'s approbation. It was a quadrangle of 200 foote square after the dimensions of the larger quadrangle at Christ Church, Oxford, for the accomodation of 440 persons, with governor and officers. This was agreed on.'

Wren was not only a Commissioner of the Hospital and architect for its buildings, but also President of the Royal Society, from whom the site was purchased. Sir Stephen Fox, formerly Paymaster General (hence Evelyn's reference to the fortune he had made out of the Army), figures prominently in these transactions. He actually bought the site for £1,300, subsequently increased his gifts to £13,000 and acted as treasurer during the building operations. The King in person laid the foundation-stone on February 16, 1682. According to a memorandum of that time, almost certainly drafted by Wren, there were to be sixteen 'galleries' on four floors, each gallery containing cubicles for twenty-four soldiers and two larger cubicles for corporals, making 416 beds in all. Each gallery had a staircase at both ends, and 'two large chimnies and cisternes and conveniencys for water'. The galleries were to be 12 feet high, and the whole block covered a space '382 feet from north to south and 348 feet from east to west'. This work seems to have been carried out according to plan, with a central block containing Hall, Chapel and domed vestibule uniting the two gallery-blocks, all as it survives today.

In 1685 it was decided to increase the number of pensioners to 500, so in 1688-9 four low 'pavilions' were added, running east and west from the corners of the main block. In December 1687, an additional space of fourteen acres in front of the building was acquired from Lord Cheney for £840. The new chapel was consecrated on August 30, 1691, and during the following seven years various stables and other outbuildings were erected. On September 3, 1692, Wren, who had hitherto given his services gratis, submitted a claim for professional fees covering the previous ten years: 'Petition of Christopher Wren Knt., Shewing that the building of the Hospitall of Chelsea, now finished by their Majestys, was put into his care to Purchase the Land, Designe and Survey the Building, and Correct and Audit the Bills contained in severall Volumes, which he hath justly performed without any Allowance. Prays her Majesty to order upon the Fund wth. which the Hospitall is built such Allowance as yr. Commissioners of the Treasury shall think reasonable for his Expence in 10 years attendance on so considerable a Building.' As a result of this appeal, Wren was awarded a honorarium after a long delay: '4 June 1693. £1000 paid to Sir Christopher Wren for his great Care and Paines in Directing and Overseeing the Building of the said Hospitall and in Stating and Settling the Workmen's Bills relating thereto for ten years past.' (Treasury Warrant.)

Save for damage by bombing during the two world wars, the main group of buildings survives almost unaltered from Wren's time (Figs. 24, 25, XLVI, XLVII). The full effect of the scheme is, however, lessened by certain modern changes in the lay-out along the north-south axis through the central cupola and portico. This axis originally extended from King's Road to the river, a distance of almost exactly half a mile. It is now cut by two roads—Royal Hospital Road and St Leonard's Terrace. The enclosed open space between them—now known as 'Burton Court', still belonging to the Hospital, and used as a recreation ground—represents the original forecourt, and the fine though weatherbeaten gate-piers which still stand in the centre of its northern boundary, with flanking lodges, are all coeval with the Hospital. Thus the approach to the Hospital from King's Road was through 'Royal Avenue' (laid out by Wren) and these gates, across the forecourt, to the north portico. Continued south, the axis traverses the 'Figure Court', with a bronze status of Charles II, attributed to Grinling Gibbons, as its central feature, and then continues to the Embankment boundary. The Figure Court retains its original appearance, but south of it there was originally an elaborate formal garden, laid out in 1687-92 and extending right to the river-bank, the Embankment being a creation of 1871.

This north-south axis bisected the original site, which was only about 500 feet wide. On this limited area was erected the building described on p. 195, with a frontage of 348 feet east to west, and a depth of 382 feet

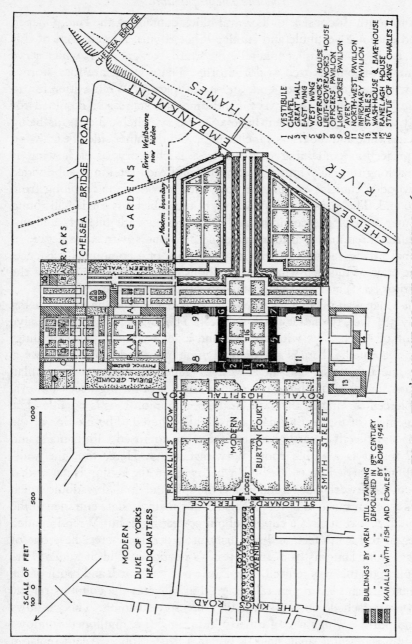

FIG. 24.—WREN'S LAY-OUT FOR CHELSEA HOSPITAL, 1691

Based upon a plan in the Bodleian Library, but with modern streets, embankment, etc., added by the author

1 VESTIBULE
2 CHAPEL
3 GREAT HALL
4 EAST WING
5 WEST WING
6 GOVERNOR'S HOUSE
7 LIEUT-GOVERNOR'S HOUSE
8 OFFICERS' PAVILION
9 LIGHT HORSE PAVILION
10 "AVERY"
11 NORTH-WEST PAVILION
12 INFIRMARY PAVILION
13 STABLES
14 WASH-HOUSE & BAKE-HOUSE
15 RANELAGH HOUSE
16 STATUE OF KING CHARLES II

BUILDINGS BY WREN STILL STANDING
DEMOLISHED IN 19TH CENTURY
DEMOLISHED BY BOMB 1945 .

"KANALLS WITH FISH AND FOWLES"

SCALE OF FEET
100 0   500   1000

north to south. It consists of a central block containing the Hall, Chapel, domed entrance vestibule and sundry other rooms. At each end of this block, a wing runs south, containing the 'wards' or 'galleries', which serve as common-rooms as well as dormitories. These wings are four storeys high with staircases at each end, and it is typical of Wren's attention to practical details that these very handsome oak staircases, designed for elderly and often infirm men, have a very easy 'pitch', the treads being 15 inches wide and the risers 5 inches high. On the outer side of each wing is a projection containing conveniences. Each story of each wing is divided longitudinally into two sections, and each section is subdivided into wooden cubicles opening on to a wide corridor 200 feet long from end to end. The massive oak panelling of the cubicles is carried all round the outer wall of the corridor, and is decorated with pilasters and entablature. Wren managed to provide the pensioners with some degree of personal privacy as well as with the amenities of a communal existence. At the ends of the two wings are pavilions containing the houses of the Governor (east) and the Lieutenant-Governor (west) respectively.

The Chapel and Hall are approximately equal in size, the former being 113 by 38½ feet, the latter 115 by 38 feet. The Chapel has an impressive interior of seven bays with an apse and a semi-circular plaster ceiling, richly decorated. There is a particularly fine oak reredos or altar-piece, a handsome oak organ-case in a western gallery resting on Corinthian columns, and oak panelling carried up to the sills of the high-set windows. The pierced carving of the gates in the communion-rails is notable. The arrangement of the seating has been slightly altered. The interior of the Hall is less effective, partly because it is more confused with banners and relics, but it is a noble room notwithstanding. Here, too, the wall-panelling is carried up to the high windows, but the ceiling is flat with a deep cove. Between Chapel and Hall is the splendid domed vestibule which serves as an entrance to both, and also as the main or state entrance to the Hospital. Above it rises a cupola, about 90 feet high; but Wren intended its height to be 130 feet, and seriously proposed to re-erect here one of the two stone lanterns from Inigo Jones's portico at Old St Paul's! Permission to do this was refused. The Doric porticos north and south of the vestibule are similar in general design, but whereas the columns on the north are attached, on the south they are free-standing. The windows throughout the wings were formerly 'transums' (i.e. mullioned windows with transomes and small panes), but in 1783-6 Robert Adam replaced them by sash-windows. The cost of this main group of buildings was about £45,000, almost double the estimate accepted.

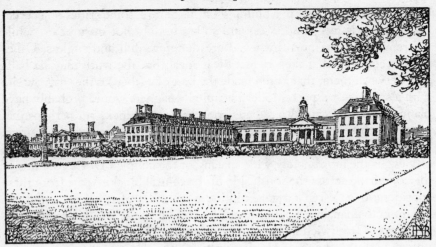

FIG. 25.—CHELSEA HOSPITAL: RIVER FRONT

The four pavilions added in 1688-9, to increase the accommodation, are uniform and most agreeable in design. They raised the total frontage of the buildings to 800 feet, each pavilion being about 150 feet long, with enclosed yards containing outbuildings at each end. The central portion of each pavilion projects slightly, and is two storeys high with a pediment, the rest of the block being one storey high with an attic. Externally, all the buildings are of rather dark red brick, with dressings of bright red brick on the wings and of Portland stone on the central block. The roofs are slated. A fine wooden cornice runs right round the main building. Thomas Carlyle is seldom quoted on aesthetic questions, in which he took little interest, but his recorded opinion on Chelsea Hospital is a discriminating testimony to Wren's ability: 'I had passed it almost daily for many years without thinking much about it, and one day I began to reflect that it had always been a pleasure to me to see it, and I looked at it more attentively and saw that it was quiet and dignified and the work of a gentleman.' Nearly all connoisseurs of architecture agree with this judgment, but some of them have more or less severe criticisms of detail.

While admitting the excellence of the general grouping, and the masterly emphasis created by the needlessly massive chimney-stacks of the four pavilions, they see a defect in the great depth of the Figure Court on the south, resulting in the diminished prominence of the central cupola and portico at the end; but, like so many critics, they are unable to suggest a better solution. On the orientation of the wards, functionally the most important requirement in a building of this nature, some critics object that half the wards face south-west and so are unduly hot in summer, while the remainder face north-east and are therefore dull and sunless. Other writers consider that the orientation is ideal; but the truth may lie half-way between them, that Wren made the best of a (then) rather narrow site with a south-east aspect. Modern hospital designers would probably have planned the four wings to radiate from the centre block, but perhaps that is too much to expect from an architect of the late seventeenth century. Yet another possible ground of criticism, this time from the aesthetic point of view, is the inordinately wide spacing of the coupled Doric columns of the colonnade across the south side of the central block. Apart from these considerations, Wren's great building is a model of good taste and ex-cellent craftsmanship; possibly because at Chelsea he was left to himself, whereas at Greenwich he had the very active assistance of Vanbrugh. It is unfortunate that none of his drawings for this Hospital have been pre-served.

After the group of buildings just described were finished in 1691, Wren acted for many years as one of the five Commissioners of the Hospital. The stable-yard buildings on the west were added in 1692-8. The Infirmary was designed by Sir John Soane in 1810. The Hospital suffered severely from bombing in both the world wars. Part of the north-east pavilion was destroyed during a Zeppelin attack in 1918, and, after being rebuilt, the whole block was demolished by a rocket in January 1945. The east wing was hit in October 1940. In these attacks, one of the original stair-cases to the wards was destroyed by a direct hit, but has since been re-placed. The Hall and Chapel escaped without serious structural damage, but there were numerous casualties among the inmates when Soane's Infirmary was struck, and largely destroyed, in April 1941.

The design of the Royal Naval Hospital at Greenwich (Figs. 26, 27, XLVIII to LI) provided a contrast, in many ways. At Chelsea, Wren seems to have had complete independence of action on an open if restricted site, and his problem was relatively simple. At Greenwich, two buildings were already there to cramp his style, and the indefatigable Queen Mary was constantly at his elbow, in the earlier stages, with most determined ideas, while the erratic genius of Vanbrugh as his colleague must have sometimes been a source of worry. The Tudor palace of Placentia, pic-tured in some old paintings in the Royal Naval Museum, occupied a part of the site, and the 'Queen's House', erected (c. 1618-35) by Inigo Jones, was completely detached from it and entirely different in style. The next venture was the block begun by Charles II from the designs of John Webb

XLVI   CHELSEA HOSPITAL; EXTERIOR FROM THE NORTH-WEST

XLVII   CHELSEA HOSPITAL; INTERIOR OF CHAPEL   *R.C.H.M.*

XLVIII GREENWICH HOSPITAL; EXTERIOR OF KING WILLIAM BLOCK

R.C.H.M.

XLIX   GREENWICH HOSPITAL; EXTERIOR OF DOME, ETC   *R.C.H.M.*

in 1662, when the old Tudor palace was razed to the ground. This was intended to be the first instalment of an altogether new palace, one more to add to Charles's list; but he must have become tired of this particular scheme, for, after it had been roofed in 1669, nothing much seems to have occurred until January 1693 when, according to Narcissus Luttrell, the Lords of the Admiralty paid a visit to Greenwich with a view to converting the unfinished royal palace there into a seamen's hospital—a naval counterpart to Chelsea, just completed.

It is uncertain whether Mary herself,[1] or her husband, or even Wren, was the first person to make this proposal. The author of *Parentalia* has this to say (p. 327): 'The Surveyor [Wren] was among the first who address'd their Majesties King William and Queen Mary, to convert the Site and Buildings of their royal Palace to this most charitable Use. . . . After the Grant had passed the Great Seal, and an ample Commission appointed . . . and the Surveyor nominated a Director, and chief Architect of this great Undertaking; he chearfully engag'd in the Work, gratis, and contriv'd the new Fabrick extensive, durable and magnificent, conformable to the graceful Pavilion, which had been erected there by King Charles the Second, and originally intended for his own Palace; contributing his Time, Labour & Skill, and prosecuting the Works for several Years, with all the Expedition the Circumstances of Affairs would allow; without any Salary, Emolument or Reward (which good Example 'tis to be hoped has since been follow'd); preferring in this, as in every Passage of his Life, the publick Service to any private Advantage of his own, by the Acquest of Wealth, of which he had always a great Contempt.'

Evelyn's *Diary* sheds no light upon the inception of the scheme, his first reference to it being two years later than Luttrell's, but he became one of the Commissioners appointed in 1695. There is, however, a rare pamphlet published in 1728 by Nicholas Hawksmoor, Wren's lieutenant at Greenwich, which gives further particulars of the Queen's close concern with the arrangements up to her sudden death in December 1694. It also refers to her insistence upon the preservation of the Queen's House, a condition which not only frustrated Wren's first sweeping proposals but actually dictated, in large measure, the plan of lay-out subsequently adopted. Here is Hawksmoor's account of the proceedings:

'Her Majesty, ever sollicitous for the Prosecution of the Design, had several times honor'd Greenwich with her personal Views of the Building

[1] According to the official guidebook to *Greenwich Palace*: 'In 1691 she ordered the "Commissioners of the Sick and Hurt" to report on the suitability as Hospitals of the unfinished King's House and also of Carisbrooke Castle.'

erected by King Charles II, as part of his Palace, and that built by Mr Inigo Jones, called the Queen's House, etc. On which Views, she was unwilling to demolish either, as was propos'd by some. This occasioned the keeping of an Approach from the Thames quite up to the Queen's House, of 115 Feet broad . . . that her Majesty might have an Access to that House by Water as well as by Land; and she retained a Desire to add the Four Pavilions to that Palace, according to Inigo Jones' Design, that she might make that little Palace compleat, as a Royal Villa for her own Retirement, or whence Embassadors, or publick Ministers might make their Entry into London. . . . And now as to the New Wing built by King Charles II, it was debated much by the Commissioners, whether it should be demolish'd or remain; and the Dispute went so far, that sundry Workmen were sent from London to give their Opinion. They, as it is indifferent to all Workmen whether they get Money by destroying or erecting Fabricks, gave their Opinion that it was nothing but a Heap of Stones, and that it might lawfully and reasonably be destroyed, and turn'd into Ornaments for slighter Buildings, such as the private Hotels, or the Houses commonly built by the London Workmen, often burning, and frequently tumbling down.

'The Expense of this Building being Considerable, and the Materials of it, when destroyed, not being able to answer a Quarter of that Sum which it stood in, adding also the great Opinion the World had of the Works of Inigo Jones, or Mr Webb, occasion'd further Considerations, till the Queen should be again acquainted with what was proposed; and again asked whether she would please to consent to pull it down. But her Majesty received the Proposal of pulling down that Wing, with as much Indignation as her excellent good Temper would suffer her, order'd it should remain, and the other Side of the Royal Court made answerable to it, in a proper Time. And in consideration that this Wing, part of the Grand Design intended by her Uncle King Charles II, was both beautiful and durable, and even Proof against so scandalous a Fate, as that of Demolition by sacrilegious Hands, which was dedicated to the publick Use; and also that it was placed to answer the regular Designs of that most admirable Person Monsieur Le Nôtre, in the Esplanades, Walks, Vistas, Plantations and Lines of that beautiful Park. There was no Argument for its being taken down could prevail. . . . This her Majesty's absolute Determination to preserve the Wing built by her Uncle King Charles II; to keep the Queen's House, and the Approach to it, on the Considerations above mentioned, naturally drew on the Disposition of the Buildings, as they are now placed and situated.'

The following is a brief account of the complicated sequence of Wren's numerous designs from 1694 to 1702, which are not dated and are dispersed among several collections. They are not even arranged in chronological order in the volumes of the Wren Society. His first scheme, in the All Souls Collection (Wren Society Vol. VIII, Plate XVII) is almost a replica of John Webb's plan for completing Charles II's unfinished palace by duplicating the block, built in 1662-5, on the east side of a square court open towards the river and closed on the south side by a wing in the same style. Wren's only substantial modification was the addition of a chapel on the east side of the new east wing. This scheme would have blocked the view of the Queen's House, hence Queen Mary's successful opposition to it. It was also inadequate to provide the accommodation required for hospital purposes. His next design, at the Soane Museum (Wren Society Vol. VI, Plate XXI and p. 83), is a grandiose project, with a much deeper court terminating on the south in a colonnaded hemicycle leading to a great block with a fine central dome, and with a 'Base Wing' added abreast of King Charles' Wing and also to the corresponding wing east of the court. This was open to the same objection as its predecessor, that it blocked the view of the Queen's House, so it was consequently discarded. Wren followed it with another scheme (Wren Society Vol. VI, Plate X) in which the whole group of buildings was moved further east, thus allowing a clear view of the Queen's House from the river, but this entailed the demolition of King Charles' Wing, and was therefore vetoed by the Queen's wishes, as Hawksmoor relates. On April 29, 1696, a Royal Warrant authorized work to be commenced forthwith on the remodelling of King Charles' Wing and the addition of a 'Base Wing' beside it, to accommodate '350 disabled seamen and their necessary attendants as part of the said Hospitall'. The alterations to King Charles' Wing cost £17,408 and took three years to carry out. The Base Wing, replaced a century later by a new wing duplicating King Charles' fragment, was a plain narrow two-storey block with pavilions at each end of rather French type having 'Mansard' roofs (Wren Society Vol. VI, Plates I-IX). By 1699, an engraved plan issued to subscribers (Wren Society Vol. VI, p. 83) showed the general lay-out much as it exists today, with the view of the Queen's House preserved, as well as King Charles' Wing, and also with Hall, Chapel and colonnades as today, but there was a central ward in each of the courts of the King William and Queen Mary Blocks that was ultimately omitted. The fine domes on these two blocks were certainly projected before 1702, although their form was modified, and greatly improved, in the later stages, and by that date the two central wards just

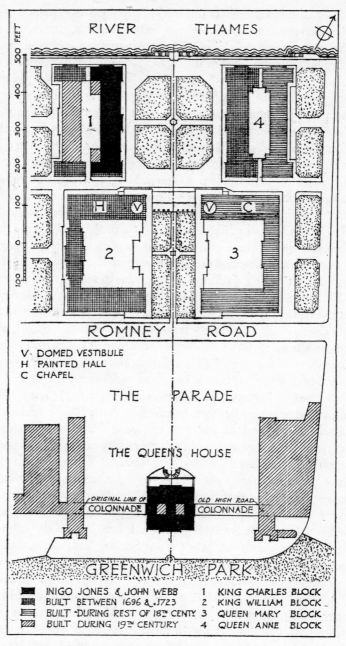

FIG. 26.—WREN'S LAY-OUT FOR GREENWICH HOSPITAL

mentioned had been discarded (Wren Society Vol. VI, Plates XII, XXI).

Evelyn's *Diary* describes the early meetings of the Commissioners, during 1695: '17 February. Called to London by Lord Godolphin, one of the Lords of the Treasury, offering me the Treasurership of the Hospital design'd to be built at Greenwich for worn-out seamen.

'5 May. I came to Deptford [his house at Sayes Court] from Wotton, in order to the first meeting of the Commissioners for endowing an Hospital for Seamen at Greenwich: it was at the Guildhall, London. Present the Abp. of Canterbury, Lord Keeper, Lord Privy Seal, Lord Godolphin, Duke of Shrewsbury, Duke of Leeds, Earls of Dorset and Monmouth, Commissioners of the Admiralty and Navy, Sir Robert Clayton, Sir Christopher Wren, and severall more. . . .

'17 May. Second meeting of the Commissioners, and a Committee appointed to go to Greenwich to survey the place, I being one of them.

'21 May. We went to survey Greenwich, Sir Robert Clayton, Sir Christopher Wren, Mr Travers, the King's Surveyor, Capt. Sanders and myselfe.

'24 May. We made report of the state of Greenwich House, and how the standing part might be made serviceable at present for £6000, and what ground would be requisite for the whole designe. My Lord Keeper order'd me to prepare a book for subscriptions, and a preamble to it.

'31 May. Met again. Mr Vanbrugh was made Secretary of the Commission, by my nomination of him to the Lords, which was all don that day.

'7 June. The Commissioners met at Guildhall, when there were scruples and contests of the Lord Mayor (Sir W. Ashurst) who would not meet, not being named as one of the Quorum, so that a new Commission was requir'd, though the Lord Keeper and the rest thought it too nice a punctilio.

'June 14. Met at Guildhall, but could do nothing for want of a Quorum.

'5 July. At Guildhall; account of subscriptions, about £7000 or £8000.

'11 July. Met at Guildhall: not a full Committee, so nothing don.'

Up to Queen Anne's accession in 1702, Wren appears to have had complete charge and control of the undertaking, subject to the approval of the Commissioners. Nicholas Hawksmoor was appointed his clerk-of-works in 1698. Towards the end of 1698, the Minutes show that, though three of the four blocks were already in hand, no part of the Hospital was ready for occupation. '4 November 1698. Mr Surveyor is desired at the next Meeting to lay before the Committee a scheme of what work may be done this Winter Season, and particularly to finish some part for the reception of

FIG. 27.—GREENWICH HOSPITAL, FROM NORTH GREENWICH
In background, Queen's House; in distance on top of hill, Royal Observatory

some seamen, who are entitled to the benefit of the Hospitall.' On December 20, Hawksmoor was ordered to 'prepare a draught of the Hospitall in perspective by direction of Mr Surveyor and bring it to the Committee as soon as perfected, in order to be graven and printed'. This instruction was fulfilled within ten days, in spite of the Christmas holiday—if any—and 100 copies were soon printed, a proportion of them being mounted on cloth and framed in black frames. In the following autumn a similar number of engravings of the plan were ordered and printed, twenty-four being framed. It appears from an entry of May 9, 1700, that this was all a part of a campaign for additional funds. On that date, Wren reported that he, with Evelyn and Dr Cade, had presented prints to the King, together with a scheme of government for the institution. The Committee resolved that 'sets of the draughts of the Hospital be delivered out to such of the Subscribers as have paid their Subscription'. (Similar steps were taken again in 1711.)

Meetings of the Commissioners on February 26 and March 26, 1701, were fruitless for want of a quorum, only Wren and Evelyn being present; but on June 3 and June 12, 1702, the meetings had to be abandoned owing to Wren's absence, only three members being present on each occasion. In that year, a new 'Board of Directors' was appointed with Wren as chairman, and Vanbrugh among the directors. Evelyn, now an old man, resigned the Treasurership of the Hospital after a long spell of devoted service. From that date onwards, Vanbrugh's influence on design as well as administration steadily increased up to the time of Wren's resignation in 1716, and Wren seems to have welcomed rather than resented the younger man's intervention, indeed his attendance at board meetings ceased in 1710. There are some dramatic details in the design of Greenwich, especially the domes over the two southern blocks, that recall Vanbrugh's work at Castle Howard, where building began in 1701. Nevertheless, the magnificent lay-out and grouping of the Hospital as it stands today is primarily Wren's, whatever additions and modifications were made to it by later architects. The Minutes recall the circumstances of his resignation: '8 June 1716. The Secretary is ordered to attend Sir Chr. Wren and desire whether he is willing to take upon him the constant inspection of the Works at Greenwich and bring his answer to the Admiralty Board.

'1 August 1716. Sir Chr. Wren having excused himself (upon account of his age) from taking upon himself the constant inspection of the Works at Greenwich Hospitall, the Court thought it absolutely necessary that there should be such an Officer as Surveyor, and accordingly have appointed Sir John Vanbrugh.'

The later history of the buildings is outside the scope of this book, but it is interesting to note that when a statement of finance was prepared after the death of George I in 1727, the cost to date had amounted to £210,741 13s. 9d., and the estimated cost of completion was £131,750, making a total of £342,491 13s. 9d. In 1779 the Chapel was gutted by a fire, and the interior remodelled by James Stuart in a neo-Greek style. During the Second World War, the Royal Hospital—which became the Royal Naval College in 1873—was damaged by bombs on five occasions. The parts most seriously affected were King Charles' Block and Queen Anne's Block.

The Museum contains a very fine wooden model, made *c.* 1702, showing the buildings as they were then intended, but it has been altered since it was first constructed. When in use as a hospital, the buildings provided accommodation for some 1,500 persons in all, of whom 1,352 were seamen and the remainder were officers and servants. The seamen were housed in large dormitory-blocks. Besides these, and the necessary administrative rooms, the chief apartments are the splendid Painted Hall (1698-1705) with its ceiling by Sir James Thornhill, the vaulted hall beneath it, and the Chapel (rebuilt, as just stated, at the end of the eighteenth century). Apart from these buildings, with their imposing vestibules, the architectural interest of Greenwich Hospital is mainly external rather than internal. Above everything else, the magnificence of the lay-out is its most impressive feature. The site itself, at the end of a bold loop of the river, gave the architect a great opportunity, and the slopes of the park provided a fine background; but the skill with which Wren contrived to create a monumental scheme without a dominating central feature is remarkable, for the relatively small and unassuming Queen's House lies so far back from the river that it forms an incident rather than a dramatic centre-piece. Although Queen Mary died before a single stone of the new Hospital had been laid, the tremendous impact of her personality ensured the survival of this architectural gem; and the genius of Wren was able to embody her expressed wishes in his final scheme, so different from his first design. He achieved this success mainly by means of the two noble domed towers that rise above the King William and Queen Mary blocks, and he tied the detached blocks together with immense Doric colonnades. Some critics have found fault with his duplication of Webb's building in order to form King Charles' Block, and then with his subsequent duplication of the resultant composition on the east side of the central axis, to form Queen Anne's Block; but to me it appears as a triumph of genius over difficulties, and a great improvement upon his first idea of a small 'Base Wing' as junior partner to Webb's imposing fragment. There are some aspects of the buildings, e.g. the east front of King William's Block, that are manifestly inferior to the rest, and it is uncertain which of them are attributable to Wren himself; but the view of the whole group from the river remains an abiding tribute to his skill as an architect.

L. GREENWICH HOSPITAL; THE PAINTED HALL

R.C.H.M.

LI GREENWICH HOSPITAL; DINING HALL

LII   TEMPLE BAR IN 1797, FROM AN AQUATINT BY B. COOPER

R.C.H.M.

LIIIb   LONDON, THE MIDDLE TEMPLE GATEWAY

R.C.H.M.

LIIIa   LONDON, THE MONUMENT; DETAIL OF BASE

XII

WREN'S OTHER BUILDINGS
FROM 1669 ONWARDS

IN Chapters II and III, Wren's early works in architecture up to 1669 were described; and in that year he was appointed Surveyor-General, so that the date forms an obvious landmark in his career. Thereafter, he was engaged in such an enormous practice that a study of his buildings in strict chronological sequence becomes an impossibility, or at least confusing to a reader. For that reason, as already explained on p. 86, it seems more satisfactory to deal with his architectural work by categories. Previous chapters have described in turn St Paul's Cathedral, the City churches, other churches, Westminster Abbey, later work at Oxford and Cambridge, royal houses and royal hospitals. This method of treatment has the disadvantage that it becomes necessary to defer to my final chapters all general consideration of Wren's methods of work and of the develop-ment of his genius, together with some account of his routine duties as Surveyor-General, his scientific and political interests, and his personal life as a man; nevertheless, this method appears to me preferable to any of the alternatives.

There remains, however, after dealing with the various categories named above, a miscellaneous residue of secular buildings, erected or pro-jected after the year 1669, with which the present chapter is concerned. Many of them were for private clients, in no way connected with his Surveyorship, but two at least resulted directly from the Great Fire. Temple Bar (LII; 1670-2) took the place of a stone gateway erected in 1533, though there is a record of some sort of a barrier at this point as early as 1301. In designing the new gateway, Wren broke right away from the traditional form of the old City gateways with their towers and medieval trappings, adopting a style so Palladian that it suggests the hand of Inigo Jones rather than his own. As it happens, Inigo Jones had made a design for Temple Bar in 1638 (illustrated in J. A. Gotch's *Inigo Jones*, Plate XXVI), but that took the form of a triumphal arch of approximately equal width and height, completely Roman in style. Compared with his design, Wren's scheme is very original, much less Italian and better suited to the practical needs of the situation. His instructions were to provide 'a digni-fied structure, worthy to define the exact spot where a Royal Visitor might be welcomed within the City Gates'. Jones's central arch was only 15 feet wide, Wren's is more than 20 feet; whereas Wren's side arches are slightly narrower than Inigo's. Wren adopted an elliptical arch for the central open-ing in view of the wide span, and placed a guard-room above it. The total width or frontage of the structure is 43 feet. The upper stage is crowned by a segmental pediment that nearly echoes the curve of the wide arch below, and the upper part of the central feature is connected with the lower stage by great Baroque brackets or scrolls. Statues of English kings and queens occupy the niches on both fronts. It has been aptly suggested that the design resembles a French Renaissance church façade on a bridge.[1] On the other hand, it may have been inspired by the famous 'Bridge of Sighs' at Venice, or by the Acqua Paola (1612) at Rome, both probably known to Wren by engravings.

It must be stated here that Wren's responsibility for this design has been questioned[2] for lack of documentary evidence; but the Wren Society illustrates it among his works without comment. It is a picturesque if somewhat amateur composition, and the ignoble erection known as the Temple Bar Memorial that now occupies the site is no credit to Victorian taste. Wren's building was demolished in 1878, having been reported un-safe for many years previously, when the new Law Courts were built. For nearly a decade its stones, carefully numbered, lay in a mason's yard in Farringdon Road; then they were bought by Sir Henry Meux, proprietor of the famous brewery, and re-erected at the entrance to his park at Theobalds near Cheshunt, in 1887. There Temple Bar still stands amid rural surroundings, a strange contrast to its former situation astride one of the busiest streets in the world; but, at the time of writing (1952), its present owner has offered to restore it to London if a suitable and dignified place for it can be found in the new plan of the City of London. Like most of Wren's civic buildings, it is constructed of Portland stone.

The same material, over 28,000 cubic feet of it according to *Parentalia* (p. 323), was used for the Monument, built in 1677 (LIII*a*). An Act of Parliament of that year sets forth the reasons for its erection: 'The better to preserve the memory of this dreadful visitation; Be it further enacted that a Columne or Pillar of Brase or stone be erected on or as neare unto the place where the said Fire soe unhappily began as Conveniently may be, in perpetuall Remembrance thereof, with such Inscription thereon, as

---

[1] G. Webb, *Wren*, p. 74.

[2] T. F. Reddaway, *The Rebuilding of London*, p. 216.

hereafter by the Mayor and Court of Aldermen in that behalfe be directed.' Three drawings in the Sloane Collection at the British Museum show that Wren had begun to prepare designs for the Monument before 1677. His first scheme took the form of a tall stone obelisk on a massive pedestal, with a phoenix on the top: the total height was 90 feet. His second design proposed a plain Doric column without flutings, surmounted by a flaming urn. The shaft was sprayed with brass 'flames' at intervals, these serving to conceal tiny windows lighting the internal staircase, as well as meeting their symbolic purpose. Reporting to the City Lands Committee on July 27, 1675, Wren wrote that: 'A Phoenix was first thought of, and is the ornament of the wooden Modell of the Pillar, which I caused to be made before it was begun; but upon second thoughts, I rejected it, because it will be costly, not easily understood at that highth, and worse understood at a distance, and lastly dangerous by reason of the sayle, the spread winges will carry in the winde.' Instead, he recommended a brass statue 15 feet high if it could be cast for £1,000; failing that, a copper ball with flames, fixed complete with the necessary ironwork for about £350. This latter proposal was accepted, and Robert Hooke was instructed to have a wooden ball made, of 9 feet diameter, covered with copper. The total cost of the amended design as we now see it, with flutes on the column but no brass flames, was £13,450 11s. 9d. This amount probably included the cost of the site, but excluded four dragons on the base, which cost £50 each.

The dimensions as stated in *Parentalia* are correct, viz. total height above the original pavement level (since slightly raised) 202 feet, height of pedestal 40 feet, diameter of column 15 feet. The number of steps up to the gallery, enclosed by an iron cage since 1842, is said in *Parentalia* in one place to be 345, but in another passage 343 steps of black marble are mentioned. The Monument was restored in 1834, again in 1888, and fortunately survived the air-raids of 1940-5. It is believed that Robert Hooke played some part in its design, which, in any case, was merely an adaptation of an antique form. Wren is said to have intended to use it as a 'giant telescope', and to carry out there certain experiments for which the Royal Society had no facilities; but, as might have been expected, the vibration caused by traffic rendered these intentions fruitless. *Parentalia* contains this comment on building operations: 'The Artificers were oblig'd to wait sometimes for Stones of proper Scantlings; which occasion'd the Work to be longer in Execution than otherwise it would have been.'

The sculptures on the pedestal, by Caius Gabriel Cibber, are of some merit. Those on the western panel represent King Charles with the Duke of York, offering protection to the stricken City, both men being in Roman costume. Dr Gale, the Master of St Paul's School, was presented with a piece of plate valued at ten guineas, as 'a loving remembrance' for composing the long Latin inscription recording the Fire. Wren had to provide a permanent and massive 'vertical feature', in the jargon of today, to rise high above the huddle of surrounding roofs, but the Monument of the Fire of London is not generally regarded as one of his masterpieces.

Nineteenth-century writers on Wren attributed to him the rebuilding of many of the City Companies' Halls, of which forty-four were destroyed in the Great Fire. James Elmes and Miss Phillimore both credit him with thirty-seven, Wyatt Papworth says he designed the Painter-Stainers', Plaisterers', Vintners' and Tallow Chandlers' himself; that he or Jarman was responsible for the Haberdashers'; and that he designed the Innholders' with Jarman. (Of these, the Painter-Stainers' was destroyed during the Blitz and the Innholders' severely damaged; the Haberdashers' was rebuilt in 1864; and the Plaisterers' ceased to exist long ago.) Mr W. H. Godfrey, writing in 1911, states that 'probably several . . . have to be put to his credit'; and Sir Reginald Blomfield (1900) hazards the suggestion that, though many Halls are known to have been designed by others, 'the designs were doubtless submitted to Wren for his approval'. Miss Milman (1908) ascribes to him Pewterers' Hall, Brewers' Hall and the front of Mercers' Hall. (Of these, the first has been much altered, and the other two destroyed in the air-raids.) Modern scholarship, however, is now unanimous that most of the Halls are known to have been designed by the companies' own surveyors, or by Jarman or Mills, the City Surveyors[1]; and that there is not a single instance where Wren is proved to have been the architect, though in point of fact many of the buildings do closely resemble his work.

In the Temple, Wren carried out an uncertain but substantial amount of building between 1678 and 1684. This was necessitated not only by the Great Fire of 1666 but also by a series of fires which took place in the next few years, notably in 1677-8. The fine House of the Master of the Temple (LIV*b*) was rebuilt in 1667 and totally demolished in the air-raids of 1940-1. It was a handsome building, three storeys high plus attics, and seven windows wide, with a central pediment, all in the characteristic style of Wren; but the name of its architect is not stated in the lengthy description of it in the *City* volume of the Historical Monuments Commission. The same authority states that Lamb Building was erected in

---

[1] In his *British Architects and Craftsmen* (1945, p. 64) Mr Sacheverell Sitwell states that Talman built halls for the Fishmongers, Haberdashers, Drapers and 'Taylors'.

1666-7, but does not mention Wren. It is an isolated brick block, four storeys high plus attics and basement, again closely resembling Wren's style. The buildings of Essex Court, Pump Court and New Court—all in the Middle Temple—are considered to form part of a project entrusted by the Society in 1676-7 to Dr Nicholas Barbon who, although a medical practitioner by profession, turned to speculative building; and it appears that, after the fires of 1677-8, Wren was called in, either to direct his work or to supersede him. Nos. 2 and 3 Brick Court are of that period, and No. 4 King's Bench Walk was then rebuilt and may well have been designed by Wren, as also some others in the same block which are of an earlier date than the 1677-8 fires. The range of chambers north of Fig Tree Court was also erected after 1677-8.

The only buildings in the Temple which are definitely known to be by Wren are the cloister forming the east end of Pump Court, with chambers above the cloister (LIV*a*); and the gateway or frontage of the Middle Temple in Fleet Street (LIII*b*). The former was built in 1681 on the site of earlier cloisters, destroyed by fire in 1678-9, and was a four-storey block with brick walls and stone dressings. There were round-headed arches on each front with a central range of Doric columns. This building was completely demolished by bombing in the air-raids of 1940-1.

The Middle Temple Gateway, which fortunately escaped that fate, is an austere classic façade to Fleet Street, the lower part of rusticated masonry and the three upper storeys in brickwork. This, and the now destroyed south front of Christ's Hospital in Newgate Street (see p. 220), are the only known examples of a street façade designed by Wren, both characterized by a simple dignity. He made effective use of rubbed brickwork here, as in the doorways often attributed to him in King's Bench Walk. *Parentalia* contains this description of the Gateway: 'The Frontispiece of the Middle-temple, towards Fleet-street, was erected in the Year 1684, of Stone and Brick. The Basis is a Rustick Arcade of Stone, supporting four Pilasters. Entablature, and triangular Pediment of the Ionick Order, and the rest of rubbed Brick.' For his work in the Inner and Middle Temple, the Societies presented Wren with twelve silver trencher plates, then valued at about £48, when his task had been completed.

At the other end of the Strand, the fine statue of Charles I, which faces Whitehall, stands on a noble pedestal designed by Wren and erected in 1674. The bronze statue itself, by Hubert le Sueur, was cast in 1633, hidden during the Civil War, and brought out again after the Restoration. Wren's pedestal is illustrated in drawings by Wren in the All Souls Collection (reproduced as Plates 38-40 in the Wren Society's Vol. V); but the boldly delineated sculpture on those drawings is attributed to the pencil of Grinling Gibbons. The actual carving was executed by Joshua Marshall. The statue, being rightly regarded as one of the most excellent artistically, as well as perhaps the most significant historically, that we possess, was removed to Mentmore during the Second World War; but the pedestal remained, shielded and camouflaged as an 'information-bureau', with this would-be humorous inscription: 'Closed on Sundays—not open all the week.'

The All Souls Collection also contains a design by Wren for 'A Theatre', unnamed, but believed to be Drury Lane, first built in 1663 and rebuilt in 1672-4. The maximum width is 113 feet and the auditorium is 35 feet high. The walls are decorated with Corinthian pilasters and there are elliptical arches over the boxes. The drawing in question is a carefully rendered section in ink and wash.

Frequent reference has been made earlier in this book (pp. 20, 22-4, 25-6) to Wren's status and ability as a clever astronomer. It was, however, apparently as an architect—more precisely in his capacity as Surveyor-General—that he was instructed in 1675 to prepare designs for a royal observatory on the site of the old castle in Greenwich Park. According to *Parentalia*: 'Sir Christopher Wren was one of the Commissioners who, at the Motion of Sir Jonas Moore, Surveyor-General of the Ordnance, had been appointed by his Majesty to find a proper Place for erecting a royal Observatory; and he proposed Greenwich, which was approved of: And August 10, 1675, the Foundation of the Building was laid, and when finished, under the Conduct of Sir Jonas, with the Advice and Assistance of Sir Christopher, was furnished with the best Instruments for making astronomical Observations, and the celebrated Mr John Flamstead constituted his Majesty's first Professor there.' Professor Hinks considers[1] that 'it seems that Wren had more to do with the design than is generally allowed', observing that 'Wren was above all other men in England at that time practically conversant with the construction of large instruments, having made them himself, and being in particular interested in the grinding of objectives . . . yet there is no evidence that he took much interest in a project that he might have been expected to make his particular care and delight'. This criticism seems rather unfair, partly because it assumes a lack of interest on the sole ground of lack of evidence, and partly because Wren, at that time, was immersed in the greatest architectural practice that any man has ever had. The Royal Warrant was dated June 22, 1675, and in exactly six months the new Observatory was finished,

[1] In the *Wren Bicentenary Volume* (1923), p. 252.

roofed, equipped and occupied—a truly remarkable achievement, whatever part Wren may have played in it! The Historical Monuments Commission's Volume on *East London* cautiously states that the design is 'attributed to Wren'; but an order to the Ordnance Department (not, be it noted, to the Office of Works) says that the building was to be erected according 'to such plot and design as shall be given you by Sir Christopher Wren'.

The building is now known as Flamsteed House (to give the usual spelling for the name of the first Astronomer Royal, 1646-1719), and is of two storeys, the lower portion about 36 feet square and divided into four rooms, the upper storey a single octagonal room called the 'Camera Stellata' in Flamsteed's day. This fine apartment has a panelled dado and a saucer-dome above a deep cove. There is a staircase in a small square wing. Numerous excrescences and alterations have marred the former simplicity of the exterior, but the octagon is clearly visible, with its tall sash-windows and its balustrade. It was the first building of its kind in England, and when Bishop Fell proposed to install an observatory in 'Tom Tower' at Oxford (cf. p. 156), Wren wrote to him on December 3, 1681, that 'Wee built indeed an Observatory not unlike what your Tower will prove, it was for the Observator's Habitation and a little for Pompe'. Indeed, the Camera Stellata was more of a State apartment than a scientific laboratory; but the foundation of the Observatory there was intended by the astute King to improve the science of navigation, and was therefore a strictly utilitarian project. In recent years the locality of Greenwich has become unsuitable for exact astronomical observation, and the Royal Observatory is being moved elsewhere. As it stands today (1952), still bearing the marks of war damage, 'Flamsteed House' is a curious building and, even if all the excrescences were removed, it does not exhibit Wren at his best.

The public library and school which Wren designed in 1685 for Archbishop Tenison, in Castle Street, St Martin's, was sold in 1861 and now no longer exists. The exterior, as it appeared in 1850, is illustrated in *The Survey of London*, Vol. XX, Plate 99.

Bromley College, in Kent (LV), is a charming group of almshouses attributed to Wren (Wren Society Vol. XIX, Plate XIII) and erected some time between 1666 and 1672. The former date indicates the foundation of the charity by the Bishop of Rochester, the latter probably the completion and occupation of the buildings, but the date of their commencement seems to have been 1670. The first group comprised twenty houses for the widows of clergymen of the Church of England. Further bequests towards the end of the eighteenth century enabled ten more

FIG. 28.—ABINGDON MARKET HOUSE OR 'COUNTY HALL'

dwellings to be built. This beautiful, dignified and reticent design resembles that of Morden College (pp. 226-7), built by Wren some twenty-five years later.

At Arbury House in Warwickshire, the seat of the Newdigate family, Wren carried out sundry works in the house itself and in the stables in 1674. The Wren Society's Vol. XII contains illustrations of two doorways there for which he made designs. The following letter, which he wrote to his client on November 11, 1674, is typical of his correspondence:
'Sir,

'I received your letter and have endeavoured to observe your commands by sending another designe wherein the stone will be somewhat less scantlings and the shield will be weathered, but I believe your workmen are such as can read noe book but their own, otherwise much of that stone of which you sent me a note might have been imployed in the designe, but the second designe will imploy most of the same stone if a man of Judgement manage it. I have no more at present, but my humble service and thanks for your favours.

'Your most humble servant,
'Chr. Wren.'

One of the most attractive buildings of this period is the variously named Market House, or Town Hall, or County Hall at Abingdon in

LIVa   LONDON, THE MIDDLE TEMPLE; THE CLOISTERS   *R.C.H.M.*

LIVb   LONDON, HOUSE OF THE MASTER OF THE TEMPLE   *N.B.R.*

LV   BROMLEY COLLEGE, KENT; EXTERIOR

The late N. Lloyd

LVI   WINDSOR CASTLE, WREN'S DESIGN FOR MAUSOLEUM

LVII LONDON: CHRIST'S HOSPITAL

Berkshire, built in 1678-81 (Fig. 28). Sir Reginald Blomfield, a learned and careful scholar, wrote in 1900 that though this building 'would not have disgraced' Wren's reputation, the name of its designer is not known. Elsewhere he remarks that 'the skill and knowledge displayed make it improbable that it was designed by a mason only, yet there are other buildings ... of a simpler character, but hardly less excellent, which were quite within the competence of any good builder of the time'. The Editors of the Wren Society (Vol. XIX, p. 100) are more confident: 'No hesitation need be felt in accepting this charming little building as the design of Sir Christopher Wren. It is reminiscent of the College of the Four Nations opposite the Louvre in Paris', which Wren knew, and 'apart from this, the set-out in four bays by two, where anybody else would have made it five by three, is characteristic'. It appealed to those two discriminating contemporary travellers Celia Fiennes and Daniel Defoe; and their enthusiasm for a building which they admired because it was so 'modern' is echoed by all discerning critics of today. It is comparatively small, measuring only 64 by 36 feet over all, but the fine room upstairs is 57 by 30 feet, and has tall round-headed windows with leaded lights. Corinthian pilasters, separating the bays and the windows, rise from the ground to the splendid cornice. The steep roof above them is covered with lead and crowned by a balustrade enclosing a lead flat. Above this is a bold lantern. The lower storey has open arches between the pilasters, and serves as a covered market. Since 1931, the room upstairs has housed a museum of local antiquities. The cost of this building was only £2,840, of which sum £1,552 was paid to the master-mason, Christopher Kempster (1627-1715), who has sometimes been credited with the design. He owned a quarry at Burford, worked for a time at St Paul's, and while he was erecting this Market House at Abingdon was also rebuilding St James Garlickhithe (pp. 124, etc.) under the direction of Wren, who had a high opinion of his abilities and recommended him strongly to Bishop Fell in 1681 in connection with 'Tom Tower' at Oxford.

Most of Wren's architecture is to be found in, or within eight miles of London, but at Lincoln Cathedral he built the Honywood Library in 1674 for the Dean of that name. The north 'alley' of the Gothic cloister was then in ruins, and Wren decided to ignore the medieval tradition completely, whereas in many cases—as we have seen—he endeavoured to produce some modified form of Gothic design. He also ignored the height of the existing cloister, and designed a tall open arcade supported on plain Doric columns. In the upper storey is the Library, with large sash windows 8 feet by 4 feet, and a massive stone cornice 32 feet above the ground. The

exterior is successful, even if inappropriate—in the eyes of some critics—
to its Gothic surroundings, and the long line of windows is relieved from
monotony by the use of a cornice over every third opening. The Library
is a fine room, nearly 120 feet long, but only 13 feet 4 inches high and
therefore producing a rather low effect internally. The subsequent addition of bookcases on the window-wall may have been unavoidable, but is
certain regrettable on aesthetic grounds; yet, from a practical point of
view, the new Library—bright and spacious—provided a welcome contrast to the ill-lit and cramped medieval book-room. The work was completed in six months at a cost of only £680, but this modest sum may not
have included the decorations and fittings. The contract prescribed that
the roof was to be covered with 7 lb. lead, that no 'firre' was to be used
except for flooring, stairs and roof-boarding (which was to be at least
1 inch thick), that all other timber was to be oak, that the lime was to be
obtained from 'the Church lime-kiln', and that the contractor must maintain the building for ten years! Unlike most of Wren's work, where Portland stone was used, the walls here are faced with fine yellow limestone
from Ancaster near Lincoln.

Adjoining the church of All Saints at Northampton already described
(pp. 132-3) stands the Sessions House, erected almost simultaneously in
1673-6. The Editors of the Wren Society (Vol. XIX, p. 58) ascribe this to
Wren and Henry Jones jointly, arguing that circumstances make it natural
to assume that Wren was, at least, consulted as to its design. One document indicates that Jones was working as a carpenter in Northampton in
1673, another that he was practising as an architect in the town in 1678.
There is nothing inherently contradictory in these two statements: the
metamorphosis from carpenter to architect was common enough in the
seventeenth and eighteenth centuries. At any rate, the design is creditable
if not brilliant. The frontage of the building is 78 feet, and the interior
comprises one large room with a flat ceiling. Externally, the stone façade
has two slightly projecting wings, each with a large doorway flanked by
coupled Corinthian columns under a curved pediment. Between these
wings is a range of mullioned windows, high up, separated by Corinthian
pilasters. The roof is hipped and somewhat steep.

In 1678, Wren prepared designs for a mausoleum for King Charles I,
adjoining St George's Chapel at Windsor. *Parentalia* gives this descrip-
tion of his scheme: 'King Charles the Second was pleased to order the
Surveyor [Wren] to design a Mausolèum, or Tomb, for his Father, the
Royal Martyr.' On January 29, 1678, the House of Commons voted 'the
Sum of Seventy Thousand Pounds, for a solemn Funeral of his Late

Majesty King Charles the First, and to erect a Monument for the said Prince of glorious Memory; the said Sum to be raised by a two Months Tax, to begin at the Expiration of the present Tax for building Ships. . . . The Form of this Structure (as appears by the Surveyor's original Drawings, which were laid before the King) is a Rotundo, with a beautiful Dome and Lantern; a circular Colonade without, of the Corinthian Order, resembling the Temple of Vesta'. This design was approved by the King, but 'after some time', the drawings, 'through Incidents of the Times, or Motives unknown to the Publick, were laid aside'. *Parentalia* explains that 'a little Gothick building raised by Cardinal Wolsey' at 'the East-end of St George's Chapel' was 'demolished in April 1646, by Command of the Long Parliament'; and that 'this Place, King Charles the First, of ever blessed and glorious Memory, intended to enlarge and make fit and capable, not only for the Interment of his own royal Body, but also for the Bodies of his Successors Kings of England, had not bad Times drawn on'.

Wren's design, never executed (LVI), is illustrated in six highly finished drawings in ink and wash, now in the All Souls Collection (see Plates XLI-XLIII in Wren Society Vol. V). The statuary on two of these designs was drawn by Grinling Gibbons, with whom Wren was now closely associated. The mausoleum, as *Parentalia* says, was to be a rotunda or domed structure, 60 feet in diameter and rising 90 feet above the floor. The memorial proper took the form of an allegorical group of sculptured figures, including Charles I, executed in marble and bronze, and standing in a niche within the domed chamber. The interior was to be richly ornamented with bronze, marble and mosaics. Wren estimated the total cost at £43,663 2s. 0d. Intrinsically a very fine design, the building would have been completely out of harmony with the medieval surroundings of Windsor Castle and of the adjoining St George's Chapel.

In 1678 Wren designed a monument, in the form of a stone urn or small cenotaph, to the two young Princes murdered in 1483, whose bodies had been found in the Tower of London just before. This memorial stands on the east wall of the north aisle of Henry VII's Chapel, Westminster, in a recess simply framed in black marble. A label beneath it bears the inscription 'Said to have been designed by Sir Christopher Wren', but *Parentalia* definitely claims it as his work.

In 1680-2, and again in 1694-5, he made important additions to the famous school for boys and girls at Christ's Hospital in Newgate Street, commonly known as the 'Bluecoat School' (LVII). Of this institution he was a governor, and his friends Samuel Pepys and Sir Charles Scarburgh (cf. p. 17) were also members of the governing body. The school was a picturesque group of medieval buildings at the time of the Great Fire, and sundry additions were made to it soon afterwards, apparently under the direction of Peter Mills, Clerk of Works to the City Corporation, who was succeeded by Hooke and Oliver. This work included the earlier Writing School. It is possible that Wren rebuilt the Hall in 1680, and quite certain that he designed the Mathematical School facing Newgate Street in 1682. This delightful façade was fortunately recorded in a fine drawing made by Professor A. E. Richardson in 1900 and now deposited in the Victoria and Albert Museum.[1] It had a frontage of *c.* 150 feet and was two storeys high, with dormers in the roof. Most of the windows had wood mullions and leaded lights. It was divided into eleven bays by pilasters, mainly Doric, but had coupled Ionic pilasters on the two end bays. All this work, except the fine modillion cornice in wood, was of brick, the pilasters and other details being in gauged brick. The central three bays were spanned by a curved pediment, the end bays by triangular pediments. In the east end bay was an archway through which one descended by a flight of nine steps to the large inner quadrangle, and above this doorway a niche contained a statue of the founder, King Edward VI. The scale of the design made the building appear larger than it really was. Evidently the work was completed in the autumn of 1684, for a Minute of the Court of Governors in October 1684 records that: 'The Court gave Orders that convenient Fires should be made in the Mathematicall Schools and Ward, for the well airing of them before the Children enter therein.'

Two later Minutes explain Wren's second commission. '16 *December* 1691: The Court was acquainted that a worthy Gentleman (who desired not to be named) had some thought of building at his own cost and charge a New Writing Schoole for the Children in this Hospital, if the Court be willing for him soe to doe. The Court unanimously granted such permission, withall returning their humble and hearty thanks for such benefaction. And, whereas the place where the School should be erected is not fully agreed upon, Sir Chr. Wren has yet the draught thereof in his hands.

'2 *March* 1692. To this Committee, Sir Chr. Wren presented the draught of the New intended Writing Schoole. The Committee gave him their hearty thanks for his pains therein.' The unknown donor was later revealed as Sir John Moore, Kt, Lord Mayor in 1681, and 'now President of this House'. Work commenced on the new building in 1692 and finished in April 1695. The School provided 'long writing boards sufficient for 300

---

[1] Reproduced as Plate XLVI in Wren Society Vol. XI, and elsewhere; some illustrations wrongly describe it as the 'Latin School'.

boys to sit and write upon'. The original estimate was £3,000, the actual cost over £4,000. The building was described as 'a most modern edifice of brick and stone, elevated on pillars fronting the Town Ditch', a circumstance which led to calamity a century later, when the rash addition of another storey overstrained the inadequate foundation, and the building had to be demolished. The opening of the New Writing School took place with great ceremony on April 10, 1695. The Court ordered that an anthem should be sung, but decided that the names of the architect and the treasurer need not be mentioned during the proceedings! Wren is reputed to have been a modest man, and certainly he was a Governor, but, unless there is some sinister explanation, such excessive anonymity seems inhuman.

Other Minutes refer to Grinling Gibbons, the famous sculptor:

'20 *December* 1695. Mr Parrey (Clerk) to call on Mr Gibbons, the Carver, to know the reason of his delaying the finishing of Sir John Moore's Statue which is to be set up in the New Writing Schoole by Order of the Court Dec. 10, 1694, and render some account of it to the next Court, and withall to get Mr Gibbons to appeare at the same time if he can.

'3 *January* 1696. Mr Gibbons, the Carver, appeared and declared he cannot finish the Statue until Sir John Moore hath sat once, upon that Sir John Moore was pleased to promise that upon Monday come 7 night he will meet Mr Gibbons for that purpose, and in a month after Mr Gibbons promised to finish the same.' (It may be added that Gibbons was paid £90 for this statue, in marble.)

Wren's Mathematical School was demolished, with all the other buildings, when the boys of Christ's Hospital were transferred to West Horsham, Sussex, in 1902. At the same time, the girls were moved to the old buildings in Fore Street, Hertford, which hitherto had accommodated the younger children of both sexes. A site for that purpose was bought in 1683, and buildings of brick in the style characteristic of Wren's domestic work were erected in 1693-5. Of these, three remain: the schoolroom, the steward's house (since altered) and some fine gateways. Minutes of the Court show that funds were collected from January 1692 and estimates discussed early in 1693. Other Minutes show that the work was directed by John Oliver, Wren's deputy at St Paul's, who was himself a Governor; and it is assumed that the design was Sir Christopher's, probably in the form of sketch-drawings. The institution is now restricted to girls, and has nearly 300 pupils in eight boarding-houses.

At some date in Charles II's reign, probably 1671, the building of the

College of Physicians in Warwick Lane in the City of London was begun. This has been attributed to Wren, but is not mentioned in the Index to *Parentalia*, and is now generally regarded as the work of Robert Hooke. Writing in *The Wren Bicentenary Volume* in 1923 (pp. 128-30), Professor A. E. Richardson praises it highly, and says that most authorities ascribe it to Wren 'although there is the probability that Dr Hooke . . . may have been associated with him to arrange the internal requirements and fitments'; but the Editors of Hooke's *Diary*, published in 1935, say that 'what evidence exists rather points to Hooke as the architect', and the Editors of the Wren Society (Vol. XIX, p. xii) concur in this opinion.

There is some uncertainty about the authorship of Easton Neston House in Northamptonshire, included in Papworth's list of Wren's executed buildings under the date *c.* 1680, but with a note that Wren was responsible for the wings only, the body of the house being rebuilt by Hawksmoor in 1702 on the site of a much older structure. The wings in question have since been pulled down, and the house as it stands is a fine Palladian block in the style of Hawksmoor or Vanbrugh rather than of Wren, but is also reminiscent of Sir Roger Pratt's Coleshill. It is a simple oblong in form, two storeys high above a basement, with its roof concealed behind a stone balustrade. It is known that Hawksmoor's work was based upon a model that he made, showing skilful planning that recalled some of Wren's early drawings for Hampton Court: it is also a fact that Wren was consulted about the house *c.* 1682, and may conceivably have inspired its design. On balance, the main credit must be ascribed to Hawksmoor (see Wren Society Vol. XII, pp. 19, 22).

In the case of Fawley Court near Henley (1684-8), the long-established tradition of Wren's authorship is supported by the circumstance that its owner William Freeman (1645-1717) and Wren had many friends in common; and in Langley's *History of the Hundred of Desborough*, published in 1797, Wren is named as the designer (LVIII). It was redecorated internally by James Wyatt in 1771. The subsequent replacement of small panes by plate-glass in the windows, and the pointing of the brickwork with black mortar, have spoiled its external appearance; but as one sees it from the river or the towpath, on the left bank about a mile below Henley Bridge, it displays the familiar characteristics of Wren's domestic architecture. It is a substantial brick building of two storeys and attics, with stone dressings. The original windows had mullions, transomes and lead glazing. There is a fine modillion cornice, above which is a slated roof with dormers. On the west side is an Ionic tetrastyle portico crowned by

FIG. 29.—WOLVESEY PALACE, WINCHESTER

a balustrade. Internally, there is an imposing entrance hall, 42 by 28 feet, on the central axis.

The handsome building known as 'School' at Winchester College (LIX) was commenced in 1683 for Warden Nicholas, and finished in 1687. Some authorities have attributed it to Wren, others have hesitated to offer an opinion, but no alternative name appears to have been suggested. It is not mentioned in *Parentalia*, and no drawings of it are in the All Souls Collection, but the Editors of the Wren Society (XIX, p. xiii) regard it as 'a very probable work by Wren'. It is undoubtedly very like some of his other work, and is also refreshingly English, with no pervading hint of Italian Baroque or French Renaissance. Externally it is a simple composition, with a central doorway, and above it a bronze statue of William of Wykeham presented by the sculptor himself, Caius Julius Cibber, in 1692. On each side of the doorway are three large round-headed windows divided into small panes. Above them are carved swags of foliage, then a fine modillion cornice repeated in a central pediment, and a plain roof of moderate pitch. Internally it is a splendid single room measuring 78 by 35 feet, with a richly carved cornice and ceiling. The dado-panelling, seating and dais for the masters were added in 1848, and an organ was afterwards installed. The whole design is mellow, dignified, scholarly and pleasing. The walls are of dark red brickwork, with dressings of gauged brick and Portland stone. In style it resembles to some extent the Mauritshuis (1633-44) at The Hague (cf. p. 261).

In Winchester, too, there is a portion of the episcopal Wolvesey Palace, now used once more for its original purpose after having served for many years as a diocesan clergy-house and certainly designed by Wren (Fig. 29). There is some confusion about the date, as Papworth in his list of Wren's buildings gives '1662-84', but the former date must be much too early, because several authorities agree that its erection was inspired by the King's large palace just outside Winchester, of which the foundation stone was not laid until March 23, 1683 (see p. 162). The following extract from *Parentalia* (p. 326) explains how the project came into being: 'Bishop Morley, seeing his Majesty designing to make Winchester a royal Residence, thought himself obliged to keep pace with the King; and therefore pulled down a great Part of the old episcopal Palace, and under the direction of the same Architect, Sir Christopher Wren, began a new one; but he dying about the Time with the King, his Palace stood still with the King's. However he had compleated one Wing in his Lifetime, & left Money for finishing the rest; but Bishop Mew, his Successor (1684), seeing no Probability of a Court at Winchester, never minded it. Sir John Trelawny, succeeding Bishop Mew in Queen Anne's time (1707), called for the Money left by Bishop Morley, and finished it. It is a very handsome Palace, à la Moderne.' The accounts show that the cost of the building was c. £2,800. The surviving portion of Wolvesey Palace has a main frontage of about 120 feet to the garden (see Fig. 29) and is beautifully situated adjoining the ruins of the old Wolvesey Castle. The walls are of stone, the roofs tiled, and the tall mullioned windows have leaded panes, though at this date Wren was beginning to use sash-windows. For dignity, reticence and formal domestic charm it ranks high in the list of his buildings.

The College of Matrons at Salisbury (1682) is regarded by the Editors of the Wren Society (XIX, p. xiii) as 'a very probable work by Wren'. Apart from its characteristic style, this attribution seems the more likely because the Bishop, Seth Ward, who paid for it was a very old friend of Wren's (cf. pp. 17, 18, 23, 24). It provided accommodation for ten widows of clergymen of the Church of England, and is a long low picturesque building of brick. Standing just inside the North Gate, and thus within the Cathedral precincts, it is in fairly good preservation, though the small panes have been removed from the windows, and the chimney-stacks have

LVIII   FAWLEY COURT, BUCKINGHAMSHIRE; EXTERIOR

N.B.R.

LIX   WINCHESTER COLLEGE; 'SCHOOL' EXTERIOR   *The late N. Lloyd*

LX   ETON COLLEGE; 'UPPER SCHOOL' FROM QUADRANGLE

N.B.R.

R.C.H.M.

LXI   MORDEN COLLEGE, BLACKHEATH; EXTERIOR

FIG. 30.—THE COLLEGE OF MATRONS, SALISBURY, 1682

been faced with cement and otherwise altered. Behind it lies a little enclosed garden (Fig. 30).

When Charles II died in 1685, Wren lost a good friend and patron. Sir
Christopher was then 63 years of age, and enormously busy with the
numerous important commissions already described, as well as with his
miscellaneous but considerable routine duties as Surveyor-General. The
only private commission that he carried out during the short reign of
James II, apart from various buildings in progress previously mentioned,
appears to have been the rebuilding of 'Upper School' at Eton College
(LX), and in fact that work did not actually begin till 1689, being
completed in 1691. Papworth attributes it to him but gives it the obviously
incorrect date of 1670; and the Editors of the Wren Society (Vol. XIX,
pp. 108-10) also ascribe it to Wren, who succeeded Hugh May as architect
to the neighbouring Windsor Castle in 1684. The total cost was
£2,286 9s. 1½d.[1] It is a simple rectangular block, *c.* 120 by 30 feet, of brick
with dressings of Portland and Burford stone and a slated roof. The front
towards the Slough Road is divided into seven bays, with large windows
in both storeys, subdivided by wood mullions and transomes, and

[1] Hakewill's *History of Windsor* (1813, p. 212) gives the cost as £1,500.

glazed in small leaded panes. The cornice is of stone and is crowned by a stone balustrade. The inner front, towards the quadrangle, is similar in its upper part, but the lower storey has an open arcade with coupled Doric columns between the arches, all of stone. This treatment recalls work at Trinity College, Cambridge. Internally, the ground floor has been much altered, but the fine original staircase remains. Upstairs the spacious 'Upper School' has hardly been changed, and still possesses its original wood panelling, seats and desks. About a third of the building was seriously damaged by a bomb in 1941.

Another school building of a very different type with which Wren was concerned is the 'Free School' (1693-7) at Appleby in Leicestershire, built for Sir John Moore, who has been mentioned (p. 220) as President of Christ's Hospital in London, where Wren was busy at the same time. At Appleby, however, Wren was associated with Sir William Wilson (1640-1710), previously named in this book (p. 134) as the possible or probable designer of the nave and tower of St Mary's, Warwick. The Wren Society devote some thirty pages of their Vol. XI to this building at Appleby and to the career of Sir William Wilson, who is revealed as the author of several notable houses in the Midlands. It seems that when the school at Appleby was projected, Wilson offered his services as a local collaborator and supervisor of the work; but he also submitted various criticisms of Wren's designs with the support of sundry influential persons in the district. He then went up to London to put his suggestions before Moore, and claimed that these were favoured by Wren. His collaboration was in no way gratuitous, and he eventually sent in a claim for £250 as architect's fees, but this was ultimately reduced to £126. The effect of a provincial collaborator upon Wren's fashionable London-made design was remarkable, for the building as actually erected completely misleads a visitor sufficiently interested and informed to guess its date, which—upon its architectural character—might be supposed to be 1640 instead of 1693-7. It is, indeed, very unlike most of Wren's work in its picturesque jumbling of classical features, and is just what one would expect from Wilson, impartially described as 'mason, sculptor and architect'. It is a building of some size with a frontage of rather more than 100 feet, three storeys high, in brick and stone with tall mullioned and leaded windows, a roof concealed by a parapet, and a central lantern.

Morden College at Blackheath (1695-1702) is a delightful building which ought to be attributable to Wren on its style alone (LXI), and is so accepted by the Wren Society and Historical Monuments Commission. This authorship is the more probable because its founder—Sir John

Morden—sat, with Wren, on the Commission for Greenwich Hospital not far away. It was founded as 'an asylum for decayed Turkey merchants', and statues of the founder and his wife stand above the entrance. It has been very little altered since it was erected. It is built round a quadrangle about 100 feet square, and is two storeys high, the upper floor extending over the Doric colonnade that surrounds the court. The walls are of brick with stone dressings, and sash-windows are used throughout. The main (west) front has a slightly projecting central feature with a wide pediment over. Above this pediment rises a graceful cupola or belfry, remodelled in 1755. The north and south wings project forward from the main front, and contain the Treasurer's House (now converted into a hospital) and the Chaplain's House. On the far side of the quadrangle, the chapel is placed on the central axis. A small building, 40 by 20 feet, it has a segmental plaster ceiling, a western gallery, a pulpit with sounding-board, panelled walls and pews, a fine reredos or altar-piece and a splendid doorway.

Marlborough House (1709-11) is generally ascribed to Wren, but Professor Geoffrey Webb, in his biography (p. 126), hazards the suggestion that the building may have been designed by Sir Christopher's son of the same name, adding that 'young Christopher was at this time certainly turning towards architecture, and Campbell, who knew them both, gives Marlborough House to the son'. On the other hand, the Wren Society and the Historical Monuments Commission both attribute it to Wren the elder. It was originally only two storeys high, plus a basement, but two more storeys were subsequently added in the eighteenth and nineteenth centuries, thus completely altering (and spoiling) Wren's design externally. Originally there were projecting wings on both fronts, those on the north having open loggias on to the garden, but later additions have altered all these features and have abolished the loggias. The interior has likewise been transformed out of recognition, but both the main staircase and the visitors' staircase with their fine balustrading have been preserved, together with the magnificent central saloon, about 30 by 35 feet and two storeys high with a cupola in the ceiling. This noble apartment is decorated with large wall-paintings by Laguerre and others of the Battle of Blenheim. The plan of the house was not particularly convenient, as all the reception rooms were arranged *en suite*, without a connecting corridor behind them. This shows no advance in planning technique since the days of Inigo Jones, and is hardly in keeping with Wren's usual practice.

The lease of the site of Marlborough House was granted by the Crown to the Duchess in 1708-9 in two stages, at a ground rent of £14, on condition that not less than £8,000 should be spent on buildings and improvements within three years. The total area of the site was 4¾ acres, formerly divided between 'The Friary' and 'The Royal Garden'. The Duchess has acquired a place in architectural history as one of the most difficult clients ever known[1]; and though in this instance she did not figure quite so ferociously as in her famous passages with Vanbrugh about Blenheim, she must have tried Wren sorely, and she made her husband's life a burden. He disapproved of her intention to build Marlborough House, and wrote to her to that effect from his military headquarters abroad on July 1, 1708: 'You know that I have no great opinion of this project, for I am very confident that this building will cost you much more money than the thing is worth, for you may build a better apartment than you have, but you will never have so many conveniences as you have in your lodgings, and you may depend upon it that it will cost you double the money of the first estimate. It is not a proper place for a great house, and I am sure when you have built a little one you will not like it, so that if you have set your heart upon it, I should advise you would think well upon it, for it is certainly more advisable to buy a house than to build one.'

But Sarah was not the sort of woman to be deflected from her purpose by advice like that, and in May 1709 she laid the foundation stone of her new home. The Duke, as usual, accepted the situation philosophically, and wrote to her thus on July 18, 1709: 'I am glad of the general approval your house meets with, since I am sure it gives you pleasure, and for the same reason be not uneasy that it costs more money than you thought it would, for upon my word I shall think nothing too much for the making you easy.' (There is a world of meaning in that last sentence!) While the Duke was campaigning abroad, his wife insisted that he should collect materials at bargain prices for her project. Thus in 1710 she arranged with him to purchase some 14,200 white Dutch tiles; and also six large mirrors, to be passed duty-free through the Customs. Six statues purchased in Florence were to be conveyed gratis in naval craft; and small red Dutch bricks, for facing the house, were to be loaded as ballast in returning transports. One can only comment on such transactions: 'Those were the days!'—for our old and not-so-old nobility.

The Duchess had a gift for creating scandal and suspicion, whatever she did; and one of the rare instances of Wren's professional integrity being impugned occurred in 1712, when a 'round robin' was signed by all the leading master-craftsmen at Marlborough House, repudiating the suggestion that he had been accepting bribes or commissions in connection

[1] See Chapter XV, 'Marlborough and his Duchess', in my book *Men of Taste* (1947).

with the building, then just completed. By an extraordinary and ironical coincidence, the first signatory was 'John Churchill, Carpenter'! The ultimate cost of the house was stated by the Duchess herself, in a letter *c.* 1742 to Sir Robert Walpole, to have been nearly £50,000, but it is uncertain what that total may have included. It would be interesting if a complete *dossier* of her correspondence with Wren could be made available for comparison with her virulent exchanges with Vanbrugh, himself an expert in the gentle art of repartee.

On the Green at Hampton Court, just outside the Palace gates, is an old brick house bearing this inscription: 'Sir Christopher Wren lived here 1706-23.' It is commonly called the 'Old Court House', and there is some reference to it in the Wren Society's Vol. XII, pp. 18-9, where a survey plan of it from the Bodleian is reproduced. This house, built a few years earlier, was leased to him in 1708 and occupied by him until his death in 1723. Originally it was a gabled house with a frontage of 39 feet, two storeys high with attics. Sundry alterations have taken place since the survey was made, possibly by Wren, and by Kent and others since his day. The bold modillion cornice, which now continues round the added portions, ties the design together. Inside, there is a panelled room which may well have served Wren as a dining-room, and there is a handsome staircase.

Close to Windsor Bridge there is a dignified old brick house, now a hotel ('The Old House'), which bears a plaque inscribed as follows: 'This house was built and occupied by Sir Christopher Wren, 1676.' It is certainly a pleasant building, inside and out, with a Doric portico and some excellent joinery, but has obviously been altered, and no evidence is known to exist proving it to be Wren's work.

Wren was M.P. for Windsor in 1689 (see p. 276), as well as Surveyor to Windsor Castle after 1684, and other houses in the town are also vaguely attributed to him, including Bank House, now used as offices by a firm of brewers, at the foot of the 'Hundred Steps'; and 'Ann Foord's House', No. 5 Park Street, believed to have been built *c.* 1702, with a fine geometrical staircase.

The Old Court House at Windsor, commonly called the Town Hall, has often been ascribed to Wren, but the Editors of the Wren Society credit it to Sir Thomas Fitz, Surveyor of the Cinque Ports, adding 'completed only by Wren', after Fitz's death in 1689, and remarking that 'it does not look like the work of Wren'. It is a small building of no special merit or importance, but it has given rise to an anecdote about Wren which is amusing if apocryphal. The story runs that when the Mayor and

Corporation came to make an inspection after the building was completed, they complained that the Doric columns of the open lower storey, serving as a market, were insufficient to carry the weight of the superstructure. Wren replied that he was quite confident that their fears were groundless; but eventually, under pressure, he agreed to add two more columns. The objectors were then satisfied, but many years later it was discovered that Sir Christopher had left a space of an inch or so between the capitals of the new columns and the beams above, so that the added columns were doing no work whatsoever! This trick or jest, worthy of Michelangelo in his dealings with the Vatican, is not mentioned in *Parentalia* or by Elmes; and the first mention of it that I can trace occurs in the Rev John Stoughton's *Windsor Castle and Town* (1862). It is not referred to in Tighe and Davis's *Annals of Windsor* (1858). The anecdote does not appear in *The Windsor and Cheltenham Guide* (1800), and there is no reference to it in James Hakewill's *History of Windsor* (1813), though the 'Town Hall' is described in both books. The story has since been repeated by several of Wren's biographers.

Winslow Hall in Buckinghamshire (1700) was built for Sir William Lowndes, Secretary of the Treasury at a time when Wren, as Surveyor-General, was in close touch with him; and is generally attributed to Wren nowadays, though no correspondence or other documentary evidence about its erection is known to exist, and it is not mentioned by any of his numerous biographers. Internally and externally, its design is entirely characteristic of Wren (LXII), and has many points of similarity with Fawley Court. It is in excellent condition and has hardly been altered. Its cost is recorded with pedantic accuracy as £6,585 10s. 2¼d., excluding a good deal of timber supplied. It has three storeys besides attics and vaulted cellars. The material is purple brick with Portland stone dressings and a slated roof. The roof is of unusual design, with sloping sides and a lead flat on top. There is a fine modillion cornice. In plan the house is a simple oblong, 63 by 44 feet, with a slightly projecting central bay on each of the four sides. The plan is, however, rather abnormal in having a staircase at each end, with massive oak newels and balusters. Internally, most of the rooms are panelled in oak, and there is a 'Painted Chamber' on the first floor. Unfortunately, the original sash-bars in the windows have been replaced by plate-glass. The gardens were laid out by London and Wise, the same men who were employed by Wren at Hampton Court and Kensington Palace. A single-storey wing has been added on the east side.

Besides the houses and other buildings described in this chapter, there are several other buildings attributed to Wren on slender evidence. Of

FIG. 31.—GROOMBRIDGE PLACE, KENT
Attributed to Wren

these, the Editors of the Wren Society consider that the Citadel Gate at Plymouth may be definitely ruled out, as it is known to have been built by Sir Thomas Fitz in 1670. The Guildhall at Rochester (1687), Groombridge Place in Kent, Honington Hall in Warwickshire (1680) and Melton Constable Hall in Norfolk (1687) are not even mentioned in the Wren Society's index. The Editors state that there is no evidence for the following: Belton House near Grantham (1685-9), the two beautiful houses in West Street at Chichester (1696), the charming Wren-like houses in the Close at Salisbury, the Trinity Almshouses at Mile End (1695), and Newby Hall near Ripon in Yorkshire (1705). Many of these are similar in character to Wren's known work, most of them are worthy of his genius, and it is still possible that some future scholar may unearth evidence which has hitherto escaped the eagle eye and the patient researches of the Wren Society's Editors.

Finally there is William and Mary College at Williamsburg in Virginia, U.S.A. (LXIII), built in 1695, and ascribed to Wren ever since Hugh Jones, a professor or lecturer in mathematics at that institution, wrote in 1724 that 'The College is beautiful and commodious, being first modelled by Sir Christopher Wren adapted to the nature of the country there . . . and is not unlike Chelsea Hospital'. The comparison is apt enough, and it seems possible that Wren did send designs or sketches from England, perhaps to be carried out by one Thomas Hadley who appears in early documents as surveyor or architect. Records also show that two bricklayers were dispatched from England in 1697. Queen Mary and the Archbishop of Canterbury were both interested in the project, and may well have consulted Wren, with whom the Queen was then constantly in touch about the royal buildings. The walls of the College were still standing, though it had twice sustained serious damage by fire, when, in 1927, the local clergyman induced Mr John D. Rockefeller, Junior, to embark upon the sensational undertaking of rebuilding the whole town complete in its original form, at a total estimated cost of £1,250,000. The work had just been finished when the Second World War began. It is unnecessary here to recount all the elaborate researches carried out in order to transform the little town into a period-piece, extending even to the analysis of the original paint to ensure an exact reproduction. Hundreds of modern buildings of inharmonious character were demolished, cinemas and other essentials of contemporary civilization were carefully camouflaged to be precisely in keeping with the period, and all the best brains among American architects, historians and archaeologists were enlisted for a task which some people regard as meritorious and others as an indefensible archaism. At all events, William and Mary College emerged from the process looking more like Wren's handiwork than ever, and is now set amidst the most Wrennish surroundings in the world.

LXII   WINSLOW HALL, BUCKINGHAMSHIRE; EXTERIOR   *R.C.H.M.*

LXIII   WILLIAMSBURG, U.S.A., WILLIAM AND MARY COLLEGE

XIII

WREN'S COLLABORATORS
AND CRAFTSMEN

THE number of names and personalities associated with Wren's architectural work is enormous. This circumstance is due partly to the length of his professional career (extending over fifty years although he entered architecture so late), partly owing to the size and importance of many of his buildings, but also to the immense mass of surviving documents relating to them, notably to St Paul's Cathedral, the City churches and the royal palaces and hospitals. The work of the Wren Society has made the greater part of this mass of important material available to modern students, but here only a selection can be made of those men who were most intimately concerned with him as an architect.

Mention has already been made of certain architects who crossed his path in the early stages of his architectural practice, especially Sir Roger Pratt (pp. 29, 47, etc.) who died in 1684, and who cannot have influenced, or have been influenced by, Wren: in fact, Pratt's main *rôle* was that of a rival and critic of Wren; but, as I have stated (p. 47), he was appointed in 1666, jointly with Wren and Hugh May, one of the Crown Commissioners for the rebuilding of London. Hugh May (1622-84) was a candidate for the post of Surveyor-General (pp. 61-2) to which Wren was appointed in 1669, May having been made Paymaster of the King's Works in 1660 and subsequently Comptroller. When Wren became Surveyor-General, May continued to act as Comptroller of Works, and in that capacity carried out, *inter alia*, important works at Windsor Castle already described (p. 164). William Talman (1650-1719), a much younger man—younger indeed than Wren—has figured in these pages as Wren's colleague but bitter opponent at Hampton Court, and though he may reasonably be supposed to have been influenced by Wren in matters of design, it seems unnecessary to dwell any further upon an association that was for the most part unhappy (see p. 187).

Much more significant in the story of Wren's long architectural career is his long and intimate association with Robert Hooke (1635-1703), upon whose *Diary*, published in 1935, we rely for a great deal of miscellaneous information about Sir Christopher's work, habits, recreations and scientific interests. Although Hooke has been mentioned on several previous pages in connection with specific buildings, it is worth while recalling here the facts of his life, so closely resembling Wren's own. Like Wren—three years his senior—Hooke was a delicate little boy, so sensitive that when he was apprenticed to Lely the painter in early youth, the smell of paint affected his head. Next he went to Westminster School, in 1648, where his recreations were organ-playing and experiments in flying; but he was not at school with Wren, who left Westminster in 1646 (p. 14). Thence Hooke proceeded to Oxford, entering Christ Church as a chorister in 1653. Wren graduated M.A. in that year, so was well ahead of Hooke; but, as we have seen, the two met in the famous gatherings at Wadham College, which ultimately led to the foundation of the Royal Society, and it is clear that they already shared an enthusiasm for scientific inquiry and 'gadgetry'. Hooke became the first 'Curator of Experiments' at the Royal Society in 1662, a Fellow in 1663, and acted as Secretary from 1677 to 1682. Even more than Wren, he was closely concerned with its activities right up to his death. After a spell as deputy for the Professor of Geometry at Gresham College—the same institution in which Wren had become Professor of Astronomy in 1657 at twenty-five years of age, moving thence to Oxford in 1661—Hooke was appointed to the Chair of Geometry there in 1665 at thirty years of age.

In the following year he was one of those who submitted plans for the rebuilding of London after the Great Fire (p. 49); and it was as a reward for that effort, which was supported by the Royal Society and the City Corporation, that he was made City Surveyor (p. 54). Thereafter he constantly figures as Wren's colleague and deputy, almost his partner, in connection with St Paul's Cathedral, the City churches, the Monument, etc.

His training was thus almost identical with Wren's; and, up to the time of his appointment as City Surveyor, he had had no experience whatever of architectural design or of building. Especially since the publication of his *Diary* in 1935, the tercentenary of his birth, he has been recognized as a scientist of the first order and one of the leading members of the infant Royal Society. His book on the microscope is a scientific classic, and among his more important inventions were the balance-spring for clocks and watches, the air-pump and the fitting of a piston into a cylinder. He also experimented with flying, and claimed that he had solved that problem.

When Hooke became City Surveyor, Wren had already acquired considerable knowledge and experience of architecture, so maintained his three years' seniority in age, and his influence upon Hooke continued to be strong all through their long association. Hooke's *Diary* covers the years 1672-80, the period of their closest partnership, and is a truly remarkable document. Clearly it was never intended for publication. It is a staccato, concise and shockingly frank series of jottings about his health, his domestic affairs, his pay, his architectural and official work, his scientific interests and his frequent meetings with his friends. Many of the details are far more indiscreet than anything that Pepys ever recorded in cypher, and some are almost unprintable but are disguised by cryptic signs. Whether it should have been published is arguable: the fact remains that it is invaluable in enabling us to amplify the meagre personal details about Wren's life that have survived.

In order to disentangle these, the reader has to wade through a host of daily details about Hooke's state of health, his food and its effects, his aperients and other medicines, for he was a confirmed and genuine dyspeptic. Though naturally sociable, this burden made him sensitive and touchy, but on the whole his relations with Wren were uniformly happy, both at work and in their innumerable walks and talks together. The following excerpts, culled from thousands of the same kind, are typical of the items that Hooke recorded day by day. January 14, 1674, 'Tumbled down'; January 15, 1674, 'Tryd shoos'; October 3, 1674, 'Bought 1 pint brandy 6d'; October 17, 1674, 'Lady Cutler not civil'; November 3, 1675, 'Eat goos and apple. Agreed well'; December 4, 1675, 'Smoked 2 Pipes'; September 18, 1676, 'Rainy day'; December 16, 1676, 'Received from shoomaker 1 pair cloth shoos and goloshoos'; December 25, 1676, 'Christmas Day. Tom a Slug'; July 18, 1678, 'Weary'; July 28, 1678, 'Strangely recovered by taking tobacco, Drinking Double Tea'; April 27, 1679, 'Left off Wastcoat—catch cold'; August 31, 1679, 'Shave'; June 6, 1680, 'Griped with pruins'; August 28, 1680, 'Smoaked noe tobacco'; November 24, 1680, 'Gave Grace 35sh. for striped gown'; December 18, 1680, 'Burnt pipes'.

From this welter of trivialities is derived much of the information given in the next two chapters about Wren's methods of work, his views on architecture, recreations, friends, scientific interests and family affairs; but there is hardly a mention of political or religious questions. If such matters were ever discussed in these endless conversations between learned men, at coffee-houses and taverns in the City, there is no record of them; and the *Diary* is so voluminous that one must assume that Wren and Hooke—unlike Pepys and Evelyn—talked mainly of other things. Hooke in due course became a successful architect and, despite his routine duties in the

City, found time to design several large buildings on his own account, of which the most important were Bedlam Hospital in Moorfields, Montague House on the site of the British Museum and, almost certainly, the College of Physicians in Warwick Lane (p. 222), all of which have since disappeared. Mr Geoffrey Webb (*Wren*, p. 32) interprets an entry in Hooke's *Diary* to prove that he and Wren were distantly connected by marriage. Their intercourse was less frequent in the last years of Hooke's life, when he became a complete invalid.

The story of Nicholas Hawksmoor (1661-1736) is very different. Born in Nottinghamshire, he is said to have first entered Wren's service in 1671, and afterwards to have become his pupil. He worked with Sir Christopher all through the latter's subsequent career, eventually succeeding him at Westminster Abbey (p. 144) and elsewhere. As is natural enough, his name does not appear in Hooke's *Diary*, and first occurs at Winchester Palace in 1683 as clerk of works, and at Chelsea Hospital soon afterwards as deputy-surveyor. At this stage he was engaged both in measuring and in draughtsmanship. As time advanced, he became Wren's right-hand man in the office, also doing much of the work that would be entrusted to a quantity surveyor nowadays. He was paid £10 'for taking the plann and out parts of Hampton Court for Mr London', the gardener (p. 188). Evidently he worked well with Wren, and in due course came to be recommended by him to private clients.

The Minute Books of St Paul's Cathedral (March 5, 1691) record that 'Upon Sir Chr. Wren's application to the Commissioners that he might have the assistance of a Servant in drawing Designes for the Works and other necessary bussiness of this Church, when his health or their Majesties service may hinder him, the Commissioners did agree that such person as he shall nominate be Entered with the labourers to be paid att 20d. *per diem* for all working days'. Hawksmoor was duly appointed. A document of 1693-4 describes him as 'Sir Chr. Wren's gentleman', suggesting the status of a pupil. At Greenwich he soon came into prominence, first as 'Clarke to the Surveyor' in 1696 with a salary of £50 *per annum*, and then as Clerk of Works in 1698 with an additional 4s. *per diem*. On the latter occasion, he was preferred to John James, another competent candidate, probably on account of his superior energy and business ability, but in taste and temper he was somewhat erratic. For some years there was intermittent friction between the two men, so that in 1706 Wren and Vanbrugh (then joint architects to the Hospital) had to interfere and prescribe James's duties as storekeeper: 'He shall constantly reside at the Works, and shall not absent himself but by Leave in writing from the Directors, the Surveyor, or the Clark of the Works [Hawksmoor] and shall be Assistant to the said Clark of the Works, and observe such orders as he shall receive from time to time, and put the same in execution, in all matters relating to the works of the Hospitall.' Later, James was promoted, and was also commissioned to build Greenwich parish church, probably on Wren's recommendation and possibly with his actual collaboration. In the end he became a prosperous architect, designed some important churches, and succeeded Hawksmoor as Surveyor of Westminster Abbey in 1736.

Both James and Hawksmoor owed a good deal to Wren, but both were also heavily indebted to Sir John Vanbrugh (1664-1726), who has already been mentioned in connection with St James's, Kensington and Hampton Court Palaces (pp. 168-9, 180-1, 190) as well as Greenwich Hospital (pp. 206-7), where he became one of the 'Directors' in 1702, under Wren's chairmanship, succeeding Wren as Surveyor in 1716. In spite of his unconventional approach to architecture by way of soldiering, play-writing and scene-painting, Vanbrugh appears to have carried out his duties conscientiously; but his tendency to scene-painting in stone, developing at times into Baroque megalomania, is mildly reflected in some of the work of Hawksmoor and James, preventing us from labelling them as disciples of Wren alone. In spite of obvious divergencies of age, taste and temperament, Wren and Vanbrugh appear to have worked together in reasonable amity, and Wren displayed no jealousy.

Among other architect-colleagues of Wren in London, reference has already been made to William Dickinson at Westminster (pp. 146-7), and to Peter Mills and Edward Jerman or Jarman the City Surveyors (pp. 47, 49, 55, 72, 212, 220). To these must be added the name of John Oliver, who figures with Hooke in 1676 as 'Surveyor of New Buildings' in connection with the Monument, and in the same years as 'Deputy for Sir Chr. Wren' in the accounts of St Paul's, where his name occurs at intervals up to his death in 1701. His duties are thus defined: 'John Oliver, Assistant Surveyor and Purveyor. Who is constantly attending the work, giving directions to the workmen according to the Surveyor's direction given to him; he measures all the masons' worke, buyes in all materialls, that are to be had without travelling into the country, keepes an account of what stores are delivered to the store-keeper, and also an account of what stores are brought into the Church; assists Mr Surveyor [Wren] in making of Contracts and examines all Accounts, etc. His salary is £100 *per annum.*'

Outside London mention has been made in this book of Wren's somewhat vague relations with Dean Aldrich at Oxford (pp. 157-8), Sir

William Wilson at Warwick (pp. 134, 135) and at Appleby Free School (p. 226), Henry Jones at Northampton (p. 218), Thomas Hadley at Williamsburg in Virginia (p. 232) and one Samuel at Newmarket (pp. 160-1). Dean Aldrich was certainly an amateur architect, Wilson—according to the latest researches—was probably more of an architect than a builder, but the status of the remaining three is very uncertain.

James Gibbs (1682-1754) has been described as 'a disciple of Wren', but, famous as he rightly has become, there seems to be no knowledge of his training; and all one can safely comment is that, of all Wren's followers, Gibbs followed most closely in Wren's tradition. There is some doubt concerning Thomas White of Worcester (died *c.* 1738). The only information relating to his early life is given in Nash's *Worcestershire*, 1781 (Vol. II, Appendix cxvi): 'He was put apprentice to a statuary and stone cutter in Piccadilly near Hyde Park corner: as soon as he had finished his apprenticeship, being an ingenious young man, Sir Christopher Wren took him with him to Rome, and placed him with a statuary there. . . . At his return to England, Wren would have retained him as his foreman, to superintend the building of St Paul's, but Mr White . . . chose rather to return to his native city, where he lived in great reputation as a master-builder and architect', and built the fine Guildhall there in 1721-3. Wren never went to Rome, and the reference to St Paul's is doubtful, but the Editors of the Wren Society (Vol. IV, p. 17) accept White as one of Wren's pupils.

Robert Grumbold, who carried out work for Wren at Cambridge (pp. 151, 154), was apparently both architect and master-mason, the son of a mason, and was evidently employed by Wren as a sort of clerk of works. The staff of some of Wren's larger buildings included other technical and financial officials besides those named, such as L. Spencer, 'Clark of the Workes and Paymaster', and Thomas Russell, 'Clark of the Cheque', both at St Paul's, who were paid £100 and £50 *per annum* respectively.

Coming next to the contractors and craftsmen, we find the names of Joshua Marshall and Thomas Strong signing the first contracts for St Paul's in 1676. Both carried on the sound tradition of Inigo Jones and John Webb. It was fortunate for Wren, himself so much an amateur, that men of this calibre were available when he tried his prentice hand at architecture. The Strongs were a Somersetshire family who possessed stone quarries at Taynton, Oxon. So far as we are concerned, Thomas Strong may be regarded as the founder of the dynasty. He is alleged to have laid the foundation of the new St Paul's on June 21, 1675 (p. 84). He died in

1681, and was succeeded as 'King's Master-Mason' by his brother Edward, who retained that office until he died, within a few weeks of Wren, in 1723. Edward's son, who subsequently became Master-Mason, was so much trusted by Sir Christopher that he sent his son, Christopher junior, to France under his charge in 1698 (pp. 272-4). Edward Strong senior worked in partnership with Christopher Kempster on the Market House at Abingdon (p. 217), on Winchester Palace and on St Stephen's Walbrook; and on his own account executed the masonry of six other City churches. Edward Strong junior was employed on Marlborough House in 1712.

Kempster, who erected three other City churches on his own account from Wren's designs, and became Master-Mason at St Paul's in 1700, was one of Wren's most dependable masons; and what Sir Christopher thought of him is recorded in a letter written to the Bishop of Oxford about 'Tom Tower' (p. 156). In this, Wren promises the Bishop that, as soon as he [Wren] receives certain outstanding particulars, he will arrange a building contract, 'to have it well and securely performed by Xtmas twelve-month. But by whome? I cannot boast of Oxford Artists though they have a good opinion of themselves. My Ld. with submission I have thought of a very able Man, modest, honest, and Treatable, and one that Your masons will submit to worke with because of his interest in the Quarries at Burford, and therefore You will have the stone from him at first hand. His name Xtopher Kempter. He wrought the Town house at Abbington and goeing now to the Quarrie, I persuaded him to return by Oxford and wait upon Your Lp. I have used him in good workes he is very carefull to work trew to his designe and strong well banded worke, and I can rely upon him, I have talked with him and indeed promised to recommend him to Yr. Lp., and I am confident he will promise little advantage to himselfe soe he may have the honor of the Worke.' Among the twelve master-masons employed during the whole period of rebuilding St Paul's under Wren's directions, there were two Strongs, two Kempsters, two Wises and six others, of whom Joshua Marshall was the most notable. He also erected six City churches, two on his own account and four in partnership.

With certain notable exceptions, most of the carving on Wren's buildings was undertaken by the masonry contractors; but Grinling Gibbons, C. G. Cibber, Jonathan Maine and Francis Bird generally confined themselves to architectural ornament and statuary. Francis Bird carved the immense pediment on the west front of St Paul's; but Joshua Marshall carved the pedestal of King Charles I's statue at Charing Cross (p. 214) and Edward Pearce, another of the master-masons at St Paul's, did much stone carving at Hampton Court. Thus he was paid £2,003 13s. od. for the following items there:

Carving in Portland Stone two Dolphins & a cisterne for a fountain	£16	0	0
Carving a great vauze of white marble, all the figures enricht with leaves, and festoons of shells, and Pedestal of Portland likewise all members enricht	£250	0	0
Carving done about the ffountaine in P.G. carving 8 scrowles & 4 festoons with shells & sevll foot of sup. in the gt. stones under the Cornish	£1262	3	0
A great white marble Urne with divers figures & other ornaments	£475	10	0
In all	£2003	13	0

Work at Hampton Court and on the Monument by another notable stone-carver, Caius Gabriel Cibber, has already been mentioned (pp. 188, 190, 211). Wren's relations with his carvers at St Paul's are illuminated by the following entries in the Cathedral Minute Book: July 17, 1696. 'That Mr Oliver do compare the measurement set downe in Mr Gibbons' Bill of Carver's work, with his owne measurement thereof, and that Mr Gibbons do then put such Prices to the same as he does intend to stand by, which he is Ordered to deliver to Mr Dean of St Paul's, who is desired to procure (if he thinks it necessary) some skillful persons in the same Art to view the Work, and report their opinions of the Prices; and it was also Ordered, that no money be paid to the said Mr Gibbons untill the same shall be agreed.'

September 18, 1696. 'Ordered, that it be transferred to Sir Chr. Wren to adjust with Mr Gibbons the Prices of the Carved Capitals mentioned in his Bill, which could not be agreed on by the Carvers who were appointed to view and examine the Prices of the said Bill, and that he report the same to this Board at their next meeting.'

Grinling Gibbons (1648-1720) was first employed at St Paul's in 1694, but his association with Wren began long before that date. Accurate information about his early life is lacking, but the *Dictionary of National Biography*, usually reliable, gives Rotterdam as the place of his birth. Between 1648 and his 'discovery' by Evelyn in 1670, related at length below, there is a tradition, lately resuscitated by Mr J. B. Morrell (in his *Woodwork in York*, 1950, p. 180), that Gibbons came to York at the age of fifteen and was apprenticed to one John Etty (d. 1709) who had 'acquired great knowledge of mathematics especially geometry and architecture', so may have been either a joiner-carver or an architect, or both. Mr Morrell adds that 'unfortunately there is no work in the city that can be attributed to him' (i.e. Gibbons), but that 'Mr J. E. K. Esdaile considers that the influence of Gibbons on York sculptors is most striking, not the least because it is so persistent, lasting for more than a generation'. The D.N.B. quotes the *Diary* of Ralph Thoresby, a contemporary, in support of the tradition that Gibbons was a Yorkshireman.

The dramatic story of Evelyn's discovery of the young carver, and subsequent introduction of him to Charles II and to Wren, is so rich in the human interest that is normally lacking in architectural history that quotation *in extenso* from Evelyn's *Diary* seems to be justified here, lengthy as are the passages in question.

December 18, 1670. 'This day I first acquainted his Majesty with that incomparable young man Gibbon, whom I had lately met with in an obscure place by meere accident as I was walking neere a poore solitary thatched house, in a field in our parish, neere Sayes Court [Deptford]. I found him shut in; but looking in at the window I perceiv'd him carving that large cartoon or crucifix of Tintoret, a copy of which I had myselfe brought from Venice, where the original painting remaines. I asked if I might enter; he open'd the door civilly to me, and I saw him about such a work as for the curiosity of handling, drawing and studious exactnesse, I never had before seene in all my travells. I questioned him why he worked in such an obscure and lonesome place; he told me it was that he might apply himselfe to his profession without interruption, and wondred not a little how I had found him out. I asked if he was unwilling to be made knowne to some greate man, for that I believed it might turn to his profit; he answer'd he was yet but a beginner, but would not be sorry to sell off that piece; on demanding the price, he said £100. In good earnest the very frame was worth the money, there being nothing in nature so tender and delicate as the flowers and festoons about it, and yet the worke was very strong; in the piece were more than 100 figures of men, &c. I found he was likewise musical, and very civil, sober, and discreete in his discourse. There was onely an old woman in the house. So desiring leave to visite him sometimes, I went away.

'Of this young artist, together with my manner of finding him out, I acquainted the King, and begg'd that he would give me leave to bring him and his worke to White-hall, for that I would adventure my reputation with his Majesty that he had never seene any thing approch it, and that he would be exceedingly pleased, and employ him. The King said he would himselfe go see him. This was the first notice his Majestie ever had of Mr Gibbon.'

February 19, 1671. 'This day din'd with me Mr Surveyor Dr Christopher Wren, and Mr Pepys, two extraordinary ingenious and knowing persons, and other friends. I carried them to see the piece of carving which I had recommended to the King.'

March 1, 1671. 'I caused Mr Gibbon to bring to White-hall his excellent piece of carving, where being come I advertis'd his Majestie, who ask'd me where it was; I told him in Sir Richard Browne's (my father-in-law) chamber, and that if it pleas'd his Majesty to appoint whither it should be brought, being large and tho' of wood heavy, I would take care for it; "No," says the King, "shew me the way, I'll go to Sir Richard's chamber", which he immediately did, walking along the entries after me; as far as the ewrie, till he came up into the roome where I also lay. No sooner was he enter'd and cast his eye on the work but he was astonish'd at the curiositie of it, and having consider'd it a long time and discours'd with Mr Gibbon, whom I brought to kisse his hand, he commanded it should be immediately carried to the Queenes side to shew her. It was carried up into her bed chamber, where she and the King looked on and admired it againe; the King being call'd away left us with the Queene, believing she would have bought it, being a crucifix; but when his Majesty was gon, a French pedling woman, one Mad. de Boord, who us'd to bring peticoates and fanns, and baubles out of France to the Ladys, began to find fault with severall things in the worke, which she understood no more than an asse or a monkey, so as in a kind of indignation, I caused the person who brought it to carry it back to the chamber, finding the Queene so much govern'd by an ignorant French woman, and this incomparable artist had his labour onely for his paines, which not a little displeas'd me, and he was faine to send it downe to his cottage againe; he not long after sold it for £80 tho' well worth £100 without the frame, to Sir George Viner.

'His Majesty's Surveyor, Mr Wren, faithfully promis'd me to employ him. I having also bespoke his Majesty for his worke at Windsor, which my friend Mr May the architect there was going to alter and repaire universally; for on the next day I had a fair opportunity of talking to his Majesty about it, in the lobby next the Queenes side.'

Evelyn's powerful influence, both with the King and with Wren, soon launched Gibbons upon a prosperous career, so that his name has already occurred many times in this book, but nowadays his share in decorating the City churches is discounted. According to modern ideas, it may seem strange that a carver and sculptor should come to be appointed 'Master-

Carpenter' at St Paul's, as Gibbons was in 1718. He does not figure as an intimate of Wren or Evelyn in contemporary diaries; perhaps because he was an artist pure and simple, immersed in his work, whereas the other members of Wren's learned circle were all or nearly all university men interested in scientific discourse and the affairs of the Royal Society. Gibbons was employed by May at Windsor Castle soon after Evelyn's introduction, but his first work for Wren seems to have been in connection with the Windsor Mausoleum design in 1678 (pp. 218-9), and next at Whitehall Palace a few years later. Thereafter he was constantly working under Wren, as we have seen. Apart from the ingenuity and beauty of his intensely individual carving, he is notable for his use of lime wood for ornamental features, and he also supplied many of the decorative details on Wren's drawings, as previously noted. Evelyn was very proud of his protégé's success, and as early as 1683 wrote of his work at Windsor: 'Stupendous and beyond all description the incomparable carving of our Gibbons, who is without controversie the greatest master both for invention and rareness of work that the world ever had in any age; nor doubt I at all that he will prove as greate a master in the statuary art.' Jonathan Maine, whose lovely wood-carvings are to be seen in the library and western chapels at St Paul's, was a pupil of Gibbons; he also executed much carved work in stone.

The Master-Carpenters at St Paul's were, successively, John Longland, Israel Knowles, Thomas Woodstock and Richard Jennings. The last-named, already mentioned in this book (pp. 94, 96), carried out most of the structural carpentry in the roof, all of oak. On his dismissal in 1711, he was replaced as Master-Carpenter by John James of Greenwich, the architect! The chief joiners at St Paul's were William Cleere, Charles and John Hopson, Roger Davis, Hugh Webb and John Smallwell. Of these, Charles Hopson was knighted *c.* 1709, an unusual honour for a man of his craft. He also did the joinery for Winslow Hall in 1700. An amusing item in the St Paul's accounts is a record that John Smallwell was paid 'for stuff and time in altering the bishop's throne to make room for his feet'. Among many models made by joiners, the famous Great Model for St Paul's cost £600 in 1670, at a period when money was worth perhaps ten times as much as it is today (pp. 80-1).

The chief Master-Bricklayer employed by Wren was Maurice or Morris Emmett, who was in charge of several of Sir Christopher's most important buildings, but at St Paul's the leading figure was Richard Billingshurst.

The plasterwork which is one of the most splendid and attractive features of so many of Wren's buildings, large and small, was mainly carried out by two or three leading firms: Henry Doogood, John Grove (senior and junior), and Sherwood. Of Wren's fifty-one City churches, forty-one were plastered by Doogood and the two Groves, and seven by Sherwood. Doogood was also employed at St Paul's, Greenwich Hospital, Winchester Palace, Whitehall and elsewhere; the Groves at Winchester, Whitehall, Kensington and St James's Palaces, etc. Edward Pearce, already named as a contractor, mason and carver in stone, may also have acted as a modeller in plaster. Doogood was succeeded at St Paul's by Chrysostom Williams in 1707.

The chief plumbing and leadwork of Wren's buildings came from the important workshop in Piccadilly of John van Nost, a Dutchman who crossed to England with William III. Here were modelled and cast most of the fine lead statues, cisterns and rainwater-heads of the period. The lead used on the roof of St Paul's weighs 20 lb. per square foot: that is, about three times as thick as would be used today in the same positions; and it is jointed with welts, not turned over rolls as in modern practice. The rainwater is carried away through large square lead pipes concealed in the thickness of the walls.

The outstanding figure among Wren's smiths was Jean Tijou, about whom singularly little is known considering the magnitude of his achievement, especially at Hampton Court, and at St Paul's where he made the heavy iron window-frames as well as the more celebrated screens, balustrades and railings. Neither Evelyn nor Pepys mention him in their voluminous diaries. He came over from France some time after the Restoration, and it has been suggested by Sir Reginald Blomfield that Wren may have induced him to do so. Considering how interested Wren was in the workshops that he visited in Paris during his tour in 1665, that certainly seems possible. At all events, Tijou worked constantly for Wren between 1689 and 1711. In that year or the next he returned to Paris and died there in poverty. A contemporary describes his 'strongly marked face with a heavy moustache but forbidding expression'. His assistant at Hampton Court was one Huntingdon Shaw (1660-1710). Tijou also did much work at Greenwich Hospital and Kensington Palace. In March 1691 he was paid £80 'for making two Iron Vanes with movements to show the points of the winds within and without, having eight supporters of Iron finely wrought in scrowle worke and bands to each supporter'. This was at Hampton Court, but a similar contrivance exists in the King's Gallery at Kensington Palace, though there is no evidence that it was made by Tijou.

At Greenwich in 1707, 'a proposition was laid before the Board by Mr Tejou for Ironwork for the Stairs in the Hall and Vestibule, and the

Stone Stairs in King Charles' Building, and agreement was made with him for the stairs in King Charles' Building at £6 a yard run, according to the pattern delivered, or such alteration therein, as shall be approved by Mr Hawksmoor'. This record is interesting not only because of the basis of payment by the 'yard run', but also because it seems to prove that Tijou's ornamental ironwork was designed by himself, not by the architect, who, however, reserved the right of control and modification. Tijou published in 1693 a book of designs, which are generally agreed to be inferior to his executed work. This is of the highest order, unsurpassed at any period, and completely different in character and execution from anything that had preceded it in this country, as might be expected from a craftsman born and trained in France at a particularly favourable moment.

For decorative painting in his larger buildings, Wren employed both English and foreign artists. One of the former, Robert Streeter or Streater (1624-80) held the post of 'Sergeant Painter' to the Crown. He figures several times in the *Diary* of John Evelyn, e.g. July 1, 1664: 'Went to Mr Povey's elegant house in Lincoln's-inn-fields, where the perspective in his court, painted by Streeter, is indeed excellent'; February 9, 1671: 'I saw the greate ball . . . at White-hall Theater. . . . There were indeede very glorious sceanes and perspectives, the worke of Mr Streeter, who well understands it'; August 26, 1672: 'Sir Robert Clayton's new house [in Old Jewry] has a cedar dining-roome painted with the historie of the Gyants War, incomparably don by Mr Streeter, but the figures are too neere the eye'. Pepys, a much less fastidious critic, records on February 1, 1669, a visit to 'Mr Streeter's, the famous history-painter . . . whom I have often heard of, but did never see him before; and there I found him, with Dr Wren, and several Virtuosos, looking upon the paintings which he is making for the new [Sheldonian] Theatre at Oxford; and, indeed, they look as if they would be very fine, and the rest think better than those of Rubens, in the Banqueting-house at White Hall, but I do not fully think so. But they will certainly be very noble; and I am mightily pleased to have had the fortune to see this man and his work, which is very famous; he is a very civil little man, and lame, but lives very handsomely'. A contemporary writer, Robert Whithall, in *Urania* (1669, a whole epic in praise of the Sheldonian ceiling), was very fulsome, claiming that
'Future ages must confess they owe,
To Streater more than Michael Angelo.'
The ceiling was, in fact, a remarkable example of Baroque painting, then new to England and having its origin in Italy. Streeter carried out painting for Wren at the palaces of Hampton Court, Winchester, Whitehall and

Kensington; at Windsor Castle and in at least thirteen of the City churches, but twenty-four of the remainder were painted by Edward Bird.

The two foreign artists chiefly employed by Wren for decorative painting were Antonio Verrio (1639?-1707) and Louis Laguerre (1663-1721). It was of their tremendous Baroque compositions that Pope wrote:

'. . . On painted ceilings you devoutly stare,

'Where sprawl the saints of Verrio, the angels of Laguerre.'

The former artist came from the remote city of Lecce in Southern Italy, renowned for its Baroque architecture[1]; and then migrated to France, where Charles II found him and brought him over to England. He decorated the chapel at Whitehall (p. 173), some rooms at Windsor (p. 165) and at Hampton Court (p. 190), but his work, although described at some length in Horace Walpole's *Anecdotes of Painting*, is of no great merit. He covered a large area of canvas at Chatsworth. Laguerre was a more talented artist, French by birth, who worked for Verrio and, incidentally, married Tijou's daughter. He also drew the frontispiece for Tijou's book of designs of ironwork (p. 245). He carried out much work at Hampton Court and at Marlborough House (p. 227).

Sir James Thornhill (1675-1734) played a prominent part in Wren's career. Returning to England about 1700 from his studies abroad, he soon became a rival of Laguerre, and in 1708 was commissioned to paint the ceiling and walls of the Great Hall of Greenwich Hospital, a work which occupied him during no less than nineteen years.[2] The following extracts from the Minute Books of the Hospital illustrate his progress.

May 20, 1708. 'Mr Thornhill came to the Board, in relation to the Painting the Hall, and it was resolved he should proceed with all expedition, and he left it to the Board to pay him for the same, as they shall judge he deserves. Mr James was ordered to get the scaffolding ready as soon as possible.'

May 23, 1712. 'A Memorial by Mr Thornhill was read desiring the Board will appoint such persons as they think fit to inspect his painting in the great Hall who may be judges of the value. The Board will represent it to the Generall Court and desire an order to give him some imprest money on account of his Work to encourage his speedy finishing the Hall.'

July 12, 1712. Thornhill's Memorial was read, he 'promising to employ his whole time thereon till it be finished', and £300 was granted to him on account.

March 6, 1714. 'Mr Thornhill acquainted the Board that he shall clear

[1] See my book *In the Heel of Italy* (1910); pp. 264-8 deal with Verrio.

[2] His *modello* for the ceiling is in the Victoria and Albert Museum.

away the Scaffolding from the Hall ceiling by the end of May. He is ordered to prime the West End of Upper Hall, and Mr Tompson the other walls and ceiling there, in order to the painting them, and it is to be fenced off from the other Hall.'

March 10, 1714. 'Ordered £200 on account to Thornhill when the scaffolding is struck.'

On July 27, 1717, just after Wren's retirement at Greenwich, Thornhill complained that he had only received £635, to date, for all his work; and a month later submitted a long memorandum citing the large sums paid to other famous 'History Painters', including Rubens and Verrio, whereas at Hampton Court he had received only £3 15s. per square yard. He now asked for £5 a yard for ceilings and £1 for walls or 'sides'. A few months afterwards, he accepted a rate of £3 and £1 respectively together with a substantial payment on account.

At St Paul's (pp. 87, 95, 106) Wren had always intended that the interior of the dome should be lined with mosaics, as at St Peter's, but this was judged impracticable on the ground of cost, and Thornhill was employed instead. The Minute Books of the Cathedral show that some sort of competition took place.

April 5, 1709. 'This day the Designes for painting the inside of the Dome were brought in to the Commissioners by Mr James Thornhill, Mr Pellegrini [b. Venice 1674], Mr Cattenaro, Mr Berchett [1659-1720], Mr Cheron [1660-1713], and allso proposalls for price & time of performing the same, as by their proposalls under their hands appeares.'

The five competitors were then reduced to two, the following Minute being revealing. February 11, 1710. 'It was ordered that a little Cupolo be prepared against this day sevenit for Mr Pelegrini to paint a specimen for the Cupolo of St Paul's in Fresco, according to the Stories directed and he, being called in, did promise, if he be employed, to do all the work of the said Cupolo, which is properly painting, with his own hand in the two following Summers. And it was Ordered, that another little Cupolo be also forthwith made for Mr Thornhill to paint a specimen for the said Cupolo of St Paul's, according to his proposal brought in this day, which he promises to do in a week after the said little Cupolo shall be ready for him.' (It was five years later, however, when Thornhill was finally commissioned.) June 28, 1715. 'Sir James Thornhill was this day chosen to paint the great Dome of St Paul's . . . after the midlemost of the 3 Designes which now hang in the Chapter House . . . and he is to receive for the whole Worke not exceeding the sume of £4000.' (Wren was present at all the three meetings recorded above.) Thornhill's decorative paintings adorn many great mansions of the early eighteenth century—Chatsworth, Blenheim, Moor Park, Stoke Edith and others—but his work, thoroughly Baroque as it is, nowhere appears to greater advantage than in the 'Painted Hall' of Greenwich Hospital.

The principal gardeners employed by Wren were the firm of London and Wise, who seem to have undertaken design as well as horticulture, and owned, jointly with other firms, a great central nursery at Brompton. Although the influence of the famous French gardener Le Nôtre is apparent in all their work, it seems to have been indirect. Charles II had employed one Rose at Hampton Court, who had learned his craft under Le Nôtre himself, and George London was a pupil of Rose. As has been noted before (p. 188), London occupied the post of 'Deputy Superintendent of the Earl of Portland' at a salary of £200 *per annum*, and was also 'Page of the Backstairs' to Queen Mary. He and Henry Wise are frequently mentioned in the Hampton Court accounts, and there is a note in 1698-9 of a payment of £10 to 'William Deeplove, Clerk of the Gardens', for measuring and checking their bills. The firm carried out work at Kensington, Whitehall and St James's Palaces for Wren; also at Blenheim, Chatsworth, Wanstead and other famous mansions under other architects. They borrowed ideas of lay-out and planting from Holland as well as from France.

Wren's relations with the various craftsmen and contractors employed on his numerous buildings appear to have been generally harmonious, and records indicate that, in spite of his enormous responsibilities, he managed to keep in close touch with them. His temperament must have been equable and his manners pleasant, in order to maintain this happy state of affairs. Occasionally he had to exert pressure, especially when he himself was being hustled by impatient clients. Thus at Greenwich Hospital on October 3, 1706, the Directors summoned Doogood, Wren's favourite plasterer, to explain why he had not yet begun work on two of the 'galleries' or dormitories. His explanation being deemed unsatisfactory, he was superseded; and two months later the Directors notified the joiners that unless work on the 'cabbins' (cubicles) was expedited, other firms would be brought in to hasten completion. Occasionally Wren utilized the specialized knowledge of experts for matters beyond his own extensive repertoire, e.g. in the design of the organ at St Paul's. According to a Cathedral Minute of May 10, 1694: 'The Commissioners [including Wren] consulted with Mr Smith and Dr Blow about making the Organ for St Paul's, and it was thought fit that the same should be 22 ft. high, 6 ft. over (besides the seat for the Organist) and 18 ft. long. That there should be 18 stops in the upper set of Keys, 3 of them wood, the rest metall, and 6 stops in the under set of Keys, and that it should be as big and loud as the place for it will bear (bigger and louder than the Temple organ). Whereupon it was Ordered that Mr Smith do bring to this Board a copy of a Contract for some other Organ by him formerly made, and the Draft of a Contract for this Organ also, with his Prices for the same.'

For his private commissions outside London, where frequent visits and constant personal supervision were impracticable owing to his other commitments, Wren must often have provided no more than a small sketch-design, leaving its elaboration and execution to a trusted representative—builder or architect—on the spot. This seems to have happened at the Abingdon Market House (p. 217), at the Trinity College Library (p. 154) and at several other provincial buildings. In the case of the Free School at Appleby, as we have seen (p. 226), the result of handing over so much responsibility to an old-fashioned deputy steeped in local tradition was a building typical of a generation earlier than Wren's day.

His correspondence with his friend Bishop Sprat about 'Tom Tower' at Oxford (cf. p. 156) shows how Wren managed to carry out that complicated building with the aid of his trusty henchman Christopher Kempster: May 26, 1681. 'I pray Your Lp. when You have viewed the designe You would please to returne it again in the Box. If You doe not follow it I would be glad to have it again in my possession having noe copy and I would not delay You till I had. If you resolve to follow it, tis necessary to have 2 Copies 1 for me and another for the workmen with some parts more at large.'

December 3, 1681. 'As farre as I can perceive by discourse with Mr Kempter You have hitherto proceeded very well in Your Building & I hope I shall have noe reason to believe otherwise when I see it. . . .'

September 9, 1682. '. . . I thinke the Mason understandes what to doe with the Towers, I discoursed it with him, if he doubts he shall have further directions.'

In spite of his reliance upon subordinates, Wren retained control in the last resort, and the building contract for 'Tom Tower' stipulates 'that if any matter of doubt or difference shall arise in the premises it be entirely submitted to the determination of Sr. Christopher Wren'.

✪ XIV ✪

WREN THE ARCHITECT

Iₙ this chapter an attempt is made to generalize about Wren's work as an architect after 1669 (the year in which he became Surveyor-General); and to examine his duties as Surveyor-General, his methods of work, his sources of inspiration, his remuneration and finally the quality of his architecture. Previous chapters have contained a number of facts and anecdotes showing the immense variety of matters referred to him in his official capacity, and proving the triviality of some of the questions to which he had to give his attention at the height of his busy career. The specimens quoted on p. 169, in connection with St James's Palace and Park, are only typical of thousands of others recorded in the voluminous files of the Office of Works, now rendered accessible to students through their publication in the twenty volumes of the Wren Society. Some items are ludicrously petty, and it seems strange that anything like the following should ever have had to be signed by the Surveyor-General himself, considering that he had subordinates at his command: 'Mr Manning: You are desired to send for his Majesty's Service at the Tower of London. 2 M. of plumber's nailes and 2 shovells. Ch. Wren. July 5, 1700.'

Sometimes the Lords of the Treasury, his employers, were unreasonable and peremptory in dealing with a man who occupied an important position, as this trio of letters shows, and it is amusing to see how Sir Christopher managed to convey a snub to Mr Speaker without being positively rude.

[I. TREASURY TO WREN]

'Sir,

The Lords Commissioners of their Majesty's Treasury haveing received a Letter from the Speaker of the House of Commons wherein he desires that the East Windowes of that house may be doubly shassed,[1] to keep out the could weather, their Lordships direct you to bring them this afternoone an Estimate what the Charge of Double Shashing those windowes, and the windowes in the passage underneathe them will amount unto.

I am Sir

Your most humble Servant

Treasury Chambers
September 20 1693

Hen. Guy.'

[1] 'Sash' was at first spelt 'Shass', being derived from the French *chassis* =frame.

[II. TREASURY TO WREN]

'Sir,

I sent you a Letter this morning by order of the Lords Commissioners of their Majesty's Treasury, wherein you were directed to bring their Lordships this afternoone an Estimate of the Charge in Double Shashing the East windowes of the House of Commons, and the windows in the passage underneath them, but you not haveing brought any such Estimate, their Lordships Direct you not to fail in bringing such an Estimate to-morrow at four of the Clock in the afternoon.

I am,

Treasury Chambers
September 20 1693

Your most humble Servant
Henry Guy.'

[III. WREN TO TREASURY]

'May it please your Lordships,

In pursuance of your Lordships Commands by two letters yesterday signyfieing that haveing received a Letter from the Speaker that the win-dowes of the East end of the house of Commons and the passage behind might be Double Shassed to keep out the Could, and Directing that I should give an Estimate thereof. I humbly represent that I have with my officers viewed those shasshes, which have been since the first objection screwed so close that wee were of opinion nothing could be made warmer; and wee suppose where cold was perceived, it was from those who opened the windowes of the passage to look out on the Thames, which windowes I have therefore decided to be fastened close for winter Sessions, and that the dore behind the Speaker be made to shut very close: Notwithstanding to observe your Lordships Commands, wee find this to be the charge of doubling the said shasshes

The Joyner's part	£23 14 0
The Glaicers with Crowne Glass	19 9 0
Totall	£42 0 0[1]

All of which is humbly submitted

Chr. Wren.   September 21, 1693.'

Sometimes Wren's duties were stretched beyond an architect's or even a surveyor's normal routine, as in a curious instance recorded by Narcissus Luttrell in February 1690: 'Sir Xtopher Wren hath completed the itinerant

[1] There is an obvious error in arithmetic here, but the figures are as given in the Wren Society's Vol. XI, p. 48.

house for His Majesty into Ireland for him to lye in in the field; it is to be taken to pieces and carried on two waggons that may be quickly fixt up.' (One recalls that Kent, a generation or so later, designed a royal barge for the Prince of Wales.) Some of Wren's instructions must have been distasteful to a man of his tolerant nature, as when in June 1670, acting under orders, he 'disfurnished four or five places erected by Nonconformists of several persuasions in and about the City'. The most comprehensive view of Wren's minor duties as Surveyor-General, apart from such important work as the maintenance, enlargement and rebuilding of the royal palaces (described in Chapter X), is found in the manuscript book of Court Orders from 1671 to 1695, collected by Wren himself, acquired by James Elmes, sold by him to Sir John Soane in 1823, and published in the Wren Society's Vol. XVIII. From these hundreds of documents I give nine specimens to show the variety of matters dealt with personally by Wren in his official capacity. (1) 1671. Colonel Panton's proposal to build on the two Bowling Greens fronting the Haymarket. Wren commends this as 'very usefull to the Publique, especially by opening a new street from the Hay market into Leicester Fields which will ease in some manner the great passage of the Strand, and will cure the noysomness of that part'.

(2) 1671. Describes the 'small and meane habitations recently built without licence in Dog Fields, Windmill Fields, and the Fields adjoining to So Hoe, which will prove only receptacles for the poorer Sort, and the Offensive Trades'; and recommends that all further erection of unlicensed buildings on the site be prohibited.

(3) 1671. Wren approves the building of John Bill's Printing House in 'Blackfryers' provided that the proposed building complies with a schedule of wall-thicknesses (appended), that the carpentry is of oak and that certain rights of light are preserved.

(4) 1672. Wren complains that 'Mr Bull continues to build stables & meane buildings on new foundations contrary to yr. Majesty's proclamation'.

(5) 1674. Wren instructs Peter Brent, 'His Majesty's Plumber', and other officers to search houses in which the inhabitants are suspected of drawing water illicitly from the conduits serving 'His Majesty's Pallace & the Mewes'.

(6) 1674. Wren approves a proposal of Ralph Bucknell and Ralph Wayne for the 'raysing of Thames water & conveying the same from Yorke house garden to such persons as shall desire it'. He says that he has 'viewed the place & seene the Designe of the Engine', and considers that it will work without noise and will not constitute a nuisance.

(7) 1676. John Blythman reports 'that one of his Majesty's lodges called Chappell Henalt Lodge within the forrest of Waltham-stoe in the County of Essex is very much decayed & out of repaire', and asks that it be surveyed and repaired. Wren reports that he has had it surveyed by 'a faithfull & able carpenter employed by the Office of his Majesty's Workes', who says that it is ruinous and not worth repairing. In a second report, Wren estimates the cost of repair, if carried out, to be £640 after deduction for value of old materials reused.

(8) 1695. Wren submits an estimate for fitting up a room 'neare the House of Peers' as a bishops' robing-room, including panelling: £147.

(9) 1689. Wren submits a very detailed account of day-work, task-work, and materials, amounting in all to £1,670 0s. 7d., for erecting scaffolds in Westminster Hall and Westminster Abbey, and for 'railing and Gravilling the Streets', as at the last Coronation; but adds that, as 'Timber and boards are at this time dearer one fifth part, it probably may raise the charge to £1800'. (The reference to rising prices of timber has a curiously modern sound.)

Among important buildings designed by Wren as Surveyor-General and not previously mentioned in this book were two enormous groups of barracks in Hyde Park, for infantry and cavalry respectively, which were never carried out (see Wren Society Vol. XII, p. 19). His work at the Tower of London included the 'Great Storehouse' built early in the reign of William III and burnt down in 1842, and the 'Horse Armoury', now in use as an Army Ordnance store and erected a few years earlier than the Great Storehouse. It is a plain brick building serving its utilitarian purpose well, but deriving dignity from its good proportions, its lofty roof and its fine wood cornice—characteristic of Wren. About 1709, the remodelling of the White Tower began, and Miss Milman (*Wren*, p. 186) credits him with the perky and rather Baroque lead roofs or domes crowning the four Norman turrets, but she does not give her authority for the statement. Certainly they add picturesqueness to the austere lines of the great stone keep.

The staff of the Office of Works were thus expected to be able to deal with anything from a town planning scheme or the design of a royal palace, down to the repair of a hen-house, the clearing of a drain, or the equipment of lodgings for a foreign visitor. Partly with a view to checking sundry abuses, the Office was reorganized soon after the Restoration, shortly before Wren became Surveyor-General, and the salaries of the various officials were then raised in order to remove or diminish the temptation to accept perquisites. There was another reorganization in 1714 on George I's accession, when Vanbrugh relieved Sir Christopher, who was then a very old man, of some of his responsibilities, but that was a personal arrangement on account of Wren's age, rather than a drastic overhaul. In the hierarchy of officials, the two most important posts were those of the Surveyor-General, held by Wren from 1669 to 1718, and of the Comptroller. Then came the 'Patent Artisans'—including the King's Master-Mason, the King's Master-Carpenter, the Sergeant Plumber, the Sergeant Painter, etc.—the Clerk Engrosser (an office requiring some knowledge of architecture and held for many years by Christopher Wren junior), the Paymaster, the Purveyor and four Clerks of Works. A good deal of Wren's own time, as well as that of Hawksmoor and other subordinates, was devoted to drawing up contracts, measuring work and checking builders' accounts. It is perfectly clear from the huge mass of accounts that have been preserved that he took these duties very seriously, though it has been suggested that in later life his supervision of contractors became more easy-going. Much of the work at St Paul's was 'task-work' (i.e. under contract), but some was 'day-work' (paid by time). The Commissioners of St Paul's usually bought building materials direct from the producer or importer; less frequently from contractors (e.g. stone from Strong the master-mason and quarry-owner).

The matter of Wren's earnings as an architect would not normally interest modern non-architectural readers, had not some of his non-architectural biographers made so much of the idea that he was entirely unselfish in matters of finance, that he was grossly underpaid and that he gave much of his time gratuitously in the case of some important buildings which served a charitable purpose. Against these easy assumptions, we have to face the facts that he lived in considerable comfort and in a style befitting a man of his high official and social standing; and that in 1713 he purchased for £19,600 a large house and estate at Wroxall Abbey in Warwickshire for his son Christopher. When one reads in Hooke's *Diary* of his frequent tips to Wren's coachman and footman, one can dismiss any notion of 'chill penury'. One biographer hazards the suggestion that Sir Christopher possessed ample private means, possibly derived from one or both of his two wives, but no documentary proof is given. It would be interesting to see a record of his personal income and expenditure, but nothing of the sort has yet been discovered. Any estimate is complicated by the fact that he undertook private commissions for unknown fees while he was drawing official salaries from several sources simultaneously.

During his first years of architectural practice, up to 1673, he was enjoying a stipend as Savilian Professor of Astronomy at Oxford.

Presumably he was paid the ordinary fee of 5 per cent for his early work at Oxford and Cambridge described in Chapter II. It is not known whether he was paid a fee, or, if so, of what amount, for his preliminary report on Old St Paul's in May 1666; but at that stage he had not yet been appointed Surveyor-General. For his work in rebuilding London after the Great Fire of 1666 he was not paid a regular salary by the Corporation, but received frequent presents in money, amounting on two occasions to 100 guineas in gold.[1] For St Paul's he received a salary of £200 a year from 1675 to 1711, i.e. £5,400 in all. As Surveyor-General his salary was 13s. 2d. a day, and 'availes' of £80 per quarter or £320 a year, by way of retaining fee; though that amount was reduced at a later stage.[2] It may have been augmented, however, as one biographer presumes, by additional fees for specific commissions. For the City churches he was paid 'twelve-pence in the pound', i.e. 5 per cent, out of which he may have had to meet office expenses. On a known outlay of £263,706 he must thus have received over £13,000 from that source, not £100 *per annum* as incorrectly stated in *Parentalia*. For Chelsea Hospital, he was paid £1,000 in 1693 as an honorarium for his ten years' work there (p. 196), although it seems to have been assumed, up to that date, that he was giving his services gratuitously. At Greenwich Hospital, on the other hand, he did work for nothing (p. 201), and that was a considerable undertaking; but the salaries of Hawksmoor, James and his other subordinates were certainly met by the Commissioners. He also worked gratis at Trinity College, Cambridge (on the Library), and at St Clement Danes. For Westminster Abbey, Wren drew £100 *per annum* salary as Surveyor from 1698 to 1722. Except, perhaps, in the case of the City churches, all these payments were probably exclusive of the salaries of his assistants, office rent and other office expenses. The Surveyor-General also occupied rent-free a commodious official residence of sixteen rooms and cellarage in Scotland Yard (Whitehall), and other free quarters were available for him at Hampton Court, Windsor, St Paul's, Greenwich and probably Westminster, together with stabling for his horses.

The difficulty of computing the total value of his income from official sources is greatly complicated by payments for miscellaneous fees, allowances and 'riding charges'. Two examples may be cited from Treasury Papers. The first is a claim made in August 1691 for five years' 'allowances and riding-charges', amounting in all to £2,213 12s. 4d. Of this total, the chief item was an 'allowance' of £325 11s. 2d. *per annum*, 'and his rideing

[1] T. F. Reddaway, *The Rebuilding of London*, p. 195.

[2] Sir Lawrence Weaver, *Sir Christopher Wren*, p. 124.

charges only when he travells at 7s. 10d. *per diem*', plus arrears of salary 'out of their Majesties Exchequer' at £45 12s. 6d. for four years, £182 10s.; plus 'an allowance out of the Great Wardrobe at £12 15s. 0d.' for two years, £25 11s. 8d. The following paragraph was added by Talman and another official when urging the Treasury to settle this overdue claim: 'Considering there is noe other Fees nor perquisites, That the rideing charges settled in the dayes of Queen Elizabeth is not a third part of the Charge in this age, That the Livery in the Wardrobe is what was allowed in Henry the VIII's dayes, That the Office is a place of Skill, Trust and perpetuall Attendance & that the Petitioner's allegations are true; Wee humbly conceive that he may justly receive yor Lopps. favour.'

Another claim submitted by Wren in 1714 for allowances due to himself and to his son Christopher as Clerk Engrosser refers to six months' visits to Windsor Castle during January-June in that year. In all, this claim amounts to £253 14s. 2d. for Wren and his man, plus £32 6s. 2d. for Christopher junior. The former item includes an average of about £26 per month for 'allowances', about £3 10s. 0d. a month for 'riding charges', about £2 a month 'ditto' for his man, and a mysterious item of about £3 a month for 'Windsor'. The total seems to be exclusive of six months' salary to Sir Christopher at the rate of £45 12s. 6d. *per annum*, and about half as much again for his son. At Kensington Palace, during seven years from 1689 to 1696, Wren drew £208 for 'travelling and riding charges' at 4s. 10d. a day, plus 3s. a day for 'his man'. As we have already seen (p. 188), he was paid at a similar rate for Hampton Court. Add to these confusing and complicated extracts from official documents the fact that we have no information of his professional charges for private commissions, including all those mentioned in Chapters X and XII, and it will be realized that no exact estimate can be made of his income.

It seems justifiable to infer, however, that during most of the fifty years or so of his architectural practice he must have enjoyed a clear net income, after including all 'allowances' and deducting office expenses, of nearer £1,000 than £500 *per annum*. To make any comparison with the purchasing power of money today (1952), it is necessary to multiply that figure by nearly ten, implying a contemporary income nearer to £10,000 than £5,000, but when we do that the comparison becomes absurd; for how many professional men today have that amount to spend when they have paid all their taxes, and how much must one earn today in order to have £10,000 or even £5,000 a year to spend? My main reason for dwelling at such length upon this sordid question of finance is to explode the myth that Wren was scandalously underpaid. Whether he was, in fact, as modest and altruistic as some of his biographers have assumed is a question to be considered in the next chapter, when his character and temperament will come in for comment.

Mention has already been made of gifts to him (and occasionally to his wife) by grateful 'clients' for his work on the City churches and the Temple. Queen Anne presented him on one occasion with a fine watch, now in the Soane Museum; and on another with a bureau made by Sir Charles Hopson. The most lavish present of this sort that he received was a gift of gold plate, valued at £200, bestowed on him by Archbishop Sheldon after the completion of the Sheldonian Theatre at Oxford; but possibly this was in lieu of ordinary professional fees, which are not mentioned in the building accounts. His house at Hampton Court seems to have been granted to him rent free in lieu of a pension.

Evidently the Treasury placed no embargo upon the numerous commissions that he undertook for private clients while drawing various emoluments from public funds; but these did not exhaust his profitable activities. A document of 1688 reveals that he purchased, jointly with one Roger Jackson, land at the Barbican in the City of London for £4,400, no small amount at that date. Presumably a speculation in sites or building was involved, for that was the period when the speculative builder had just become busy in London; and only four years earlier Wren had had to deal with a troublesome case involving Dr Nicholas Barbon, a notable or notorious dabbler in that lucrative traffic. Yet Barbon and Wren were somehow concerned jointly, as previously noted (p. 213), in building operations in the Temple. One way and another, Wren cannot have been quite so guileless and unworldly as some of his panegyrists would have us believe. Generous he must have been, naïve he certainly was not.

Another aspect of his work that has aroused much controversy is his ability, or lack of ability, as a draughtsman. Evidence of precocious early skill in drawing is available, and has already been quoted (p. 24). Nothing has survived from his trip to France in 1665, unless, as the Editors of the Wren Society have suggested (Vol. V, p. 9), two compositions or studies signed by Wren and now in the Soane Museum are souvenirs of that excursion. Incidentally, they are on paper bearing an Auvergne watermark. Wren favoured instruction in drawing as a useful item in education and in 1694 he wrote this oft-quoted letter to the Treasurer of Christ's Hospital:

'Sir, 24 November 1694

I perceive your extraordinary diligence, and that the improvement of your charge is always in your thoughts, by your importuning me to

I

recollect what passed in discourse some time since at your House. I intended to have waited on you severall times but have been prevented sometimes by business and at present by sickness which detaines me. It was observed by somebody then present that our English Artists are dull enough at Inventions, but when once a forreigne patterne is sett, they imitate soe well that commonly they exceed the originall. I confess the observation is generally true, but this shows that our Natives want not a Genius, but education in that which is the ffoundation of all Mechanick Arts, a practice in designing or drawing, to which every body in Italy, France, and the Low Countries pretends to more or less.

'I cannot imagine that, next to good writing, anything could be more usefully taught your Children, especially such as will naturally take to it, and many such you will find amongst your numbers, who will have a natural genius to it, which it is a pity should be stifled. It will prepare them for many Trades, and they will be more usefull and profitable to their Masters, who shall take them, the first yeare than a boy untaught will be in three or four yeares, and consequently they will be desired and sooner taken from you at cheaper rates.

'It is not Painters, Sculptors, and Gravers onely that will find an advantage in such boyes, but many other Artificers too long to enumerate, noe Art but will be mended and improved, By which not onely the Charity of this House will be enlarged but the Nation advantaged, and this I am confident is obvious to any Ingenious person who hath been abroad.

'I was surprised to see what Mr Smith hath shewn me, performed by some of the Boyes already, by which you may perceive how soon they imitate and teach one another. This is what we were discoursing which I repeate in pursuance of your request and remaine

'Your Affectionate and humble Servant

'To Mr Nathaniel Hawes   'Chr. Wren.'
Treasurer of Christ Hospital'

Sir Reginald Blomfield is very critical of Wren's ability as an architectural draughtsman. In one book he writes that Wren was 'a poor draughtsman, and he was the last man in the world to be deceived by his own drawings'.[1] Elsewhere we are told that, at the time of Wren's appointment as Surveyor-General, he was 'the merest amateur, both in architecture and draughtsmanship; and though in architecture he rose to unequalled eminence, he never was a fine draughtsman. . . . He relied largely on such men as Grinling Gibbons for his detail. The drawing in the All Souls Collection of the design for St Paul's, with the open pineapple at

[1] Blomfield, *Short History of Renaissance Architecture in England*, p. 128.

the top, dated 1666, is by Wren himself, and is as bad in drawing as it is in design. The "Warrant" design, made in 1675, shows a considerable advance in both'.[1] Sir Lawrence Weaver regards him as 'a competent but not a good performer'; while Mr Geoffrey Webb more charitably notes that 'an engraved view, by Wenceslas Hollar, of Windsor Castle from the north . . . dated 1667 . . . is an interesting and charming example of Wren as a landscape draughtsman and, as far as is known, the only one'.[2]

The number of architectural drawings, made by Wren himself or under his personal supervision, that have survived is large. When his son's collection was disposed of at the sale in 1749, the Editors of the Wren Society (Vol. III, pp. 3-6) have calculated that it contained 924 such drawings in all, of which 914 were in bound volumes and ten were loose in a portfolio. Of these 584 could be accounted for, up to 1926, in the collections in St Paul's Library, at All Souls College and in the Soane Museum; others were subsequently found in the Sloane Collection at the British Museum, and in 1930 a further volume containing thirty-two additional drawings was discovered in the Library of All Souls.[3]

This new volume, containing some of his best work for the period 1694-8, may have been, as the Wren Society's Editors suggest (Vol. XX, p. 33), his own pet selection which he would bring out to show to his friends. The total number of Wren's drawings is certainly large enough to enable one to form some opinion upon his capacity as a draughtsman. Even if one admits that Grinling Gibbons inserted many of the human figures and much of the ornamental detail, even if Hawksmoor is responsible for some of the rest, it must be conceded that Hawksmoor was trained by Wren himself and that Grinling Gibbons' assistance was only supplementary. My own view is that, after 1675 or so, when Wren had thoroughly got into his stride as an architect, his drawing was excellent by any reasonable standard. If it was inferior to the beautiful perspectives produced a century or so later by Soane, Gandon and Cockerell, it was equal to that of most famous architects of the nineteenth century and since, and indeed was remarkable in quality for so busy a man as Wren was. These drawings were not prepared for display, or for exhibition to students, and should not be judged accordingly. The Royal Academy and its Diploma Gallery

[1] Blomfield, *Architectural Drawing and Draughtsmen*, p. 76.

[2] Webb, *Wren*, p. 58.

[3] In May 1951, 122 hitherto unknown drawings by Wren from the Marquess of Bute's collection were sold in London, 59 of them relating to the City churches. Many of these are now in the R.I.B.A. Library. (See article by J. Summerson, *R.I.B.A. Journal*, Vol. LIX, pp. 126-9.)

had not then been established, and Wren's chief concern was to produce fine buildings.

Most previous writers on Wren have given some attention to the influence of foreign buildings upon his design. Any such influence was derived mainly from France, Italy and Holland. As his only tour abroad was in France, early in his architectural career (pp. 38-43), it follows that inspiration from Italy and Holland must have been second-hand, through the medium of books and engravings. It was in France, however, that he met Bernini, the acknowledged leader of the Baroque movement in Italy. Wren's fondness for domes cannot be attributed wholly to France, but it is a fact that when he visited Paris in 1665 he must have seen, studied and admired François Mansart's domed church of Ste Marie in the Rue St Antoine (1633-4) and the great dome of the Val-de-Grâce (1645-65), while the same architect's design for the domed church of the Minimes in the Place Royale, though not carried out, was available in engravings. Then there was Lemercier's fine domed church of the Sorbonne (1635-53), the octagonal dome of the Salpêtrière (begun 1656), the church of the Collège des Quatre Nations (1660-8), and Guarini's Theatine church. The noble dome of the Invalides was not begun till a generation after Wren's visit, and is thus more likely to have been based upon St Paul's than vice versa. For the rest, Wren would see coupled columns at the Val-de-Grâce and other buildings, he would obtain ideas of monumental lay-out from several great *châteaux*, and in his later work he certainly made use of Daniel Marot's published books of designs for ornamental details such as ceilings, chimney-pieces, doorways, altar-pieces, pulpits and organ-cases. The gardeners whom he employed at Hampton Court and elsewhere were disciples of Le Nôtre (p. 248); and Tijou, a French craftsman, seems to have been allowed considerable latitude by Wren in designing ironwork. Laguerre was another French artist who has been mentioned (p. 246).

Italian influence, even if derived from books, is apparent in much of Wren's work, and is particularly evident in the Sheldonian Theatre at Oxford, based upon Serlio's drawings of the Theatre of Marcellus at Rome. Wren must have used books about the Orders and their application by Alberti, Serlio, Vignola, Palladio and Scamozzi from the beginning of his architectural career; and between 1665 and 1673 were published large folios by G. B. Falda and D. Rossi on the ancient monuments and other important buildings in Rome. Such designs as Temple Bar and the Monument were based upon classical precedent, French or Italian; and the City churches also owe much to foreign influence, though they were planned to meet ritual requirements halfway between those of Catholic and

Protestant churches on the Continent. It was considered blasphemous, two generations ago, to label any of Wren's work (which most people admired) with the opprobious name of 'Baroque' (which we had been taught to condemn), but critics of today apply it to many of his buildings without the slightest shudder and detect in them the influence of Borromini, especially of that architect's fine church of S. Agnese at Rome. Above all, St Peter's must have been in Wren's mind when designing St Paul's.

Dutch influence is most apparent in his least formal buildings and their gardens—in fact, in the most 'English' of his designs and those mainly of brick, such as Chelsea Hospital, Kensington Palace, Hampton Court to some extent, Morden College and the School Room at Winchester. It is often ascribed entirely to William III who certainly and inevitably arrived here imbued with Dutch ideas; but one must remember that Charles II, before the Restoration, had divided his exile between France and the Low Countries. The earldoms of Portland and Albemarle were given to two Dutchmen—Bentinck and Keppel—who came to England in the train of William III, as also did the famous French engraver, architect and garden designer Daniel Marot. Some English buildings of the late sixteenth and early seventeenth centuries, e.g. Gresham's Royal Exchange in London, had their counterparts in Antwerp or Amsterdam, and from both those famous cities there issued a steady stream of folios illustrating classical architecture, of a sort: notably the volumes of Philip Vingbooms, of which Hooke certainly possessed a copy. Wren's admirable taste in the use of brickwork may have had some stimulus from Holland, but he never visited that country, and none of his bricklayers seem to have been Dutchmen. Mr Sacheverell Sitwell has recently suggested that perhaps 'the Great Schoolroom at Winchester College ... could not have existed without the Mauritshuis at The Hague [1633-44], a town Wren never visited, but his genius absorbed the Dutch example and made it his own. ... Wren is only under Dutch influence till we have been to Holland. Then nevermore.'[1] Yet I have seen streets and buildings, in Haarlem and elsewhere, that resemble Wren's domestic brick style so closely that Mr Sitwell's dictum does not convince me. In another book, however (*The Netherlands*, p. 5), Mr Sitwell writes that 'the characteristic steeples of the City churches owe their form to Dutch examples, such as the towers of town halls and city gateways'. About the alleged introduction of sash-windows into England by William III, I have already written (p. 174). Evelyn travelled extensively in Holland, and bought architectural books there. As one of Wren's closest friends, very influential at court, he may have played a part in

[1] Sitwell, *British Architects and Craftsmen*, p. 44.

popularizing Dutch fashions. As for his protégé, Grinling Gibbons, that fine artist was probably born in Holland, but a slender tradition apprentices him to an architect or joiner in York (p. 240).

When Wren's son Christopher died in 1749, there was a sale, lasting over three days, of 'The Genuine and Entire Collection of Curious Greek and Roman Medals and Medallions in Silver and Brass; Antique Marble Statues, Busts, Urns and Inscriptions, Bronzes, Gems, and other Curiosities, of Christopher Wren, Esq., late of Hampton Court, Deceased; together with the Collection of Drawings of Architecture of the late Sir Christopher Wren, his Father.' Nothing is said here of books, but in fact a fair number of architectural books were comprised in the sale. If one deducts from the list all those published after Sir Christopher's death in 1723, there remain about 120 volumes, or 100 titles, of which about 60 are folios, the remainder about equally divided between quarto and smaller sizes. The first thing that strikes anyone examining the list is the dearth of treatises on scientific, mathematical and mechanical subjects: there are only three or four in all. About twenty deal with travel in Italy, France, the Alps, the Levant, Greece, Persia and the East Indies. There are half a dozen works on English archaeology and medieval architecture, including Inigo Jones's *Stone Heng* and Dugdale's *Monasticon*; and three manuals of perspective and geometry. The remaining seventy volumes are nearly all concerned with the Orders, Rome and its antiques, and architectural theory. It stands to reason that Sir Christopher must have possessed a far more comprehensive collection than this, and one must assume that either he himself or his son, after the older man's death, disposed of his presumably large scientific library.

What concerns us here is that he did own and use some seventy standard books on Roman and Renaissance architecture, mostly in Italian and French. Hooke, as his *Diary* informs us incidentally, likewise possessed a number of similar works, mainly in French, and a very large collection of French engravings by Pérelle, Israel, Sylvestre and others, together with some Italian prints. Of Wren's general or recreational reading we know nothing. He may have been too busy to have had much time for such relief, or he may have been one of those supermen who can always find time for anything. Hooke has little to tell us on this point—never a mention of poetry or fiction.

Wren, like Hooke, was so phenomenally versatile that he combined an interest in archaeology with a scientific curiosity that was devastatingly modern. His intellect was capable of comprehending both, and he was singularly free from prejudice. This attitude was characteristic of his period, and especially notable in the case of those inquisitive scientists at Wadham College who transformed themselves so easily and so surprisingly, one after another, into bishops and deans. We find Wren and Hooke discoursing one day on Lars Porsena's tomb or the Mausoleum at Halicarnassus, and next day on aviation or astronomy. Everything was fish that came into their net—except, as I have suggested, religion, politics, poetry, fiction and the foibles of human nature. Yet Hooke was human enough in his private *Diary*. (There were some things that he did not discuss with Wren, whose private life seems to have been exemplary.)

Sir Christopher, after his practice had become very large, had little time for writing about architecture, old or new; and even in his retirement, which occurred very late in life, he did not produce any book. His two long reports on Old St Paul's (pp. 67-70, 72-5) give some indication of his views on certain aspects of architectural design and history; while those on Westminster Abbey, 1713 (pp. 141-6), and on modern church building, 1710 (pp. 135-8), embody the mature conclusions of an experienced practitioner, and were intended for the guidance of his successors. In *Parentalia*, however, are printed five so-called 'Tracts' on architecture, and also an interesting statement of his views on Roman London. This last document (*Parentalia*, pp. 164-7) is evidently written by his son from memory or from Sir Christopher's notes. Archaeology was then in its infancy, but the surmises that Wren's paper contains accord, for the most part, with the results of modern research. The title is: 'Of London in ancient Times, and the Boundary of the Roman Colony, discern'd by the Surveyor, after the Great Fire.' Beginning with the ancient Britons, Wren suggests that 'surely we cannot think them so barbarous, at least in that Age (and the Accounts before that are too fabulous), as is commonly believ'd'. Explaining the choice of London as a site, he continues: 'Here the Romans fix'd a civil, or trading Colony. . . . The Extent of the Roman Colony, or Praefecture, particularly Northward, the Surveyor had Occasion to discover by this Accident. The parochial Church of St Mary le Bow . . . requir'd to be rebuilt after the great Fire. . . . Upon opening the Ground, a Foundation was discern'd firm enough for the new intended Fabrick, which (on further Inspection) appear'd to be the Walls, with the Windows also and the Pavement of a Temple, or Church, of Roman Workmanship, intirely bury'd under the Level of the present Street. Hereupon, he determin'd to erect his new Church over the old.' In this case, however, Wren's archaeology was at fault, for the old building that he discovered, and converted into a crypt for his new church, is now known to be Norman. He placed his new steeple north of it, fronting on to Cheapside. 'Here, to his surprise, he sunk about 18 Feet deep through made-ground, and then imagin'd he was come to the natural Soil, and hard Gravel, but upon full Examination, it appear'd to be a Roman Causeway of rough Stone, close and well rammed, with Roman Brick and Rubbish at the Bottom, for a Foundation, and all firmly cemented. This Causeway was four Feet thick.... Underneath this Causeway lay the natural Clay, over which that Part of the City stands, and which descends at least forty Feet lower. He concluded then to lay the Foundation of the Tower upon the very Roman Causeway, as most proper to bear what he had design'd, a weighty and lofty Structure.

'He was of opinion for divers Reasons, that this High-way ran along the North Boundary of the Colony. The Breadth then North and South was from the Causeway near Cheapside, to the River Thames; the Extent East and West, from Tower-hill to Ludgate, and the principal middle Street, or Praetorian Way, was Watling-street.

'The Colony was wall'd next the Thames, and had a Gate there called Dow-gate, but anciently Dour-gate, which signified the Water-gate. On the North Side, beyond the Causeway, was a great Fen, or Morass, in those Times; which the Surveyor discover'd more particularly when he had to build a new East-front to the parochial Church of St Laurence near Guildhall; for the Foundation of which, after sinking seven Feet, he was obliged to pile twelve Feet deeper; and if there was no Causeway over the Bog, there could be no reason for a Gate that Way. At length, about the Year 1414, all this moorish Ground was drain'd . . . and still retains the name of Moorfields, and the Gate, Moor-gate.'

He dismissed the common belief that 'London Stone' was a Roman milestone, and 'was of Opinion, by Reason of the large Foundation, it was rather some considerable Monument in the Forum; for in the adjoining Ground on the South Side (upon digging for Cellars, after the great Fire) were discovered some tessellated Pavements, and other extensive Remains of Roman Workmanship, and Buildings.[1]

'On the West-side was situated the Praetorian Camp, which was also walled-in to Ludgate, in the Vallum of which was dug near the Gate, after the Fire, a Stone, with an Inscription, and the Figure of a Roman Soldier which the Surveyor presented to the Archbishop of Canterbury, who sent it to Oxford, and it is reposited among the Arundellian Marbles.' Wren concludes his statement with an account of Roman burials and their relation to later interments, British and Saxon, revealed in digging the

[1] The Historical Monuments Commission's Volume on *Roman London* (1928), p. 111, states that 'there is no evidence of its original use'.

foundations of St Paul's, and describes various urns and other objects discovered in the process. He doubtless learned something from his close friend Aubrey, the father of English archaeology, and he was, for his period, a thoughtful and conscientious archaeologist, as appears also in the first paragraphs of his report on Westminster Abbey.

Of the five incomplete essays or papers, miscalled 'Tracts', which are printed in *Parentalia*, the first consists of a series of rather disjointed aphorisms on architectural aesthetics, and the remainder are mainly concerned with specialized aspects of ancient and classical building. The following extracts from Tract No. 1 contain all its salient matter:

'Architecture aims at Eternity; and therefore the only Thing uncapable of Modes and Fashions in its Principals the Orders.

'The Orders are not only Roman and Greek, but Phoenician, Hebrew, and Assyrian; therefore being founded upon the Experience of all Ages. . . .

'Vitruvius hath led us the true Way to find out the Originals of the Orders. When Man first cohabited in civil Commerce, there was Necessity of Forums and publick Places of Meeting. In cold Countries, People were obliged to shut out the Air, the Cold, and the Rain; but in the hot Countries, where Civility first began, they desired to exclude the Sun only, and admit all possible Air for Coolness and Health; this brought in naturally the Use of Porticoes, or Roofs for Shade, set upon Pillars.'

So for their pillars 'they imitated Nature, most Trees in their Prime, that are not Saplings, or Dotards, observe near the Proportion of Dorick Pillars in the length of their Bole, before they part into Branches. This I think the more natural Comparison, than that to the Body of a Man, in which there is little Resemblance of a cylindrical Body. . . .

'Beauty, Firmness and Convenience, are the Principles; the two first depend upon geometrical Reasons of Opticks and Staticks; the third only makes the Variety.

'There are natural Causes of Beauty. Beauty is a Harmony of Objects, begetting Pleasure by the Eye. There are two Causes of Beauty, natural and customary. Natural is from Geometry, consisting in Uniformity (that is Equality) and Proportion. Customary Beauty is begotten by the Use of our Senses to those Objects which are usually pleasing to us for other Causes, as Familiarity or particular Inclination breeds a Love to Things not in themselves lovely. Here lies the great Occasion of Errors; here is tried the Architect's Judgment; but always the true Test is natural or geometrical Beauty.

'Geometrical Figures are naturally more beautiful than other irregular; in this all consent as to a Law of Nature. Of geometrical Figures, the

Square and the Circle are most Beautiful; next, the Parallelogram and the Oval. Strait Lines are more beautiful than curve; next to strait lines, equal and geometrical Flexures; an Object elevated in the Middle is more beautiful than depressed. Position is necessary for perfecting Beauty. There are only two beautiful Positions of strait Lines, perpendicular and horizontal; this is from Nature, and consequently Necessity, no other than upright being firm. Oblique Positions are Discord to the Eye, unless answered in Pairs, as in the Sides of an Equicrural Triangle; Therefore Gothick Buttresses are ill-favoured, and were avoided by the Ancients, and no Roofs almost but spherick raised to be visible, except in the Front, where the Lines answer. In spherick, in all Positions, the Ribs answer.

'In Things to be seen at once, much Variety makes Confusion, another Vice of Beauty. In Things that are not to be seen at once, and have no Respect one to another, great Variety is commendable provided this Variety transgress not the Rules of Opticks and Geometry.

'An Architect ought to be jealous of Novelties, in which Fancy blinds the Judgment; and to think his Judges, as well those that are to live five Centuries after him, as those of his own Time. That which is commendable now for Novelty, will not be a new Invention to Posterity, when his Works are often imitated, and when it is unknown which was the Original; but the Glory of that which is good of itself is eternal.'

He then says that the architect, above all things, ought to be well skilled in perspective, and discusses its principles, composition and the disposition of ornament on a building.

'No sort of Pinnacle is worthy enough to appear in the Air but Statue [?s]. Pyramids are Gothick; Pots are modern French. Chimnies ought to be hid, if not, to be well adorned. No Roof can have Dignity enough to appear above a Cornice, but the circular; in private Building it is excusable. The Ancients affected Flatness. In Buildings where the View is sideways, as in Streets, it is absolutely required, that the Composition be square. Intercolumniations equal, Projectures not great, the Cornices unbroken, and everything strait, equal, and uniform. Breaks in the Cornice, Projectures of the upright Members, Variety, Inequality in the Parts, various Heights of the Roof, serve only to confound the Perspective, and make it deformed, while the Breaches and Projectures are cast one upon another, and obscure all Symmetry.'

The contents of the four remaining 'Tracts' are very miscellaneous. The second one develops his theory of the origin of the Orders from tree-trunks, argues that the spacing of columns was reduced when stone lintels came into use, explains why ornamental capitals were added, discusses the proper abutment of arches, and then describes in some detail the science of vaulting as practised by the Romans, the 'Saracens', and 'Gothick' builders. Tract III deals with the origins of the Doric Order, the speed and magnitude of ancient building, the use of large blocks of stone and their preparation at the quarries. Tract IV speculates on the type of building pulled down by Samson, offers a conjectural restoration of the Temple of Diana at Ephesus (with plans by Wren and Flitcroft), describes the design and construction of the Temple of Peace at Rome and also of the Temple of Mars Ultor; finally there is a conjectural restoration of the Mausoleum at Halicarnassus, though the accompanying drawing, 'being imperfect', is omitted in *Parentalia*.[1] This last subject is treated in some detail, with quotations from Pliny. The fifth Tract, though headed 'Discourse on Architecture', contains a medley of comments upon primitive and pre-Hellenic buildings, including Cain's first city of Enos, the Tower of Babel, the Pyramids of Egypt, the Pillar of Absolom, the two Temples of Jerusalem, the walls of Babylon, and the Tomb of Lars Porsena. Several of these topics figure in Hooke's record of talks with Wren, who referred to Herodotus and other ancient authorities in preparing his 'Tracts'. Professor Lethaby, though hardly an admirer of the Renaissance, drew attention to them and to Wren's discerning judgment in a lecture delivered to the R.I.B.A. on April 18, 1910, and subsequently published in his *Form in Civilization*, pp. 80-8. Incidentally, it is curious that men so scholarly as Wren and Hooke should be so inconsistent and careless in their spelling, as is evident from the copious quotations given in these pages.

Some recent critics have shown a tendency to disparage Wren's achievement as an architect; others have been, perhaps, too prone to accept everything that he designed as faultless. The truth lies between the two extremes, but much nearer to the latter than the former. His earliest works, particularly the Sheldonian Theatre (though that is a structural and functional masterpiece), were inferior in quality to those of his middle and later years. Even Sir Reginald Blomfield, one of his most fervent admirers, writes of the Sheldonian as an 'artistic fiasco', and his two chapels at Cambridge are generally considered to be amateur if picturesque designs. His 'pine-apple' scheme for St Paul's prepared before the Fire (p. 71) and the hideous telescopic steeple of the 'Warrant' design immediately after the Fire (pp. 83-4) are stigmatized by all critics as inferior work, but thereafter his powers rapidly developed, and from 1675 to the end he maintained a consistently high level. The change took place during the period 1670-5, when he had the wonderful opportunity of experimenting with

[1] But is reproduced as Plate LXXVII in Wren Society Vol. XIX.

more than fifty City churches, by no means all successful in the result, while preparing the working drawings and details for St Paul's, so that that noble building gained immensely in quality as it rose slowly from the foundations.

It seems superfluous to recapitulate here the familiar criticisms already discussed in previous chapters, of St Paul's Cathedral (pp. 103-6) and of the City churches (pp. 115-21). As for his designs, carried out or merely projected, for the various royal palaces, those were conceived on a monumental scale hitherto unimagined in England, though Wren borrowed inspiration freely from France and Italy. The same statement applies equally to Greenwich Hospital, where his success consisted rather in the splendid lay-out than in the design of specific buildings, for at Greenwich his conception was governed from the outset by Inigo Jones's surviving block, and in later stages by Vanbrugh's increasing share in the undertaking. At Chelsea Hospital, where he had an entirely free hand, he produced a dignified, homely and individual type of building, beautifully grouped, which is entirely his own. It is also definitely English in appearance, as are several of his smaller works, and it is undoubtedly picturesque in spite of its austerity.

It has often been argued that Wren's work is less 'scholarly' than that of his predecessor Inigo Jones or that of his Palladian successors. It may be so, in the sense of being less rigidly controlled by Roman precedent, but it has other qualities of grace and charm that redeem any shortcomings detected by the pedants. It is doubtful if Inigo Jones, or any of the eighteenth-century Palladians, could have produced so splendid a monument as St Paul's; it seems certain that none of them could have imagined a building so pleasing as Chelsea Hospital. If he toyed with Baroque elements, as he certainly did, in some of his steeples and much of his decorative detail, he never ventured as far as Vanbrugh went at Seaton Delaval and Blenheim in the way of megalomania, or in eccentricity to the extent that Continental architects did almost everywhere. One of Wren's biographers who is an organist acutely compares his architecture with the music of Bach, suggesting that the main theme of each composition remains constant, but brilliant improvizations are introduced. Sir Thomas Jackson compares his independence of mind and freedom with that of Michelangelo. Another authority praises his eye for colour in building. All these comments seem to me sound.

Modern writers, whether architects or laymen, who attempt an estimate of Wren's achievement in architecture, must remember—in explanation rather than in extenuation—the immense burden that he carried for forty years or so from about 1670 to about 1710. Any reader of this book who cares to amuse himself by compiling, from the dates given in my previous chapters, a chart or table of the number of buildings that Wren had in hand at any given moment during that period, can obtain some idea of the volume of his work; but only an architect with experience of practice can realize fully the magnitude of his output and the heavy strain that it threw upon his brain and his energy. Sir Reginald Blomfield, himself an architect, writes in one place that 'Wren's career was one of incessant labour', and elsewhere refers to 'his unwearied labour and indomitable effort'. Admitting all this, as any honest man must, with admiration, it becomes the more remarkable that he contrived to devote so much personal attention to small details of craftsmanship and to trumpery items of finance; yet the evidence of our eyes in the beautiful accessories of his churches and palaces on the one hand, and the published accounts of St Paul's and his other buildings on the other, supply evidence of his meticulous care in such matters.

A letter written by Wren to Dean Sancroft on August 5, 1666, about his first design for Old St Paul's, forms an appropriate tail-piece to this chapter:

'I have with a great deale of paines finished the designes for it, if they may be usefull, if it happen they bee not thought soe I shall not repent the great satisfaction and pleasure I have taken in the contrivance, which aequalls that of poetry or compositions in Musick. It hath been my constant Recreation when Journies, buisinesse or friends left me vacant, which is not often, for Oxford in sumer is noe retirement, I think lesse than London.'

❦ XV ❦

WREN THE MAN

ALTHOUGH an enormous amount of information relating to Wren's numerous buildings has been preserved, there is a lamentable lack of material concerning his personal life. A diary would have been most valuable. The following chapter is an attempt to picture him as a human being, after 1669 or so, the earlier years of his life having been described in Chapters I-IV. We have seen that he was small of stature and delicate of constitution. In *Parentalia*, after an account of his last illness and death, it is stated that 'his bodily Constitution . . . was naturally rather delicate than strong, especially in his Youth, which seem'd consumptive; and yet, by a judicious Regularity and Temperance (having acquir'd good Knowledge in Physick), he continued healthy, with little Intermission, even to this extreme old Age'.

Hooke, who was morbidly interested in matters of health, occasionally makes mention of slight ailments suffered by Wren during the period (1672-80) covered by his *Diary*; October 30, 1673. 'At Dr Wren's, he very sick with physick taking day before'; November 1, 1673. 'To Dr Wren's with Mr Aubrey. Dr Wren recovered'; March 30, 1675. 'Went to Sir Chr. Wren. He took physick'; March 31, 1675. 'At Sir Chr. Wren's, he sick of stone, &c.'; December 1, 1677. 'At Sir Chr. Wren's, he sick, had taken north hall waters evaporated which he affirms was the best physick and had given him ease.' This record covering eight years does not suggest that Wren suffered much illness, yet he was working tremendously hard and putting a severe strain on his health. A letter written to his son Christopher at a much later date (p. 273), when he was approaching seventy years of age, seems to indicate that at that time he did not expect to live much longer; but in fact he lasted for another quarter of a century. It appears that in his case—as with many other famous men—a temperate life and an interest in his work enabled him to conquer his delicate constitution and to achieve an enormous output.

It is only natural that the physical appearance of a man so prominent in artistic and intellectual circles as well as at Court should have been commemorated in a number of busts, oil paintings and engravings. In order of date, the earliest would normally be the painting by H. Gascar, reproduced as frontispiece to the Wren Society Vol. II, depicting a quite young man holding in his hand a print of St Paul's; but expert examination has now revealed that it has been 'faked', and that it can no longer be regarded as an authentic portrait of Wren. It belongs to the Duke of Portland and is at Welbeck Abbey. There is another painting by an unknown artist, illustrated in Sir Lawrence Weaver's *Wren*, Plate II, with the caption 'Wren as a man of forty', and said to be in the possession of the Bishop of Southwell (in 1923), but the picture suggests a youth rather than a man of forty. The splendid marble bust and pedestal by Wren's favourite sculptor Edward Pearce, now in the Ashmolean Museum at Oxford, may be dated with some confidence as 1673, when Wren was forty-one years of age. Then comes the Wadham College portrait (Weaver, *op. cit.*, Plate XIII), said to be 'an 1825 copy by John Smith of Oxford based on the Sheldonian portrait', and showing Wren about 1675, but it is a feeble effort. The fine Royal Society portrait, commemorating Wren's presidency, is usually attributed to Sir Godfrey Kneller and is so titled in the Wren Society's Vol. VIII (Frontispiece), without comment; however, according to Sir Lawrence Weaver (*op. cit.*, p. 165), 'the legend on the frame says this picture is by Michael Wright, but Mr Collins Baker attributes it, on the ground of style, to Riley and Closterman in collaboration. . . . I suggest it shows a man of seventy'. A fine mezzotint, engraved by Kirkall from a painting by Closterman (possibly the Royal Society portrait), is reproduced as frontispiece to the Wren Society's Vol. I. The excellent painting by Kneller in the National Portrait Gallery (see Frontispiece) is considered to have been made *c.* 1711, when Wren was eighty years of age. There is an inferior copy of it in the Deanery of St Paul's Cathedral. Lastly must be mentioned the death-mask of 1723, preserved at All Souls College, Oxford; and the terracotta bust by Rysbrack at Queen's College, Oxford, modelled in 1726-7 from the death-mask.

Wren's first wife, Faith Coghill, to whom he was married in 1669 (p. 62), lived to become Lady Wren when he was knighted in 1673, but died two years later. His first son, Gilbert, died in infancy. Hooke's *Diary* contains some brief references to that event: October 13, 1672. 'Dr Wren's son born about 8 at night'; October 15, 1672. 'Dr Bradford assured Dr Wren that his next child would be a boy, this being born in the increase of the moon.' About a fortnight later, Hooke records another visit to the house, when he gave the nurse 5s. Then, on March 23, 1673. 'Sir Chr. Wren's child died suddenly.' Hooke's next reference to Lady Wren is peevish: August 15, 1674. 'At Paules with Lady Wren, &c. Slighted', but he continued to meet her husband as frequently as ever. In the following February, Christopher junior was born. Only a few months afterwards Hooke notes: August 28, 1675. 'Lady Wren 5 days sick of small pox'; September 4, 1675, 'Lady Wren died last night of small pox. Buried to-night', in St Martin's Church. A year later, Hooke ordered a rocking-horse for young Christopher: September 9, 1676. 'Coxes cheapened cradle horse for Little Wren'; October 21, 1676. 'Sent Sir Chr. Wren's son a hobby horse, 14 sh. paid.'

On February 24, 1677, Wren married Jane, daughter of Lord Fitz-william of Lifford, at the Chapel Royal in St James's Palace. Evidently Hooke had never heard or had forgotten her name, for the entry in his *Diary* is: 'Sir Chr. Wren married to ——'; but on April 7 we read: 'To Sir Chr. Wren, saw his lady'; and on July 21, 'saluted Lady Wren'—not very gushing or illuminating comments. Pepys would have done better than that!

But at this point we encounter in Hooke's staccato and surprising jottings one of those delightful trivialities that relieve the often arid tedium of research: August 16, 1677. 'At the Crown, Sir Christopher told of killing the wormes with burnt oyle, and of curing his Lady of a thrush by hanging a bag of live bog-lice about her neck.' On November 1, 1677, the arrival of Jane Wren, Sir Christopher's favourite child, is recorded: 'Sir Chr. Wren's lady first deliver'd of a daughter.' On February 1, 1679, Hooke notes: 'I gave Christopher [junior] 5 sh.'; and he became a frequent visitor to Wren's house, apparently discussing literature and history with his wife, for he notes: 'Promis'd Lady Wren Mahomet's book', but he did not redeem his promise for three months. In the autumn she fell ill. Hooke notes on September 18 that she had recovered, but records her death at the beginning of October. She had borne another son, William, in June 1679. He was a delicate child, but lived to be sixty. Her daughter Jane died at the age of twenty-six in 1702 and is buried in the crypt of St Paul's, where a white marble tablet by Francis Bird has a relief showing her seated at an organ, recalling her devotion to music.

These bare facts are almost all we know of Wren's two wives and his four children, save a certain amount of additional information about Christopher's later career, some of which has already been mentioned (p. 272). In or about 1698, Christopher junior was sent by his father on a tour abroad, under the care of Edward Strong the younger, son of the master-mason of St Paul's. Wren wrote a letter to his son, then aged about twenty-three, which is worth quoting here for several reasons. It contains Sir Christopher's mature views on the relative value of various modes of foreign travel, it displays a good deal of parental affection, and it reveals a premonition, to be proved groundless, that his life was nearing its end.

'My dear Son,

I hope by this time you are pretty well satisfied of the condition of the Climat you are in: if not, I believe you will ere Lent be over, and will learne to dine upon Sallad. . . . If you thinke you can dine better cheape in Italy you may trie, but I thinke the passing the Alpes and other dangers of disbanded armies and abominable Lodgings will ballance that advantage: but the seeing of fine buildings I perceive temptes you, and your companion Mr Strong, whose inclination and interest leades him, by neither of which I can find you are moved; but how doth it concerne you? You would have it to say hereafter that you have seen Rome, Naples and other fine places, a hundred others can say as much and more; calculate whether this be worth the expence and hazard as to any advantage at youre returne. I sent you to France at a time of businesse and when you might make your observations and find acquaintance who might hereafter be usefull to you in the future concernes of your life: if this be your ayme I willingly let you proceed, provided you will soon returne, for these reasons, the little I have to leave you is unfortunately involved in trouble, and your presence would be a comfort to me to assist me, not only for my sake, but for your own that you might understand your affaires, before it shall please God to take me from you, which if suddenly will leave you in perplexity and losse. I do not say all this out of parsimony, for what you spend will be out of what will, in a short time, be your owne, but I would have you be a man of businesse as early as you can bring your thoughts to it. I hope, by the next you will give me account of the reception of our ambassador; of the intrigues at this time between the two nations, of the establishment of the commerce, and of anything that may be innocently talked of without danger and reflection, that I may perceive whither you look about you or noe and penetrate into what occurres, or whither the world passes like a pleasant dream, or the amusement of fine scenes in a play without considering the plot. If you have in ten weeks spent half your bill of exchange besides your gold, I confesse your money will not hold out, especially if you goe for Italy, which voyage forward and back-ward will take up more than twenty weekes; thinke well of it, and let me hear more from you, for though I would advise you, I will not discontent you. Mr Strong hath profered credit by the same merchant he uses for his son, and I will thinke of it, but before I change, you must make up your account with your merchant, and send it to me. My hearty service to young Mr Strong and tell him I am obliged to him for your sake. I bless God for your health and pray for the continuance of it through all adventures till it pleases Him to restore you to me and your Sister and friends who wish the same as doth

Your most affectionate Father

Chr. Wren.

Poor Billy[1] continues in his indisposition and I fear is lost to me and the world to my great discomfort and your future trouble.'

Hardly anything is known of the various houses in which Wren and his family lived from 1669 onwards, but they were all in or near London. His appointment as Surveyor-General carried with it, as I have already said (p. 255), the use of a comparatively large house in Scotland Yard (*not* New Scotland Yard) within the precinct of the palace of Whitehall. Wren must have been entitled to live there up to the time of his dismissal from the Surveyorship in 1718, but as early as 1676 he seems to have had another house of his own, probably in Bloomsbury, for on March 18, 1676, Hooke records that 'Sir Christopher let his house for £32 per annum for one year'. After 1718, up to his death in 1723, he possessed a house in St James's Street. During that period, he continued to live mainly at Hampton Court in the Old Court House which had served as one of his numerous subsidiary official residences (p. 229) until 1718, and thereafter had been granted to him in lieu of a pension. Elsewhere I have contended that the claims made for the 'Old House' at Windsor to be included among his places of residence cannot be substantiated. As for the house on Bankside opposite St Paul's (p. 103), the recent Vol. XXII of the London Survey Committee, dealing with Bankside, states on p. 58 that no confirmation can be found in the records for that tradition, though a plaque so affirms and although a watercolour drawing in the Guildhall Collection illustrates a house near the Falcon Inn (since demolished) and bears a similar statement.

I have referred briefly to Wren's religious views in connection with his designs for St Paul's (p. 82) and the City churches (pp. 115-6), and his memorandum on the churches to be built in Queen Anne's reign (pp. 135-8). He seems to have maintained the tolerant attitude of a philosophical scientist towards the advanced Protestant or Nonconformist wing on the one hand and the extreme Roman Catholic attitude of James II's court on the other, remaining a Protestant Churchman through all the controversies, and he was by birth and upbringing a confirmed Erastian. He was also a devout and God-fearing man at heart, objecting to loose living and

[1] Sir Christopher Wren's son William. He lived to be 60 (see p. 272).

loose language. During the building of St Paul's Cathedral, he caused the following notice to be exhibited: 'Whereas, among labourers, &c., that ungodly custom of swearing is too frequently heard, to the dishonour of God and contempt of Authority; and to the end, therefore, that such impiety may be utterly banished from these works, intended for the service of God and the honour of religion—it is ordered that customary swearing shall be a sufficient crime to dismiss any labourer that comes to the call, and the Clerk of Works, upon sufficient proof, shall dismiss them accordingly, and if any master, working by task, shall not, upon admonition, reform this profanation among his apprentices, servants, and labourers, it shall be construed his fault; and he shall be liable to be censured by the Commissioners.'

On p. 189 I wrote that Wren, 'who was then Grand Master of Masons, initiated the King into the mysteries of that craft'. The statement is based upon a sentence to that effect in Ernest Law's learned *History of Hampton Court Palace* (1891, Vol. III, p. 63). James Elmes also has the following paragraph on Wren's alleged connection with Freemasonry in his biography of Wren, pp. 485-6: 'In 1666 Sir Christopher Wren was appointed Deputy Grand Master under Earl Rivers, and distinguished himself beyond any of his predecessors, in legislating for, and promoting, the success of the lodges under his care. He was master of the St Paul's Lodge, now the Lodge of Antiquity . . . and attended their meetings regularly for upwards of 18 years. . . . During the short reign of James II they were much neglected; but in 1685 Sir Christopher Wren was elected Grand Master, and appointed Cibber the sculptor and Edward Strong . . . his wardens. . . . In 1698 he was elected a second time . . . Grand Master of the Order of Freemasons, and continued to exercise the duties of his office till 1702.' This is categorical enough, but Elmes was notoriously inaccurate, and Sir Lawrence Weaver (*Wren*, p. 116), is sceptical of the whole story: 'Some candlesticks, and a mallet bearing an inscription which suggests that it was used at a St Paul's ceremonial, remain in possession of the Antiquity Lodge.' It is necessary, however, to add that Gould, in his *History of Freemasonry*, gives it as his opinion, after careful investigation of the architect's connection with the craft, that the evidence points to Wren not having belonged to a lodge, or to a society which was not in existence until 1717, and he goes on to allege that there are three misstatements on the mallet inscription. I have no knowledge of these matters, but assume that Gould's opinion is competent. There is no reference to Freemasonry in any Wren document or in *Parentalia*, but so far as the latter is concerned the omission means nothing. The Editors of the Wren Society (Vol.

XVIII, p. 181 *n*.) take much the same view: 'There is no conclusive evidence that Sir Christopher Wren was a Freemason. Christopher Wren his son was installed as Master of the Lodge of Antiquity No. 1, now No. 2, on July 26, 1729. (Information supplied by Sir Algernon Tudor Craig, Librarian, Freemasons.)' Nevertheless two obituary notices in newssheets of March 1723 refer to him as 'that worthy Freemason Sir Christopher Wren'.

Because he was M.P. for various constituencies intermittently between 1685 and 1702, there has been much speculation as to his precise political views and his work in Parliament. Nothing is known of important speeches made by him, and no record exists of measures introduced or supported by him, except that in June 1685 he was concerned with a Bill for financing Chelsea Hospital by means of a tax on hackney coaches; and yet notable events took place during that period, including the decision to invite William of Orange to become King. Knowing what we do of Wren's training, tastes and temperament, it is difficult to imagine him as anything but a High Church Tory; on the other hand, we may assume that he was all for toleration, and probably for Protestantism. He could not have been a bigoted party man or a fanatic. The lack of information about his work as M.P. is, however, partially explained by a critical examination of the facts, which reveal that the time when he actually held a seat in the House of Commons was quite brief.

His first attempt to enter Parliament was in 1674 at Oxford, as Hooke relates in his *Diary* for January 21, 1674. 'Heard Dr Wren had lost Election last Friday at Oxon.' Eleven years later he was more successful, and represented Plympton St Maurice (Devon) from 1685 to 1687. In 1689 he and the Rt Hon H. Powle, the Speaker, were returned jointly as members for the Borough of New Windsor, under an indenture, by the mayor, bailiffs and a select number of burgesses. Both returns were then petitioned against, Powle's by William Adderley and Wren's by Sir Algernon May. For ten years previously there had been strife between the mayor and bailiffs on the one hand, and the inhabitants of the town in general on the other, as to the right to elect Members of Parliament; but in 1689 the case against Wren was that Sir A. May had twelve votes without the mayor, and Wren the same number including the mayor. The whole petition was referred to a Committee of Privileges, who declared the entire election void, and in this decision the Committee was upheld by 107 to 72 votes in the Commons. In the following year, Wren and Baptist May were returned by the mayor, bailiffs and selected burgesses, but William Adderley and Sir Charles Porter were returned by the inhabitants. Again the matter was referred to a Committee of Privileges, who pronounced in favour of Wren and May, but this finding was reversed in the House of Commons by 152 to 140 votes. From December 1701 to July 1702 Wren sat as Member for the Borough of Weymouth and Melcombe Regis. Thus the sum total of his experience as M.P. cannot have been more than three years and may have been slightly less, spread over a total period of seventeen years, 1685-1702. This fact explains, to some extent, why so little has been recorded of his Parliamentary career, which was relatively negligible. In any case, the story is confused by the circumstance that his own son Christopher was elected M.P. for New Windsor in 1715, but was unseated by the House of Commons on the ground of bribery and corrupt practices.[1]

Much more is known about Wren's scientific interests, though he had to curtail those drastically after he became Surveyor-General in 1669. Notwithstanding, he still held his Savilian Chair at Oxford, until 1673; and he continued to take a most active part in the affairs of the Royal Society, becoming Vice-President in 1674. On January 12, 1681, he was elected President, and held that distinguished office for two years. As Hooke was Secretary from 1677 to 1682, it was only natural that the two friends, closely associated since their youth in so many ways, as we have seen, and so intimately associated throughout the period of Hooke's own *Diary* (1672-80) as colleagues in architectural practice, should discuss the doings of the Society constantly in their frequent meetings; and indeed the brief records of their conversations on scientific matters form the most important part of the *Diary*. From its voluminous pages I have culled the following topics of their talks:

1674. 'The way of Casting capitalls in tin in a flat and to bend them', 'horizontall sayles'; fire engines.

1675. 'His new way of raising ballast'; 'spring watch'; 'Springs; told him my theory was from the Aether, &c.'; 'The beginning of a clubb for Natural Philosophy and Mechanicks'.

1676. Logarithms; musical instruments and ways of improving them; 'To Dr Wren's. Dr Holder and I discours'd of musick. He read my notes and saw my designs, then he read his which was more imperfect'; 'I told Sir Chr. Wren of my new Barometer and of my oares to swim by a float'; 'Discours'd about watches and for longitude'; flying and rowing engines; chariots; 'my theory of musical ear'; 'Told him of my flying chariott by horses, he liked it, and gave me liberty to print his

[1] The above particulars of the various Windsor elections are drawn from R. R. Tighe and J. E. Davis, *Annals of Windsor* (1858), Vol. II, pp. 445-50 and pp. 499-500; and from the Rev J. Stoughton, *Windsor* (1862), p. 181.

geometricall proposition about 5 lines and told me of his examination about flying'; 'Told Sir Chr. Wren my Invention of flying, air pump, and my anagram. He approved it'; 'Sir Christopher shew'd his projection of mapps, supposing the eye at the distance of the Radius which reduced the parallels to equall Distances'; 'He told me his way of calculating Eclipses of the Sun by an instrument. His double cranks. His double and treble Planisphere and analemma by parallel indices, &c'; 'Sir Chr. Wren's way of printing by hobby plate'.

1677. 'A way of polishing a barrell'; 'Much discourse about Trade. &c.'; springs; 'experiments of smoke'; comets; rowing. 'Making of tyles for Enamelling like the pipe metal or Porcelain'; 'Falling sicknesse, catts, the curious gardener of Amsterdam'.

1678. Air poise; 'His theory of Respiration, muscular motion, &c. Advised me to finish air pump'; 'About Vibrative motion of comet, phosphorus, mapps, &c'; 'Could not procure his judgement of springs'; 'Told him my new way of sayling by slope sayles'; 'Talked about the Alexandrian Bible of Tecla. Sir Chr. Wren would have it printed from copper plates'.

1679. 'About refracting and reflecting glasses and marble tooles'; 'Told Sir Chr. Wren about flying module, limewater and iron hardening and Pappin's softening, shew'd him New Baths'; 'About Planetary catena and coyled cone for Celestiall theory'; 'He told me that he had found [how] to make a circle equall in periphery to Ellipse, about centrall attraction'.

1680. 'Planetary Motion'; 'Told him of my Universall Algebra, my observation about use of air, Blood Ephemera, &c.'

Even to a non-scientific mind, the range of interests shared by these two remarkable cronies is astounding: it speaks for itself, but the frequent mention of flying shows how far ahead they were both thinking. Apart from Hooke's *Diary*, there is an interesting letter from Wren to the Bishop of Oxford in 1681, about the latter's proposal to establish an observatory in 'Tom Tower'. Wren did not favour the idea but, as usual, showed himself obliging and furnished the Bishop with a list of equipment, prefaced by these words: 'Were I to set up the Trade again I was once well acquainted with, & I thinke the World doth or may justly own some improvements of to me, I should require nothing else but these things . . .' (then follows the list).

At all the numerous meetings of the Royal Society for many years after 1669, Wren attended regularly and often took the chair, sometimes serving on special committees to examine inventions submitted to them. In 1674 he, Hooke and his old friend Seth Ward were appointed as a special commission to try to devise an efficient method of finding longitude at sea. Other problems that he discussed were the birth of eels and the making of jessamine-scented gloves. In 1680 we find him describing a pheasant from Surinam, the next day theorizing on the sweetening of salt water by freezing, and soon afterwards, with Evelyn, interviewing the French traveller Chardin, who told them about Nineveh and Persepolis. Enough has been said to prove Wren's versatility, and his continued interest in scientific work at a time when one might reasonably expect him to be completely swamped by his enormous architectural practice.

It stands to reason that in such a crowded life there was little or no room for recreation. There are no records of any indulgence in sport. A reference to riding occurs in the letter to the Bishop of Oxford just quoted: 'I have been using my Horses and enjoy the summer a little, or Yr. Lp had heard from me ere this,' but probably he was only riding from one building to another. Certainly he did not play tennis, as a previous quotation has proved (p. 189). Occasionally the two friends discussed a 'theater', and once they attended a performance of *The Tempest* at the Playhouse. A rare specimen of lighter amusement occurs in the *Diary* for September 1, 1679: 'At Bartholomew Fair [with Wren]. Saw elephant wave colours, shoot a gun, bend and kneel, carry a castle and a man, &c.'

His chief relaxations were walks and talks with Hooke and other friends. The walks were mostly in St James's Park, which was close to his official residence and office. Apart from fairly frequent entertaining in private houses, his own included, the gatherings of Wren, Hooke and their circle took place mainly in coffee-houses, the one most often mentioned in Hooke's *Diary* being Garaway's in Cornhill. It was an economical way of meeting one's friends. They must have drunk quantities of coffee, but cocoa and 'soft drinks' were also provided there, and both men smoked regularly though Hooke tried to cure himself of the habit. The taverns were more expensive. On one occasion Hooke chronicles a dinner at Palsgrave's Head (October 20, 1676): 'Sir Christopher Wren's birthday. He paid all. . . . Good discourse.' Wren was evidently generous in such things, but the traffic was not all one way, and on May 17, 1679, Hooke notes: 'At Tompions, paid him £8 for the Watch with seconds. He would have had more . . . I gave Sir Chr. Wren the Watch I paid Tompion for today.' (It may be added that £8 was a very large sum in those days.) Other taverns favoured by the pair were the Crown and the Three Swans.

There are occasional references to Wren in Samuel Pepys' *Diary*, but none of them really important, and Pepys was evidently never very intimate with him, or with Hooke who mentions him twice: August 28, 1676. 'I was twice with Mr Pepys who was very civill and kind'; December 19, 1676. 'Mr Pepys, Master of the Trinity House, made a long speech to noe great purpose.' John Evelyn, on the other hand, was a close friend of Wren, and records on June 17, 1679, that 'I was godfather to a sonn [William] of Sir Christopher Wren . . . that most excellent and learned person, with Sir William Fermor and my Lady Viscountesse Newport, wife of the Treasurer of the Household'. Frequent reference to Evelyn has been made in previous chapters of this book. It appears from Hooke's *Diary* that, in later years at any rate, John Aubrey the antiquary and Sir John Hoskins—who followed Wren as President of the Royal Society— were among Sir Christopher's chief cronies; but he survived them all. His brother-in-law, Dr Holder, died in 1698, Hooke in 1703, Aubrey and Hoskins in 1705, Evelyn in 1706, Dr Sprat in 1713. During his last years he must have been a very lonely old man.

In attempting any estimate of Wren's temperament and character, one is hampered by the lack of documents, due in part—it has been suggested —to his extreme modesty. He was certainly not excessively emotional, and the story that he wept when his favourite design for St Paul's was rejected, if it be true, is a solitary example of a normally reserved disposition breaking down under severe provocation. It is clear that he did not suffer fools gladly—whether crowned heads, eminent divines or workmen; but his manners must have been good, for heavy demands were often made upon his patience. The list of his major disappointments in practice is a long one, when one starts counting the number of unrealized projects that he prepared. Some of his 'clients' were impatient, unreasonable and fractious—among them certainly Queen Mary and her husband, even his patron and admirer King Charles II at times, and perhaps one ought to add Queen Anne. We do not know enough of his dealings with the Duchess of Marlborough to be sure that he fared any better at the hands of that tempestuous woman than Vanbrugh did afterwards; but the presumption is that Wren's patience, tact and courtesy averted any open quarrel. He must have found Nell Gwyn and the Duchess of Portsmouth something of a social problem; but there is nothing in his letters or in contemporary diaries to suggest that he was a sycophant. From the early days of the Restoration, when Charles II had recognized his great abilities, he had been able to hold his head up at Court, and he continued to serve Charles's successors through all the turmoil of the following reigns without becoming a Vicar of Bray or a Quisling. His tactful letters to King William are a model of respectful independence. Hooke knew him intimately, but through all the eight years spanned by the *Diary* there are very few references to any loss of temper on Wren's part, yet it is certain that Hooke suppressed nothing of that sort in his notes. These are the few exceptions: June 1, 1675. 'At Sir Chr. Wren, but noe money or favour. He seem'd jealous of me'; November 13, 1675. 'Sir Chr. Wren. Importunate woman about party church wall. Sir Christopher surly'; January 16, 1679. 'At Sir Chr. Wren's, Mrs Marshall angry. Sir Christopher not kind.'

Although Hooke and other diarists make frequent references to Wren's conversational powers, there is hardly an indication of any humour in his make-up. Once, and once only, in the case of the Windsor Court House or 'Town Hall', a welcome streak of Puckishness appears (p. 229). His normal demeanour must have been grave, dignified and quiet, as befitted a man of his powers, status and responsibilities. It is inconceivable that he would do anything mean, cheap, vulgar or strident. He was certainly generous and on several occasions he intentionally or negligently omitted to claim credit where it was due to him, either for scientific inventions or for some of his architectural work. To that extent he was modest and even altruistic, but this attribute of his character has been absurdly magnified by hero-worshippers determined to provide him with a halo at all costs. He was such a great man that exaggeration is superfluous. The fact is that Wren was a most enterprising person, as was proved by his promptitude in submitting to the King a plan for rebuilding London before the ashes of the Fire were cold. His schemes for enlarging the royal palaces were most ambitious and lavish, with no hint of higgardly parsimony about them. Far from being a retiring scholar or wayward artist, he was a diplomatic courtier, worldly-wise and confident of his own abilities. No donnish recluse could have controlled the immense practice that came to him by reason of his own herculean efforts. The scholars with whom he discussed scientific problems at Wadham in his early days became his 'clients' after he had turned to architecture, and after they themselves had become bishops or deans; and they remained his friends and patrons after he had carried out buildings for them, because he justified their confidence. While his extensive scientific and mathematical knowledge enabled him to produce such a structural marvel as the dome of St Paul's, his anxiety to please impatient royal employers sometimes led him to adopt or countenance hasty and shoddy construction which led to disaster, as at Hampton Court and Kensington Palace.

In a masterly study of Wren's mind,[1] Mr John Summerson has related

[1] J. Summerson, *The Tyranny of Intellect*. R.I.B.A. Prize Essay, 1936; since republished in *Heavenly Mansions* (1950).

his architectural achievement to the philosophical thought of the day, concluding that 'the vein of psychological inconsistency which runs through all Wren's work' is due to 'that tyranny of intellect which the seventeenth century established'; but admitting also that 'one of the highest peaks' in that brilliant period 'was the mind of Sir Christopher Wren'. The latter statement is generally accepted, but an analysis of so commanding an intellect, reaching over so vast a field of science as well as of architecture, is beyond my powers, and it would be presumptuous on my part to attempt it.

The story of Wren's last years and death has been told in differing ways by his various biographers. The tale, or legend, of his visits to St Paul's in old age is derived in part from the usually spiteful Duchess of Marlborough, who stated that he was dragged up to the top of the dome in a basket; but in this case there is no need to doubt her statement, for the ingenious apparatus used for that purpose is still preserved at the Cathedral. Wren was then 78 years of age. In his last years, he used to be driven up to St Paul's and would sit beneath his glorious dome to meditate. Miss Phillimore wrote that it was on one of those occasions, in February 1723, that he caught cold, dying soon afterwards at his house in St James's Street; but the Editors of the Wren Society consider (Vol. XVIII, 184-5) that it was most unlikely that so old a man would risk a visit to the Cathedral in such inclement weather, and that more probably he caught cold in travelling from Hampton Court to St James's Street. The local tradition that places his death at the Old Court House at Hampton Court is no longer accepted by scholars, and contemporary newspapers stated that the funeral procession started for St Paul's from his house in St James's Street.

Parentalia gives the following account of his end: In 1718, after his supersession in the post of Surveyor-General, Wren 'betook himself to a Country Retirement [at Hampton Court]. In which Recess, free from Worldly Affairs, he passed the greatest Part of the five last following Years of his Life in Contemplation and Studies, and principally in the Consolation of the Holy Scriptures; chearful in Solitude, & as well pleased to die in the Shade as in the Light. . . . Though Time had enfeebled his Limbs (which was his chief Ailment), yet had it little Influence on the Vigour of his Mind, which continued, with a Vivacity rarely found at that Age, till within a few Days of his Dissolution; & not till then could cease the continued Aim of his whole Life, to be (in his own words) *beneficus humano generi*; for his great Humanity appeared to the last, in Benevolence and Complacency free from all Moroseness in Behaviour or Aspect. After a short Indisposition', he died on February 25, 1723, in his ninety-first year.

He passed away peacefully, alone in his chair during his midday nap, a quiet and fitting end to a long life which, though always strenuous and laborious, was never undignified. The noble Latin inscription which his devoted son Christopher composed may be seen inside St Paul's, his greatest building, and must inevitably be quoted here: 'SUBTUS CONDITUR HUJUS ECCLESIAE ET URBIS CONDITOR CHRISTOPHORUS WREN QUI VIXIT ANNOS ULTRA NONAGINTA, NON SIBI, SED BONO PUBLICO: LECTOR, SI MONUMENTUM REQUIRIS, CIRCUMSPICE.' (Beneath lies buried the Founder of this Church and City, Christopher Wren, who lived for more than ninety years, not for himself, but for the public good. Reader, if you seek his monument, look around you.)

Long afterwards, *Punch* printed, as a joke, a Latin epitaph considered appropriate for a later but lesser architect, Sir William Tite, years before his death, in which one sentence stated that 'he never wasted a day'. That claim might have been made with even greater force for Wren, whose great achievement was lauded in many obituary notices in 1723; but the most glowing eulogy of his work was written by John Evelyn in dedicating to him a book on architecture during his lifetime, in 1706. 'That I take the Boldness to adorn this little Work with the Name of the Master of the Works . . . I have no Excuse for, but an Ambition of publicly declaring the great Esteem I have ever had of his Virtues and Accomplishments; not only in the Art of Building, but through all the learned Cycle of the most useful Knowledge, and abstruser Sciences, as well as of the polite and shining. All of which is so justly allowed him, that he needs no Panegyrick, or other History to eternize them; than the greatest City of the Universe, which he hath rebuilt & beautified, and is still improving; witness the Churches, the royal Courts, stately Halls, Magazines, Palaces and other publick Structures; beside what he has built of great and magnificent at both the Universities, at Chelsea, and in the Country; and is now advancing of the Royal Marine Hospital at Greenwich, &c. All of them so many Trophies of his Skill and Industry and conducted with that Success, that if the whole Art of Building were lost, it might be recovered, and found again in St Paul's, the historical Pillar, and those other Monuments of his happy Talent and extraordinary Genius.'

A SELECT BIBLIOGRAPHY

I. BIOGRAPHIES (in order of publication)

Wren, Christopher (jun.) and Stephen: *Parentalia* 1750
Elmes, James: *Memoirs . . . of Sir C. Wren* 1823
Clayton, John: *Works of Sir C. Wren: Parochial Churches* 1848-9
Phillimore, Lucy: *Sir Christopher Wren* 1881
Loftie, Rev W. J.: *Inigo Jones and Wren* 1893
Milman, Lena: *Sir Christopher Wren* 1908
Weaver, Sir L.: *Sir Christopher Wren* 1923
Dircks, R. (ed.): *The Wren Bicentenary Volume* 1923
Whitaker-Wilson, C.: *Sir Christopher Wren* 1932
Webb, Geoffrey: *Wren* ('Great Lives' series) 1937
Briggs, M. S.: *Christopher Wren* [for children] 1951
Dutton, Ralph: *The Age of Wren* 1951
Lindsey, J.: *Wren* 1951

II. THE WREN SOCIETY'S VOLUMES (with summary of contents)

I. St Paul's Cathedral: Original Drawings from
   All Souls, Oxford 1924
II-III. St Paul's Cathedral: Original Drawings in
   Cathedral Library 1925-6
IV. Hampton Court Palace: Original Drawings 1927
V. Designs for Oxford, Cambridge, London,
   Windsor, etc. 1928
VI. Original Drawings for Greenwich Hospital 1929
VII. Royal Palaces: Winchester, Whitehall, Ken-
   sington, St James's 1930
VIII. Designs for Whitehall, Windsor and Green-
   wich 1931
IX-X. Parochial Churches, 1666-1718 1932-3
XI. Designs for Westminster Abbey, Christ's Hos-
   pital, etc. 1934
XII. Miscellaneous designs: plans for rebuilding
   London 1935
XIII. St Paul's Cathedral: designs, accounts, Dean-
   ery, etc. 1936
XIV. St Paul's Cathedral: accounts 1685-95, engrav-
   ings up to 1800 1937
XV. St Paul's Cathedral: accounts 1695-1713; photo-
   graphs 1938
XVI. St Paul's Cathedral: constructional drawings;
   Minutes 1939
XVII. Miscellaneous Designs (supplement to Vol.
   XII) 1940
XVIII. Wren's Work as Surveyor-General; Court
   Orders 1941
XIX. Churches; Chelsea Hospital; Wren's 'Tracts',
   etc. 1942
XX. Catalogue of Wren's Drawings; Index to all
   Volumes 1943

INDEX

Roman numbers refer to the Plates